A CENTURY OF

WHITMAN
CRITICISM

A CENTURY

OF

WHITMAN
CRITICISM

EDITED BY

Edwin Haviland Miller

Indiana University Press

BLOOMINGTON / LONDON

To Gay Wilson Allen

whose writings illustrate the simple
but often forgotten fact that a prose
style is a life style

C O N T E N T S

Contents

Contents

I N T R O D U C T I O N

IN 1872 A NEWSPAPER REPORTED WALT WHITMAN'S READ-
ing of a commencement poem at Dartmouth College in customary journalistic prose until the conclusion, where an editorial
speculation was introduced:

> . . . if it should turn out that in this plain unsuspected old
> customer, dressed in gray & wearing no neck tie, America and
> her republican institutions are possessing that *rara avis* a real
> national poet, chanting, putting in form, in her own proud spirit,
> first class style, for present & future time, her democratic shapes
> even as the bards of Judah put in song, for all time to come, the
> Hebrew spirit, and Homer the war-life of prehistoric Greece, and
> Shakespeare the feudal shapes of Europe's kings and lords!
>   Whether or not the future will justify such extravagant claims
> of his admirers, only that future itself can show. But Walt
> Whitman is certainly taking position as an original force and new
> power in literature.[1]

"A real national poet . . . dressed in gray & wearing no neck
tie" was in the writer's opinion the democratic successor of the
Hebrew singers, Homer, and Shakespeare—"an original force
and new power in literature."

The writer was Walt Whitman.

Sometimes anonymously, as in this instance, sometimes in
articles approved and edited before publication by the poet
himself, Whitman and his coterie indeed made "extravagant
claims." There was to be no middle ground: one was either for

or against Walt Whitman. As they decreed, so it has turned out: the critical response has tended toward extremes.

Throughout his life Whitman affected unconcern about what critics said of his works—or his person, since the writer and his poetry have been inseparable from the beginning. Yet probably no poet in history has been more concerned with public opinion. In the photographs and portraits there is the air of imperturbability and geniality, but such were his caution and secretive nature that he left nothing to chance as far as his "image" was concerned.

The image was by no means consistent. In 1855 in the preface to *Leaves of Grass*, he made abundantly clear that he scorned pretty, emasculated versifiers and that he was the athletic spokesman of a virile America. He insisted too that he was the poet of the body and good health and continued to say so even though, beginning in 1873, his body was wracked with pain and his gait was that of a partial cripple. He welcomed the mantle of "the good gray poet" which William D. O'Connor bestowed upon him—and the transposition of glory from Olympus to Brooklyn (or Washington or Camden, as the case may be). The emphasis upon masculinity was too insistent to be wholly convincing, but then nineteenth-century America, it sometimes seemed, liked to assume the hirsute pose—manly style, manly behavior, muscular Christianity, the "strenuous life," the rough riders, and so forth. Behind these masculine clichés lay deep social and personal fears—of mothers, of the effeminacy attributed by the "roughs" to artists, of their own feminine sensibilities. The body, except in Whitman's case, was rarely allowed to exist, and sexuality was denied anything more than a procreative function—except in Victorian pornography and in the dives of New York's Five Points. As time passed and Whitman retreated to the role of "the good gray poet," he inclined to minimize the physical element to emphasize what he vaguely called the "religious" character of *Leaves of Grass*. He had no false modesty, as we have seen, in placing himself in most august company.

He aspired to be the democratic "national poet" but at the same time to be more than a poet or a literary man: "I do not value literature as a profession. I feel about literature what Grant did about war. He hated war. I hate literature. I am not a literary West Pointer: I do not love a literary man as a literary man . . . : it is a means to an end, that is all there is to it." Some time later he said to his Boswell, Horace Traubel: "When you talk to me of 'style' it is as though you had brought me artificial flowers. . . . What's the use of the wax flowers when you can go out for yourself and pick the real flowers?" Or on still another occasion: "The stylists object to me—but they lack just what Matthew Arnold lacks. They talk about form, rule, canons, and all the time forget the real point, which is the substance of poetry."

Few major writers have had so many derogatory things to say about literature, yet *Democratic Vistas* alleges that America can be saved only by poets. And this is stated stridently: "America demands a poetry that is bold, modern, and all-surrounding and kosmical, as she is herself. . . . America needs, and the world needs, a class of bards who will, now and ever, so link and tally the rational physical being of man, with the ensembles of time and space." These are the words of a man whose own family could not understand his verse, and who concealed from the semiliterate boys he befriended the fact that he was a poet. This bachelor-artist once observed: "We scribble, scribble, scribble —eternally scribble: God looks on—it turns his stomach: and while we scribble we neglect life."[2]

Since Whitman directed attention to the content of his poetry, not to his artistic expression, it is hardly surprising that his admirers followed suit. In a eulogistic essay included in *The New Spirit* (1890), Havelock Ellis speaks for his age when he observes, "It is not as an artist that Whitman is chiefly interesting to us," and then proceeds to have Whitman epitomize "the new spirit" he seeks in the shackled Victorian age. To Ellis, Whitman is "one of the very greatest emotional forces of modern times": his doctrine comprises an "intense sense of individuality," "strenuousness," "sublime audacity," and the "sword of love . . . adhesiveness" which is "deeper than religion, underneath Socrates, underneath Christ." We cannot miss Ellis' impassioned hyberbole and we may squirm a little that he like so many others (including the poet himself) must introduce Jesus and Socrates—that dubious tactic of argument by analogy and of name-dropping—but there can be no doubt of the impact of Whitman upon Ellis.

Whitman, although he was the descendant of Socrates, Jesus, and Buddha—or so he and others alleged—was not to be considered a systematizer. At some length he discussed this matter with Traubel toward the end of his life:

> I do not teach a definite philosophy—I have no cocked and primed system—I but outline, suggest, hint—tell what I see—then each may make up the rest for himself. He who goes to my book expecting a cocked and primed philosophy, will depart utterly disappointed—and deserve to! . . . The last thing the world needs is a cut and dried philosophy, and the last man to announce a cut and dried philosophy would be Walt Whitman. Why, boy, there's just the secret of it—which you have always so well grasped: including all philosophies, as I do, how could I nail myself to any one, or single specimen—except it be this, only—that my philosophy is to include all philosophies.[3]

Much of the early commentary on Whitman is actually an expression of love for a leader who seems to promise release from the desperation of desperate lives in a desperate age. Throughout his life men and women, important and obscure, wrote fervid letters to the poet which, if one is nasty, one can term the effusions of the emotionally unstable, but nineteenth-century Americans and Englishmen were perhaps not so much unstable as they were desirous of a hero. William D. O'Connor and Anne Gilchrist, the one a novelist and the other a highly intelligent woman who completed her husband's biography of William Blake, ventured into print in articles that were more erotic than conventionally critical. John Addington Symonds and Robert Louis Stevenson muffled their intense responses in print. A few—like Bayard Taylor, Algernon Swinburne, and Sidney Lanier—recanted their early avowals with a fury that stems from love gone sour.

We can smile, in condescension or (concealed) envy, at the ardent responses to Whitman. We can also debunk the reports of contemporaries who, when they watched the hobbling gait of Whitman beneath his serene, ruddy, bountifully whiskered face, spoke of his Olympian majesty. We can belittle the hero worship of those who came from Europe to seek out a nondescript "shanty" on a nondescript street in Camden in order to gain a glimpse of or exchange a "howdy" with its occupant. But the aura was a reality to those who came into the presence of greatness. The reality cannot be recaptured in its immediacy after the hero's death, when the radiant face with the soft eyes is frozen in portraits and photographs. For any hero is at least in part a creation of a cultural context and emotional need.

And yet this is not completely true, although the best twentieth-century criticism of Whitman is more detached and less idolatrous than that of the previous century. A few years ago I gave (I thought) a charming but restrained address on Whitman. I was followed by a nonacademician who, with an impassioned eye and in sonorous tones, thawed the chill of my professorial reserve: "There are three great men in history—Jesus, Buddha, and Walt Whitman! And the greatest of these is Walt!" With his trinity and his god, the speaker worried not at all about content and reason: he had the certitude of his faith. And if Whitman had been listening, I am certain that he would have nodded, with a pleasant and perhaps pitying twinkle, to the editor of his letters and applauded the man of conviction.

I am equally certain that he would have approved of those critics who dwell upon the message of his poems and who depict him as an inspired prophet, just as he thoroughly approved of Gabriel Sarrazin's essay in 1888, which, scarcely acute or original, abounds in superlatives. He would have termed many of the critics collected here, as he termed Sir Edmund Gosse, "amiable conventional wall-flowers of literature . . . good harmless well-fed sleek well-tamed fellows, like well-order'd parlors, crowded all over with wealth of books (generally gilt & morocco) & statuary & pictures & bric-a-brac . . . but no more real *pulse and appreciation* than the wood floors or lime & sand walls."[4]

"The real *pulse and appreciation*" appears in the essays of Edward Dowden, Standish James O'Grady, and Symonds, who find, for example, momentous cultural significance in the friendship theme unfolded in the "Calamus" poems and in the portrait of a future democracy of comrades presented in *Democratic Vistas*. We can say, as James E. Miller in effect says, that here Whitman speaks of Christian brotherhood, of a universal world order based on love. But I suspect that the nineteenth-century fascination with this theme stems not so much from a belief in the possibility of a new utopian social order, although it may be rationalized in that fashion, as from the emotional starvation of disadvantaged members of the middle class who felt themselves isolated from the new technocracy and affluence. I also suspect, as the essays in this volume appear to indicate, that "adhesiveness" had a greater appeal to intellectuals in industrialized England, which was already facing the human problems that still lay ahead for America, although our writers intuited the situation long before the public was ready to recognize the human costs of industrialization. A generally sympathetic review of Whitman's poetry in the *New York Sun* on November 19, 1881, protests "the abstract idea of universal brotherhood, of which the kiss between man and man is his not agreeable poetic type." This is genuine Yankee caution, perhaps also reflective of the vehement American overresponse to the homosexual implications of "Calamus."

That the nineteenth-century and particularly the romantic writers sought a hero and even an heroic philosophy is a truism, although Nietzsche had far too much nerve for many hero-worshipers. The hero that emerges from Whitman's poetry and his personal presence is a new kind of hero. Not only does he wear plain clothing over his muscular frame and blatantly proclaim all the body's appendages, but also he is a lover who attempts— and successfully for many readers—to transcend the typeface of the printed page. Like a most aggressive (masculine) lover he speaks to "whoever you are holding me now in your hand"—an assault that seems like rape to the timid and the unsympathetic. But the "me" that is a book is also a human held like a child in the reader's hands. For Whitman's hero is both masculine and feminine, adult and child, actor and receiver. The hand freely offered in the poetry is the authority and blessing of the father-adult and the loving touch is the gentle mother-child. The male prophet—"the true son of God" in "Passage to India"—speaks of a future race of athletic comrades who bask in an eternal maternal glow. The emotional referents of Whitman's hero are far more complex and subterranean in their appeal than the cold intellectual constructs of Carlyle, Emerson, and Nietzsche.

Whitman speaks of "power," Ellis of "strenuousness," and O'Grady and others of "energy." Yet this is the man who begins his longest and finest poem with a picture of the protagonist lying on Mother Earth at his "ease observing a spear of summer grass." This is the man who recreates a moment of artistic awareness as alone he listens to and gradually understands the grief of a bird that has lost its mate and sings its threnody of lost love above the "angry moans" of "the fierce old mother," the sea. This is the man who retreats to the "pondwaters" in order to "celebrate the needs of comrades" and who retires to "deep secluded recesses" to hear the thrush's lullaby, "Come lovely and soothing death." Whitman is the lyrical (or feminine) poet who attempts an epic (or masculine) statement. If one is not intent upon deriving a message from the poetry, it is clear that passiveness rather than activeness characterizes the verse.

The nineteenth century was too eager for a message to look closely beneath the rhetoric of the verse. With few exceptions, notably George Saintsbury, few early critics examined Whitman's art seriously, although many assailed the rhymeless, meterless lines as barbaric. To them, Whitman was either a prophet or a barbarian—and of course he was neither.

In the twentieth century a new kind of "energy"—Henry Adams's dynamo—magnified nineteenth-century fears of impending decline and fall: whether in Adams's defensively impersonal "song of myself"; in Thomas Mann's prophetic treatment of the artist in a bourgeois culture; in T. S. Eliot's waste land of hollow men and ineffectual Prufrocks; in F. Scott Fitzgerald's tragic parody of the American dream; or in Hart Crane's Whitmanesque *Bridge*, which, unlike "Crossing Brooklyn Ferry," reflects the anguish of an age of steel and macadam, of people running for their lives, not finding "dumb, beautiful ministers" that "furnish your parts to the soul." "The machine in the garden" was no longer romanticized with "recitatives": it was now the ominous lights of Norris's octopus.

Whitman, the urban poet, had not anticipated urbanization, and his easy faith in progress was no longer convincing. Also his thinly disguised pastoralism made his poetry and his rhetoric quaint and even outdated, although, as the popular media demonstrate, there still remains a paradoxical nostalgia for a simple rural America even as we approve more bond issues for new improved superhighways. In short, what Ellis found meaningful and emotionally charged in Whitman's poetry, the new century, with a distrust of abstractions that was more self-pity than evidence of maturity, found irrelevant, and until Whitman shed the prophetic mantle of "the good gray poet" and emerged as an artist, and a great one, he was rarely evaluated at his true worth.

About the turn of the century, the first of the important new poets, Edwin Arlington Robinson, composed a bittersweet elegy to Whitman which says indelibly what I have been struggling to suggest.

> The master-songs are ended, and the man
> That sang them is a name. And so is God
> A name; and so is love, and life, and death,
> And everything. But we, who are too blind
> To read what we have written, or what faith
> Has written for us, do not understand:
> We only blink, and wonder.
>
> Last night it was the song that was the man,
> But now it is the man that is the song.
> We do not hear him very much to-day:
> His piercing and eternal cadence rings
> Too pure for us—too powerfully pure,
> Too lovingly triumphant, and too large;
> But there are some that hear him, and they know
> That he shall sing to-morrow for all men,
> And that all time shall listen.
>
> The master-songs are ended? Rather say
> No songs are ended that are ever sung,
> And that no names are dead names. When we write
> Men's letters on proud marble or on sand,
> We write them there forever.

In 1902 Whitman's literary executors—Richard Maurice Bucke, Thomas B. Harned, and Horace Traubel—issued a ten-volume edition of *The Writings of Walt Whitman*, which is not so much an act of scholarship as of faith in a man they knew and loved. In 1906 appeared the first of the academic biographies, the sane and well-told account by Bliss Perry, still one of the most readable. Perry did not slight Whitman's prosody for the sake of the life story: he was one of the first Americans to attempt an explanation of the appropriateness of the style to the subject matter. Another Harvard professor, George Santayana, however, renewed the offensive against the "poetry of barbarism," which is basically a sensational and clumsy rubric that no philosopher should have succumbed to. Only reluctantly did the "new poetry" fathered by Pound and Eliot admit a tradition that included Whitman, but sons must be ingrates in order to be sons. Poets affecting the pose of impersonality were always uneasy about a poet who revelled in his own skin. D. H. Lawrence after his own eccentric fashion and later Henry Miller after his were among the few who attributed philosophical and social relevancy to Whitman. Academicians, of course, issued special studies about Whitman's reputation here and abroad, his indebtedness to music, and so forth; but their books often illuminated only the peripheral aspects of Whitman's genius. It was, however, these professors—inspired and uninspired—who kept Whitman alive during the first part of the twentieth century.

It was inevitable that the preoccupation with the artist so characteristic of this century should eventually catch up with Whitman. Perhaps the most influential work was F. O. Matthiessen's treatment of Whitman's language in *The American Renaissance* in 1941. Writing in the period of the so-called "new criticism" and explication of texts, Matthiessen was able to bring new tools and new insights to a man whose themes had been endlessly and repetitively evaluated but whose artistry had rarely been scrutinized with similar attention and devotion. And so it is that in roughly the past twenty-five years we have had some of the most perceptive analyses of America's greatest poet.

With this new direction, "The Song of the Open Road"—the basis for John Jay Chapman's "tramp"—and "I Sing the Body Electric" were no longer the touchstones of Whitman's genius. Critics began to find unity in "Song of Myself." "As I Ebb'd with the Ocean of Life" and "The Sleepers" became more important: "the doubts of daytime and . . . nighttime" awoke a sympathetic response in an age of anxiety. In the process Whitman is no longer quite the same old nineteenth-century bard or Olympian figure: the father-lover has become the anguished son in an era that feels more comfortable, and empathic, with struggling, stumbling man than with the hero. Actually, as close reading of his poetry demonstrates, the change in response only reflects the various roles the poetic "I" assumes in his journey from darkness to light. Whitman has never been so limited or one-dimensional as his critics and readers have averred.

Something of Whitman has been lost, I suppose, since in one sense he has been reduced to our troubled image of ourselves. In another sense he is not the victim at all. If each age must create its own Whitman, this is glorious testimony to his larger and timeless dimensions: no age will grasp his totality—he is destined to remain in death as elusive as he was in life—but each age in making its "pact" witnesses eloquently to his greatness and enduring vitality.

Literary history is composed of stereotypes, of false distinctions that place everything in neat packages with wrappings as deceptive as the cartons in modern supermarkets. If we were to trust literary history as composed and stridently insisted upon by Whitman's idolators, we would believe that his strange looking and eccentrically titled book *Leaves of Grass* met only a hostile response in 1855 and later. If we were, on the other hand, to accept the genteel tradition as the dominant art movement in mid-nineteenth-century America, we would separate Brooklyn's "rough" from the sages of Concord and Cambridge. Yet within one month of the publication of the first edition of *Leaves of Grass*, America's wisest man composed the most amazing letter in our literature as he greeted an unknown poet at the "beginning of a great career." Ralph Waldo Emerson, intimate of many of the most august people in the United States and England, soon made a pilgrimage to Whitman's humble home in Brooklyn—one of the early visitors to a poet who was before the end of his career to hold open house to the world in one democratic "shanty" after another. Henry David Thoreau, that wonderful recluse who seldom traveled far from Concord, journeyed to Brooklyn in 1856. A. Bronson Alcott—termed by Carlyle "a venerable Don Quixote, whom nobody can laugh at without loving"—was still another visitor, and further evidence that Concord went to Brooklyn.

Neither Emerson nor Thoreau published his impressions, but Charles Eliot Norton, later a professor at Harvard and the translator of Dante's *Divine Comedy*, reviewed *Leaves of Grass* in September 1855. Although Norton had reservations, he was willing to do what only the rare critic or reviewer does: he judged the poet on the poet's terms, not on his own. Emerson's personal letter became a public statement when Whitman gave a transcription to Charles A. Dana, who printed it in the *New-York Tribune* on October 10, 1855. This was the second important statement in Horace Greeley's *Tribune*, which had carried on July 23 Dana's laudatory but qualified notice ("His language is too frequently reckless and indecent, though this appears to arise from a naive unconsciousness rather than from an impure mind").[5] The story of Whitman's unauthorized use of Emerson's letter, both in its release to Dana and in the second edition of *Leaves of Grass* in the following year, is too well known to be repeated. It is pointless (and untrue) to say that Whitman did not realize fully what he was doing: as an experienced journalist and editor he understood publicity, and no poet in history has been more zealous in creating an "image" and utilizing newspapers and magazines for maximum exposure. Whitman, so far as I am aware, never termed himself naive; late in life he likened himself to "a furtive hen"—a most apt description of his secretive and calculating nature. Critics, on the other hand, have too often converted him into a primitive (note Thoreau), sometimes because of their embarrassment before the frank sexuality of his poetry (Dana, for example) and sometimes because of the irregularity and unconventionality of his verse. But it is a truism (or at least should be) that no great artist is naive. Whitman's lines, Charles Ives's notes, and Jackson Pollack's drippings "happen" as the artist consciously orders the unconscious.

Emerson, Norton, and Thoreau are as one in their exhilarated response to the freshness of Whitman's verse: they recognize the authenticity of the first American voice in poetry. Although Whitman in 1889 was to observe without censure that "letting-go was not an element in his character,"[6] Emerson really let himself go in his letter. Both Emerson and Norton note what has been too seldom observed until Richard Chase's treatment—the poet's comic exuberance. A harmonious "mixture of Yankee transcendentalism and New York rowdyism," though much too neat and quotable to be precise, is not an unhappy way to characterize the tensions of the oratorical surface of the preacher who explores Everyman's instinctual depths. Interestingly, Thoreau is the first to introduce the affinities of Whitman's poetry with Oriental mysticism, a topic which has been much explored recently. Whitman's response to Thoreau ("No: tell me about them") may have been disingenuous (he was to deny having read Emerson before the appearance of *Leaves of Grass*), but it is of some importance, I believe, that while he never discouraged those who, like his friend Dr. Richard Maurice Bucke, insisted upon finding mystical revelations in his poems, he made no such claims himself. Of course, characteristically, he neither agreed nor disagreed—a defensive tactic that he delighted in. On one occasion he handed his Boswell, Horace Traubel, some papers: "They are papers of the mystic esoteric sort, . . . I can't go them: they tell me I am a mystic myself: maybe that's the reason I don't like mystics." I suspect that his friends failed to observe the skeptical tendencies of Whitman's mind, just as many readers have ignored the personal anxiety behind the sometimes unduly optimistic public utterances.

It would be unfair to leave even for a moment the impression that these three commentators summed up New England's attitude toward the "rough" Brooklyn poet. James Russell Lowell, the most brahmin of the brahmins, decreed that Whitman was "solemn humbug." Henry Wadsworth Longfellow was not quite so pontifical: according to James T. Field's wife, he "finds some good in the 'yawp.'" John Greenleaf Whittier reportedly threw *Leaves of Grass* into the fireplace, although he graciously acknowledged in 1889 Whitman's tribute on the occasion of his seventieth birthday.

The publication of *Drum-Taps* in 1865 was the occasion of reviews by William Dean Howells and Henry James, Jr. Although they did not know that what has been called the American Renaissance was past and that the American literary scene was to be sterile for several decades, the new generation, as represented by two of its most distinguished members, was much more hostile in its attitude toward Whitman than toward

Emerson and Thoreau. The reaction is understandable: Howells and James disliked confessional literature and revered the impersonal art of certain foreign writers, and they consciously strove to give American literature dignity, normality, and conventional morality. Although Howells and James were to become arbiters of good taste, their initial responses to Whitman were churlish and bad-mannered. It is tasteless to report that some people held their noses when they read *Leaves of Grass*. It is arrogance to speak of an arrogant poet's taste as "monstrous" and to question Whitman's sincerity. (Any artist should know that all artists are liars.) Worst of all, Howells and James condemned Whitman because he failed to meet their standards of art and decorum. But I am unfair perhaps, for these two uncertain young men, who in 1865 had not established their reputations, had to attack a giant who stood in their paths. Sons —and Ezra Pound was a later one—must topple fathers.

Like Pound, both Howells and James eventually made pacts with Whitman. Howells in the "Editor's Study" in *Harper's Monthly* later reversed himself, although his subservience to public morality compelled him to mention the innocence of *November Boughs*—a sop that he should have been big enough to have forgone. And then there is Howells' poem "To Walt Whitman," which reveals an insight into "the voice of our mother benignant" (a marvelous and revealing line) but which also demonstrates Howells' tight, constricted nature in contrast with Whitman's open embrace of the cosmos.

In *A Small Boy and Others*, written in his old age, James refers to Whitman on two occasions. Early in his recollections he observes that "Walt Whitman broke out in the later fifties— and I was to know nothing of that happy genius till long after" —a statement which is, to say the least, a prose fiction since his review appeared in 1865. At another point James describes the "wasted melancholy" of the Civil War soldier—"an effect that somehow corresponds for memory, I bethink myself, with the tender elegiac tone in which Walt Whitman was later on so admirably to commemorate him."[8] It is perhaps not unkind to remark that "sincerity" should have led James to retract the sentiments expressed in *The Nation*. Perhaps James's later reaction was influenced by his brother William's consistent empathy with the poet. It matters little, however, whether James changed his mind "for reasons." One of the most touching scenes in our literature is Edith Wharton's account of Henry James reading "Out of the Cradle Endlessly Rocking" and "When Lilacs Last in the Dooryard Bloom'd."

The other part of the story is Whitman's reaction to Howells and James. He found Howells' notice in *Harper's Monthly* only "so-so" but "friendly." He observed to Traubel on January 25, 1889, that Howells had "so little virility" that he was "unable to follow up radically the lead of his rather remarkable intellect"[9]—a comment which, though not scrupulously fair and certainly not without vagueness in its use of that overworked word "virility," does single out Howells' flaws and strengths. Whitman was less fair about James, whom he may not have read but only sampled as was his wont in his haphazard reading (a tendency which would have kept him from the dense textures of James's canvasses). In one conversation he remarked: "James is only feathers to me." At another time: "I don't see anything above common in him: he has a vogue—but surely his vogue won't last: he don't stand permanently for anything."[10] Which only proves that as a prophet Whitman was all too human.

On June 30, 1865, Whitman lost his post in the Interior Department because the Secretary, James Harlan, refused to employ the author of indecent verse. Although the poet was given a position in the Attorney General's Office on the following day, his friends jubilantly seized upon the incident to begin the process of deification and to answer the abuse hurled at *Leaves of Grass* from the beginning. Whitman's most vigorous and hyperbolic champion was William D. O'Connor, a minor novelist, formerly an editor of the *Saturday Evening Post*, and at the time an employee in the Life Saving Bureau in Washington. As his style indicates, O'Connor was an incurable enthusiast, incapable of fine distinctions and contemptuous of nuances. He saw himself as a later Tom Paine, the defender of his friend against the abuse of government, critics, and a prudish public. In truth, O'Connor was somewhat of a Don Quixote, for he surrounded Whitman with a more hostile world than the one he in fact lived in—consciously to justify the vehemence of his attacks and unconsciously perhaps to glorify his own role as a defender of the faith. His intemperateness frequently antagonized Whitman's other friends, and his outbursts were too caustic and emotional to convince the nonbelievers. Yet the poet himself had only praise for O'Connor's colored prose.

"The Good Gray Poet," which provided an epithet and a mantle for Whitman, is, despite its polemical nature, a love poem in prose. It begins with an icon which may be a rhetorical device but is also the fantasy of a lover who may love unwisely but who loves completely a man-god:

> The dark sombrero he usually wears was, when I saw him just now, the day being warm, held for the moment in his hand; rich light an artist would have chosen, lay upon his uncovered head, majestic, large, Homeric, and set upon his strong shoulders with the grandeur of ancient sculpture. I marked the countenance, serene, proud, cheerful, florid, grave; the brow seamed with noble wrinkles; the features, massive and handsome, with firm blue eyes; the eyebrows and eyelids especially showing that fulness of arch seldom seen save in the antique busts; the flowing hair and fleecy beard, both very gray, and tempering with a look of age the youthful aspect of one who is but forty-five; the simplicity and purity of his dress, cheap and plain, but spotless, from snowy falling collar to burnished boot, and exhaling faint fragrance; the whole form surrounded with manliness as with a nimbus, and breathing, in its perfect health and vigor, the august charm of the strong.

One cannot argue with the eroticized feelings in such a passage. Indeed, it is futile to say, "wait a minute," anywhere in the entire essay, for the words relentlessly gush forth; and the adjectives, the phrases, and the exclamation points almost compel submission to the virtuoso display. And yet we sense that O'Connor is not discussing Whitman but a fantasy ("a nimbus"). His friends always lamented that he never produced a book worthy of his verbal skills, but in their kindness they erred: it was O'Connor's fate to achieve immortality in the only way possible to a man incapable of artistic or even emotional control. No artist wears his heart on his sleeve.

John Burroughs, the famous naturalist, met Whitman in Washington during the Civil War. It was the most meaningful event in the young man's life. "I love him very much," he wrote to a friend at the time. "The more I see and talk with him, the greater he becomes to me. He is as vast as the earth, and as loving and noble." In 1888, when Whitman appeared to be dying, Burroughs wrote in his journal: "How life will seem to me with Whitman gone, I cannot imagine. He is my larger, greater, earlier self. No man alive seems quite so near to me."[11] Burroughs was no starry-faced romantic; he was a sophisticated and intelligent man, the intimate of many of the most distinguished people of his era. He wrote two books and a number of essays about Whitman and invariably emphasized the poet's treatment of nature. His temperament did not permit O'Connor's excesses, and perhaps in the long run his judiciousness aided the cause more than the other's passionate outbursts.

It must be noted that O'Connor and Burroughs never wrote about the poet without submitting their manuscripts to him for correction and approval. How much Whitman altered we cannot know; but probably he corrected factual errors, supplied additional information, and occasionally excised certain phrases or passages. Certainly he did not rewrite the manuscripts, for O'Connor's style is consistently his own as is Burroughs'. The important point is not the revision, but the supervision Whitman exercised over his public image. He was, as he always admitted, a cautious man.

Ferdinand Freiligrath, a friend of Longfellow, became acquainted with Whitman through William Michael Rossetti's book of selections (1868). His was among the first voices to herald Whitman on the continent, and the translations which he made a few years later were also among the first to appear. Freiligrath had nothing original to say about Whitman except in his last two sentences; it is a pity that he did not pursue the comparison with Wagner, a point which is still in need of development. The significance of his essay is that it shows *Leaves of Grass* had begun to disturb the European establishment: Whitman was about to become a world force.

Rossetti declared that Anne Gilchrist's was "about the fullest, farthest-reaching, and most eloquent appreciation of Whitman yet put into writing, and certainly the most valuable." Whitman pronounced her essay "the proudest word that ever came to me from a woman."[12] Certainly it is one of the most personal and courageous evaluations to appear in the poet's lifetime. For Mrs. Gilchrist, an eminently respectable widow with four children and a friend of the Carlyles and the Tennysons, dared to defend even the language and the sexual passages in *Leaves of Grass* in an age of prudery on both sides of the Atlantic Ocean. Hers was an amorous critique, a love letter masquerading as criticism.

As soon as Rossetti gave her a complete edition of *Leaves of Grass* to read, she literally fell in love with the poet. Her response to Whitman's orgiastic rhythms was equally erotic: "I am breathless, bewildered, half-dead." When Whitman did not write to her after the publication of her essay, she had a nervous collapse and finally, on September 3, 1871, she wrote one of the most extraordinary love letters in the language.[13] This well-bred Victorian lady swept aside conventions to declare her love and to offer her soul and body to the poet. She rapturously envisaged herself as the poet's spiritual mate and the mother of a noble progeny. And so we have an amazing spectacle, the stuff of tragedy for some writers, of comedy to others. The poet who shocked the world because of his anatomical candor and who boldly summoned lovers to embrace him wherever he walked did not know how to handle a woman whose ardor his verses had inflamed. She exposed her feelings without shame and without stint; he was awed—and frightened—by her emotional excesses. He retreated as she pursued. When, against his wishes, she came to America in 1876 with three of her children, she learned that the fantasy which she extracted from the poetry had no counterpart in the flesh. Her disappointment, this wonderful middle-aged lady, aching with youthful ardor, never recorded.

Although Whitman was not overawed by professors and genteel literary critics, unless they had the good sense to admire his verse, he was rarely so well served in his lifetime as he was by Edward Dowden and George Saintsbury. Dowden, the distinguished professor of English literature at Trinity College, Dublin, and a noted Shakespearian scholar, was the first academician to analyze Whitman's poetry systematically. Although Dowden has reservations about the frank sexual passages and the poet's attack upon reason, he does not permit his own standards of decorum or his own rational philosophy to keep him from appreciating Whitman's unsystematic "philosophy." Dowden is the first to cite Whitman as confirmation of de Tocqueville's speculations about poetry in a democracy. However, he is so interested in content that he does not do justice to Whitman's art, and, as he acknowledges in a letter in which he included his review: "I ought to say that the article expresses very partially the impression which your writings have made on me. It keeps, as is obvious, at a single point of view, & regards only what becomes visible from that point. But also I wrote more cooly than I feel because I wanted those, who being ignorant of your writings are perhaps prejudiced against them, to say 'Here is a cool, judicious, impartial critic who finds a great deal in Whitman—perhaps, after all, we are mistaken.' "[14] For the next two decades poet and scholar corresponded, and Dowden imbued his students with a love of the American poet. (Standish James O'Grady, later a pioneer in the Celtic Renaissance, was one of the students who venerated the New World spokesman of joy and friendship.) Whitman, in 1888, summed up the relationship with a terseness that he often brought to such matters despite his alleged diffuseness: "Dowden is a book-man: but he is also and more particularly a man-man: I guess that is where we connect."[15]

How refreshing after all the talk of Whitman's "power" is Saintsbury's discussion of his greatest power—his verse! Saintsbury's defense of the much maligned and parodied catalogues is perceptive and certainly valid, and profoundly sensible is the observation: "In passages, and many of them, the marriage of matter and form justifies itself as a true marriage." The observation is not married, however, to sufficient concrete examples to be wholly convincing. Gerard Manley Hopkins apparently became acquainted with Whitman through Saintsbury's essay, and his letter to his friend Robert Bridges is another of the rare pieces of metrical commentary in early Whitman criticism. That Hopkins was fascinated by the American's experimentation is understandable, but one hungers to know the whole meaning behind Hopkins' wonderfully evasive remark: "I always knew in my heart Walt Whitman's mind to be more like my own than any other man's living."

When Robert Louis Stevenson's essay on Whitman was reprinted in *Familiar Studies of Men and Books*, Burroughs, on October 29, 1882, wrote to the poet: "It does not amount to much. He has the American vice of smartness and flippancy." In 1888 Whitman observed to Traubel: "Stevenson was friendly to me. . . . he was complimentary to the Leaves: not outrightly so—saying yes with reservations: but being a man in whom I dare not waits upon I would, he does not state his conviction unequivocally." Whitman went on to say that Mrs. Stevenson, who made a pilgrimage to Camden, "assured me that he felt far more strongly on the subject than he wrote."[16] Whitman rightly detected the "yes but" tone in Stevenson's piece, just as Burroughs spotted the flippancy, which, however, was probably the author's way of handling his ambivalence toward a book that attracted him as much as it unsettled him.

Sidney Lanier—the "Sir Galahad" of American literature, according to Thomas Wentworth Higginson—made a mistake not committed by Stevenson. On May 5, 1878, he informed Whitman that, after finding a copy of *Leaves of Grass* in Bayard Taylor's library, he took it to his hotel room and "spent a night of glory and delight":

> Although I entirely disagree with you in all points connected with artistic form, and in so much of the outcome of your doctrine as is involved in those poetic exposures of the person which your pages so unreservedly make, yet I feel sure that I understand you therein, and my dissent in these particulars becomes a very insignificant consideration in the presence of that unbounded delight which I take in all the bigness and bravery of all your ways and thoughts. It is not known to me where I can find another modern song at once so large and so naive; and the time needs to be told few things so much as the absolute personality of the person, the sufficiency of the man's manhood *to* the man, which you have propounded in such strong and beautiful rhythms. I beg you to count me among your most earnest lovers, and to believe that it would make me very happy to be of the least humble service to you at any time.[17]

Three years later in his Johns Hopkins lectures Lanier completely shifted his position, just as Taylor had recanted the effusions expressed in a letter to Whitman to become implacably hostile. In the lecture, except for his tribute to one of Whitman's least successful poems, Lanier is no longer one of the "most earnest lovers"; now he rues that "night of glory" and finds the "kosmos" a chaos. In commenting upon Lanier's letter Whitman was probably pretty close to the truth: "Lanier was a beautiful spirit: he had his work to do: did his work: I can see how the Leaves may at first blush have carried him by storm— then how, analyzing his feeling, he became less sure of his enthusiasm. It was after all rather a rough dish for so delicate a palate."[18]

Lanier makes a number of valid points: Whitman is a poseur, but Lanier forgets that all artists (and most people) are too. The poet's delight in tough guys, not unlike Hemingway's, is wish-fulfillment and cannot be considered seriously as a desirable social goal, but Lanier fails to see that Whitman, like Emerson and Thoreau, is assailing the deadening conformity of American life. Whitman's claim to be the spokesman of the democratic public, is, as Lanier suggests, cant, but Whitman knew as well as his critic that the masses are not interested in poetry. Lanier upholds decorum, standards, and sound sense; but the future is Whitman's, not Lanier's, even though Lanier's "pipe-stem-legged young man" has easily triumphed over Whitman's "rough."

The story of Swinburne's response to Whitman has often been narrated, since he was the first important contemporary English poet to extol the American in print. Swinburne sent Whitman a copy of *William Blake: A Critical Essay*, in which he devoted four pages to discussing similarities between Blake and Whitman. A few years later Swinburne included in *Songs Before Sunrise* "To Walt Whitman in America." Although Whitman was flattered by the critical notice, he was not impressed by the Blake analogy—"funny" was his word for it. O'Connor was more forthright: "The resemblance is extremely superficial—about as much as between the Gregorian chant, bellowed by bull-necked priests with donkey lips, and a first-class, infinitely varied, complex-melodied Italian opera, sung by voices half-human, half-divine."[19] This, of course, is a wild-eyed attempt to protest Whitman's originality. Swinburne's recantation in 1887 came as a shock to the Whitmanites and was the literary scandal of the year. The only one not upset was Whitman, who actually had no reason to become involved since his followers on both sides of the Atlantic Ocean were all too eager to defend him. The replies were inferior to Swinburne's rather wonderful, though grossly unfair, tirade which, among Whitman's friends, only O'Connor (who was critically ill at the time) could have matched in verbal energy, literary allusiveness, and intemperateness. That "drunken apple-woman" (Eve) and "that Hottentot wench under the influence of cantharides and adulterated rum" (Venus) are worthy of Hogarth.

When Gabriel Sarrazin's article was translated for him, Whitman pronounced that "this man has said the best things yet about us." To a friend he wrote on February 11, 1889: "It is a wonderfully *consoling* piece to me—coming from so evidently a fully equipt, sharp-eyed, sharp-nosed, sharp-ear'd Parisian Frenchman."[20] Rare is the recipient of such praise as Sarrazin heaps upon Whitman who can resist the flattery to the ego. But Sarrazin is not so "penetrative" as earlier, calmer critics; and the name-dropping in which he indulges without restraint borders at times on the ludicrous. There is no question of Sarrazin's sincerity, or of the impact of *Leaves of Grass* upon him, but only the converted can read such idolatry without reacting against the idol.

Whitman considered John Addington Symonds "a critic scholar of the first international all-time rank," and over the years he read *Greek Poets* several times, not merely because Symonds likened Whitman's to the Greek spirit. On one occasion Whitman said to Traubel: "Symonds is as tall as a mountain peak—and gentle: always gentle. . . . for pure grace and suavity of phrase, for a certain element of literary as distinguished from oratorical eloquence, he is unexcelled. Symonds is a craftsman of the first order—pure as crystal—fine, fine, fine—dangerously near the superfine in his weaker moments."[21] When Symonds wrote to the poet on October 7, 1871, it was clear that he responded—perhaps overresponded—to the "Calamus" poems. For the next twenty years he pressed Whitman for clarification of "adhesiveness"; such perhaps was his guilt over his own homosexual tendencies and such was his desire to find consolation in having a revered father figure approve deviancy. To silence Symonds Whitman was finally driven to concoct the biggest whopper of his career: he claimed he had fathered six bastards. Although Symonds' discussion of "Calamus" is associated with a personal conflict, he probes the implications of Whitman's sequence as no one before him had done in print.

At the beginning of his section on Whitman, John Jay Chapman enunciates his critical principle: "true criticism means an attempt to find out what something is, not for the purpose of judging it, or of imitating it, nor for the purpose of illustrating something else, nor for any other ulterior purpose whatever." Despite his excellently stated position, Chapman is too rooted in the principles of common sense to comprehend Whitman's achievement. It is simply naive to insist that Whitman's mind was "utterly incoherent and unintellectual," that "When Lilacs Last in the Dooryard Bloom'd" is "without a trace of self-consciousness," and that Whitman is little different from quacks. Chapman's is, I fear, a well-intentioned but simplistic mind that becomes too preoccupied with egomania and the surface traits of the poetry in order to evade the "personal" depths. But it may be fairer to say that, as the shifts in his essay from praise to censure indicate, Chapman does not fully comprehend his own unconscious response to the poet.

Barrett Wendell, one of the first professors of American literature, writes with the authority of the establishment, and Harvard College, when he attempts his survey of native writers at the dawn of the twentieth century. From his New England academic chair, he sees himself as the maintainer of standards —"excellence," it will be noted, is one of his favorite words, as indeed it is of his successors in the establishment—and somewhat anxiously Wendell defends the United States from the "decadent" standards of Europe. In doing so he comes close to making Whitman an unrepresentative American man, for his mistaken conception of American life and literature makes abnormal the normal eccentricity of some of its greatest writers who, like Thoreau, "follow the bent of my genius, which is a very crooked one."

Dr. Richard Maurice Bucke, the enlightened superintendent of an insane asylum in Canada, became acquainted with *Leaves of Grass* in the 1870's, which is too prosaic a way to describe the impact of Whitman's poetry on a man who discovered in it an illumination which he was eventually to term "cosmic consciousness." Bucke's is not a reasoned argument or view of the world: it is a statement of faith which must be respected, if not accepted. Bucke prepared a biography of Whitman (1883) which the poet, as was his custom, completely supervised and from which he ruthlessly excised the doctor's mystical and moral disquisitions. In their lengthy correspondence in the last years of Whitman's life, the poet never responded to Bucke's cosmic flights. In the prosaic life that Whitman the man had to lead, as even artists must, he was not given to illuminations of the kind Bucke discusses. In his *Commonplace-Book*, in which appear the day-by-day recordings of his last sixteen years, he notes on February 25, 1887: "Am I not having a 'happy hour,' or as near an approximation to it (the *suspicion* of it)—as is allowed? . . . (Is it not largely or really good condition of the stomach, liver & excretory apparatus?)—I was quite ill all yesterday—(how quickly the thermometer slides up or down!)." Whitman's wings were grounded to the earth more than Bucke allows in his desire to elevate the poet above Buddha, St. Paul, and Jesus.

William James's later remarks are anticipated in a comment in *The Nation* in 1875: "As far as the outward animal life goes, the existence of Walt Whitman confounds Schopenhauer quite as thoroughly as the existence of a Leopardi refutes Dr. Pangloss."[22] Later Whitman becomes James's example of "healthy-mindedness," a concept which, I feel, gives a one-dimensional view of the poet. For only by selecting evidence carefully and by confining himself to a surface reading of the poetry can James arrive at the erroneous conclusions stated in his first two sentences; many passages proving the opposite can readily be found. Santayana converts Whitman into the very model of barbarism; James converts him into the very model of "healthy-mindedness." Somehow their treatment shrinks the multifaceted poet into an ideological tool. Geniuses, like lesser men, read into a book what they want to find there, and too often because they are intent upon generalizations they neglect the all too contradictory nature of their subject matter. James's delightful enthusiasm is that of the amateur (and the word is not pejorative here): he comes only slightly closer to understanding the poet than does his brother.

Neither Henry nor William James commented upon the fact that Whitman's "I"—a persona perhaps but also the poet—plays the role of the son, embracing the voluptuous earth, hearkening fearfully to the "hissing" of the maternal sea until the boy-poet rocks in the cradle-coffin, and addressing motherland as a child who has despoiled a nation and violated maternal love—

(Say O Mother, have I not to your thought been faithful? Have I not through life kept you and yours before me?)[23]

But at the turn of the century the son became the father of American poetry, and a new generation of poets had to make "pacts" with him. To Ezra Pound Whitman is a "pig-headed father" with whom he reluctantly makes his peace: "We have one sap and one root— / Let there be commerce between us." Although Pound has many contradictory things to say about Whitman, the piece included here is candid revelation, even to its erratic spelling. It is not important for any new insights into his predecessor but surely significant in its description of the egocentric son in the presence of the egocentric father. Pound was never to outgrow his ambivalence—a son rarely does—and a disrespectful (and unsuccessful) parody in *The Spirit of Romance* ("Lo, behold, I eat water-melons. When I eat water-melons the world eats water-melons through me") proves Whitman inimitable and his paternal advice all too (annoyingly) sagacious: "Shoulder your duds dear son, and I will mine, and let us hasten forth."

When pure mind meets pure emotion—to create a polarity that contains the falsity inherent in all polarities—we witness the exhilarating confrontation of George Santayana and Walt Whitman, the philosopher with a precise mind nurtured on ideals and the poet with a sensuous heart exploding in vague idealisms. Yet Santayana's poetic distinctions are deceptive and fuzzy: "barbarism" is a most inexact word for Whitman's poetry, which is scarcely "the innocent style of Adam"; to say that "with Whitman the surface is absolutely all" is to miss his obliquities or "indirections," to use one of his favorite expressions. The reference to the poet's "canine devotion" during the Civil War is an intellectual judgment (possibly barbaric at that) that simplifies the emotional complexities of a strife not only destructive of untold young lives but also, like a family brawl, destructive of the basic social and political framework. Icy intellectualizations aside, Santayana clearly recognizes that the future Whitman speaks of "was in reality the survival of the past"; that the poet, despite the claims of those who speak of "energy" and "strenuousness," unfolds in his verse a passive rather than active personality; and that Whitman never attempts to grasp the complexities of the hearts of those people he lists in his catalogues. In the last instance, however, fairness demands acknowledgment of the fact that Whitman generalizes from a ruthlessly honest analysis of his own being, which is to "go beyond a sensuous sympathy." After reading Santayana's book, William James commented: "Bah! Give me Walt Whitman and Browning ten times over, much as the perverse ugliness of the latter at times irritates me, and intensely as I have enjoyed Santayana's attack. The barbarians are in the line of mental growth."[24] Perhaps it would be even more accurate to say that man's fate is to wrestle with his innate "barbarism," as Santayana does with his lovely intellectual defenses and as Whitman does with his extraordinary candor.

Although Basil De Selincourt's analysis lacks the sweep and scope of Santayana's essay, his discussion of poetic form goes beyond Saintsbury's to relate the line to the larger unit, the stanza or paragraph. He is especially acute in his comments on the organic justification of the parenthetical elements and in his analogy of the ebb and flow in music with Whitman's verse. The latter is not a new point since the poet himself talked often of his fondness for music, but De Selincourt endeavors to make the real but almost indescribable relationship meaningful and somewhat concrete. Unfortunately, he confines his observations primarily to two poems and does not come to grips with the difficulties of Whitman's greatest work, "Song of Myself."

Lawrence's is one of the classic statements in American literature, brilliantly insightful but also brilliantly wrongheaded. It is stimulating to watch Lawrence seize upon certain aspects of our literature and to see what he considers our literary glory and our national failures, but in the process the author of *Leaves of Grass* becomes the author of *Women in Love*, an extraordinary novel which the poet of "Calamus" could not have written. In his own apocalyptic way Lawrence, like the uninspired idolators in Whitman's lifetime, is so intent upon converting Whitman into a man-god and smoothing out contradictions and inconsistencies which the poet insisted upon that the portrait is a half truth and the program which Lawrence attributes to him one that the "furtive" poet would no doubt have repudiated.

It is easy to fault Parrington's magisterial review of our literature in *Main Currents in American Thought:* his economic interpretation is such a marked bias that he fails to do justice to many writers and frequently subordinates art to socio-economic concerns. Yet his bias is only slightly more limiting than those of moralists or intellectual historians whose theories slight almost completely the affectiveness of art, which in final analysis is the most important aspect of the artistic experience. Parrington, despite his preoccupation with democratic and political thought, has a genuine feeling for his version of Whitman, as his sensitive introductory paragraphs reveal. He presents his case with logic and a skillful (and correct) use of evidence, a trait absent in far too much Whitman criticism. There is something touching in Parrington's romantic liberalism with its abiding faith in Whitman's democracy.

Like Parrington's work, Matthiessen's *American Renaissance* is one of the great works of American scholarship, a lasting monument to one of our most perceptive literary historians. How many articles and books, in agreement, disagreement, and elaboration, it has produced, no one can ever know. In the well-known section reprinted here, the intent is perhaps more rewarding than the execution: Matthiessen devotes too much attention to Whitman's loose remarks on diction and too little to the language of the poetry. He lacks Burke's psychoanalytic insights and Chase's awareness of Whitman's conscious comic effects. Surely, as Matthiessen observes, Whitman indulges in the American tendency "to talk big"—perhaps a sign of cultural and personal feelings of inferiority—but I am not at all sure that we should deplore his "intoxication with mere sound." For I somehow have the feeling that Whitman was not unaware of what Matthiessen calls the "intense inane" in the line, "How plenteous! how spiritual! how resumé!"—which may be logically and syntactically absurd but which nevertheless has a joyous and aural clarity that harmonizes with the poet's undiscriminating love of the very sounds of life.

Muriel Rukeyser has a keen, sensitive, unconventional mind. Dismissing consideration of Whitman's sense of evil—that all too glib tombstone of moralists—she rightly focuses on the poet's treatment of what she terms the "problem of good" or his search for identity, which is the quintessential human problem. She finds the search revealing itself in the poetry: "Each poem follows the curves of its own life in passion." Her discussion of the catalogues is one of the most stimulating treatments of a device that has been likened to almost everything, including a Sears Roebuck catalogue. Perhaps one day some adventurous moviemaker will test Whitman's cinematic skill—a consummation most devoutly to be wished, since then the man who desired to be the people's poet would speak and sound in the medium the masses love.

Somewhere in his writings Henry Miller sees himself as the heir of Emerson, Thoreau, and Whitman, by which, I suppose, he means that he shares their radical (almost anarchistic) tendencies, their love of nature, and their somewhat vague faith in a vague harmony given only to the free spirits of artists to unravel. There is a link between them, tenuous as it may seem, although Miller only on rare occasions can order his disorderly talent to approximate the eccentrically ordered achievements of his predecessors. Miller is at his best in his tender but unusual comparison of Dostoevski and Whitman. In truth, like Whitman, Miller is truly moving when he abandons clowning and exhibitionism and the supposed "big statement" to voice the delicacy of his essentially unflamboyant nature.

Although there were psychologically oriented studies earlier, chiefly centered about the poet's sexual abnormality, Dr. Gustav Bychowski, a psychiatrist, is the first professional to explore in depth the oedipal situation and sublimation with only incidental attention to the homosexual question. At times Bychowski is too clinical and employs psychoanalytic jargon where ordinary language would be clearer and more humane. He also is too insistent, I believe, upon smoothing out the stresses in Whitman's life: the progression to serene old age did not follow a straight path nor, as every psychiatrist knows, did compensation through artistic expression assuage the poet's longing for human relationships. Bychowski overlooks the hard core in Whitman's nature which was somewhat at variance with his sometimes glib optimism. In his old age he wrote to Bucke: "Don't be uneasy ab't me in any respect—nature has not only endowed me with immense emotionality but immense bufferism (so to call it) or placid resignation to what happens."[25] Whitman reconciled himself—at what price we cannot know, since he was closemouthed about such things—to the ultimate reality: whatever is, is. Like most critical amateurs, Bychowski weakens his case through overreliance upon one or two sources and carelessness in citations. These faults aside, his conclusions are for the most part valid, and Whitman criticism is the richer for this psychoanalytic investigation.

With the same omnivorous appetite with which Whitman consumes experiences and life in his famous catalogues, particularly in "Song of Myself," Randall Jarrell feasts on Whitman's poetry and creates a veritable banquet of quotable phrases and passages. He is a hedonist whose eye seizes a lovely line and whose ear luxuriates in a quivering phrase. With the exception of Powys's essay, which is too delicate and warm to be spoiled by editorial comment, this is unlike any other in the collection: it is the kind of thing that all of us critics want to write and that after we have read we wonder why it was not written before. In 1855 Emerson with his marvelous eye and ear (we tend to slight his sensuous nature) saw and heard in *Leaves of Grass* what few after him perceived—"the most extraordinary piece of wit & wisdom that America has yet contributed." Jarrell abundantly illustrates Emerson's insight, and although he worries not at all about philosophy, content, or explication, he reveres Whitman for his greatest accomplishment—his poetry. He also gives the lie to Whitman's assertion that *Leaves of Grass* was too unified to be presented in extracts or in collections of poetic gems. Gems there are aplenty.

Jarrell's essay leads to a series of close readings of Whitman's major poems in the presentation of which I have for the first time ignored chronology. Although these explications follow a modern critical fashion and perhaps are sometimes intended only for serious students—since the average reader

scorns reading an explanation as long as the work it explains—
they do reveal most conclusively the seriousness with which
Whitman the poet is now taken. As noted before, Whitman
criticism has gradually centered on the artist and his artifacts
rather than on his doctrines. The poet was not speaking of
explications in the modern sense when with his usual realism he
observed to Horace Traubel: "I always saw that explications
did not explicate—that certain people were eligible to understand me, would understand me—that certain other people were
not to be reached—would only negative me whatever—that no
sort of a plea, no figures quoted, even, would affect them—reduce the quality, quantity, vehemence of their prejudice."[26]

Malcolm Cowley has made two significant contributions to
Whitman criticism: his argument for the superiority of the
1855 edition over subsequent editions and his linkage of the
American poet and Eastern mysticism, which has renewed interest in Whitman's philosophical position. Several Indian scholars, schooled in a tradition which is Cowley's only at second-
hand, have argued the similarity in book-length studies. In my
judgment these studies reveal the flaws of the familiar "source"
studies of academic scholarship—magnification of sometimes
suggestive but often vague parallels, a freewheeling treatment
of context, and an (understandably) ardent desire to prove a
point. Although it is possible to demonstrate almost anything
through careful selection from the poetry and from Whitman's
contradictory statements about *Leaves of Grass*, he does not
reveal any very profound interest in mysticism. One can characterize Section 5 in "Song of Myself" as a mystical experience
but also as a Joyce-like epiphany of an awakening artist. Cowley, like his successors, has to weaken his argument by noting
that Whitman's body worship makes him an eccentric Eastern
(or Christian) mystic. This is part of Whitman's fascination:
he simply does not fit into any of the critical or philosophical
rubrics, or perhaps he fits into all of them.

Richard Chase's commentary on the comic dimensions of
"Song of Myself" corrects a critical imbalance—the almost
unanimous tendency of students to deny Whitman a sense of
humor. The poet had no such solemn opinion of himself: he
thought that there was a worse fate than to be deemed a humor-

ist, and on one occasion he remarked to Traubel: "The humor in the Shakespearean comedies is very broad, obvious, often brutal, coarse: but in some of the tragedies—take Lear for instance—you will find another kind of humor, a humor more remote (subtle, illusive, not present)—the sort of humor William [O'Connor] declares he finds in the Leaves and in me."[27] Chase goes but one step further than the poet in placing him in the tradition of high comedy, with Congreve and Jane Austen. Although Chase's interpretation improves upon the elementary but seminal study of Constance Rourke in *American Humor: A Study of the National Character*, the argument is asserted more often than demonstrated; his insights suggest further comic elaboration.

Leo Spitzer brings to the discussion of "Out of the Cradle Endlessly Rocking" an impressive knowledge of other literatures and cultures, and with his persuasiveness Whitman's poem emerges as an American variation upon one of the oldest forms of poetry, the ode. The concreteness of his analysis enables him to avoid the weakness of the comparative approach, the tenuous and often irrelevant analogy which displays the critic's learning but sheds little light upon the poem under examination. Spitzer is especially sensitive to the complex grammatical structure and musical affinities of the poem. Whitman and Wagner have often been linked but usually in a foggy way, except for the obvious point that both were innovators at mid-century. In short, this is explication at its best.

Where Spitzer analyzes "Out of the Cradle Endlessly Rocking" as the culmination of a cultural and poetical history, Stephen E. Whicher sees it as the culmination of an "emotional crisis" stemming from "some sort of homosexual 'love affair.' " Although one can be accused of the historical fallacy and the other of the biographical fallacy, both readings have one purpose—the universalization of the experience that takes place on the shores of Paumanok, which is literally Long Island and figuratively the world—or, to put it another way, the portrait of a boy reconciling himself to loss as well as the portrait of an artist as a boy.

Although it is Matthiessen who speaks of *Leaves of Grass* as a language experiment, it is Kenneth Burke who scrutinizes the verbal texture of Whitman's prose and poetry. His closely argued essay makes great demands upon readers, but it unfolds, to borrow a Whitmanesque word that Burke calls attention to, layers of meaning that perhaps only Bychowski from his psychoanalytic base has given equal attention to. Burke's is a splendid example of what we may call psycholinguistic explication. Its weakness may be, I suspect, that it subordinates the poem in its own way to the critical technique. However, Burke's study, of which only one-third is printed here, offers exciting new approaches to Whitman's art.

James E. Miller, Jr., offers a vigorous defense of the spiritual and democratic intent (which the poet himself states in *Democratic Vistas*) behind the "Calamus" poems. He has two purposes: to defend the sequence against Van Doren's charges and to deny what the majority of Whitman scholars now accept, the homosexual component in Whitman's art. In short, the controversy set off by Symonds still rages. Miller sees as evidence of "romantic love" what others interpret as deviant sexuality, and he consistently spiritualizes the sexual passages in the poems. His is a well-reasoned defense until he succumbs to invective in his last few sentences. Surely the time has long passed when we have to talk about "unwholesomeness," and certainly one does not have to accept Miller's reading in whole or part in order to accept the fact that "Calamus" is the greatest love sequence in American literature.

Appropriateness demands that the last critical word in this volume be that of the man to whom it is dedicated—Gay Wilson Allen. He is the author of the indispensable *Walt Whitman Handbook* (1946), the definitive biographical study *The Solitary Singer* (1955), important critical and bibliographical material collected in *Walt Whitman as Man, Poet, and Legend* (1961), and many other works. In this collection he is represented by one of his finest critical essays, written in collaboration with one of his students, Professor Charles T. Davis. From a firm critical base in the nineteenth-century milieux, the essay expands, as Whitman's poetry expands, to explore time and spatial form in Whitman's writings and in effect to demonstrate that Whitman intuits what Bergson was to formulate systematically.

Introduction

The last critical word in this volume, of course, is but the first word in the next collection of Whitman criticism. Future readers will come to Whitman as though no one had read him before, and they will reinterpret him, sometimes in the light of previous criticism, often in terms of the social and critical currents of the new age.

Ideas presented here may be refined, modified, and corrected, although *corrected* is hardly the word for the personal art of interpretation. The comic aspects of Whitman's art are far from exhausted. To the psychoanalytic approaches of Bychowski and Burke may be grafted Jungian insights beyond Maude Bodkin's brief references as well as newer psychological theories. Examination of Whitman's "music" may lead to greater illumination of the Wagnerian analogies or to an exploration of the affinities between Whitman and Charles Ives or for that matter John Cage. Although Whitman and Millet have often been compared, more significant analyses will investigate, I suspect, the esthetic theories of contemporary painters like Courbet; and surely more can be done with the vaguely observed continuity of American painting from Whitman's age to that of Jackson Pollock, whose eye, external and internal, has more in common with the poet's (and Emerson's) than is apparent upon superficial examination. An adequate history of American art, verbal and pictorial, has yet to be written. Whitman's diction and prosody remain fertile fields for commentary. Close reading of the poems, despite some excellent examples gathered here, has only begun. But it is redundant and perhaps even presumptuous to predict the course of Whitman criticism.

Somewhere Robert Frost points out with characteristic facetiousness that every poet deserves all the interpretations critics advance. Whitman's most sympathetic and greatest critic has touched on the same subject—with characteristic caution: "I find anyhow that a great many of my readers credit my writings with things that do not attach to the writings themselves but to the persons who read them—things they supply, bring with them."[28]

A WORD ABOUT THE TEXT

THE EDITORIAL PROCEDURES IN THIS BOOK are quite simple. I have frequently abridged articles without, I believe, damage to the exposition. Since quotations from Whitman tend to be extensive, I have referred in brackets or in a note to the lines which the critic quotes. If, however, he offers a close reading of a passage, I have retained it. Quotations from Whitman always pose difficulties if the writer does not clearly indicate which edition he follows. I have verified all readings and have used the new *Comprehensive Reader's Edition*, issued by the New York University Press, as my authority; this monumental work of Professors Blodgett and Bradley supersedes all previous editions. In almost all cases I have identified quotations, through extensive use of Edwin Harold Eby's *Concordance* (1955), a most indispensable tool of Whitman scholarship. These identifications have swelled the notes, but it seems to me that the reader deserves to know the exact context if he is to check the validity of an interpretation. Where I have reproduced existent notes, I have placed the author's initials in brackets at the conclusion. I have standardized the format of the notes as well as of the quotations in order to avoid confusion.

Errors in transcriptions—and they are alarmingly numerous —are silently corrected without pretentious brackets or obnoxious *sics*. Careless scholars and nonscholars have forgotten that Walt Whitman was an editor and proofreader who took great pride in the accuracy of his books. A book about him deserves the same care.

A CENTURY OF

WHITMAN
CRITICISM

RALPH WALDO EMERSON

[1803–1882]

Letter to Walt Whitman (*July 21, 1855*)

Concord | Massachusetts | 21 July | 1855

DEAR SIR,

I am not blind to the worth of the wonderful gift of "Leaves of Grass." I find it the most extraordinary piece of wit & wisdom that America has yet contributed. I am very happy in reading it, as great power makes us happy. It meets the demand I am always making of what seemed the sterile & stingy Nature, as if too much handiwork or too much lymph in the temperament were making our western wits fat & mean.

I give you joy of your free & brave thought. I have great joy in it. I find incomparable things said incomparably well, as they must be. I find the courage of *treatment*, which so delights us, & which large perception only can inspire.

I greet you at the beginning of a great career, which yet must have had a long foreground somewhere, for such a start. I rubbed my eyes a little to see if this sunbeam were no illusion; but the solid sense of the book is a sober certainty. It has the best merits, namely, of fortifying & encouraging.

I did not know until I, last night, saw the book advertised in a newspaper, that I could trust the name as real &

This famous letter, the most famous in our literature, now in the Charles E. Feinberg Collection, has been often reprinted; see *Correspondence*, I, 41.

available for a Post-office. I wish to see my benefactor, & have felt much like striking my tasks, & visiting New York to pay you my respects.

R. W. EMERSON.

Mr Walter Whitman.

CHARLES ELIOT NORTON

[1827–1908]

Whitman's LEAVES OF GRASS (*1855*)

OUR ACCOUNT of the last month's literature would be incomplete without some notice of a curious and lawless collection of poems, called *Leaves of Grass*, and issued in a thin quarto without the name of publisher or author. The poems, twelve in number, are neither in rhyme nor blank verse, but in a sort of excited prose broken into lines without any attempt at measure or regularity, and, as many readers will perhaps think, without any idea of sense or reason. The writer's scorn for the wonted usages of good writing extends to the vocabulary he adopts; words usually banished from polite society are here employed without reserve and with perfect indifference to their effect on the reader's mind; and not only is the book one not to be read aloud to a mixed audience, but the introduction of terms never before heard or seen, and of slang expressions, often renders an otherwise striking passage altogether laughable. But, as the writer is a new light in poetry, it is only fair to let him state his theory for himself. We extract from the preface: —

The art of art, the glory of expression, is simplicity. Nothing is better than simplicity, and the sunlight of letters is simplicity.

Reprinted from *Putnam's Monthly*, Sept. 1855; the text used here was reprinted by Kenneth B. Murdoch in *A Leaf of Grass from Shady Hill* (Boston, 1928).

2]

Nothing is better than simplicity—nothing can make up for excess, or for the lack of definiteness. . . . To speak in literature, with the perfect rectitude and the insouciance of the movements of animals and the unimpeachableness of the sentiment of trees in the woods, is the flawless triumph of art. . . . The greatest poet has less a marked style, and is more the channel of thought and things, without increase or diminution, and is the free channel of himself. He swears to his art, I will not be meddlesome, I will not have in my writing any elegance, or effect, or originality to hang in the way between me and the rest, like curtains. What I feel, I feel for precisely what it is. Let who may exalt, or startle, or fascinate, or soothe, I will have purposes, as health, or heat, or snow has, and be as regardless of observation. What I experience or portray shall go from my composition without a shred of my composition. You shall stand by my side to look in the mirror with me.[1]

The application of these principles, and of many others equally peculiar, which are expounded in a style equally oracular throughout the long preface,—is made *passim*, and often with comical success, in the poems themselves, which may briefly be described as a compound of the New England transcendentalist and New York rowdy. A fireman or omnibus driver, who had intelligence enough to absorb the speculations of that school of thought which culminated at Boston some fifteen or eighteen years ago, and resources of expression to put them forth again in a form of his own, with sufficient self-conceit and contempt for public taste to affront all usual propriety of diction, might have written this gross yet elevated, this superficial yet profound, this preposterous yet somehow fascinating book. As we say, it is a mixture of Yankee transcendentalism and New York rowdyism, and, what must be surprising to both these elements, they here seem to fuse and combine with the most perfect harmony. The vast and vague conceptions of the one, lose nothing of their quality in passing through the coarse and odd intellectual medium of the other; while there is an original perception of nature, a manly brawn, and an epic directness in our new poet, which belong to no other adept of the transcendental school. But we have no intention of regularly criticising this very irregular production; our aim is rather to cull, from the rough and ragged thicket of its pages, a few passages equally remarkable in point of thought and expression. Of course we do not select those which are the most transcendental or the most bold: —. . . .[2]

As seems very proper in a book of transcendental poetry, the author withholds his name from the title page, and presents his portrait, neatly engraved on steel, instead. This, no doubt, is upon the principle that the name is merely accidental; while the portrait affords an idea of the essential being from whom these utterances proceed. We must add, however, that this significant reticence does not prevail throughout the volume, for we learn on p. 29, that our poet is "Walt Whitman, an American, one of the roughs, a kosmos." That he was an American, we knew before, for, aside from America, there is no quarter of the universe where such a production could have had a genesis. That he was one of the roughs was also tolerably plain; but that he was a kosmos, is a piece of news we were hardly prepared for. Precisely what a kosmos is, we trust Mr. Whitman will take an early occasion to inform the impatient public.

HENRY DAVID THOREAU

[1 8 1 7 – 1 8 6 2]

Letters to H. G. O. Blake (1856)

ALCOTT HAS BEEN HERE three times, and, Saturday before last, I went with him and Greeley, by invitation of the last, to G.'s farm, thirty-six miles north of New York. The next day A.

The excerpts are from letters written on Nov. 19 and Dec. 6–7, 1856; see *The Correspondence of Henry David Thoreau,* ed. Walter Harding and Carl Bode (New York, 1958), 441–442, 444–445.

and I heard Beecher[1] preach; and what was more, we visited Whitman the next morning (A. had already seen him), and were much interested and provoked. He is apparently the greatest democrat the world has seen. Kings and aristocracy go by the board at once, as they have long deserved to. A remarkably strong though coarse nature, of a sweet disposition, and much prized by his friends. Though peculiar and rough in his exterior, his skin (all over (?)) red, he is essentially a gentleman. I am still somewhat in a quandary about him,—feel that he is essentially strange to me, at any rate; but I am surprised by the sight of him. He is very broad, but, as I have said, not fine. He said that I misapprehended him. I am not quite sure that I do. He told us that he loved to ride up and down Broadway all day on an omnibus, sitting beside the driver, listening to the roar of the carts, and sometimes gesticulating and declaiming Homer at the top of his voice. He has long been an editor and writer for the newspapers,—was editor of the "New Orleans Crescent" once; but now has no employment but to read and write in the forenoon, and walk in the afternoon, like all the rest of the scribbling gentry. . . .

That Walt Whitman, of whom I wrote to you, is the most interesting fact to me at present. I have just read his 2nd edition (which he gave me) and it has done me more good than any reading for a long time. Perhaps I remember best the poem of Walt Whitman an American & the Sun Down Poem.[2] There are 2 or 3 pieces in the book which are disagreeable to say the least, simply sensual. He does not celebrate love at all. It is as if the beasts spoke. I think that men have not been ashamed of themselves without reason. No doubt, there have always been dens where such deeds were unblushingly recited, and it is no merit to compete with their inhabitants. But even on this side, he has spoken more truth than any American or modern that I know. I have found his poem exhilirating encouraging. As for its sensuality,—& it may turn out to be less sensual than it appeared—I do not so much wish that those parts were not written, as that men & women were so pure that they could read them without harm, that is, without understanding them. One woman told me that no woman could read it as if a man could read what a woman could not. Of course Walt Whitman can communicate

[5

to us no experience, and if we are shocked, whose experience is it that we are reminded of?

On the whole it sounds to me very brave & American after whatever deductions. I do not believe that all the sermons so called that have been preached in this land put together are equal to it for preaching—

We ought to rejoice greatly in him. He occasionally suggests something a little more than human. You cant confound him with the other inhabitants of Brooklyn or New York. How they must shudder when they read him! He is awfully good.

To be sure I sometimes feel a little imposed on. By his heartiness & broad generalities he puts me into a liberal frame of mind prepared to see wonders—as it were sets me upon a hill or in the midst of a plain—stirs me well up, and then—throws in a thousand of brick. Though rude & sometimes ineffectual, it is a great primitive poem,—an alarum or trumpet-note ringing through the American camp. Wonderfully like the Orientals, too, considering that when I asked him if he had read them, he answered, "No: tell me about them."

I did not get far in conversation with him,—two more being present,—and among the few things which I chanced to say, I remember that one was, in answer to him as representing America, that I did not think much of America or of politics, and so on, which may have been somewhat of a damper to him.

Since I have seen him, I find that I am not disturbed by any brag or egoism in his book. He may turn out the least of a braggart of all, having a better right to be confident.

He is a great fellow.

WILLIAM DEAN HOWELLS

[1837–1920]

"Drum-Taps" (1865)

WILL SALTPETER EXPLODE? Is Walt Whitman a true poet? Doubts to be solved by the wise futurity which shall pay off our national debt. Poet or not, however, there was that in Walt Whitman's first book which compels attention to his second. There are obvious differences between the two: this is much smaller than that; and whereas you had at times to hold your nose (as a great sage observed) in reading "Leaves of Grass," there is not an indecent thing in "Drum-Taps." The artistic method of the poet remains, however, the same, and we must think it mistaken. The trouble about it is that it does not give you sensation in a portable shape; the thought is as intangible as aroma; it is no more put up than the atmosphere.

We are to suppose that Mr. Whitman first adopted his method as something that came to him of its own motion. This is the best possible reason, and only possible excuse, for it. In its way, it is quite as artificial as that of any other poet, while it is unspeakably inartistic. On this account it is a failure. The method of talking to one's self in rhythmic and ecstatic prose is one that surprises at first, but, in the end, the talker can only have the devil for a listener, as happens in other cases when people address their own individualities; not, however, the devil of the proverb, but the devil of reasonless, hopeless, all-defying egotism. An ingenious French critic said very acutely of Mr.

Reprinted from *The Round Table* (Nov. 1865), 147–148.

[7

Whitman that he made you partner of the poetical enterprise, which is perfectly true; but no one wants to share the enterprise. We want its effect, its success; we do not want to plant corn, to hoe it, to drive the crows away, to gather it, husk it, grind it, sift it, bake it, and butter it, before eating it, and then take the risk of its being at last moldy in our mouths. And this is what you have to do in reading Mr. Whitman's rhythm.

At first, a favorable impression is made by the lawlessness of this poet, and one asks himself if this is not the form which the unconscious poetry of American life would take, if it could find a general utterance. But there is really no evidence that such is the case. It is certain that among the rudest peoples the lurking sublimity of nature has always sought expression in artistic form, and there is no good reason to believe that the sentiment of a people with our high average culture would seek expression more rude and formless than that of the savagest tribes. Is it not more probable that, if the passional principle of American life could find utterance, it would choose the highest, least dubious, most articulate speech? Could the finest, most shapely expression be too good for it?

If we are to judge the worth of Mr. Whitman's poetic theory (or impulse, or possession) by its popular success, we must confess that he is wrong. It is already many years since he first appeared with his claim of poet, and in that time he has employed criticism as much as any literary man in our country, and he has enjoyed the fructifying extremes of blame and praise. Yet he is, perhaps, less known to the popular mind, to which he has attempted to give an utterance, than the newest growth of the magazines and the newspaper notices. The people fairly rejected his former revelation, letter and spirit, and those who enjoyed it were readers with a cultivated taste for the quaint and the outlandish. The time to denounce or to ridicule Mr. Whitman for his first book is past. The case of "Leaves of Grass" was long ago taken out the hands of counsel and referred to the great jury. They have pronounced no audible verdict; but what does their silence mean? There were reasons in the preponderant beastliness of that book why a decent public should reject it; but now the poet has cleansed the old channels of their filth, and pours through them a stream of blameless purity, and the public has again to decide, and this time more directly, on the question of his poethood. As we said, his method remains the same, and he himself declares that, so far as concerns it, he has not changed nor grown in any way since we saw him last:

Beginning my studies, the first step pleased me so much,
The mere fact, consciousness—these forms—the power of motion,
The least insect or animal—the senses—eye-sight;
The first step, I say, aw'd me and pleas'd me so much,
I have never gone, and never wish'd to go, any further,
But stop and loiter all my life to sing it in ecstatic songs.

Mr. Whitman has summed up his own poetical theory so well in these lines, that no criticism could possibly have done it better. It makes us doubt, indeed, if all we have said in consideration of him has not been said idly, and certainly releases us from further explanation of his method.

In "Drum-Taps," there is far more equality than in "Leaves of Grass," and though the poet is not the least changed in purpose, he is certainly changed in fact. The pieces of the new book are nearly all very brief, but generally his expression is freer and fuller than ever before. The reader understands, doubtless, from the title, that nearly all these pieces relate to the war; and they celebrate many of the experiences of the author in the noble part he took in the war. One imagines the burly tenderness of the man who went to supply the

——lack of woman's nursing

that there was in the hospitals of the field, and woman's tears creep unconsciously to the eyes as the pity of his heart communicates itself to his reader's. No doubt the pathos of many of the poems gains something from the quaintness of the poet's speech. One is touched in reading them by the same inarticulate feeling as that which dwells in music; and is sensible that the poet conveys to the heart certain emotions which the brain cannot analyze, and only remotely perceives. This is especially true of his inspirations from nature; memories and yearnings come to you folded, mute, and motionless in his verse, as they come in the breath of a familiar perfume. They give a strange, shadowy sort of pleasure, but they do not satisfy, and you rise from the perusal of this man's book as you issue from the presence of one whose personal magnetism is very subtle and strong, but who has not added to this tacit attraction the charm of spoken ideas. We must not mistake this fascination for a higher quality. In the tender eyes of an ox lurks a melancholy, soft and pleasing to the glance as the pensive sweetness of a woman's eyes; but in the orb of the brute there is no hope of expression, and in the woman's look there is the endless delight of history, the heavenly possibility of utterance.

Art cannot greatly employ itself with things in embryo. The instinct of the beast may interest science; but poetry, which is nobler than science, must concern itself with natural instincts only as they can be developed into the sentiments and ideas of the soul of man. The mind will absorb from nature all that is speechless in her influences; and it will demand from kindred mind those higher things which can be spoken. Let us say our say here against the nonsense, long current, that there is, or can be, poetry *between the lines*, as is often sillily asserted. *Expression* will always suggest; but mere *suggestion* in art is unworthy of existence, vexes the heart, and shall not live. Every man has tender, and beautiful, and lofty emotions; but the poet was sent into this world to give these a tangible utterance, and if he do not this, but only give us back dumb emotion for dumb emotion, he is a cumberer of the earth. There is a yearning, almost to agony at times, in the human heart, to throw off the burden of inarticulate feeling, and if the poet will not help it in this effort, if, on the contrary, he shall seek to weigh it and sink it down under heavier burdens, he has not any reason to be.

So long, then, as Mr. Whitman chooses to stop at mere consciousness, he cannot be called a true poet. We all have consciousness; but we ask of art an utterance. We do not so much care in what way we get this expression; we will take it in ecstatic prose, though we think it is better subjected to the laws of prosody, since every good thing is subject to some law; but the expression we must have. Often, in spite of himself, Mr. Whitman grants it in this volume, and there is some hope that he will hereafter grant it more and more. There are such rich possibilities in the man that it is lamentable to contemplate his error of theory. He has truly and thoroughly absorbed the idea of our American life, and we say to him as he says to himself,

"You've got enough in you, Walt; why don't you get it out?"[1] A man's greatness is good for nothing folded up in him, and if emitted in barbaric yawps, it is not more filling than Ossian or the east wind.

Editor's Study (1889)

MR. WALT WHITMAN calls his latest book *November Boughs*, and in more ways than one it testifies and it appeals beyond the letter to the reader's interest. For the poet the long fight is over; he rests his cause with what he has done; and we think no one now would like to consider the result without respect, without deference, even if one cannot approach it with entire submission. It is time, certainly, while such a poet is still with us, to own that his literary intention was as generous as his spirit was bold, and that if he has not accomplished all he intended, he has been a force that is by no means spent. Apart from the social import of his first book ("without yielding an inch, the working-man and working-woman were to be in my pages from first to last"), he aimed in it at the emancipation of poetry from what he felt to be the trammels of rhyme and metre. He did not achieve this; but he produced a new kind in literature, which we may or may not allow to be poetry, but which we cannot deny is something eloquent, suggestive, moving, with a lawless, formless beauty of its own. He dealt literary conventionality one of those blows which eventually show as internal injuries, whatever the immediate effect seems to be. He made it possible for poetry hereafter to be more direct and natural than hitherto; the hearing which he has braved nearly half a century of contumely and mockery to win would now be granted on very different terms to a man of

Reprinted from *Harper's Monthly*, LXXVIII (Feb. 1889), 448.

[*11*

his greatness. This is always the way; and it is always the way that the reformer (perhaps in helpless confession of the weakness he shares with all humankind) champions some error which seems as dear to him as the truth he was born to proclaim. Walt Whitman was not the first to observe that we are all naked under our clothes, but he was one of the greatest, if not the first, to preach a gospel of nudity; not as one of his Quaker ancestry might have done for a witness against the spiritual nakedness of his hearers, but in celebration of the five senses and their equal origin with the three virtues of which the greatest is charity. His offence, if rank, is quantitatively small; a few lines at most; and it is one which the judicious pencil of the editor will some day remove for him, though for the present he "takes occasion to confirm those lines with the settled convictions and deliberate renewals of thirty years." We hope for that day, not only because it will give to all a kind in poetry which none can afford to ignore, and which his cherished lines bar to most of those who read most in our time and country, but because we think the five senses do not need any celebration. In that duality which every thoughtful person must have noticed composes him, we believe the universal experience is that the beast half from first to last is fully able to take care of itself. But it is a vast subject, and, as the poet says, "it does not stand by itself; the vitality of it is altogether in its relations, bearings, significance."[2] In the mean while we can assure the reader that these *November Boughs* are as innocent as so many sprays of apple blossom, and that he may take the book home without misgiving.

We think he will find in reading it that the prose passages are, some of them, more poetic than the most poetic of the rhythmical passages. "Some War Memoranda," and "The Last of the War Cases"—notes made twenty-five years ago—are alive with a simple pathos and instinct with a love of truth which recall the best new Russian work, and which make the poet's psalms seem vague and thin as wandering smoke in comparison. Yet these have the beauty of undulant, sinuous, desultory smoke forms, and they sometimes take the light with a response of such color as dwells in autumn sunsets. The book is well named *November Boughs:* it is meditative and reminiscent, with a sober fragrance in it like the scent of fallen leaves in woods where the leaves that still linger overhead,

> Or few, or none, do shake against the cold—
> Bare ruined choirs where late the sweet birds sang.

It is the hymn of the runner resting after the race, and much the same as he chants always, whether the race has been lost or won.

HENRY JAMES

[1 8 4 3 – 1 9 1 6]

Mr. Walt Whitman (*1865*)

IT HAS BEEN a melancholy task to read this book; and it is a still more melancholy one to write about it. Perhaps since the day of Mr. Tupper's *Philosophy*[1] there has been no more difficult reading of the poetic sort. It exhibits the effort of an essentially prosaic mind to lift itself, by a prolonged muscular strain, into poetry. Like hundreds of other good patriots, during the last four years, Mr. Walt Whitman has imagined that a certain amount of violent sympathy with the great deeds and sufferings of our soldiers, and of admiration for our national energy, together with a ready command of picturesque language, are sufficient inspiration for a poet. If this were the case, we had been a nation of poets. The constant developments of the war moved us continually to strong feeling and to strong expression of it. But in those cases in which these expressions were written

An unsigned review in *The Nation* on Nov. 15, 1865; the text used here was reprinted in *Views and Reviews* (New York, 1908), 101–110.

out and printed with all due regard to prosody, they failed to make poetry, as any one may see by consulting now in cold blood the back volumes of the *Rebellion Record*.

Of course the city of Manhattan, as Mr. Whitman delights to call it, when regiments poured through it in the first months of the war, and its own sole god, to borrow the words of a real poet, ceased for a while to be the millionaire, was a noble spectacle, and a poetical statement to this effect is possible. *Of course* the tumult of a battle is grand, the results of a battle tragic, and the untimely deaths of young men a theme for elegies. But he is not a poet who merely reiterates these plain facts *ore rotundo*. He only sings them worthily who views them from a height. Every tragic event collects about it a number of persons who delight to dwell upon its superficial points—of minds which are bullied by the *accidents* of the affair. The temper of such minds seems to us to be the reverse of the poetic temper; for the poet, although he incidentally masters, grasps, and uses the superficial traits of his theme, is really a poet only in so far as he extracts its latent meaning and holds it up to common eyes. And yet from such minds most of our war-verses have come, and Mr. Whitman's utterances, much as the assertion may surprise his friends, are in this respect no exception to general fashion. They are an exception, however, in that they openly pretend to be something better; and this it is that makes them melancholy reading.

Mr. Whitman is very fond of blowing his own trumpet, and he has made very explicit claims for his books. "Shut not your doors," he exclaims at the outset—

Shut not your doors to me, proud libraries,
For that which was lacking among you all, yet needed most, I bring;
A book I have made for your dear sake, O soldiers,
And for you, O soul of man, and you, love of comrades;
The words of my book nothing, the life of it everything;
A book separate, not link'd with the rest, nor felt by the intellect;
But you will feel every word, O Libertad! arm'd Libertad!
It shall pass by the intellect to swim the sea, the air,
With joy with you, O soul of man.[2]

These are great pretensions, but it seems to us that the following are even greater:

From Paumanok starting, I fly like a bird,
Around and around to soar, to sing the idea of all;
To the north betaking myself, to sing there arctic songs,
To Kanada, 'till I absorb Kanada in myself—to Michigan then,
To Wisconsin, Iowa, Minnesota, to sing their songs (they are
    inimitable);
Then to Ohio and Indiana, to sing theirs—to Missouri and Kansas
    and Arkansas to sing theirs,
To Tennessee and Kentucky—to the Carolinas and Georgia, to sing
    theirs,
To Texas, and so along up toward California, to roam accepted
    everywhere;
To sing first (to the tap of the war-drum, if need be)
The idea of all—of the western world, one and inseparable,
And then the song of each member of these States.[3]

Mr. Whitman's primary purpose is to celebrate the greatness of our armies; his secondary purpose is to celebrate the greatness of the city of New York. He pursues these objects through a hundred pages of matter which remind us irresistibly of the story of the college professor who, on a venturesome youth bringing him a theme done in blank verse, reminded him that it was not customary in writing prose to begin each line with a capital. The frequent capitals are the only marks of verse in Mr. Whitman's writings. There is, fortunately, but one attempt at rhyme. We say fortunately, for if the inequality of Mr. Whitman's lines were self-registering, as it would be in the case of an anticipated syllable at their close, the effect would be painful in the extreme. As the case stands, each line stands off by itself, in resolute independence of its companions, without a visible goal.

But if Mr. Whitman does not write verse, he does not write ordinary prose. The reader has seen that liberty is "libertad." In like manner, comrade is "camerado"; Americans are "Americanos"; a pavement is a "trottoir," and Mr. Whitman himself is a "chansonnier." If there is one thing that Mr. Whitman is not, it is this, for Béranger was a *chansonnier*.[4] To appreciate the force of our conjunction, the reader should compare his military lyrics with Mr. Whitman's declamations. Our author's novelty, however, is not in his words, but in the form of his writing. As we have said, it begins for all the world like verse and turns out to be arrant prose. It is more like Mr. Tupper's proverbs than anything we have met.

But what if, in form, it *is* prose? it may be asked. Very good poetry has come out of prose before this. To this we would reply that it must first have gone into it. Prose, in order to be good poetry, must first be good prose. As a general principle, we know of no circumstance more likely to impugn a writer's earnestness than the adoption of an anomalous style. He must have something very original to say if none of the old vehicles will carry his thoughts. Of course he *may* be surprisingly original. Still, presumption is against him. If on examination the matter of his discourse proves very valuable, it justifies, or at any rate excuses, his literary innovation.

But if, on the other hand, it is of a common quality, with nothing new about it but its manners, the public will judge the writer harshly. The most that can be said of Mr. Whitman's vaticinations is, that, cast in a fluent and familiar manner, the average substance of them might escape unchallenged. But we have seen that Mr. Whitman prides himself especially on the substance—the life—of his poetry. It may be rough, it may be grim, it may be clumsy—such we take to be the author's argument—but it is sincere, it is sublime, it appeals to the soul of man, it is the voice of a people. He tells us, in the lines quoted, that the words of his book are nothing. To our perception they are everything, and very little at that.

A great deal of verse that is nothing but words has, during the war, been sympathetically sighed over and cut out of newspaper corners, because it has possessed a certain simple melody. But Mr. Whitman's verse, we are confident, would have failed even of this triumph, for the simple reason that no triumph, however small, is won but through the exercise of art, and that this volume is an offence against art. It is not enough to be grim and rough and careless; common sense is also necessary, for it is by common sense that we are judged. There exists in even the commonest minds, in literary matters, a certain precise instinct of conservatism, which is very shrewd in detecting wanton eccentricities.

To this instinct Mr. Whitman's attitude seems monstrous. It is monstrous because it pretends to persuade the soul while it slights the intellect; because it pretends to gratify the feelings while it outrages the taste. The point is that it does this *on theory*, wilfully, consciously, arrogantly. It is the little nursery game of "open your mouth and shut your eyes." Our hearts are often touched through a compromise with the artistic sense, but never in direct violation of it. Mr. Whitman sits down at the outset and counts out the intelligence. This were indeed a wise precaution on his part if the intelligence were only submissive! But when she is deliberately insulted, she takes her revenge by simply standing erect and open-eyed. This is assuredly the best she can do. And if she could find a voice she would probably address Mr. Whitman as follows: —

"You came to woo my sister, the human soul. Instead of giving me a kick as you approach, you should either greet me courteously, or, at least, steal in unobserved. But now you have me on your hands. Your chances are poor. What the human heart desires above all is sincerity, and you do not appear to me sincere. For a lover you talk entirely too much about yourself. In one place you threaten to absorb Kanada. In another you call upon the city of New York to incarnate you, as you have incarnated it. In another you inform us that neither youth pertains to you nor 'delicatesse,' that you are awkward in the parlour, that you do not dance, and that you have neither bearing, beauty, knowledge, nor fortune. In another place, by an allusion to your 'little songs,' you seem to identify yourself with the third person of the Trinity.

"For a poet who claims to sing 'the idea of all,' this is tolerably egotistical. We look in vain, however, through your book for a single idea. We find nothing but flashy imitations of ideas. We find a medley of extravagances and commonplaces. We find art, measure, grace, sense sneered at on every page, and nothing positive given us in their stead. To be positive one must have something to say; to be positive requires reason, labour, and art; and art requires, above all things, a suppression of one's self, a subordination of one's self to an idea. This will never do for you, whose plan is to adapt the scheme of the universe to your own limitations. You cannot entertain and exhibit ideas; but, as we have seen, you are prepared to incarnate them. It is for this reason, doubtless, that when once you have planted yourself squarely before the public, and in view of the great service you have done to the ideal, have become, as you say, 'accepted everywhere,' you can afford to deal exclusively in words. What would be bald nonsense and dreary platitudes in any one else becomes sublimity in you.

"But all this is a mistake. To become adopted as a national poet, it is not enough to discard everything in particular and to accept everything in general, to amass crudity upon crudity, to discharge the undigested contents of your blotting-book into the lap of the public. You must respect the public which you address; for it has taste, if you have not. It delights in the grand, the heroic, and the masculine; but it delights to see these conceptions cast into worthy form. It is indifferent to brute sublimity. It will never do for you to thrust your hands into your pockets and cry out that, as the research of form is an intolerable bore, the shortest and most economical way for the public to embrace its idols—for the nation to realise its genius—is in your own person.

"This democratic, liberty-loving, American populace, this stern and war-tried people, is a great civiliser. It is devoted to refinement. If it has sustained a monstrous war, and practised human nature's best in so many ways for the last five years, it is not to put up with spurious poetry afterwards. To sing aright our battles and our glories it is not enough to have served in a hospital (however praiseworthy the task in itself), to be aggressively careless, inelegant, and ignorant, and to be constantly preoccupied with yourself. It is not enough to be rude, lugubrious, and grim. You must also be serious. You must forget yourself in your ideas. Your personal qualities—the vigour of your temperament, the manly independence of your nature, the tenderness of your heart—these facts are impertinent. You must be *possessed*, and you must thrive to possess your possession. If in your striving you break into divine eloquence, then you are a poet. If the idea which possesses you is the idea of your country's greatness, then you are a national poet; and not otherwise."

WILLIAM D. O'CONNOR

[1832–1889]

The Good Gray Poet (1866)

I HAVE HAD THE HONOR, which I esteem a very high one, to know Walt Whitman intimately for several years, and am conversant with the details of his life and history. Scores and scores of persons, who know him well, can confirm my own report of him, and I have therefore no hesitation in saying that the scandalous assertions of Mr. Harlan, derived from whom I know not, as to his being a bad man, a free lover, etc., belong to the category of those calumnies at which, as Napoleon said, innocence itself is confounded. A better man in all respects, or one more irreproachable in his relations to the other sex, lives not upon this earth. His is the great goodness, the great chastity of spiritual strength and sanity. I do not believe that from the hour of his infancy, when Lafayette held him in his arms, to the present hour, in which he bends over the last wounded and dying of the war, any one can say aught of him, which does not consort with the largest and truest manliness. . . . If I could associate the title with a really great person, or if the name of man were not radically superior, I should say that for solid nobleness of character, for native elegance and delicacy of soul, for a courtesy which is the very passion of thoughtful kindness and forbearance, for his tender and paternal respect and manly honor for woman, for love and heroism carried into the pettiest

The text used here was reprinted by Richard Maurice Bucke in *Walt Whitman* (Philadelphia, 1883), 101–129.

details of life, and for a large and homely beauty of manners, which makes the civilities of parlors fantastic and puerile in comparison, Walt Whitman deserves to be considered the grandest gentleman that treads this continent. I know well the habits and tendencies of his life. They are all simple, sane, domestic, worthy of him as one of an estimable family and a member of society. He is a tender and faithful son, a good brother, a loyal friend, an ardent and devoted citizen. . . . He has been a visitor of prisons, a protector of fugitive slaves, a constant voluntary nurse, night and day, at the hospitals, from the beginning of the war to the present time; a brother and friend through life to the neglected and the forgotten, the poor, the degraded, the criminal, the outcast, turning away from no man for his guilt, nor woman for her vileness. His is the strongest and truest compassion I have ever known. . . . I know not what talisman Walt Whitman carries, unless it be an unexcluding friendliness and goodness which is felt upon his approach like magnetism; but I know that in the subterranean life of cities, among the worst roughs, he goes safely; and I could recite instances where hands that, in mere wantonness of ferocity, assault anybody, raised against him, have of their own accord been lowered almost as quickly, or, in some cases, have been dragged promptly down by others; this, too, I mean, when he and the assaulting gang were mutual strangers. I have seen singular evidence of the mysterious quality which not only guards him, but draws to him with intuition, rapid as light, simple and rude people, as to their natural mate and friend. . . . It would be impossible to exaggerate the personal adhesion and strong, simple affection given him, in numerous instances on sight, by multitudes of plain persons, sailors, mechanics, drivers, soldiers, farmers, sempstresses, old people of the past generation, mothers of families—those powerful, unlettered persons, among whom, as he says in his book, he has gone freely, and who never in most cases even suspect as an author him whom they love as a man, and who loves them in return.

His intellectual influence upon many young men and women —spirits of the morning sort, not willing to belong to that intellectual colony of Great Britain which our literary classes compose, nor helplessly tied, like them, to the old forms—I note as kindred to that of Socrates upon the youth of ancient Attica, or Raleigh upon the gallant young England of his day. It is a power at once liberating, instructing, and inspiring.—His conversation is a university. Those who have heard him in some roused hour, when the full afflatus of his spirit moved him, will agree with me that the grandeur of talk was accomplished. He is known as a passionate lover and powerful critic of the great music and of art. He is deeply cultured by some of the best books, especially those of the Bible, which he prefers above all other great literature, but principally by contact and communion with things themselves, which literature can only mirror and celebrate. He has travelled through most of the United States,[1] intent on comprehending and absorbing the genius and history of his country, that he might do his best to start a literature worthy of her, sprung from her own polity, and tallying her own unexampled magnificence among the nations. To the same end, he has been a long, patient, and laborious student of life, mixing intimately with all varieties of experience and men, with curiosity and with love. He has given his thought, his life, to this beautiful ambition, and, still young, he has grown gray in its service. He has never married; like Giordano Bruno, he has made Thought in the service of his fellow-creatures his *bella donna*, his best beloved, his bride. His patriotism is boundless. It is no intellectual sentiment; it is a personal passion. He performs with scrupulous fidelity and zeal the duties of a citizen. . . . Who, knowing him, does not regard him as a man of the highest spiritual culture? I have never known one of greater and deeper religious feeling. To call one like him good seems an impertinence. In our sweet country phrase, he is one of God's men. And as I write these hurried and broken memoranda—as his strength and sweetness of nature, his moral health, his rich humor, his gentleness, his serenity, his charity, his simple-heartedness, his courage, his deep and varied knowledge of life and men, his calm wisdom, his singular and beautiful boy-innocence, his personal majesty, his rough scorn of mean actions, his magnetic and exterminating anger on due occasions—all that I have seen and heard of him, the testimony of associates, the anecdotes of friends, the remembrance of hours with him that should be immortal, the traits, lineaments, incidents of his life and being

—as they come crowding into memory—his seems to me a character which only the heroic pen of Plutarch could record, and which Socrates himself might emulate or envy. . . .

I have carefully counted out from Walt Whitman's poetry the lines, perfectly moral to me, whether viewed in themselves or in the light of their sublime intentions and purport, but upon which ignorant and indecent persons of respectability base their sweeping condemnation of the whole work. Taking *Leaves of Grass*, and the recent small volume, "Drum-Taps" (which was in Mr. Harlan's possession), there are in the whole about nine thousand lines or verses. From these, including matter which I can hardly imagine objectionable to any one, but counting everything which the most malignant virtue could shrink from, I have culled eighty lines. Eighty lines out of nine thousand! It is a less proportion than one finds in Shakespeare. Upon this so slender basis rests the whole crazy fabric of American and European slander and the brutal lever of the Secretary.[2]

. . . Let it be remembered that there is nothing in the book that in one form or another is not contained in all great poetic or universal literature. It has nothing either in quantity or quality so offensive as everybody knows is in Shakespeare. All that this poet has done is to mention, without levity, without low language, very seriously, often devoutly, always simply, certain facts in the natural history of man and of life, and sometimes, assuming their sanctity, to use them in illustration or imagery. Far more questionable mention and use of these facts are common to the greatest literature. Shall the presence in a book of eighty lines, similar in character to what every great and noble poetic book contains, be sufficient to shove it below even the lewd writings of Petronius Arbiter, the dirty dramas of Shirley, or the scrofulous fiction of Louvet de Couvray?[3] to lump it in with the anonymous lascivious trash spawned in holes and sold in corners, too witless and disgusting for any notice but that of the police—and to entitle its author to treatment such as only the nameless wretches of the very sewers of authorship ought to receive? . . .

What is this poem, for the giving of which to America and the world, and for that alone, its author has been dismissed with ignominy from a Government office? It is a poem which Schiller might have hailed as the noblest specimen of naïve literature, worthy of a place beside Homer. It is, in the first place, a work purely and entirely American, autochthonic, sprung from our own soil; no savor of Europe nor of the past, nor of any other literature in it; a vast carol of our own land, and of its Present and Future; the strong and haughty psalm of the Republic. There is not one other book, I care not whose, of which this can be said. I weigh my words and have considered well. Every other book by an American author implies, both in form and substance, I cannot even say the European, but the British mind. The shadow of Temple Bar and Arthur's Seat lies dark on all our letters. Intellectually, we are still a dependency of Great Britain, and one word—colonial—comprehends and stamps our literature. In no literary form, except our newspapers, has there been anything distinctively American. I note our best books—the works of Jefferson, the romances of Brockden Brown, the speeches of Webster, Everett's rhetoric, the divinity of Channing, some of Cooper's novels, the writings of Theodore Parker, the poetry of Bryant, the masterly law arguments of Lysander Spooner,[4] the miscellanies of Margaret Fuller, the histories of Hildreth,[5] Bancroft and Motley, Ticknor's "History of Spanish Literature," Judd's "Margaret,"[6] the political treatises of Calhoun, the rich, benignant poems of Longfellow, the ballads of Whittier, the delicate songs of Philip Pendleton Cooke,[7] the weird poetry of Edgar Poe, the wizard tales of Hawthorne, Irving's "Knickerbocker," Delia Bacon's[8] splendid sibyllic book on Shakespeare, the political economy of Carey,[9] the prison letters and immortal speech of John Brown, the lofty patrician eloquence of Wendell Phillips,[10] and those diamonds of the first water, the great clear essays and greater poems of Emerson. This literature has often commanding merits, and much of it is very precious to me; but in respect to its national character, all that can be said is that it is tinged, more or less deeply, with America; and the foreign model, the foreign standards, the foreign ideas, dominate over it all.

At most, our best books were but struggling beams; behold in *Leaves of Grass* the immense and absolute sunrise! It is all our own! The nation is in it! In form a series of chants, in substance it is an epic of America. It is distinctively and utterly American.

Without model, without imitation, without reminiscence, it is evolved entirely from our own polity and popular life. Look at what it celebrates and contains! hardly to be enumerated without sometimes using the powerful, wondrous phrases of its author, so indissoluble are they with the things described.[11] . . . with all these, with more, with everything transcendent, amazing, and new, undimmed by the pale cast of thought, and with the very color and brawn of actual life, the whole gigantic epic of our continental being unwinds in all its magnificent reality in these pages. To understand Greece, study the "Iliad" and "Odyssey;" study *Leaves of Grass* to understand America. Her democracy is there. Would you have a text-book of democracy? The writings of Jefferson are good; De Tocqueville is better; but the great poet always contains historian and philosopher—and to know the comprehending spirit of this country, you shall question these insulted pages.

Yet this vast and patriotic celebration and presentation of all that is our own, is but a part of this tremendous volume. Here in addition is thrown in poetic form, a philosophy of life, rich, subtle, composite, ample, adequate to these great shores. Here are presented superb types of models of manly and womanly character for the future of this country, athletic, large, naïve, free, dauntless, haughty, loving, nobly carnal, nobly spiritual, equal in body and soul, acceptive and tolerant as Nature, generous, cosmopolitan, above all, religious. Here are erected standards, drawn from the circumstances of our case, by which not merely our literature, but all our performance, our politics, art, behavior, love, conversation, dress, society, everything belonging to our lives and their conduct, will be shaped and recreated. A powerful afflatus from the Infinite has given this book life. A voice which is the manliest of human voices sounds through it all. In it is the strong spirit which will surely mould our future. Mark my words: its sentences will yet clinch the arguments of statesmen; its precepts will be the laws of the people! From the beams of this seminal sun will be generated, with tropical luxuriance, the myriad new forms of thought and life in America. And in view of the national character and national purpose of this work—in view of its vigorous re-enforcement and service to all that we hold most precious—I make the claim here, that so far from defaming and persecuting its author, the attitude of an American statesman or public officer towards him should be to the highest degree friendly and sustaining.

Beyond his country, too, this poet serves the world. He refutes by his example the saying of Goethe, one of those which stain that noble fame with baseness, that a great poet cannot be patriotic; and he dilates to a universal use which redoubles the splendors of his volume, and makes it dear to all that is human. I am not its authorized interpreter, and can only state, at the risk of imperfect expression and perhaps error, what its meanings and purpose seem to me. But I see that, in his general intention, the author has aimed to express that most common but wondrous thing—that strange assemblage of soul, body, intellect—beautiful, mystical, terrible, limited, boundless, ill-assorted, contradictory, yet singularly harmonized—a Human Being, a single separate identity—a Man—himself; but himself typically, and in his universal being. This he has done with perfect candor, including the bodily attributes and organs as necessary component parts of the creation. Every thinking person should see the value and use of such a presentation of human nature as this. I also see—and it is from these parts of the book that much of the misunderstanding and offence arises—that this poet seeks in subtle ways to rescue from the keeping of blackguards and debauchees, to which it has been abandoned, and to redeem to noble thought and use, the great element of amativeness or sexuality, with all its acts and organs. Sometimes by direct assertion, sometimes by implication, he rejects the prevailing admission that this element is vile; declares its natural or normal manifestation to be sacred and unworthy shame; awards it an equal but not superior sanctity with the other elements that compose man; and illustrates his doctrine and sets his example by applying this element, with all that pertains to it, to use as part of the imagery of poetry. Then, besides, diffused like an atmosphere throughout the poem, tincturing all its quality, and giving it that sacerdotal and prophetic character which makes it a sort of American Bible, is the pronounced and ever-recurring assertion of the divinity of all things. In a spirit like that of the Egyptian priesthood, who wore the dung-beetle in gold on their crests, perhaps as a symbol of the sacredness of even the lowest forms of life, the poet celebrates all the Creation as noble and holy—the meanest and lowest parts of it, as well as the most lofty; all equally projections of the Infinite; all emanations of the creative life of God. Perpetual hymns break from him in praise of the divineness of the universe; he sees a halo around every shape, however low; and life in all its forms inspires a rapture of worship.

. . . Nothing that America had before in literature rose above construction; this is a creation. Idle, and worse than idle, is any attempt to place this author either among or below the poets of the day. They are but singers; he is a bard. . . . I class him boldly, and the future will confirm my judgment, among the great creative minds of the world. By a quality almost incommunicable, which makes its possessor, no matter what his diversity or imperfections, equal with the Supremes of art and by the very structure of his mind, he belongs there. His place is beside Shakespeare, Æschylus, Cervantes, Dante, Homer, Isaiah—the bards of the last ascent, the brothers of the radiant summit. And if any man think this estimate extravagant, I leave him, as Lord Bacon says, to the gravity of that judgment, and pass on. Enough for me to pronounce this book grandly good and supremely great. . . .

I know not what further vicissitude of insult and outrage is in store for this great man. It may be that the devotees of a castrated literature, the earthworms that call themselves authors, the confectioners that pass for poets, the flies that are recognized as critics, the bigots, the dilettanti, the prudes and the fools, are more potent than I dream to mar the fortunes of his earthly hours; but above and beyond them uprises a more majestic civilization in the immense and sane serenities of futurity; and the man who has achieved that sublime thing, a genuine book; who has written to make his land greater, her citizens better, his race nobler; who has striven to serve men by communicating to them that which they least know, their own nature, their own experience; who has thrown into living verse a philosophy designed to exalt life to a higher level of sincerity, reality, religion; who has torn away disguises and illusions, and restored to commonest things, and the simplest and roughest people, their divine significance and natural, antique dignity, and who has wrapped his country and all created things as with splendors of sunrise, in the beams of a powerful and gorgeous poetry —that man, whatever be the clouds that close around his fame, is assured illustrious; and when every face lowers, when every hand is raised against him, turning his back upon his day and generation, he may write upon his book, with all the pride and grief of the calumniated Æschylus, the haughty dedication that poet graved upon his hundred dramas: TO TIME![12]

JOHN BURROUGHS

[1837–1921]

Notes on Walt Whitman as Poet and Person (1867)

DATING MAINLY FROM Wordsworth and his school, there is in modern literature, and especially in current poetry, a great deal of what is technically called Nature. Indeed it might seem that this subject was worn threadbare long ago, and that something else was needed. The word Nature, now, to most readers, suggests only some flower bank, or summer cloud, or pretty scene that appeals to the sentiments. None of this is in Walt Whitman. And it is because he corrects this false, artificial Nature, and shows me the real article, that I hail his appearance as the most important literary event of our times.

Wordsworth was truly a devout and loving observer of Na-

Reprinted in 1871 with "Supplementary Notes"; the present extract is from the second edition, 46–47, 54–56. For a discussion of Whitman's share in Burroughs' pamphlet, see Frederick P. Hier, Jr., "The End of a Literary Mystery," *American Mercury*, I (1924), 471–478.

ture, and perhaps has indicated more surely than any other poet the healthful moral influence of the milder aspects of rural scenery. But to have spoken in the full spirit of the least fact which he describes would have rent him to atoms. To have accepted Nature in her entirety, as the absolutely good and the absolutely beautiful, would have been to him tantamount to moral and intellectual destruction. He is simply a rural and metaphysical poet whose subjects are drawn mostly from Nature, instead of from society, or the domain of romance; and he tells in so many words what he sees and feels in the presence of natural objects. He has definite aim, like a preacher or moralist as he was, and his effects are nearer akin to those of pretty vases and parlor ornaments than to trees or hills.

In Nature everything is held in solution; there are no discriminations, or failures, or ends; there is no poetry or philosophy— but there is that which is better, and which feeds the soul, diffusing itself through the mind in calm and equable showers. To give the analogy of this in the least degree was not the success of Wordsworth. Neither has it been the success of any of the so-called poets of Nature since his time. Admirable as many of these poets are in some respects, they are but visiting-card callers upon Nature, going to her for tropes and figures only. In the products of the lesser fry of them I recognize merely a small toying with Nature—a kind of sentimental flirtation with birds and butterflies. . . .

Woe to that poet, musician, or any artist, who disengages beauty from the wide background of rudeness, darkness, and strength—and disengages her from absolute Nature! The mild and beneficent aspects of Nature—what gulfs and abysses of power underlie them! The great, ugly, barbaric earth—yet the summing up, the plenum of all we know, or can know, of beauty! So the orbic poems of the world have a foundation as of the earth itself, and are beautiful because they are something else first. Homer chose for his groundwork War, clinching, tearing, tugging war; in Dante it is Hell; in Milton, Satan and the Fall; in Shakespeare it is pride and diabolic passion. What is it in Tennyson? Soft aristocratic ennui and luxury, and love-sick sentiment. The dainty poets, "the eye singers, ear singers, love singers," have not the courage, the stamina, to accept the gross in Nature or life; that which is the basis of all else. Only the great masters accept all. It is this which gives genesis to their works.

Do I say, then, that beauty is not the object or attribute of *Leaves of Grass?* Not directly the object, but indirectly. The love of eternal beauty and of truth move the author to his work, producing a poem without a single piece of embroidery or hung-on ornament, yet in its quality and proportion dominating, in this very attribute, all rivals.

It is on the clear eye, the firm and limber step, the sweet breath, the loving lip, the magnetism of sex, the lofty and religious soul, eloquent in figure as in face, that Walt Whitman has depended for beauty's attractiveness in his poems.

He is by no means insensible to what is called the poetic aspect of things; only he uses this element sparingly, and well seasoned with the salt of the earth. Where others bring a flower from the woods or a shell from the shore, he brings the woods and the shore also, so that his charm lies in the completed integrity of his statements.

Of a long account of a battle which I once read in some old Grecian history I remember only the fact, casually mentioned by the historian, that the whereabouts of one army was betrayed to the other by the glint of the moonlight upon the shield of a soldier as he stood on a high hill. The touches in *Leaves of Grass* are of like significance, and by their singleness and peculiarity not one is lost to the mind.

But this is not the final statement. That which in every instance has been counted the defect of Walt Whitman's writings, namely, that they are not markedly poetical, as that term is used, constitutes their transcendent merit. Unlike all others, this poet's words seem dressed for work, with hands and arms bare. At first sight they appear as careless of mere beauty, or mere art, as do the leaves of the forest about numbers, or the snow-flakes as to where they shall fall; yet his poems do more to the mind, for this very reason, than the most ostentatiously elaborated works. They indicate fresh and near at hand the exhaustless sources of beauty and art. Comparatively few minds are impressed with the organic beauty of the world. That there are gleams and touches here and there which not only have no reference "to the compact truth of the world,"[1] but which are lucky exceptions to the general rule, and which it is the province of art to fix and perpetuate in color or form, is the notion of all our poets and poetlings. Outside of *Leaves of Grass* there is no theory or practice in modern letters that keeps in view the principle after which the highest artists, like Michael Angelo, have wrought, namely, that in the unimpeachable health and rectitude and latent power of the world are to be found the true sources of beauty for purposes of Art.

The perception of such high, kosmical beauty comes by a vital original process of the mind. It is in some measure a creative act, and those works that rest upon it make demands— perhaps extraordinary demands—upon the reader or beholder. We regard mere surface glitter, or mere verbal sweetness, in a mood entirely passive, and with a pleasure entirely profitless. The beauty of excellent stage scenery seems much more obvious and easy of apprehension than the beauty of the trees and hills themselves, inasmuch as the act of association in the mind is easier and inferior to the act of original perception.

Only the greatest works in any department afford any explanation of this wonder we call Nature, or aid the mind in arriving at correct notions concerning it. To copy here and there a line or a tint is no explanation; but to translate Nature into another language—to repeat, in some sort, the act of creation itself—as is done in *Leaves of Grass*, is the final and crowning triumph of poetic art.

FERDINAND FREILIGRATH

[1810–1876]

Walt Whitman (1868)

WALT WHITMAN! Who is Walt Whitman?

The answer is, a poet! A new American poet! His admirers say, the first, the only poet America has as yet produced. The only American poet of specific character. No follower in the beaten track of the European muse, but fresh from the prairie and the new settlements, fresh from the coast and the great watercourses, fresh from the thronging humanity of seaports and cities, fresh from the battle fields of the South, and from the earthy smells in hair and beard and clothing of the soil from which he sprang. A being not yet come to fulness of existence, a person standing firmly and consciously upon his own American feet, an utterer of a gross of great things, though often odd. And his admirers go still further: Walt Whitman is to them the only poet at all, in whom the age, this struggling, eagerly seeking age, in travail with thought and longing, has found its expression; the poet *par excellence*. . . .

Are these verses? The lines are arranged like verses, to be sure, but verses they are not. No metre, no rhyme, no stanzas. Rhythmical prose, ductile verses. At first sight rugged, inflexible, formless; but yet for a more delicate ear, not devoid of euphony. The language homely, hearty, straightforward, nam-

This essay appeared in the Augsburg *Allgemeinen Zeitung* on April 24, 1868; a translation appeared in *The New Eclectic Magazine*, II (July 1868), 325–329. See *Correspondence*, II, 78n.

ing everything by its true name, shrinking from nothing, sometimes obscure. The tone rhapsodical, like that of a seer, often
unequal, the sublime mingled with the trivial even to the point
of insipidity. He reminds us sometimes, with all the differences
that exist besides, of our own Hamann.[1] Or of Carlyle's oracular
wisdom. Or of the *Paroles d'un Croyant*.[2] Through all there
sounds out the Bible—its language, not its creed.

And what does the poet propound to us in this form? First of
all Himself, his *I*, Walt Whitman. This *I* however is a part of
America, a part of the earth, a part of mankind, a part of the
All. As such he is conscious of himself and revolves, knitting the
greatest to the least, ever going out from America, and coming
back to America ever again (only to a free people does the
future belong!) before our view, a vast and magnificent world-
panorama. Through this individual Walt Whitman and his
Americanism marches, we may say, a *cosmical* procession, such
as may be suitable for reflective spirits, who, face to face with
eternity, have passed solitary days on the sea-shore, solitary
nights under the starry sky of the prairie. He finds himself in all
things and all things in himself. He, the one man, Walt Whitman, is mankind and the world. And the world and mankind are
to him one great poem. What he sees and hears, what he comes
in contact with, whatever approaches him, even the meanest, the
most trifling, the most every-day matter—all is to him symbolical of a higher, of a spiritual fact. Or rather, matter and spirit,
the real and the ideal are to him one and the same. Thus,
produced by himself, he takes his stand; thus he strides along,
singing as he goes; thus he opens from his soul, a proud free
man, and *only* a man, world-wide, social and political vistas.

A wonderful appearance. We confess that it moves us, disturbs us, will not loose its hold upon us. At the same time,
however, we would remark that we are not yet ready with our
judgment of it, that we are still biased by our first impression.
Meanwhile we, probably the first in Germany to do so, will take
at least a provisional view of the scope and tendency of this new
energy. It is fitting that our poets and thinkers should have a
closer look at this strange new comrade, who threatens to over-
turn our entire *Ars Poetica* and all our theories and canons on
the subject of æsthetics. Indeed, when we have listened to all

that is within these earnest pages, when we have grown familiar with the deep, resounding roar of those, as it were, surges of the sea in their unbroken sequence of rhapsodical verses breaking upon us, then will our ordinary verse-making, our system of forcing thought into all sorts of received forms, our playing with ring and sound, our syllable-counting and measure of quantity, our sonnet-writing and construction of strophes and stanzas, seem to us almost childish. Are we really come to the point, when life, even in poetry, calls imperatively for new forms of expression? Has the age so much and such serious matter to say, that the old vessels no longer suffice for the new contents? Are we standing before a poetry of the ages to come, just as some years ago a music of the ages to come was announced to us? And is Walt Whitman a greater than Richard Wagner?

ANNE GILCHRIST

[1 8 2 8 – 1 8 8 5]

An Englishwoman's Estimate of Walt Whitman

(1870)

I THINK IT WAS very manly and kind of you to put the whole of Walt Whitman's poems into my hands; and that I have no other friend who would have judged them and me so wisely and generously.

The Radical (Boston), VII (May 1870), 345–359; the abridged text used here is from the printing by Herbert H. Gilchrist in *Anne Gilchrist —Her Life and Writings* (New York, 1887), 287–307.

I had not dreamed that words could cease to be words, and become electric streams like these. I do assure you that, strong as I am, I feel sometimes as if I had not bodily strength to read many of these poems. In the series headed "Calamus," for instance, in some of the "Songs of Parting," the "Voice out of the Sea,"[1] the poem beginning "Tears, tears,"[2] &c., there is such a weight of emotion, such a tension of the heart, that mine refuses to beat under it—stands quite still—and I am obliged to lay the book down for a while. Or again, in the piece called "Walt Whitman," and one or two others of that type, I am as one hurried through stormy seas, over high mountains, dazed with sunlight, stunned with a crowd and tumult of faces and voices, till I am breathless, bewildered, half-dead. Then come parts and whole poems in which there is such calm wisdom and strength of thought, such a cheerful breadth of sunshine, that the soul bathes in them renewed and strengthened. Living impulses flow out of these that make me exult in life, yet look longingly towards "the superb vistas of Death."[3] Those who admire this poem, and do not care for that, and talk of formlessness, absence of metre, and so forth, are quite as far from any genuine recognition of Walt Whitman as his bitter detractors. Not, of course, that all the pieces are equal in power and beauty, but that all are vital; they grew—they were not made. We criticise a palace or a cathedral; but what is the good of criticising a forest? Are not the hitherto-accepted masterpieces of literature akin rather to noble architecture; built up of material rendered precious by elaboration; planned with subtile art that makes beauty go hand in hand with rule and measure, and knows where the last stone will come, before the first is laid; the result stately, fixed, yet such as might, in every particular, have been different from what it is (therefore inviting criticism), contrasting proudly with the careless freedom of nature, opposing its own rigid adherence to symmetry to her wilful dallying with it? But not such is this book. Seeds brought by the winds from north, south, east, and west, lying long in the earth, not resting on it like the stately building, but hid in and assimilating it, shooting upwards to be nourished by the air and the sunshine and the rain which beat idly against that,—each bough and twig and leaf growing in strength and beauty its own way, a law to itself, yet, with all this freedom of spontaneous growth, the result inevitable, unalterable (therefore setting criticism at naught), above all things vital,—that is, a source of ever-generating vitality: such are these poems. . . .[4]

I see that no counting of syllables will reveal the mechanism of the music; and that this rushing spontaneity could not stay to bind itself with the fetters of metre. But I know that the music is there, and that I would not for something change ears with those who cannot hear it. And I know that poetry must be one of two things,—either own this man as equal with her highest, completest manifestors, or stand aside, and admit that there is something come into the world nobler, diviner than herself, one that is free of the universe, and can tell its secrets as none before. . . .

I am persuaded that one great source of this kindling, vitalizing power—I suppose *the* great source—is the grasp laid upon the present, the fearless and comprehensive dealing with reality. Hitherto the leaders of thought have (except in science) been men with their faces resolutely turned backwards; men who have made of the past a tyrant that beggars and scorns the present, hardly seeing any greatness but what is shrouded away in the twilight, underground past; naming the present only for disparaging comparisons, humiliating distrust that tends to create the very barrenness it complains of; bidding me warm myself at fires that went out to mortal eyes centuries ago; insisting, in religion above all, that I must either "look through dead men's eyes," or shut my own in helpless darkness. Poets fancying themselves so happy over the chill and faded beauty of the past, but not making me happy at all,—rebellious always at being dragged down out of the free air and sunshine of to-day.

But this poet, this "athlete, full of rich words, full of joys,"[5] takes you by the hand, and turns you with your face straight forwards. The present is great enough for him, because he is great enough for it. It flows through him as a "vast oceanic tide," lifting up a mighty voice. Earth, "the eloquent, dumb, great mother,"[6] is not old, has lost none of her fresh charms, none of her divine meanings; still bears great sons and daughters, if only they would possess themselves and accept their birth-right,—a richer, not a poorer, heritage than was ever pro-

vided before,—richer by all the toil and suffering of the generations that have preceded, and by the further unfolding of the
eternal purposes. Here is one come at last who can show them
how; whose songs are the breath of a glad, strong, beautiful life,
nourished sufficingly, kindled to unsurpassed intensity and
greatness by the gifts of the present. . . .[7]

See, again, in the pieces gathered together under the title
"Calamus," and elsewhere, what it means for a man to love his
fellow-man. Did you dream it before? These "evangel-poems of
comrades and of love"[8] speak, with the abiding, penetrating
power of prophecy, of a "new and superb friendship;" speak not
as beautiful dreams, unrealizable aspirations to be laid aside in
sober moods, because they breathe out what now glows within
the poet's own breast, and flows out in action toward the men
around him. Had ever any land before her poet, not only to
concentrate within himself her life, and, when she kindled with
anger against her children who were treacherous to the cause
her life is bound up with, to announce and justify her terrible
purpose in words of unsurpassable grandeur (as in the poem
beginning, "Rise, O days, from your fathomless deeps"), but
also to go and with his own hands dress the wounds, with his
powerful presence soothe and sustain and nourish her suffering
soldiers,—hundreds of them, thousands, tens of thousands,—by
day and by night, for weeks, months, years?

I sit by the restless all the dark night; some are so young,
Some suffer so much: I recall the experience sweet and sad.
Many a soldier's loving arms about this neck have crossed and
    rested,
Many a soldier's kiss dwells on these bearded lips: —[9]

Kisses, that touched with the fire of a strange, new, undying
eloquence the lips that received them! The most transcendent
genius could not, untaught by that "experience sweet and sad,"
have breathed out hymns for her dead soldiers of such ineffably
tender, sorrowful, yet triumphant beauty. . . .

Nor do I sympathize with those who grumble at the unex-
pected words that turn up now and then. A quarrel with words
is always, more or less, a quarrel with meanings; and here we
are to be as genial and as wide as nature, and quarrel with
nothing. If the thing a word stands for exists by divine appoint-

ment (and what does not so exist?), the word need never be ashamed of itself; the shorter and more direct, the better. It is a gain to make friends with it, and see it in good company. Here, at all events, "poetic diction" would not serve,—not pretty, soft, colourless words, laid by in lavender for the special uses of poetry, that have had none of the wear and tear of daily life; but such as have stood most, as tell of human heart-beats, as fit closest to the sense, and have taken deep hues of association from the varied experiences of life—those are the words wanted here. We only ask to seize and be seized swiftly, overmasteringly, by the great meanings. We see with the eyes of the soul, listen with the ears of the soul; the poor old words that have served so many generations for purposes, good, bad, and indifferent, and become warped and blurred in the process, grow young again, regenerate, translucent. . .

You [W. M. Rossetti] argued rightly that my confidence would not be betrayed by any of the poems in this book. None of them troubled me even for a moment; because I saw at a glance that it was not, as men had supposed, the heights brought down to the depths, but the depths lifted up level with the sunlit heights, that they might become clear and sunlit too. Always, for a woman, a veil woven out of her own soul—never touched upon even, with a rough hand, by this poet. But, for a man, a daring, fearless pride in himself, not a mock-modesty woven out of delusions—a very poor imitation of a woman's. Do they not see that this fearless pride, this complete acceptance of themselves, is needful for her pride, her justification? What! is it all so ignoble, so base, that it will not bear the honest light of speech from lips so gifted with "the divine power to use words?"[10] Then what hateful, bitter humiliation for her, to have to give herself up to the reality! Do you think there is ever a bride who does not taste more or less this bitterness in her cup? But who put it there? It must surely be man's fault, not God's, that she has to say to herself, "Soul, look another way—you have no part in this. Motherhood is beautiful, fatherhood is beautiful; but the dawn of fatherhood and motherhood is not beautiful." Do they really think that God is ashamed of what He has made and appointed? And, if not, surely it is somewhat superfluous that they should undertake to be so for Him.

The full-spread pride of man is calming and excellent to the soul,[11]

Of a woman above all. It is true that instinct of silence I spoke of is a beautiful, imperishable part of nature too. But it is not beautiful when it means an ignominious shame brooding darkly. Shame is like a very flexible veil, that follows faithfully the shape of what it covers,—beautiful when it hides a beautiful thing, ugly when it hides an ugly one. It has not covered what was beautiful here; it has covered a mean distrust of a man's self and of his Creator. It was needed that this silence, this evil spell, should for once be broken, and the daylight let in, that the dark cloud lying under might be scattered to the winds. It was needed that one who could here indicate for us "the path between reality and the soul" should speak. That is what these beautiful, despised poems, the "Children of Adam," do, read by the light that glows out of the rest of the volume: light of a clear, strong faith in God, of an unfathomably deep and tender love for humanity,—light shed out of a soul that is "possessed of itself."

. . . Yet I feel deeply persuaded that a perfectly fearless, candid, ennobling treatment of the life of the body (so inextricably intertwined with, so potent in its influence on the life of the soul) will prove of inestimable value to all earnest and aspiring natures, impatient of the folly of the long prevalent belief that it is because of the greatness of the spirit that it has learned to despise the body, and to ignore its influences; knowing well that it is, on the contrary, just because the spirit is not great enough, not healthy and vigorous enough, to transfuse itself into the life of the body, elevating that and making it holy by its own triumphant intensity; knowing, too, how the body avenges this by dragging the soul down to the level assigned itself. Whereas the spirit must lovingly embrace the body, as the roots of a tree embrace the ground, drawing thence rich nourishment, warmth, impulse. Or, rather, the body is itself the root of the soul,—that whereby it grows and feeds. The great tide of healthful life that carries all before it must surge through the whole man, not beat to and fro in one corner of his brain.

O the life of my senses and flesh, transcending my senses and flesh![12]

. . . He [Whitman], the beloved friend of all, initiated for

them a "new and superb friendship;"[13] whispered that secret of
a god-like pride in a man's self, and a perfect trust in woman,
whereby their love for each other, no longer poisoned and sti-
fled, but basking in the light of God's smile, and sending up to
Him a perfume of gratitude, attains at last a divine and tender
completeness. He gave a faith-compelling utterance to that "wisdom which is the certainty of the reality and immortality of
things, and of the excellence of things."[14] Happy America, that
he should be her son! One sees, indeed, that only a young giant
of a nation could produce this kind of greatness, so full of the
ardour, the elasticity, the inexhaustible vigour and freshness,
the joyousness, the audacity of youth. But I, for one, cannot
grudge anything to America. For, after all, the young giant is
the old English giant,—the great English race renewing its
youth in that magnificent land, "Mexican-breathed, Arctic-
braced,"[15] and girding up its loins to start on a new career that
shall match with the greatness of the new home.

EDWARD DOWDEN

[1 8 4 3 – 1 9 1 3]

The Poetry of Democracy: Walt Whitman (1871)

AT LAST STEPS FORWARD a man unlike any of his predecessors,
and announces himself, and is announced with a flourish of
critical trumpets, as Bard of America, and Bard of democracy.

Westminster Review, n.s., XL (July 1871), 16–32, abridged; the
text used here was reprinted in *Studies in Literature* (London, 1878).
Dowden's is ostensibly a review of three works, *Leaves of Grass*, *Passage
to India*, and *Democratic Vistas*, all published in 1871. The beginning of
the essay (here omitted) surveys the principal American writers (Longfellow, Irving, Bryant, Emerson), all of whom were more European than
American.

What cannot be questioned after an hour's acquaintance with Walt Whitman and his "Leaves of Grass" is that in him we meet a man not shaped out of old-world clay, not cast in any old-world mould, and hard to name by any old-world name. In his self-assertion there is a manner of powerful nonchalantness which is not assumed; he does not peep timidly from behind his works to glean our suffrages, but seems to say, "Take me or leave me, here I am a solid and not an inconsiderable fact of the universe." He disturbs our classifications. He attracts us; he repels us; he excites our curiosity, wonder, admiration, love; or, our extreme repugnance. He does anything except leave us indifferent. However we feel towards him we cannot despise him. He is "a summons and a challenge." He must be understood and so accepted, or must be got rid of. Passed by he cannot be. . . . His critics have, for the most part, confined their attention to the personality of the man; they have studied him, for the most part, as a phenomenon isolated from the surrounding society, the environment, the *milieu*, which has made such a phenomenon possible. In a general way it has been said that Whitman is the representative in art of American democracy, but the meaning of this has not been investigated in detail. It is purposed here to consider some of the characteristics of democratic art, and to inquire in what manner they manifest themselves in Whitman's work. . . .

Now in all these particulars the art of a democratic age exhibits characteristics precisely opposite to those of the art of an aristocracy. Form and style modelled on traditional examples are little valued. No canons of composition are agreed upon or observed without formal agreement. No critical dictator enacts laws which are accepted without dispute, and acquire additional authority during many years. Each new generation, with its new heave of life, its multitudinous energies, ideas, passions, is a law to itself. Except public opinion, there is no authority on earth above the authority of a man's own soul, and public opinion being strongly in favour of individualism, a writer is tempted to depreciate unduly the worth of order, propriety, regularity of the academic kind; he is encouraged to make new literary experiments as others make new experiments in religion; he is permitted to be true to his own instincts, whether they are beautiful instincts or the reverse. The appeal which a work of art makes is to the nation, not to a class, and diversities of style are consequently admissible. Every style can be tolerated except the vapid, everything can be accepted but that which fails to stimulate the intellect or the passions.

Turning to Whitman, we perceive at once that his work corresponds with this state of things. If he had written in England in the period of Queen Anne, if he had written in France in the period of the *grand monarque*, he must have either acknowledged the supremacy of authority in literature and submitted to it, or on the other hand revolted against it. As it is, he is remote from authority, and neither submits nor revolts. Whether we call what he has written verse or prose, we have no hesitation in saying that it is no copy, that it is something uncontrolled by any model or canon, something which takes whatever shape it possesses directly from the soul of its maker. With the Bible, Homer, and Shakespeare familiar to him, Whitman writes in the presence of great models, and some influences from each have doubtless entered into his nature; but that they should possess authority over him any more than that he should possess authority over them, does not occur to him as possible. The relation of democracy to the Past comes out very notably here. Entirely assured of its own right to the Present, it is prepared to acknowledge fully the right of past generations to the Past. It is not hostile to that Past, rather claims kinship with it, but also claims equality, as a full-grown son with a father. . . .[1]

As in all else, so with regard to the form of what he writes, Walt Whitman can find no authority superior to himself, or rather to the rights of the subject which engages him. There is, as Mr. Rossetti has observed, "a very powerful and majestic rhythmical sense," throughout his writings, prose and verse (if we consent to apply the term *verse* to any of them), and this rhythmical sense, as with every great poet, is original and inborn. His works, it may be, exhibit no perfect crystal of artistic form, but each is a menstruum saturated with form in solution. He fears to lose the instinctive in any process of elaboration, the vital in anything which looks like mechanism. He does not write with a full consciousness of the processes of creation, nor does any true poet. Certain combinations of sound are preconceived, and his imagination excited by them works towards them by a kind of reflex action, automatically. His *ars poetica* is embodied in the precept that the poet should hold himself passive in presence of the material universe, in presence of society, in presence of his own soul, and become the blind but yet unerringly guided force through which these seek artistic expression. No afterthought, no intrusion of reasoning, no calculating of effects, no stepping back to view his work is tolerated. The artist must create his art with as little hesitation, as little questioning of processes, and as much sureness of result as the beaver builds his house. . . .

. . . Science and democracy appear before Whitman as twin powers which bend over the modern world hand in hand, great and beneficent. Democracy seems to him that form of society which alone is scientifically justifiable; founded upon a recognition of the facts of nature, and a resolute denial of social fables, superstitions, and uninvestigated tradition. Moreover he looks to science for important elements which shall contribute to a new conception of nature and of man, and of their mutual relations, to be itself the ideal basis of a new poetry and art—"after the chemist, geologist, ethnologist, finally shall come the Poet worthy that name; the true Son of God shall come singing his songs."[2] Lastly, Whitman has a peculiar reason of his own for loving science; he is a mystic, and such a mystic as finds positive science not unacceptable. Whitman's mysticism is not of the Swedenborgian type. He beholds no visions of visible things in heaven or hell unseen to other men. He rather sees with extraordinary precision the realities of our earth, but he sees them, in his mystical mood, as symbols of the impalpable and spiritual. They are hieroglyphs most clear-cut, most brilliantly and definitely coloured to his eyes, but still expressive of something unseen. His own personality as far as he can give it expression or is conscious of it—that identity of himself, which is the hardest of all facts, and the only entrance to all facts, is yet no more than the image projected by another ego, the real *Me*, which stands "untouched, untold, altogether unreached:"—

Withdrawn far, mocking me with mock-congratulatory signs and
   bows,

With peals of distant ironical laughter at every word I have written,

. . . .

Now I perceive I have not understood anything—not a single object;
and that no man ever can.
I perceive Nature, here in sight of the sea, is taking advantage of
me, to dart upon me, and sting me,
Because I have dared to open my mouth to sing at all. . . .[3]

Men of every class then are interesting to Whitman. But no
individual is pre-eminently interesting to him. His sketches of
individual men and women, though wonderfully vivid and precise, are none of them longer than a page; each single figure
passes rapidly out of sight, and a stream of other figures of men
and women succeeds. Even in "Lincoln's Burial Hymn" he has
only a word to say of "the large sweet soul that has gone;" the
chords of his nocturn, with their implicated threefold sweetness,
odour and sound and light, having passed into his strain, really
speak not of Lincoln but of death. George Peabody is celebrated
briefly, because through him, a "stintless, lavish giver, tallying
the gifts of earth,"[4] a multitude of human beings have been
blessed, and the true service of riches illustrated. No single
person is the subject of Whitman's song, or can be; the individual suggests a group, and the group a multitude, each unit of
which is as interesting as every other unit, and possesses equal
claims to recognition. Hence the recurring tendency of his
poems to become catalogues of persons and things. Selection
seems forbidden to him; if he names one race of mankind the
names of all other races press into his page; if he mentions one
trade or occupation, all other trades and occupations follow. A
long procession of living forms passes before him; each several
form, keenly inspected for a moment, is then dismissed. Men
and women are seen *en masse*, and the mass is viewed not from
a distance, but close at hand, where it is felt to be a concourse of
individuals. Whitman will not have the people appear in his
poems by representatives or delegates; the people itself, in its
undiminished totality, marches through his poems, making its
greatness and variety felt. Writing down the headings of a
Trades' Directory is not poetry; but this is what Whitman never
does. His catalogues are for the poet always, if not always for
the reader, *visions*—they are delighted—not perhaps delightful
—enumerations; when his desire for the perception of greatness

and variety is satisfied, not when a really complete catalogue is made out, Whitman's enumeration ends; we may murmur, but Whitman has been happy; what has failed to interest our imaginations has deeply interested his; and even for us the impression of multitude, of variety, of equality is produced, as perhaps it could be in no other way. Whether Whitman's habit of cataloguing be justified by what has been said, or is in any way justifiable, such at least is its true interpretation and significance.

One can perceive at a glance that these characteristics of Whitman's work proceed directly from the democratic tendencies of the world of thought and feeling in which he moves. It is curious to find De Tocqueville, before there existed properly any native American literature, describing in the spirit of philosophical prophecy what we find realized in Whitman's "Leaves of Grass.". . .[5]

The democratic poet celebrates no individual hero, nor does he celebrate himself. "I celebrate myself," sings Whitman, and the longest poem in "Leaves of Grass" is named by his own name;[6] but the self-celebration throughout is celebration of himself as a man and an American; it is what he possesses in common with all others that he feels to be glorious and worthy of song, not that which differentiates him from others; manhood, and in particular American manhood, is the real subject of the poem "Walt Whitman;" and although Whitman has a most poignant feeling of personality, which indeed is a note of all he has written, it is to be remembered that in nearly every instance in which he speaks of himself the reference is as much impersonal as personal. In what is common he finds what is most precious. The true hero of the democratic poet is the nation of which he is a member, or the whole race of man to which the nation belongs. . . . But if the American nation is his hero, let it be observed that it is the American nation as the supposed leader of the human race, as the supposed possessor in ideas, in type of character, and in tendency if not in actual achievement, of all that is most powerful and promising for the progress of mankind.

. . . Thus we find our way to the centre of what has been called the "materialism" of Whitman—his vindication of the body as it might be more correctly termed. Materialist, in any proper sense of the word, he is not; on the contrary, as Mr. Rossetti has stated, "he is a most strenuous asserter of the soul," but "with the soul, of the body, as its infallible associate and vehicle in the present frame of things." And as every faculty of the soul seems admirable and sacred to him, so does every organ and function and natural act of the body. But Whitman is a poet; it is not his manner to preach doctrines in an abstract form, by means of a general statement; and the doctrine, which seems to him of vital importance, that a healthy, perfect body—male or female—is altogether worthy of honour, admiration, and desire, is accordingly preached with fulness and plainness of detail. . . . If there be any class of subjects which it is more truly natural, more truly human *not* to speak of than to speak of (such speech producing self-consciousness, whereas part of our nature, it may be maintained, is healthy only while it lives and moves in holy blindness and unconsciousness of self), if there be any sphere of silence, then Whitman has been guilty of invading that sphere of silence. But he has done this by conviction that it is best to do so, and in a spirit as remote from base curiosity as from insolent licence. He deliberately appropriates a portion of his writings to the subject of the feelings of sex, as he appropriates another, "Calamus," to that of the love of man for man, "adhesiveness," as contrasted with "amativeness," in the nomenclature of Whitman, comradeship apart from all feelings of sex. That article of the poet's creed, which declares that man is very good, that there is nothing about him which is naturally vile or dishonourable, prepares him for absolute familiarity, glad, unabashed familiarity with every part and every act of the body. . . .

The body then is not given authority over the soul by Whitman. Precisely as in the life of the nation a great material civilization seems admirable to him and worthy of honour, yet of little value in comparison with or apart from a great spiritual civilization, a noble national character, so in the life of the individual all that is external, material, sensuous, is estimated by the worth of what it can give to the soul. No Hebrew ever maintained the rights of the spiritual more absolutely. But towards certain parts of our nature, although in the poet's creed their rights are dogmatically laid down, he is practically unjust. The tendencies of his own nature lead him in his preaching to sink unduly certain articles of his creed. The logical faculty, in particular, is almost an offence to Whitman. The processes of reasoning appear to him to have elaboration for their characteristic, and nothing elaborated or manufactured seems of equal reality with what is natural and has grown. Truth he feels to be, as Wordsworth has said, "a motion or a shape instinct with vital functions;" and were Whitman to seek for formal proof of such truth, he, like Wordsworth, would lose all feeling of conviction, and yield up moral questions in despair. "A slumbering woman and child convince as an university course can never convince:"[7]

> Logic and sermons never convince,
> The damp of the night drives deeper into my soul.[8]

Whitman becomes lyrical in presence of the imagination attempting for itself an interpretation of the problems of the world; he becomes lyrical in presence of gratified senses and desires; but he remains indifferent in presence of the understanding searching after conclusions. There is something like intolerance or want of comprehensiveness here; one's heart, touched by the injustice, rises to take the part of this patient, serviceable, despised understanding. . . .

In the period of chivalry there existed a beautiful relation between man and man, of which no trace remains in existence as an institution—that of knight and squire. The protecting, encouraging, downward glance of the elder, experienced, and superior man was answered by the admiring and aspiring, upward gaze of the younger and inferior. The relation was founded upon inequality; from the inequality of the parties its essential beauty was derived. Is there any possible relation of no less beauty, corresponding to the new condition of things, and founded upon equality? Yes, there is manly comradeship. Here we catch one of the clearest and most often reiterated notes of Whitman's song. . . . One division of "Leaves of Grass," that entitled "Calamus" (Calamus being the grass with largest and hardiest spears and with fresh pungent *bouquet*), is appropriated to the theme of comradeship. And to us it seems impossible to read the poems comprised under this head without finding our interest in the poet Walt Whitman fast changing into hearty love of the man, these poems, through their tender reserves and concealments and betrayals, revealing his heart in its weakness and its strength more than any others. The chord of feeling which he strikes may be old—as old as David and Jonathan—but a fulness and peculiarity of tone are brought out, the like of which have not been heard before. For this love of man for man, as Whitman dreams of it, or rather confidently expects it, is to be no rare, no exceptional emotion, making its possessors illustrious by its singular preciousness, but it is to be widespread, common, unnoticeable.

. . . By another working of the same democratic influence (each man finding in the world what he cares to find) Whitman discovers everywhere in nature the same qualities, or types of the same qualities which he admires most in men. For his imagination the powers of the earth do not incarnate themselves in the forms of god and demi-god, faun and satyr, oread, dryad, and nymph of river and sea—meet associates, allies or antagonists of the heroes of an age, when the chiefs and shepherds of the people were themselves almost demi-gods. But the great Mother—the Earth—is one in character with her children of the democracy, who, at last, as the poet holds, have learned to live and work in her great style. She is tolerant, includes diversity, refuses nothing, shuts no one out; she is powerful, full of vitality, generous, proud, perfect in natural rectitude, does not discuss her duty to God, never apologizes, does not argue, is incomprehensible, silent, coarse, productive, charitable, rich in the organs and instincts of sex, and at the same time continent and chaste. The grass Whitman loves as much as did Chaucer himself; but his love has a certain spiritual significance which Chaucer's had not. It is not the "soft, swete, smale grass," embroidered with flowers, a fitting carpet for the feet of glad knights and sportive ladies, for which he cares. In the grass he beholds the democracy of the fields, earthborn, with close and copious companionship of blades, each blade like every other, and equal to every other, spreading in all directions with lusty life, blown upon by the open air, "coarse, sunlit, fresh, nutritious."⁹ The peculiar title of his most important volume, "Leaves of Grass," as Mr. Rossetti has finely observed, "seems to express with some aptness the simplicity, universality, and spontaneity of the poems to which it is applied."

The character of Whitman's feeling with respect to external nature bears witness to the joyous bodily health of the man. His communication with the earth, and sea, and skies, is carried on through senses that are never torpid, and never overwrought beyond the measure of health. He presses close to nature, and will not be satisfied with shy glances or a distant greeting. He enjoys the strong sensations of a vigorous nervous system, and the rest and recuperation which follow. His self-projections into external objects are never morbid; when he employs the "pathetic fallacy" the world shares in his joyousness; he does not hear in the voices of the waters or of the winds echoes of a miserable egotism, the moan of wounded vanity, or the crying of insatiable lust. He is sane and vigorous. But his relation with nature is not one in which the senses and perceptive faculty have a predominant share. He passes through the visible and sensible things, and pursues an invisible somewhat—

> A motion and a spirit that impels
> All thinking things, all objects of all thought,
> And rolls through all things;[10]

and of this he can never quite possess himself. . . .

At times this optimism leads Whitman to the entire denial of evil; "he contemplates evil as, in some sense, not existing, or, if existing, then as being of as much importance as anything else;" in some transcendental way, he believes, the opposition of God and Satan cannot really exist. Practically, however, he is not led astray by any such transcendental reducing of all things to the Divine. Any tendency of a mystical kind to ignore the distinction between good and evil, is checked by his strong democratic sense of the supreme importance of personal qualities, and the inevitable perception of the superiority of virtuous over vicious personal qualities. By one who feels profoundly that the differences between men are determined, not by rank, or birth, or hereditary name or title, but simply by the different powers belonging to the bodies and souls of men, there is small danger of the meaning of *bad* and *good* being forgotten. And Whitman never really forgets this. The formation of a noble national character, to be itself the source of all literature, art, statesman-ship, is that which above all else he desires. In that character the element of religion must, according to Whitman's ideal, occupy an important place, only inferior to that assigned to moral soundness, to conscience. "We want, for These States, for the general character, a cheerful, religious fervour, imbued with the ever-present modifications of the human emotions, friendship, benevolence, with a fair field for scientific inquiry [to check fanaticism], the right of individual judgment, and always the cooling influences of material Nature." These are not the words of one who moves the landmarks of right and wrong, and obscures their boundaries. For Whitman the worth of any man is simply the worth of his body and soul; each gift of nature, product of industry, and creation of art, is valuable in his eyes exactly in proportion to what it can afford for the benefit of body and soul. Only what belongs to these, and becomes a part of them, properly belongs to us—the rest is mere "material." This mode of estimating values is very revolutionary, but to us it seems essentially just and moral. The rich man is not he who has accumulated unappropriated matter around him, but he who possesses much of what "adheres, and goes forward, and is not dropped by death. . . ."[11]

Here we must end. We have not argued the question which many persons are most desirous to put about Walt Whitman—"Is he a poet at all?" It is not easy to argue such a question in a profitable way. One thing only need here be said,—no adequate impression of Whitman's poetical power can be obtained from this article. A single side of his mind and of his work has been studied, but we have written with an abiding remembrance of the truth expressed by Vauvenargues:[12]—"Lorsque nous croy-ons tenir la vérité par un endroit, elle nous échappe par mille autres."

GEORGE SAINTSBURY

[1845–1933]

LEAVES OF GRASS (*1874*)

FORTUNATELY, . . . admiration for a creed is easily separable from admiration for the utterance and expression of that creed, and Walt Whitman as a poet is not difficult to disengage from Walt Whitman as an evangelist and politician. The keyword of all his ideas and of all his writings is universality. His Utopia is one which shall be open to everybody; his ideal of man and woman one which shall be attainable by everybody; his favourite scenes, ideas, subjects, those which everybody, at least to some extent, can enjoy and appreciate. He cares not that by this limitation he may exclude thoughts and feelings, at any rate phases of thought and feeling, infinitely choicer and higher than any which he admits. To express this striving after universality he has recourse to methods both unusual and (to most readers) unwelcome. The extraordinary jumbles and strings of names, places, employments, which deface his pages, and which have encouraged the profane to liken them to auctioneers' catalogues or indexes of encyclopaedias, have no other object than to express this universal sympathy, reaching to the highest and penetrating to the lowest forms of life. The exclusion of culture, philosophy, manners, is owing to this desire to admit nothing but what is open to every human being of ordinary faculty and opportunities. Moreover it is to this that we may fairly trace the

The Academy, October 10, 1874; the abridged text used here was reprinted in *The Letters of Gerard Manley Hopkins to Robert Bridges*, ed. Claude Colleer Abbott (London, 1935), 311–316.

prominence in Whitman's writings of the sexual passion, a prominence which has given rise, and probably will yet give rise, to much unphilosophical hubbub. This passion, as the poet has no doubt observed, is almost the only one which is peculiar to man as man, the presence of which denotes virility if not humanity, the absence of which is a sign of abnormal temperament. Hence he elevates it to almost the principal place, and treats of it in a manner somewhat shocking to those who are accustomed to speak of such subjects (we owe the word to Southey) enfarinhadamente. As a matter of fact, however, the treatment, though outspoken, is eminently 'clean,' to use the poet's own word; there is not a vestige of prurient thought, not a syllable of prurient language. Yet it would be a great mistake to suppose that sexual passion occupies the chief place in Whitman's estimation. There is according to him something above it, something which in any ecstasies he fails not to realise, something which seems more intimately connected in his mind with the welfare of mankind, and the promotion of his ideal republic. This is what he calls 'robust American love.'[1] He is never tired of repeating 'I am the poet of comrades'—Socrates himself seems renascent in this apostle of friendship. In the ears of a world (at least on this side the Atlantic) incredulous of such things, he reiterates the expressions of Plato to Aster, of Socrates respecting Charmides, and in this respect fully justifies (making allowance for altered manners) Mr. Symonds' assertion of his essentially Greek character,[2] an assertion which most students of Whitman will heartily endorse. But we must again repeat that it is not so much in the matter as in the manner of his Evangel that the strength of Whitman lies. It is impossible not to notice his exquisite descriptive faculty, and his singular felicity in its use. Forced as he is, both by natural inclination and in the carrying out of his main idea, to take note of 'the actual earth's equalities,' he has literally filled his pages with the song of birds, the hushed murmur of waves, the quiet and multiform life of the forest and the meadow. And in these descriptions he succeeds in doing what is most difficult, in giving us the actual scene or circumstance as it impressed him, and not merely the impression itself. This is what none but the greatest poets have ever save by accident done, and what Whitman does constantly and with a sure hand. 'You shall,' he says at the beginning of his book:

You shall no longer take things at second or third hand, nor look
 through the eyes of the dead, nor feed on the spectres in books:
You shall not look through my eyes either, nor take things from me:
You shall listen to all sides and filter them from yourself.[3]

But affluent as his descriptions are, there are two subjects on which he is especially eloquent, which seem indeed to intoxicate and inspire him the moment he approaches them. These are Death and the sea. In the latter respect he is not, indeed, peculiar, but accords with all poets of all times, and especially of this time. But in his connection of the two ideas (for the one always seems to suggest the other to him), and in his special devotion to Death, he is more singular. The combined influence of the two has produced what is certainly the most perfect specimen of his work, the 'Word out of the Sea.'. . . Unfortunately it is indivisible, and its length precludes the possibility of quotation. But there is another poem almost equally beautiful, which forms part of 'President Lincoln's Burial Hymn,' and for this space may perhaps be found. . . .[4] It is easy enough to connect this cultus of Death, and the pantheism which necessarily accompanies it, with the main articles of Whitman's creed. Death is viewed as the one event of great solemnity and importance which is common to all—the one inevitable, yet not commonplace incident in every life, however commonplace; and, further, it must not be overlooked that Death is pre-eminently valuable in such a system as this, in the capacity of reconciler ready to accommodate all difficulties, to sweep away all rubbish. The cheeriest of optimists with the lowest of standards cannot pretend to assert or expect that everyone will live the ideal life—but Death pays all scores and obliterates all mistakes.

There remains, however, still to be considered a point not least in importance—the vehicle which Whitman has chosen for the conveyance of these thoughts. He employs, as most people know who know anything at all about him, neither rhyme nor even regular metre; the exceptions to this rule occurring among his more recent poems are few and insignificant. A page of his work has little or no look of poetry about it; it is not, indeed, printed continuously, but it consists of versicles, often less in extent than a line, sometimes extending to many lines. Only after reading these for some time does it become apparent that, though rhyme and metre have been abandoned, rhythm has not; and, moreover, that certain figures and tricks of language occur which are generally considered more appropriate to poetry than to prose. The total effect produced is dissimilar to that of any of the various attempts which have been made to evade the shackles of metre and rhyme, while retaining the other advantages of poetical form and diction. Whitman's style differs very much from that of such efforts as Baudelaire's 'Petits Poèmes en Prose,' for from these all rhythm, diction, and so forth not strictly appropriate to prose is conscientiously excluded. It is more like the polymeters of the poet's namesake Walt in Richter's 'Flegeljahre,' except that these latter being limited to the expression of a single thought are not divided into separate limbs or verses. Perhaps the likeness which is presented to the mind most strongly, is that which exists between our author and the verse divisions of the English Bible, especially in the poetical books, and it is not unlikely that the latter did actually exercise some influence in moulding the poet's work. It is hard to give a fair specimen of it in the way of quotation—that already given is not representative, being too avowedly lyrical—and the rhythm is as a rule too varying, complex, and subtle to be readily seized except from a comparison of many instances. Perhaps, however, the following stanza from 'Children of Adam' may convey some idea of it:

I have perceived that to be with those I like is enough;
To stop in company with the rest at evening is enough;
To be surrounded by beautiful, curious, breathing, laughing flesh is
    enough;
To pass among them, or touch any one, or rest my arm ever so
    lightly round his or her neck for a moment—what is this then?
I do not ask any more delight—I swim in it as in a sea.
There is something in staying close to men and women, and looking
    on them, and in the contact and odour of them, that pleases the
    soul well;
All things please the soul—but these please the soul well.[5]

It will be observed that the rhythm is many-centred, that it takes fresh departures as it goes on. The poet uses freely alliteration, chiasmus, antithesis, and especially the retention of the same word or words to begin and end successive lines, but none of these so freely as to render it characteristic. The result, though perhaps uncouth at first sight and hearing, is a medium of expression by no means wanting in excellence, and certainly well adapted for Whitman's purposes. Strange as it appears to a reader familiarised with the exquisite versification of modern England or France, it is by no means in disagreeable contrast therewith, being at least in its earlier forms (for in some of the later poems reminiscences of the English heroic, of Longfellow's hexameters, and even of Poe's stanzas occur) singularly fresh, light, and vigorous. Nor should the language pass unmentioned—for though of course somewhat Transatlantic in construction and vocabulary, it is not offensively American. The chief blemish in the eyes of a sensitive critic is an ugly trick of using foreign words, such as 'Libertad' for liberty,[6] '*habitan* of the Alleghanies,'[7] 'to become *élève* of mine,'[8] 'with reference to *ensemble*,'[9] and so forth; but even this does not occur very frequently. . . .

From A HISTORY OF PROSODY (*1910*)

THE GENESIS OF Whitman's dithyrambic versicles is sufficiently clear, even if we set aside the direct Emersonian suggestions which were hinted at above. I do not know his letters, and the biographical writings about him, so well as I know his poems, and so I cannot say whether he ever gave his own account of it. But, presumptuous as it may seem to say so, a poet's account of such things is by no means always the true account of them. That true account, in Whitman's case, does not need a combination of the late Professor Owen and the living Professor Sievers[10] to make out. The impulsive cause of it was,

Reprinted from *A History of Prosody* (London, 1910), 490–492.

no doubt, that natural and not disgraceful, though sometimes slightly comic, desire to be entirely original and American—to give an unadulterated product of These States,—of which Longfellow, with the best right in the world, has made such excellent fun in *Kavanagh*. The cause of pattern or suggestion was even more undoubtedly—still leaving the Emersonian following as unproved—the verse-divisions of the English Bible. How far possible secondary causes of development by hints from Blake, De Quincey, Lamennais, and others may have helped, is a more speculative division of the subject. But the last and completely formative cause was, as it always is, the idiosyncrasy of the writer. Whitman could and did write more or less regular metre, and his actual medium is often a plum-pudding-stone or conglomerate of metrical fragments. Still the form which he mainly adopts, though hybrid between poetry and prose, is a genuine thing as far as it goes—a true hybrid, and not a mere Watertonian cobbling together of unrelated elements.

The result, at its best, is not easy to specify or exemplify precisely, because it has no ruling type. Of one kind I really do not know a better example than a passage the praise of which, many years ago, excited the never-to-be-quenched wrath of one of the most "cultured" of American prints. It comes early in *Leaves of Grass*, and is one of a series of similitudes for the grass itself:

Or I guess it is the handkerchief of the Lord,
A scented gift and remembrancer designedly dropt,
Bearing the owner's name someway in the corners, that we may see
    and remark, and say, *Whose?*[11]

Here, it will be observed, there is, though no metre, a comparatively regular progression of a quasi-metrical kind, capable of several divisions no doubt, but grouping easiest into something like three, four, and six or seven examples of the "prose-feet" pæons, epitrites, or dochmiacs—which we have occasionally mentioned. The length of these versicles (which are batched in subsections of absolutely optional length) is quite irregular; they might be monosyllabic—though I do not at the moment remember, or in a casual turning over find, one; and they may extend to several lines, though they seldom do, except in the catalogue-pieces, to more than three or four. Even on these last Whitman can often inculcate an excellent rhythmical undulation and final break. But they naturally tend, at times, to something like this:

> Not a move can a man or woman make that affects him or her in a day, month, any part of the direct life-time, or the hour of death, but the same affects him or her onward afterward through the indirect life-time.[12]

That is not without rhythm—hardly any but the most abject prose is,—but it is prose pure and simple. In fact no small part of the "Verse"—he calls it "verse" himself—if printed straight on, would be indistinguishable from no small part of the prose (*Democratic Vistas*, etc.) which *is* so printed.

On the other hand, not a few of the shorter or middle-cut verses have an inefficient suggestion of ordinary verse, as where the tails of the lines, and to some extent their bodies, give confused echoes of *Evangeline* hexameters, or Ionics *a minore* clumsily and inharmoniously managed. The fact is that people have not, as a rule, treated Whitmanics sensibly. I have never myself been able to see why they should be barred, as a variety of expression, when the poet (or whatever he likes to call himself) chooses them, and can justify the choice. It is evident that the continuity of ordinary prose may be inconvenient for some subjects, and uncongenial for some moods. It is, I think, at least fair matter of contention that the regularity of verse, even with all the easements and licences possible to it, if it is to remain verse, may be subject to similar drawbacks. But I should doubt whether the medium will ever be susceptible of any but very occasional use; and I am certain that the justification mentioned above will only be secured by keeping it nearer to verse than to prose, and by rigidly excluding *purely* prosaic passages. Moreover, in a very large number of instances, verse would do even better what this does well. And from Whitman's actual experiments it is clear that had he chosen, and taken the trouble, he could have written beautiful verse proper. Yet it is clear also, that in passages, and many of them, the marriage of matter and form justifies itself as a true marriage. So let it be registered as such, with the banns and the warnings properly proclaimed and attended to.

STANDISH JAMES O'GRADY

[1846–1928]

Walt Whitman, The Poet of Joy *(1875)*

A SPIRIT OF MELANCHOLY pervades modern society. It is not superficial or ephemeral. It has got into the blood and penetrated to the bones and marrow. The modern man habilitates himself in black, and hates gay colours as the owl hates the light of the sun.

There is an almost complete absence of joyfulness in our literature. What do our books tell us of life? Do they represent existence as a boon? Do they bless the world and declare that it is a good thing to be alive? No. Our intellectual masters and pastors take a lugubrious view of the situation. They are overwhelmed with a sense either of the nothingness of things or of the vastness of the weight which destiny has laid on our shoulders. What light-hearted but imaginative and intelligent person can read Carlyle or Ruskin without rejecting all *gaieté de cœur* as a sin and disgrace in this world of awful eternal verities? These doleful prophets, with minds so constituted that in the broad sunshine they must see darkness, are our accepted teachers. . . .

I shall not waste words in the endeavour to prove that Walt Whitman is a poet, and one of high order. In the first magazines and by the first literary persons in this country he has been saluted as such. I desire to call attention to the nature of his

Reprinted from *The Gentleman's Magazine*, n.s., XV (1875), 704–716, abridged; published under the pseudonym Arthur Clive. For an account of O'Grady, see Harold Blodgett, *Walt Whitman in England* (Ithaca, N. Y., 1934), 180–182.

distinguishing merits, and first and beyond all others I would set this, that he always represents life as a boon beyond price, and is ever ready to invoke a blessing on his natal day. Doubtless he, too, has doleful moments; but these, and thoughts arising from these, he refuses to allow to stain the richness and beauty of his work. What will gladden and invigorate the mind is that which he undertakes to give expression to, and he has charged himself "to sing contentment and triumph."[1]

Poets, doubtless, are to a considerable extent liars, and palm off occasional moods as the prevailing temper of their minds; but after a long and close study of Whitman it is my opinion that the character of his life is reflected in his poetry as truly as that of any modern poet has been reflected in his. It is this in Whitman that is most admirable and most beneficent. . . .

Whitman is unceasingly gay, and fresh, and racy. He speaks of common things, and men, and the common sights of every-day life, and yet he is always artistic. The things he observes are significant and such as arrest the eye and the mind, and make a deep mark in the memory. He expresses more than happiness, he expresses exultation. The two hemispheres of the soul he describes as love and dilatation, or pride: —

I was Manhattanese, friendly, and proud.[2]

And so he often uses the word arrogant in a good sense. His poems teem with such words as superb, perfect, gigantic, divine. At his touch the dry bones of our meagre humanity are transformed, and man starts forth like a god, in body and in soul superhuman. The blurring concealing mist peels away, and we see a new heaven and a new earth. It is no longer a mean thing to be a man. From a hundred points he comes back always to this, that man is great and glorious, not little and contemptible. For you to-day who read my poems, he reminds us, this noble planet that travels round the sun gradually cohered from the nebulous float, and passed through all its initial and preparatory stages. . . .

But even exultation is not enough to satisfy the boundless ambition of this man. There is in him a suggestion of something enormous, something bursting the limits of mundane existence and pouring around on all sides, invading the supernatural world, in which, unlike most literary men, he seems fully to believe. The supernatural world is not to him a vague far-away sphere with which we have no practical connection. It is around him and its inhabitants are around him; they are only a sphere beyond. Man passes into that world carrying with him all that he has acquired in the body and in the soul in this world. To express this he employs a remarkable metaphor.

> Not the types set up by the printer return their impression, the meaning, the main concern, any more than a man's substance and life or a woman's substance and life return in the body and in the soul indifferently before death and after death.[3]

Thus death is more the beginning than the end. What it concludes is glorious, but what it begins is divine. Whitman is a mystic. He pours a glamour over the world. From the supernatural sphere, so natural to him, strange light is shed that transfigures the universe before his eyes and before ours. . . .

Whitman lays strong emphasis on physical happiness and those forms of spiritual pleasure which are more closely allied with the physical. This has been to many a stumbling-block and rock of offence. Scholastic and monkish views have evidently not yet disappeared. In real life the importance of physique and of physical health and the irresistible attractions of mere beauty are always recognised. They must be recognised. They make their mark as irresistibly as gravitation or any of the known laws of nature. Yet in our higher literature all this has been neglected for sentiment and the cultivation of pure and delicate emotions. A return to nature has been imperatively called for; and Whitman, not a moment too soon, has appeared singing the body electric.

The intellectualism which has marked the century—the cultivation of sentiment and the emotions—threatened to enfeeble and emasculate the educated classes. The strong voice of Whitman, showing again and again, in metaphors and images, in startling vivid memorable language, the supreme need of sweet blood and pure flesh, the delight of vigour and activity and of mere existence where there is health, the pleasures of mere society even without clever conversation, of bathing, swimming, riding, and the inhaling of pure air, has so arrested the mind of the world that a relapse to scholasticism is no longer possible.

. . . Words simple as grass, lawless as snow-flakes, sun-tan, freckles, unshorn beards, the beauty of wood-boys and all natural persons, the fishermen in the shallow water supported on strong legs, the butcher's boy breaking down in his repartee, the dark countenances of the miners, the vast native thoughts seen in the smutched faces, the giant negro lolling on the cart-load of corn—all the simple employments and operations in which the common people are engaged and the different aspects they present perpetually recur to him and arrest his mind at all times. It was this that at first produced the impression that he was an uneducated man. On the contrary no English poet except perhaps Shelley was so well acquainted with all that could be learned from books. But they give expression to their learning in widely different ways. Shelley's knowledge did not appear in his poetry, it went to feed his idealism and egotism. Whitman's appears as a natural growth. He alludes to the solar system and the formation of the earth, and to what he has learned from travellers and ethnologists, as he alludes to the apple-blossom or any other common thing. No poet ever assimilated his knowledge so well as Whitman or so vitalised it with his own large and joyous life.

Thus beyond all others he is the poet of the day. He knows all that can be known by one person of the stored accumulations of the *savants*, and this knowledge appears in his works as poetry. The extraordinary raciness of his language—the love of nature and of common things and men—deceived the world at first, and the opinion went abroad that he was himself a member of the labouring class and utterly untinctured by books.

. . . Certainly one cannot detect affectation in Whitman. He has at all events attained honesty. But the simplicity which would make him welcome to that class in the community which he more particularly affects he has not attained. The common people, whom he likes most, and who most like him, are not those who can comprehend or care for his poems. The young woodman will not be as ready to take the "Leaves of Grass" with him as Whitman fondly deems, and however affected by the charms of "the red-faced girl,"[4] will but poorly relish the Adamic poetry.

Whitman professes to contemn culture and education, yet he is a perfect representative of both. It is the cultivated classes who receive and recognise him, and it is to them that he is beneficial. He is subtle, profound, psychological, a mystic. He is nothing if not metaphysical, nothing if not erudite. "Grey-necked, forbidding, he has arrived at last to be wrestled with as he passes for the solid prizes of the Universe";[5] but the wrestlers will be the literary man and the scholar. He tries the muscle of the brains of young men, but only muscles that have been previously developed in literary and intellectual exercises. For the educated classes he is a splendid exercise, but to them, and to them alone, does he belong. He sees everything with the eye of a cultivated poet and philosopher—with the eye of a man who knows much and can give a reason for the faith that is in him.

Of the new ideas which Whitman has cast as seed into the American brain the importance which he attaches to friendship is the most remarkable.[6] This appears to have been a subject over which he has brooded long and deeply. It is not possible that Whitman could have written as he has upon this and kindred subjects if he were merely a cultivated brain and nothing more. A thin-blooded, weak-spirited man may, doubtless, like Swedenborg, strike profound truths through sheer force of intellect, or may use violent and swelling language with little dilatation in his spirit; but there is a genuineness and eloquence in Whitman's language concerning friendship which preclude the possibility of the suspicion that he uses strong words for weak feelings. It must not be forgotten that, though now latent, there is in human nature a capacity for friendship of a most absorbing and passionate character. . . .

There cannot be a doubt but that with highly developed races friendship is a passion, and like all passions more physical than intellectual in its sources and modes of expression.

I will sing the song of companionship, I will show what finally must compact these (the States).
I believe these are to found their own ideal of manly love indicating it in me. I will therefore let flame from me the burning fires that were threatening to consume me.
I will lift what has too long kept down those smouldering fires.
I will give them complete abandonment. I will write the evan-

gel-poem of comrades and of love. For who but I should understand love with all its sorrow and joy?

And who but I should be the poet of comrades?[7]

This is strong language and doubtless genuine. Pride and
love, I have said, Whitman considers the two hemispheres of the
brain of humanity, and by love he means not alone benevolence
and wide sympathy and the passion that embraces sexual relation, but that other passion which has existed before, and whose
latent strength the American poet here indicates as a burning
and repressed flame. Elsewhere he speaks of the sick, sick dread
of unreturned friendship, of the comrade's kiss, the arm round
the neck—but he speaks to sticks and stones; the emotion does
not exist in us, and the language of his evangel-poems appears
simply disgusting. . . .

Under a mask of extravagance, of insane intensity, Whitman
preserves a balance of mind and a sanity such as no poet since
Shakespeare has evinced. If his sympathies were fewer he would
go mad. Energy and passion so great, streaming through few
and narrow channels, would burst all barriers. His universal
sympathies have been his salvation, and have rendered his work
in the highest degree sane and true. He is always emphatic, nay
violent, but then he touches all things. Life is intense in him,
and the fire of existence burns brighter and stronger than in
other men. Thus he does his reader service: he seems out of the
fullness of his veins to pour life into those who read him. He is
electric and vitalising. All nature, books, men, countries, things,
change in appearance as we read Whitman: they present themselves under new aspects and with different faces.

No poet since Shakespeare has written with a vocabulary so
fruitful. Words the most erudite and remote, words not quite
naturalised from foreign countries, words used by the lowest of
the people, teem in his works, yet without affectation. You can
take away no word that he uses and substitute another without
spoiling the sense and marring the melody. For where Whitman
seems roughest, rudest, most prosaic, there often is his language
most profoundly melodious. . . .

Whitman is pathetic. There are touches of pathos profounder
and more tender in him than in any modern poet. One recalls the
poem on the steamship *Arctic* going down[8]—the thought of the

last moment as it drew on—the women huddled on the deck, then silence and the passionless wet flowing on—that idealism of wildest sorrow concluding with tears, tears, tears[9]—the low voice and sob which he heard in a lull of the deafening confusion when the embattled States met in deadly conflict—the soldier's funeral, flooding all the ways as with music and with tears, while the moon, like a mother's face in heaven grown brighter, looked down[10]—the picture of the hospital and its fearful sights,[11] and the flame that burned in the heart of the impassive operator, the deep sympathy with suffering and degradation at all times. If Whitman finds it a good thing to be alive it is not because he refuses to see the evil side of life, but because he would see the whole. "*Omnes, omnes*, let others ignore what they may.". . .

Whitman says that they who most loudly praise him are those who understand him least. I, perhaps, will not come under the censure, though I do under the description; for I confess that I do not understand this man. The logical sense of the words, the appositeness and accuracy of the images, one can indeed apprehend and enjoy; but there is an undertone of meaning in Whitman which can never be fully comprehended. This, doubtless, is true of all first-rate poetry; but it must be applied in a special sense to the writings of a man who is not only a poet but a mystic—a man who thoroughly enjoys this world, yet looks confidently to one diviner still beyond; who professes a passionate attachment to his friends, yet says that he has other friends, not to be seen with the eye, closer and nearer and dearer to him than these. The hardening, vulgarising influences of life have not hardened and vulgarised the spiritual sensibilities of this poet, who looks at this world with the wondering freshness of a child, and to the world beyond with the gaze of a seer. He has what Wordsworth lost, and in his old age comes trailing clouds of glory—shadows cast backward from a sphere which we have left, thrown forward from a sphere to which we are approaching.

He is the noblest literary product of modern times, and his influence is invigorating and refining beyond expression.

ROBERT LOUIS STEVENSON

[1850-1894]

The Gospel According to Walt Whitman (1878)

WHAT WHITMAN has to say is another affair from how he says
it. It is not possible to acquit any one of defective intelligence, or
else stiff prejudice, who is not interested by Whitman's matter
and the spirit it represents. Not as a poet, but as what we must
call (for lack of a more exact expression) a prophet, he occupies
a curious and prominent position. Whether he may greatly
influence the future or not, he is a notable symptom of the
present. As a sign of the times, it would be hard to find his
parallel. I should hazard a large wager, for instance, that he was
not unacquainted with the works of Herbert Spencer; and yet
where, in all the history books, shall we lay our hands on two
more incongruous contemporaries? Mr. Spencer so decorous—I
had almost said, so dandy—in dissent; and Whitman, like a
large shaggy dog, just unchained, scouring the beaches of the
world and baying at the moon. And when was an echo more
curiously like a satire, than when Mr. Spencer found his Syn-
thetic Philosophy reverberated from the other shores of the
Atlantic in the "barbaric yawp" of Whitman?

Whitman, it cannot be too soon explained, writes up to a
system. He was a theoriser about society before he was a poet.
He first perceived something wanting, and then sat down

New Quarterly, X (Oct. 1878), 461–481; reprinted in *Familiar
Studies of Men and Books* (London, 1882); the extracts given here are
from the 1924 reprint, 89–91, 96–98, 101–103, 117–119, 121–122,
124.

squarely to supply the want. The reader, running over his works, will find that he takes nearly as much pleasure in critically expounding his theory of poetry as in making poems. This is as far as it can be from the case of the spontaneous village minstrel dear to elegy, who has no theory whatever, although sometimes he may have fully as much poetry as Whitman. The whole of Whitman's work is deliberate and preconceived. A man born into a society comparatively new, full of conflicting elements and interests, could not fail, if he had any thoughts at all, to reflect upon the tendencies around him. He saw much good and evil on all sides, not yet settled down into some more or less unjust compromise as in older nations, but still in the act of settlement. And he could not but wonder what it would turn out; whether the compromise would be very just or very much the reverse, and give great or little scope for healthy human energies. From idle wonder to active speculation is but a step; and he seems to have been early struck with the inefficacy of literature and its extreme unsuitability to the conditions. What he calls "Feudal Literature" could have little living action on the tumult of American democracy; what he calls the "Literature of Wo," meaning the whole tribe of Werther and Byron, could have no action for good in any time or place. Both propositions, if art had none but a direct moral influence, would be true enough; and as this seems to be Whitman's view, they were true enough for him. He conceived the idea of a Literature which was to inhere in the life of the present; which was to be, first, human, and next, American; which was to be brave and cheerful as per contract; to give culture in a popular and poetical presentment; and, in so doing, catch and stereotype some democratic ideal of humanity which should be equally natural to all grades of wealth and education, and suited, in one of his favourite phrases, to "the average man." To the formation of some such literature as this his poems are to be regarded as so many contributions, one sometimes explaining, sometimes superseding, the other: and the whole together not so much a finished work as a body of suggestive hints. He does not profess to have built the castle, but he pretends he has traced the lines of the foundation. He has not made the poetry, but he flatters himself he has done something towards making the poets. . . .

Here we have the key to Whitman's attitude. To give a certain unity of ideal to the average population of America—to gather their activities about some conception of humanity that shall be central and normal, if only for the moment—the poet must portray that population as it is. Like human law, human poetry is simply declaratory. If any ideal is possible, it must be already in the thoughts of the people; and, by the same reason, in the thoughts of the poet, who is one of them. And hence Whitman's own formula: "The poet is individual—he is complete in himself: the others are as good as he; only he sees it, and they do not."[1] To show them how good they are, the poet must study his fellow-countrymen and himself somewhat like a traveller on the hunt for his book of travels. There is a sense, of course, in which all true books are books of travel; and all genuine poets must run their risk of being charged with the traveller's exaggeration; for to whom are such books more surprising than to those whose own life is faithfully and smartly pictured? But this danger is all upon one side; and you may judiciously flatter the portrait without any likelihood of the sitter's disowning it for a faithful likeness. And so Whitman has reasoned: that by drawing at first hand from himself and his neighbours, accepting without shame the inconsistencies and brutalities that go to make up a man, and yet treating the whole in a high, magnanimous spirit, he would make sure of belief, and at the same time encourage people forward by the means of praise. . . .

Whitman tries to reinforce this cheerfulness by keeping up a sort of outdoor atmosphere of sentiment. His book, he tells us, should be read "among the cooling influences of external nature"; and this recommendation, like that other famous one which Hawthorne prefixed to his collected tales, is in itself a character of the work. Every one who has been upon a walking or a boating tour, living in the open air, with the body in constant exercise and the mind in fallow, knows true ease and quiet. The irritating action of the brain is set at rest; we think in a plain, unfeverish temper; little things seem big enough, and great things no longer portentous; and the world is smilingly accepted as it is. This is the spirit that Whitman inculcates and parades. He thinks very ill of the atmosphere of parlours or libraries. Wisdom keeps school outdoors. And he has the art to recommend this attitude of mind by simply pluming himself upon it as a virtue; so that the reader, to keep the advantage over his author which most readers enjoy, is tricked into professing the same view. And this spirit, as it is his chief lesson, is the greatest charm of his work. Thence, in spite of an uneven and emphatic key of expression, something trenchant and straightforward, something simple and surprising, distinguishes his poems. He has sayings that come home to one like the Bible. We fall upon Whitman, after the works of so many men who write better, with a sense of relief from strain, with a sense of touching nature, as when one passes out of the flaring, noisy thoroughfares of a great city into what he himself has called, with unexcelled imaginative justice of language, "the huge and thoughtful night."[2] And his book in consequence, whatever may be the final judgment of its merit, whatever may be its influence on the future, should be in the hands of all parents and guardians as a specific for the distressing malady of being seventeen years old. Green-sickness yields to his treatment as to a charm of magic; and the youth, after a short course of reading, ceases to carry the universe upon his shoulders.

Whitman is not one of those who can be deceived by familiarity. He considers it just as wonderful that there are myriads of stars, as that one man should rise from the dead. He declares "a hair on the back of his hand just as curious as any special revelation."[3] His whole life is to him what it was to Sir Thomas Browne, one perpetual miracle. Everything is strange, everything unaccountable, everything beautiful; from a bug to the moon, from the sight of the eyes to the appetite for food. He makes it his business to see things as if he saw them for the first time, and professes astonishment on principle. . . .

Something should be said of Whitman's style, for style is of the essence of thinking. And where a man is so critically deliberate as our author, and goes solemnly about his poetry for an ulterior end, every indication is worth notice. He has chosen a rough, unrhymed, lyrical verse; sometimes instinct with a fine processional movement; often so rugged and careless that it can only be described by saying that he has not taken the trouble to write prose. I believe myself that it was selected principally because it was easy to write, although not without recollections of the marching measures of some of the prose in our English Old Testament. According to Whitman, on the other hand, "the time has arrived to essentially break down the barriers of form between Prose and Poetry . . . for the most cogent purposes of those great inland states, and for Texas, and California, and Oregon";—a statement which is among the happiest achievements of American humour. He calls his verses "recitatives," in easily followed allusion to a musical form. "Easily-written, loose-fingered chords," he cries, "I feel the thrum of your climax and close."[4] Too often, I fear, he is the only one who can perceive the rhythm; and in spite of Mr. Swinburne, a great part of his work considered as verses is poor bald stuff.[5] Considered, not as verse, but as speech, a great part of it is full of strange and admirable merits. The right detail is seized; the right word, bold and trenchant, is thrust into its place. Whitman has small regard to literary decencies, and is totally free from literary timidities. He is neither afraid of being slangy nor of being dull; nor, let me add, of being ridiculous. The result is a most surprising compound of plain grandeur, sentimental affectation, and downright nonsense. It would be useless to follow his detractors and give instances of how bad he can be at his worst; and perhaps it would be not much wiser to give extracted specimens of how happily he can write when he is at his best. These come in to most advantage in their own place; owing something, it may be, to the offset of their curious surroundings. And one thing is certain, that no one can appreciate Whitman's excellences until he has grown accustomed to his faults. Until you are content to pick poetry out of his pages almost as you must pick it out of a Greek play in Bohn's translation, your gravity will be continually upset, your ears perpetually disappointed, and the whole book will be no more to you than a particularly flagrant production by the Poet Close. . . .

One other point, where his means failed him, must be touched upon, however shortly. In his desire to accept all facts loyally and simply, it fell within his programme to speak at some length and with some plainness on what is, for I really do not know what reason, the most delicate of subjects. Seeing in that one of the most serious and interesting parts of life, he was aggrieved that it should be looked upon as ridiculous or shameful. No one speaks of maternity with his tongue in his cheek; and Whitman made a bold push to set the sanctity of fatherhood beside the sanctity of motherhood, and introduce this also among the things that can be spoken of without either a blush or a wink. But the Philistines have been too strong; and, to say truth, Whitman has rather played the fool. We may be thoroughly conscious that his end is improving; that it would be a good thing if a window were opened on these close privacies of life; that on this subject, as on all others, he now and then lets fall a pregnant saying. But we are not satisfied. We feel that he was not the man for so difficult an enterprise. He loses our sympathy in the character of a poet by attracting too much of our attention in that of a Bull in a China Shop. And where, by a little more art, we might have been solemnised ourselves, it is too often Whitman alone who is solemn in the face of an audience somewhat indecorously amused.

. . . Any reader who bears in mind Whitman's own advice and "dismisses whatever insults his own soul"[6] will find plenty that is bracing, brightening, and chastening to reward him for a little patience at first. It seems hardly possible that any being should get evil from so healthy a book as the *Leaves of Grass*, which is simply comical wherever it falls short of nobility; but if there be any such, who cannot both take and leave, who cannot let a single opportunity pass by without some unworthy and unmanly thought, I should have as great difficulty, and neither more nor less, in recommending the works of Whitman as in lending them Shakespeare, or letting them go abroad outside of the grounds of a private asylum.

SIDNEY LANIER

[1842–1881]

From THE ENGLISH NOVEL (*1881*)

HERE LET ME first carefully disclaim and condemn all that flippant and sneering tone which dominates so many discussions of Whitman. While I differ from him utterly as to every principle of artistic procedure; while he seems to me the most stupenduously mistaken man in all history as to what constitutes true democracy, and the true advance of art and man; while I am immeasurably shocked at the sweeping invasions of those reserves which depend on the very personality I have so much insisted upon, and which the whole consensus of the ages has considered more and more sacred with every year of growth in delicacy; yet, after all these prodigious allowances, I owe some keen delights to a certain combination of bigness and naïvety which make some of Whitman's passages so strong and taking, and indeed, on the one occasion when Whitman has abandoned his theory of formlessness and written in form he has made *My Captain, O my Captain* surely one of the most tender and beautiful poems in any language.

I need quote but a few scraps from characteristic sentences here and there in a recent paper of Whitman's in order to present a perfectly fair view of his whole doctrine. When, for instance, he declares that Tennyson's poetry is not the poetry of

Reprinted from *The English Novel* (New York, 1883), 45–65, an abridged version of Lanier's 1881 lectures. Whitman was Lanier's example of formlessness in contemporary literature. For the poet's balanced evaluation of Lanier, see Traubel, I, 170–171.

the future because, although it is "the highest order of verbal melody, exquisitely clean and pure and almost always perfumed like the tuberose to an extreme of sweetness," yet it has "never one democratic page," and is "never free, naïve poetry, but involved, labored, quite sophisticated;" when we find him bragging of "the measureless viciousness of the great radical republic" (the United States, of course) "with its ruffianly nominations and elections; its loud, ill-pitched voice, utterly regardless whether the verb agrees with the nominative; its fights, errors, eructations, repulsions, dishonesties, audacities; those fearful and varied, long and continued storm-and-stress stages (so offensive to the well-regulated, college-bred mind) wherewith nature, history and time block out nationalities more powerful than the past;" and when finally we hear him tenderly declaring that "meanwhile democracy waits the coming of its bards in silence and in twilight—but 'tis the twilight of dawn":[1] —we are in sufficient possession of the distinctive catch-words which summarize his doctrine.

In examining it, a circumstance occurs to me at the outset which throws a strange but effective light upon the whole argument. It seems curious to reflect that the two poets who have most avowedly written for the people, who have claimed most distinctively to represent and embody the thought of the people, and to be bone of the people's bone and flesh of the people's flesh, are precisely the two who have most signally failed of all popular acceptance and who have most exclusively found audience at the other extreme of culture. These are Wordsworth and Whitman. We all know how strenuously and faithfully Wordsworth believed that in using the simplest words and treating the lowliest themes, he was bringing poetry back near to the popular heart; yet Wordsworth's greatest admirer is Mr. Matthew Arnold, the apostle of culture, the farthest remove from anything that could be called popular: and in point of fact it is probable that many a peasant who would feel his blood stir in hearing *A man's a man for a' that*, would grin and guffaw if you should read him Wordsworth's *Lambs* and *Peter Grays*.

And a precisely similar fate has met Whitman. Professing to be a mudsill and glorying in it, chanting democracy and shirt-sleeves and equal rights, declaring that he is nothing if not one of the people, nevertheless the people, the democracy, will yet have nothing to do with him, and it is safe to say that his sole audience has lain among such representatives of the highest culture as Emerson and the English *illuminated*.

The truth is, that if closely examined, Whitman, instead of being a true democrat, is simply the most incorrigible of aristocrats masquing in a peasant's costume, and his poetry, instead of being the natural outcome of a fresh young democracy, is a product which would be impossible except in a highly civilized society. . . .[2]

Here, then, let us take up the thread of that argument. In the quotations which were given from Whitman's paper, we have really the ideal democracy and democrat of this school. It is curious to reflect in the first place that in point of fact no such democracy, no such democrat, has ever existed in this country.[3] . . . let us inquire, to what representative facts in our history does this picture correspond, what great democrat who has helped to block out this present republic sat for this portrait? Is it George Washington, that beautiful, broad, tranquil spirit whom, I sometimes think, even we Americans have never yet held quite at his true value,—is it Washington who was vicious, dishonest, audacious, combative? But Washington had some hand in blocking out this republic. Or what would our courtly and philosophic Thomas Jefferson look like if you should put this slouch hat on him, and open his shirt-front at the bosom, and set him to presiding over a ruffianly nomination? Yet he had some hand in blocking out this republic. . . .

But where are these roughs, these beards, and this combativeness? Were the Adamses and Benjamin Franklin roughs? Was it these who taught us to make ruffianly nominations? But they had some hand in blocking out this republic. In short, leaving each one to extend this list of names for himself, it may be fairly said that nowhere in history can one find less of that ruggedness which Whitman regards as the essential of democracy, nowhere more of that grace which he considers fatal to it, than among the very representative democrats who blocked out this republic. In truth, when Whitman cries "fear the mellow sweet," and "beware the mortal ripening of nature,"[4] we have an instructive instance of the extreme folly into which a man may be led by mistaking a metaphor for an argument. . . .

If therefore after an inquiry ranging from Washington and Jefferson down to William Cullen Bryant (that surely unrugged and graceful figure who was so often called the finest American gentleman) and Lowell and Longfellow and the rest who are really the men that are blocking out our republic,—if we find not a single representative American democrat to whom any of these pet adjectives apply,—not one who is measurelessly vicious, or ruffianly, or audacious, or purposely rugged, or contemptuous towards the graces of life,—then we are obliged to affirm that the whole ideal drawn by Whitman is a fancy picture with no counterpart in nature. . . .

Now if we carry the result of this inquiry over into art; if we are presented with a poetry which professes to be democratic because it—the poetry—is measurelessly vicious, purposely eructant, striving after ruggedness, despising grace, like the democracy described by Whitman; then we reply that as matter of fact there never was any such American democracy and that the poetry which represents it has no constituency. And herein seems a most abundant solution of the fact just now brought to your notice, that the actually existing democracy have never accepted Whitman's poetry. But here we are met with the cry of strength and manfulness. Everywhere throughout Whitman's poetry the "rude muscle," the brawn, the physical bigness of the American prairie, the sinew of the Western backwoodsman, are apotheosized, and all these, as Whitman claims, are fitly chanted in his "savage song."[5]

Here, then, is a great stalwart man, in perfect health, all brawn and rude muscle, set up before us as the ideal of strength. Let us examine this strength a little. For one, I declare that I do not find it impressive. Yonder, in a counting-room—alas, in how many counting-rooms! A young man with weak eyes bends over a ledger, and painfully casts up the figures day by day, on pitiful wages, to support his mother, or to send his younger brother to school, or some such matter. If we watch this young man when he takes down his hat, lays off his ink-splotched office-coat, and starts home for dinner, we perceive that he is in every respect the opposite of the stalwart Whitman ideal; his chest is not huge, his legs are inclined to be pipe-stems, and his dress is like that of any other book-keeper. Yet the weak-eyed pipe-stem-legged young man impresses me as more of a man, more of a democratic man, than the tallest of Whitman's roughs; to the eye of my spirit there is more strength in this man's daily endurance of petty care and small weariness, for love, more of the sort of stuff which makes a real democracy and a sound republic, than in an army of Whitman's unshaven loafers. . . .

Nay, when we think of it, how little is it a matter of the future, how entirely is it a matter of the past, when people come running at us with rude muscle and great mountains and such matters of purely physical bigness to shake our souls? How long ago is it that they began to put great bearskin caps on soldiers with a view to make them look grisly and formidable when advancing on the enemy? It is so long ago that the practice has survived mainly as ceremonial, and the little boys on the streets now laugh at this ferociousness when the sappers and miners come by who affect this costume.

Yet here in the nineteenth century we behold artists purposely setting bearskin caps upon their poetry to make it effective. This sort of thing never yet succeeded as against Anglo-Saxon people. . . .

In the name of all really manful democracy, in the name of the true strength that only can make our republic reputable among the nations, let us repudiate the strength that is no stronger than a human biceps, let us repudiate the manfulness that averages no more than six feet high. My democrat, the democrat whom I contemplate with pleasure, the democrat who is to write or to read the poetry of the future, may have a mere thread for his biceps, yet he shall be strong enough to handle hell, he shall play ball with the earth; and albeit his stature may be no more than a boy's, he shall still be taller than the great redwoods of California; his height shall be the height of great resolution and love and faith and beauty and knowledge and subtle meditation; his head shall be forever among the stars.

But here we are met with the cry of freedom. This poetry is free, it is asserted, because it is independent of form. But this claim is also too late. It should have been made at least before the French Revolution. We all know what that freedom means in politics which is independent of form, of law. It means myriad-fold slavery to a mob. As in politics, so in art. Once for all, in art, to be free is not to be independent of any form, it is to be master of many forms. Does the young artist of the Whitman school fancy that he is free because under the fond belief that he is yielding himself to nature, stopping not for words lest he may fail to make what Whitman proudly calls "a savage song," he allows himself to be blown about by every wind of passion? Is a ship free because, without rudder or sail, it is turned loose to the winds, and has no master but nature? Nature is the tyrant of tyrants. Now, just as that freedom of the ship on the sea means shipwreck, so independence of form in art means death. Here one recurs with pleasure to the aphorism cited in the last lecture: in art, as elsewhere, "he who will not answer to the rudder shall answer to the rocks." I find all the great artists of time striving after this same freedom; but it is not by destroying, it is by extending the forms of art, that all sane and sober souls hope to attain. . . .

And lastly, the Poetry of the Future holds that all modern poetry, Tennyson particularly,[6] is dainty and over-perfumed, and Whitman speaks of it with that contempt which he everywhere affects for the dandy. But surely—I do not mean this disrespectfully—what age of time ever yielded such a dandy as the founder of this school, Whitman himself? The simpering beau who is the product of the tailor's art is certainly absurd enough; but what difference is there between that and the other dandy-upside-down who from equal motives of affectation throws away coat and vest, dons a slouch hat, opens his shirt so as to expose his breast, and industriously circulates his portrait, thus taken, in his own books. And this dandyism—the dandyism of the roustabout—I find in Whitman's poetry from beginning to end. Everywhere it is conscious of itself, everywhere it is analyzing itself, everywhere it is posing to see if it cannot assume a naïve and striking attitude, everywhere it is screwing up its eyes, not into an eyeglass like the conventional dandy, but into an expression supposed to be fearsomely rough and barbaric and frightful to the terror-stricken reader, and it is almost safe to say that one half of Whitman's poetic work has consisted of a detailed description of the song he is going to sing. It is the extreme of sophistication in writing.

But if we must have dandyism in our art, surely the softer sort, which at least leans toward decorum and gentility, is preferable; for that at worst becomes only laughable, while the rude dandyism, when it does acquire a factitious interest by being a blasphemy against real manhood, is simply tiresome.

I have thus dwelt upon these claims of the Whitman school, not so much because of any intrinsic weight they possess, as because they are advanced in such taking and sacred names,—of democracy, of manhood, of freedom, of progress. Upon the most earnest examination, I can find it nothing but wholly undemocratic; not manful, but dandy; not free, because the slave of nature; not progressive, because its whole momentum is derived from the physical-large which ceased to astonish the world ages ago, in comparison with spiritual greatness.

Indeed, this matter has been pushed so far, with the apparent, but wholly unreal sanction of so many influential names, that in speaking to those who may be poets of the future, I cannot close these hasty words upon the Whitman school without a fervent protest, in the name of all art and all artists, against a poetry which has painted a great scrawling picture of the human body and has written under it, *"This is the soul;"* which shouts a profession of religion in every line, but of a religion that, when examined, reveals no tenet, no rubric, save that a man must be natural, must abandon himself to every passion; and which constantly roars its belief in God, but with a camerado air as if it were patting the Deity on the back and bidding Him *Cheer up* and hope for further encouragement.

It seems like a curious sarcasm of time that even the form of Whitman's poetry is not poetry of the future but tends constantly into the rhythm of

Brimmanna boda abeod eft ongean,

which is the earliest rhythm of our poetry. The only difference which Whitman makes is in rejecting the alliteration, in changing the line-division, so as to admit longer lines, and the allowance of much liberty in interrupting this general rhythm for a moment. It is remarkable indeed that this old rhythm is still distinctly the prevalent rhythm of English prose. Some years ago Walter Savage Landor remarked that the dactyl was "the bindweed of English prose," and by the dactyl he means simply a word of three syllables with the accent on the first, like *Brimmanna*. For example:

I loaf and invite my soul;
I lean and loaf at my ease, observing a spear of summer grass.
I exist as I am—that is enough:
If no other in the world be aware, I sit content;
And if each and all be aware I sit content.
Washes and razors for foofoos, and for me freckles and a bristling beard.[7]

Walt Whitman am I, a cosmos of mighty Manhattan the son.

GERARD MANLEY HOPKINS

[1844–1889]

Letter to Robert Bridges (1882)

Stonyhurst College, Blackburn. Oct. 18 1882.

DEAREST BRIDGES,—I have read of Whitman's (1) 'Pete'[1] in the library at Bedford Square (and perhaps something else; if so I forget), which you pointed out; (2) two pieces in the *Athenaeum* or *Academy*, one on the Man-of-War Bird, the other beginning 'Spirit that formed this scene';[2] (3) short extracts in a review by Saintsbury in the *Academy*:[3] this is all I remember. I cannot have read more than half a dozen pieces at most.

This, though very little, is quite enough to give a strong

Reprinted from *The Letters of Gerard Manley Hopkins to Robert Bridges*, ed. Claude Colleer Abbott (London, 1935), 154–158.

impression of his marked and original manner and way of thought and in particular of his rhythm. It might be even enough, I shall not deny, to originate or, much more, influence another's style: they say the French trace their whole modern school of landscape to a single piece of Constable's exhibited at the Salon early this century.[4]

The question then is only about the fact. But first I may as well say what I should not otherwise have said, that I always knew in my heart Walt Whitman's mind to be more like my own than any other man's living. As he is a very great scoundrel this is not a pleasant confession. And this also makes me the more desirous to read him and the more determined that I will not.

Nevertheless I believe that you are quite mistaken about this piece and that on second thoughts you will find the fancied resemblance diminish and the imitation disappear.[5]

And first of the rhythm. Of course I saw that there was to the eye something in my long lines like his, that the one would remind people of the other. And both are in irregular rhythms. There the likeness ends. The pieces of his I read were mostly in an irregular rhythmic prose: that is what they are thought to be meant for and what they seemed to me to be. Here is a fragment of a line I remember: 'or a handkerchief designedly dropped'. This is in a dactylic rhythm—or let us say anapaestic; for it is a great convenience in English to assume that the stress is always at the end of the foot; the consequence of which assumption is that in ordinary verse there are only two English feet possible, the iamb and the anapaest, and even in my regular sprung rhythm only one additional, the fourth paeon: for convenience' sake assuming this, then the above fragment is anapaestic— 'or a hand/kerchief . . ./. design/edly dropped'—and there is a break down, a designed break of rhythm, after 'handkerchief', done no doubt that the line may not become downright verse, as it would be if he had said 'or a handkerchief purposely dropped'. Now you can of course say that he meant pure verse and that the foot is a paeon—'or a hand/kerchief design/edly dropped'; or that he means, without fuss, what I should achieve by looping the syllable *de* and calling that foot an outriding foot—for the result might be attained either way. Here then I must make the answer which will apply here and to all like cases and to the examples which may be found up and down the poets of the use of sprung rhythm—*if they could have done it they would:* sprung rhythm, once you hear it, is so eminently natural a thing and so effective a thing that if they had known of it they would have used it. Many people, as we say, have been 'burning', but they all missed it; they took it up and mislaid it again. So far as I know—I am enquiring and presently I shall be able to speak more decidedly—it existed in full force in Anglo saxon verse and in great beauty; in a degraded and doggrel shape in *Piers Ploughman* (I am reading that famous poem and am coming to the conclusion that it is not worth reading); Greene[6] was the last who employed it at all consciously and he never continuously; then it disappeared—for one cadence in it here and there is not sprung rhythm and one swallow does not make a spring. (I put aside Milton's case, for it is altogether singular.) In a matter like this a thing does not exist, is not *done* unless it is wittingly and willingly done; to recognise the form you are employing and to mean it is everything. To apply this: there is (I suppose, but you will know) no sign that Whitman means to use paeons or outriding feet where these breaks in rhythm occur; it seems to me a mere extravagance to think he means people to understand of themselves what they are slow to understand even when marked or pointed out. If he does not mean it then he does not do it; or in short what he means to write—and writes—is rhythmic prose and that only. And after all, you probably grant this.

Good. Now prose rhythm in English is always one of two things (allowing my convention about scanning upwards or from slack to stress and not from stress to slack)—either iambic or anapaestic. You may make a third measure (let us call it) by intermixing them. One of these three simple measures then, all iambic or all anapaestic or mingled iambic and anapaestic, is what he in every case means to write. He dreams of no other and he *means* a rugged or, as he calls it in that very piece 'Spirit that formed this scene' (which is very instructive and should be read on this very subject), a 'savage' art and rhythm.

Extremes meet, and (I must for truth's sake say what

sounds pride) this savagery of his art, this rhythm in its last ruggedness and decomposition into common prose, comes near the last elaboration of mine. For that piece of mine is very highly wrought. The long lines are not rhythm run to seed: everything is weighed and timed in them. Wait till they have taken hold of your ear and you will find it so. No, but what it *is* like is the rhythm of Greek tragic choruses or of Pindar: which is pure sprung rhythm. And that has the same changes of cadence from point to point as this piece. If you want to try it, read one till you have settled the true places of the stress, mark these, then read it aloud, and you will see. Without this these choruses are prose bewitched; with it they are sprung rhythm like that piece of mine.

Besides, why did you not say *Binsey Poplars* was like Whitman? The present piece is in the same kind and vein, but developed, an advance. The lines and the stanzas (of which there are two in each poem and having much the same relation to one another) are both longer, but the two pieces are greatly alike: just look. If so how is this a being untrue to myself? I am sure it is no such thing.

The above remarks are not meant to run down Whitman. His 'savage' style has advantages, and he has chosen it; he says so. But you cannot eat your cake and keep it: he eats his offhand, I keep mine. It makes a very great difference. Neither do I deny all resemblance. In particular I noticed in 'Spirit that formed this scene' a preference for the alexandrine. I have the same preference: I came to it by degrees, I did not take it from him.

About diction the matter does not allow me so clearly to point out my independence as about rhythm. I cannot think that the present piece owes anything to him. I hope not, here especially, for it is not even spoken in my own person but in that of St. Winefred's maidens. It ought to sound like the thoughts of a good but lively girl and not at all like—not at all like Walt Whitman. But perhaps your mind may have changed by this.

I wish I had not spent so much time in defending the piece.

Believe me your affectionate friend

GERARD

ALGERNON SWINBURNE

[1837–1909]

Whitmania (*1887*)

THE REMARKABLE AMERICAN RHAPSODIST who has inoculated a certain number of English readers and writers with the
singular form of ethical and aesthetic rabies for which his name
supplies the proper medical term of definition is usually regarded by others than Whitmaniacs as simply a blatant quack—
a vehement and emphatic dunce, of incomparable vanity and
volubility, inconceivable pretentions, and incompetence. That
such is by no means altogether my own view I need scarcely
take the trouble to protest. Walt Whitman has written some
pages to which I have before now given praise enough to exoner-
ate me, I should presume, from any charge of prejudice or
prepossession against a writer whose claims to occasional notice
and occasional respect no man can be less desirous to dispute
than I am.[1] Nor should I have thought it necessary to comment
on the symptoms of a disorder which happily is not likely to
become epidemic in an island or on a continent not utterly
barren of poetry, had the sufferers not given such painfully
singular signs of inability to realize a condition only too obvious
to the compassionate bystander. While the preachers or the
proselytes of the gospel according to Whitman were content to
admit that he was either no poet at all, or the only poet who had

The Fortnightly Review, XLVIII (Aug. 1887), 170–176; the text
used here was reprinted in *The Eclectic Magazine*, CIX (Oct. 1887),
454–458, and in *Studies in Prose and Poetry* (London, 1894). For an
account of the two poets, see Harold Blodgett, *Walt Whitman in England* (Ithaca, N. Y., 1934), 103–121.

ever been born into this world—that those who accepted him were bound to reject all others as nullities—they had at least the merit of irrefragable logic; they could claim at least the credit of indisputable consistency. But when other gods or godlings are accepted as participants in the divine nature; when his temple is transformed into a pantheon, and a place assigned his godhead a little beneath Shakespeare, a little above Dante, or cheek by jowl with Homer; when Isaiah and Æschylus, for anything we know, may be admitted to a greater or lesser share in his incommunicable and indivisible supremacy—then, indeed, it is high time to enter a strenuous and (if it be possible) a serious protest. The first apostles alone were the depositaries of the pure and perfect evangel: these later and comparatively heterodox disciples have adulterated and debased the genuine metal of absolute, coherent, unalloyed and unqualified nonsense.

To the better qualities discernible in the voluminous and incoherent effusions of Walt Whitman it should not be difficult for any reader not unduly exasperated by the rabid idiocy of the Whitmaniacs to do full and ample justice: for these qualities are no less simple and obvious than laudable and valuable. A just enthusiasm, a genuine passion of patriotic and imaginative sympathy, a sincere though limited and distorted love of nature, an eager and earnest faith in freedom and in loyalty—in the loyalty that can only be born of liberty; a really manful and a nobly rational tone of mind with regard to the crowning questions of duty and of death; these excellent qualities of emotion and reflection find here and there a not inadequate expression in a style of rhetoric not always flatulent or inharmonious. Originality of matter or of manner, of structure or of thought, it would be equally difficult for any reader not endowed with a quite exceptional gift of ignorance of or hebetude to discover in any part of Mr. Whitman's political or ethical or physical or proverbial philosophy. But he has said wise and noble things upon such simple and eternal subjects as life and death, pity and enmity, friendship and fighting; and even the intensely conventional nature of its elaborate and artificial simplicity should not be allowed, by a magnanimous and candid reader, too absolutely to eclipse the genuine energy and the occasional beauty of his feverish and convulsive style of writing.

All this may be cordially conceded by the lovers of good work in any kind, however imperfect, incomposite, and infirm; and more than this the present writer at any rate most assuredly never intended to convey by any tribute of sympathy or admiration which may have earned for him the wholly unmerited honour of an imaginary enlistment in the noble army of Whitmaniacs. He has therefore no palinode to chant, no recantation to intone; for if it seems and is unreasonable to attribute a capacity of thought to one who has never given any sign of thinking, a faculty of song to one who has never shown ability to sing, it must be remembered, on the other hand, that such qualities of energetic emotion and sonorous expression as distinguish the happier moments and the more sincere inspirations of such writers as Whitman or as Byron have always, in common parlance, been allowed to pass muster and do duty for the faculty of thinking or the capacity of singing. Such an use of common terms is doubtless inaccurate and inexact, if judged by the "just but severe law" of logical definition or of mathematical precision: but such abuse or misuse of plain words is generally understood as conveying no more than a conventional import such as may be expressed by the terms with which we subscribe an ordinary letter, or by the formula through which we decline an untimely visit. Assuredly I never have meant to imply what most assuredly I never have said—that I regarded Mr. Whitman as a poet or a thinker in the proper sense; the sense in which the one term is applicable to Coleridge or to Shelley, the other to Bacon or to Mill. Whoever may have abdicated his natural right, as a being not born without a sense of music or a sense of reason, to protest against the judgment which discerns in *Childe Harold* or in *Drum-Taps* a masterpiece of imagination and expression, of intelligence or of song, I never have abdicated mine. The highest literary quality discoverable in either book is rhetoric: and very excellent rhetoric in either case it sometimes is; what it is at other times I see no present necessity to say. But Whitmaniacs and Byronites have yet to learn that if rhetoric were poetry John Bright would be a poet at least equal to John Milton, Demosthenes to Sophocles, and Cicero to Catullus. Poetry may be something more—I certainly am not concerned to deny it—than an art or a science; but not because it is not, strictly speaking, a science or an art. There is a science of verse as surely as there is a science of mathematics: there is an art of expression by metre as certainly as there is an art of representation by painting. To some poets the understanding of this science, the mastery of this art, would seem to come by a natural instinct which needs nothing but practice for its development, its application, and its perfection: others by patient and conscientious study of their own abilities attain a no less unmistakable and a scarcely less admirable success. But the man of genius and the dullard who cannot write good verse are equally out of the running. "Did you ask dulcet rhymes from me?" inquires Mr. Whitman of some extraordinary if not imaginary interlocutor; and proceeds, with some not ineffective energy of expression, to explain that "I lull nobody—and you will never understand me."[2] No, my dear good sir—or camerado, if that be the more courteous and conventional address (a modest reader might deferentially reply): not in the wildest visions of a distempered slumber could I ever have dreamed of doing anything of the kind. Nor do we ask them even from such other and inferior scribes or bards as the humble Homer, the modest Milton, or the obsolete and narrow-minded Shakespeare—poets of sickly feudality, of hidebound classicism, of effete and barbarous incompetence. But metre, rhythm, cadence not merely appreciable but definable and reducible to rule and measurement, though we do not expect from you, we demand from all who claim, we discern in the works of all who have achieved, any place among poets of any class whatsoever. The question whether your work is in any sense poetry has no more to do with dulcet rhymes than with the differential calculus. The question is whether you have any more right to call yourself a poet, or to be called a poet by any man who knows verse from prose, or black from white, or speech from silence, or his right hand from his left, than to call yourself or to be called, on the strength of your published writings, a mathematician, a logician, a painter, a political economist, a sculptor, a dynamiter, an old parliamentary hand, a civil engineer, a dealer in marine stores, an amphimacer, a triptych, a rhomboid, or a rectangular parallelogram. "Vois-tu bien, tu es baron comme ma pantoufle!" said old Gillenormand—the creature of one who was indeed a creator or a poet: and the humblest of critics who knows any one thing from any one other thing has a right to say to the man who offers as poetry what the exuberant incontinence of a Whitman presents for our acceptance—"Tu es poète comme mon—soulier."

But the student has other and better evidence than any merely negative indication of impotence in the case of the American as in the case of the British despiser and disclaimer of so pitiful a profession or ambition as that of a versifier. Mr. Carlyle and Mr. Whitman have both been good enough to try their hands at lyric verse: and the ear which has once absorbed their dulcet rhymes will never need to be reminded of the reason for their contemptuous abhorrence of a diversion so contemptible as the art of Coleridge and Shelley.

> Out of eternity
>   This new day is born:
> Into eternity
>   This day shall return.

Such were the flute-notes of Diogenes Devilsdung: comparable by those who would verify the value of his estimate with any stanza of Shelley's "To a Skylark." And here is a sample of the dulcet rhymes which a most tragic occasion succeeded in evoking from the orotund oratist of Manhattan.

The port is near, the bells I hear, the people all exulting,
While follow eyes the steady keel, the vessel grim and daring;
. . . .
For you bouquets and ribbon'd wreaths—for you the shores a-crowd-
    ing; (*sic*)
For you they call, the surging mass, their eager faces turning.[3]

Ἰοὺ ἰοὺ ὢ ὢ κακά. Upon the whole, I prefer Burns—or Hogg— to Carlyle, and Dibdin—or Catnach[4]—to Whitman.

A pedantic writer of poems distilled from other poems (which, as the immortal author of the imperishable *Leaves of Grass* is well aware, must "pass away")—a Wordsworth, for example, or a Tennyson—would hardly have made "eyes" follow the verb they must be supposed to govern. Nor would a poor creature whose ear was yet unattuned to the cadence of "chants democratic" have permitted his Pegasus so remarkable a capriole as to result in the rhythmic reverberation of such rhymes as these. When a boy who remains unable after many efforts to cross the Asses' Bridge expresses his opinion that Euclid was a beastly old fool, his obviously impartial verdict is generally received by his elders with exactly the same amount of respectful attention as is accorded by any competent reader to the equally valuable and judicial deliverances of Messrs. Whitman, Emerson, and Carlyle on the subject of poetry—that is, of lyrical or creative literature. The first critic of our time—perhaps the largest-minded and surest-sighted of any age—has pointed out, in an essay on poetry which should not be too long left buried in the columns of the *Eycyclopaedia Britannica,* the exhaustive accuracy of the Greek terms which define every claimant to the laurel as either a singer or a maker. There is no third term, as there is no third class. If then it appears that Mr. Walt Whitman has about as much gift of song as his precursors and apparent models in rhythmic structure and style, Mr. James Macpherson and Mr. Martin Tupper, his capacity for creation is the only thing that remains for us to consider. And on that score we find him, beyond all question, rather like the later than like the earlier of his masters. Macpherson could at least evoke shadows: Mr. Tupper and Mr. Whitman can only accumulate words. As to his originality in the matter of free speaking, it need only be observed that no remarkable mental gift is requisite to qualify man or woman for membership of a sect mentioned by Dr. Johnson—the Adamites, who believed in the virtue of public nudity. If those worthies claimed the right to bid their children run about the streets stark naked, the magistrate, observed Johnson, "would have a right to flog them into their doublets;" a right no plainer than the right of common sense and sound criticism to flog the Whitmaniacs into their strait-waistcoats; or, were there any female members of such a sect, into their strait-petticoats. If nothing that concerns the physical organism of men or of women is common or unclean or improper for literary manipulation, it may be maintained, by others than the disciples of a contemporary French novelist who has amply proved the sincerity of his own opinion to that effect, that it is not beyond the province of literature to describe with realistic exuberance of detail the functions of digestion or indigestion in all its processes—the objects and the results of an aperient or an emetic medicine. Into "the troughs of Zolaism," as Lord Tennyson calls them (a phrase which bears rather unduly hard on the quadrupedal pig), I am happy to believe that Mr. Whitman has never dipped a passing nose: he is a writer of something occasionally like English, and a man of something occasionally like genius. But in his treatment of topics usually regarded as no less unfit for public exposition and literary illustration than those which have obtained notoriety for the would-be bastard of Balzac—the Davenant of the (French) prose Shakespeare, he has contrived to make "the way of a man with a maid" (Proverbs xxx. 19) almost as loathsomely ludicrous and almost as ludicrously loathsome—I speak merely of the aesthetic or literary aspect of his effusions—as the Swiftian or Zolaesque enthusiasm of bestiality which insists on handling what "goeth into the belly, and is cast out into the draught" (St. Mark xv. 17). The Zolas and the Whitmen, to whom nothing, absolutely and literally nothing, is unclean or common, have an obvious and incalculable advantage over the unconverted who have never enjoyed the privilege of a vision like St. Peter's, and received the benefit of a supernatural prohibition to call anything common or unclean. They cannot possibly be exposed, and they cannot possibly be put to shame: for that best of all imaginable reasons which makes it proverbially difficult to "take the brecks off a Highlander."

It would really seem as though, in literary and other matters, the very plainness and certitude of a principle made it doubly necessary for those who maintain it to enforce and reinforce it over and over again; as though, the more obvious it were, the more it needed indication and demonstration, assertion and reassertion. There is no more important, no more radical and fundamental truth of criticism than this: that, in poetry perhaps above all other arts, the method of treatment, the manner of touch, the tone of expression, is the first and last thing to be considered. There is no subject which may not be treated with success (I do not say there are no subjects which on other than artistic grounds it may not be as well to avoid, it may not be better to pass by) if the poet, by instinct or by training, knows exactly how to handle it aright, to present it without danger of just or rational offence. For evidence of this truth we need look no further than the pastorals of Virgil and Theocritus. But under the dirty clumsy paws of a harper whose plectrum is a muck-rake any tune will become a chaos of discords, though the motive of the tune should be the first principle of nature—the passion of man for woman or the passion of woman for man. And the unhealthily demonstrative and obtrusive animalism of the Whitmaniad is as unnatural, as incompatible with the wholesome instincts of human passion, as even the filthy and inhuman asceticism of SS. Macarius and Simeon Stylites. If anything can justify the serious and deliberate display of merely physical emotion in literature or in art, it must be one of two things: intense depth of feeling expressed with inspired perfection of simplicity, with divine sublimity of fascination, as by Sappho; or transcendant supremacy of actual and irresistible beauty in such revelation of naked nature as was possible to Titian. But Mr. Whitman's Eve is a drunken apple-woman, indecently sprawling in the slush and garbage of the gutter amid the rotten refuse of her overturned fruit-stall: but Mr. Whitman's Venus is a Hottentot wench under the influence of cantharides and adulterated rum. Cotytto[5] herself would repudiate the ministration of such priestesses as these.

But what then, if anything, is it that a rational creature who has studied and understood the work of any poet, great or small, from Homer down to Moschus, from Lucretius down to Martial, from Dante down to Metastasio,[6] from Villon down to Voltaire, from Shakespeare down to Byron, can find to applaud, to approve, or to condone in the work of Mr. Whitman? To this very reasonable and inevitable question the answer is not far to seek. I have myself repeatedly pointed out—it may be (I have often been told so) with too unqualified sympathy and too uncritical enthusiasm—the qualities which give a certain touch of greatness to his work, the sources of inspiration which infuse into its chaotic jargon some passing or seeming notes of cosmic beauty, and diversify with something of occasional harmony the strident and barren discord of its jarring and erring atoms. His sympathies, I repeat, are usually generous, his views of life are occasionally just, and his views of death are invariably noble. In other words, he generally means well, having a good stock on hand of honest emotion; he sometimes sees well, having a natural sensibility to such aspects of nature as appeal to an eye rather quick than penetrating; he seldom writes well, being cabined, cribbed, confined, bound in, to the limits of a thoroughly unnatural, imitative, histrionic and affected style. But there is a thrilling and fiery force in his finest bursts of gusty rhetoric which makes us wonder whether with a little more sense and a good deal more cultivation he might not have made a noticeable orator. As a poet, no amount of improvement that self-knowledge and self-culture might have brought to bear upon such exceptionally raw material could ever have raised him higher than a station to which his homely and manly patriotism would be the best claim that could be preferred for him; a seat beside such writers as Ebenezer Elliot[7]—or possibly a little higher, on such an elevation as might be occupied by a poet whom careful training had reared and matured into a rather inferior kind of Southey. But to fit himself for such promotion he would have in the first place to resign all claim to the laurels of Gotham, with which the critical sages of that famous borough have bedecked his unbashful brows; he would have to recognise that he is no more, in the proper sense of the word, a poet, than Communalists or Dissolutionists are, in any sense of the word, Republicans; that he has exactly as much claim to a place beside Dante as any Vermersch or Vermorel or other verminous and murderous muckworm of the Parisian Commune to a place beside Mazzini: in other words, that the informing principle of his work is not so much the negation as the contradition of the creative principle of poetry. And this it is not to be expected that such a man should bring himself to believe, as long as he hears himself proclaimed the inheritor of a seat assigned a hundred years ago by the fantastic adulation of more or less distinguished literary eccentrics to a person of the name of Jephson— whose triumphs as a tragic poet made his admirers tremble for Shakespeare.

GABRIEL SARRAZIN

[1 8 5 3 – 1 9 4 0 ?]

Walt Whitman (*1888*)

AT THE MOMENT WHEN, in western Europe, the educated and literary classes are allowing themselves to become inoculated with the subtle poison of pessimism; when, in Russia, a nation of so grand a future, the Slav spirit gropes in the midst of utopias and contradictions, mingling tendencies toward conquest and supremacy with the idea of a mission at once humanitarian and mystical—at the self-same moment a triumphant voice is raised on the other side of the Atlantic. In this chant of a lasting and almost blinding luminary, no hesitations, no despairs; the present and the past, the universe and man, free from all concealment, confront with a serene superiority the bitter smile of the analyst. There is no need for us any longer to search for ourselves, because we have found ourselves; and from the midst of its period of development one nation at least points to its coming puissance reflected in the mirror of the future. The man who thus announces himself—himself and his race—brings at the same time a word absolutely new, a form instinctively audacious, novel, overstepping all literary conventions. He creates a rhythm of his own, less rigid than verse, more broken than prose —a rhythm adapted to the movement of his emotion, hastened as

"Poetes modernes de l'Amerique: Whitman," *La Nouvelle Revue,* LII (May 1, 1888), 164–184; expanded in *La renaissance de la poésie anglaise* (Paris, 1889), 235–279; the abridged text used here was translated by Harrison S. Morris and included in *In Re* (Philadelphia, 1893), 159–169. See also Roger Asselineau's article in *Walt Whitman Review,* V (1959), 8–11.

it hastens, precipitated, abated, and led into repose. At times he will utter almost an Hebraic chant, quitted anon as he enlarges or abandons himself to the theme. But, as he freely uses the forms of others as well as his own, the habitual employment of the artifices of literary writing is, to him, entirely unknown. If he makes literature, it is, openly and without shame, as an author ignorant of research and artistic vainglory. The word *literateur*, in the sense it assumes amongst the older civilizations, cannot in any manner be applied to him. His writings come forth glowing and direct, with an immediate significance and as if spoken. As those of the ancient prophet poets his words are addressed to the assembled people. . . .

The poetry of Walt Whitman proclaimed at the outset complete pantheism, with no extenuation, and with all its consequences (see "Song of the Universal"). At first there was an outcry. Shelley himself had dreamed of sanctifying evil—had declared it the necessary brother of good and its equal. One may perhaps be permitted to say that evil envelopes good as the fertilizer encloses and nourishes the germ of the flower; but to place the pedestal of Satan next that of the Divine—what spirit escaped from the nether regions has committed that audacity? And worst of all, most incomprehensible of all, the heart of the miscreant whence springs this blasphemy seems to have wings, joyous, light, which palpitate in ecstasy. In brief, and with the condition that one possesses an idea of the sentiment of the sublime, the explanation was simple enough, and to understand it one had but to regard the love of the great Yankee for the Cosmos—that love at once pious, profound, overflowing, ecstatic, strong as an intoxication and as a possession. Neither in the dawn of civilizations in the Orient, that region of mysticism, nor amongst the most exalted Catholics of Spain and Italy, has a spirit ever more profoundly lost itself in God than has Walt Whitman's. For him, Nature and God are one. God is the universe, or, to speak more exactly, the mystery at once visible and hidden in the universe. Wholly unlike Carlyle, who has been thought to possess traits of resemblance with Walt Whitman, but who, before the unknown divinity, could only prostrate himself and tremble with a holy terror, Walt Whitman, in his confident and lofty piety, is the direct inheritor of the great

Oriental mystics, Brahma, Proclus, Abou Said.[1] In Europe he may be compared with the German metaphysicians, disciples and developers of Spinoza; more than one trait unites him to Herder, to Hegel, to Schelling—above all, to the bizarre, chaotic and sublime Jean Paul. From these to him—Jean Paul apart, and noting that Whitman differs from Richter by a total lack of humor—there is still all the distance from the philosopher to the poet, the doctor to the dervish: more candid and more intense than they, the Yankee bard abandons himself with ecstasy into the adored hands of the Universal Being. Living in happy harmony with all the aspects of the Cosmos, even the most sombre, he exclaims at the close of "Leaves of Grass," his great collection of poems: "And henceforth I will go celebrate any thing I see or am, . . . and deny nothing."[2] And then, in effect, he says: God being in all things and everywhere, how can I help loving Him in all things and everywhere; and because the unbeliever dares judge of Him from seeing a part of one of His faces, should the believing heart follow the pitiful example? Jacob Boehm held evil to be the promoter of good—the good of strife and victory. But this position is always open to dispute, and Walt Whitman never disputes. . . .[3]

It must not be thought that his definitive optimism is free from crises; numerous are the traces of meditative sorrows, of his bitternesses as thinker and patriot. He knows that the ordinary course of the world is pitiable, and that terrors lie in wait for the solitary muser.[4] But faith supports him and the pride of feeling, with all other beings, his brothers, the eternal manifestations of Eternal Thought. From this flows that mighty and sacred joy which laughs through the whole book, joy such as one imagines of some antediluvian colossus, lashing the resplendent waves, and breathing out enormous water-spouts in the face of the earliest suns. From this his song, so to speak, pre-Adamic of the flesh; his worship of forms and of colors; his appetite for sexual embracements; his adoration of the body and the act of generation! When all is full of the Spirit, when all is divine, what evil is there in the fact that the source of life lies in bubbling passion and frenzy! Naturally enough, the whited sepulchres of America and England madly cry: "The hideous voice of rottenness denounces the august shamelessness of Walt

Whitman. Reflect: an echo of the Phallic cult fills the air; Bacchus, the conqueror, comes anew on his ear surrounded by nymphs and fauns and bacchanals. Hearken: again an appeal for the naive sensuality of primitive civilizations; the old rites are brought forth and the sacramental orgies!" So cry in defiance, with affront upon their faces, the fainting depravities and secular Sodoms! Phariseeism never pardons the poet. . . .[5]

If his pantheism celebrates the flesh, which he holds as part of the spirit—as the most innocent and primordial part—and if he proclaims joy—the drunkenness of the world-fête—he nevertheless does not fail to love and to tenderly salute endurance, now put to torture, now fallen into the lowest depths. I have already said, and it cannot be too often repeated, because it is the key to the book, that in the light of thought all things are necessary, because divine—all, even vice and crime, however inexplicable this last may seem. Let no one mistake these words, however: there is no more impetuous idealist than Whitman, nor a more indefatigable preacher of truth, of good, and of beauty. He holds that the evil will disappear, and before the ecstatic vision of the perfect and radiant future raises a long cry of triumph.[6] Yet is not that very hope a dogma of the dogmas? No, we cannot judge of evil, because that would be to judge God, and how can the lover judge that which he loves? Evil is a mystery, perhaps the most sacred of all mysteries, because it is the least comprehensible, because it may be the expiatory victim offered to good, the holocaust always smoking on the altar. Immense is the pity of Whitman for the degraded and miserable, as vast and tender as that of Shelley, of Hugo, of Tolstoi, of Dostoievsky—great spirits who bring back to our days the teachings of the purer heroes of Buddhism and Christianity, and who, from forth their march into the future, turn toward the past cycles and reach a hand to Sakya-Mouni,[7] to Jesus of Nazareth, to Francis of Assissi, to Saint Theresa, to Vincent de Paul,[8] to Fénelon, to Saint Jean de Dieu, to Jean d'Avila.[9] Whether whole peoples in distress, or the crushed and broken individual, are concerned, or simply the ordinary and middling humanity, I do not know any amongst all these who has surpassed in charity, in pity, in devotedness, in love, him who gave at the same time his words and his actions, and while caring for his fellow-creatures, dying or sick, wrote the following pieces which I cite among so many others: "The Base of All Metaphysics," "Recorders Ages Hence," "Calamus," "Salut au Monde," "Pioneers! O Pioneers!" "Old Ireland," "O Star of France," "To Him that was Crucified," "To a Common Prostitute," "The City Dead House." This last, above all, is poignant and might have been written by Dostoievsky.

"Leaves of Grass," indeed, is not purely poetic, at least in the sense of the older literatures. It is useless to seek here the refinement and impeccable virtuosity of a Tennyson. Walt Whitman is not an artist; he is above art. Not only do the words of his verse fail of being the most choice, but he laughs at proportion and composition. He is charged with affecting the rude, the overcharged, the encumbered. The religious and barbaric lyricism which Anglo-Saxon poetry possesses in common with the Bible is in "Leaves of Grass" interspersed with a multitude of prosaic images, infinity of detail and minute enumerations of all points of view. Our Latin genius soberly prunes down inequalities and knows nothing, ordinarily, of such lawless modes of expression. It takes them for chaos, and there commits the gravest of errors. Without wishing to defend exuberance or to oppose good taste, it will be permitted me to say that this last should only dominate writings which aim at pure art, where form is so paramount in importance as to relegate substance to the background. Where these larger works are in question, however—works wherein all external appearances and human masses precipitate themselves; where, at the same time, battalions of sensations, sentiments and ideas enter the breach; where science and morality and æsthetics are fused—where such creations are concerned, the horizon widens strangely. There are no other rules save those of nobility and strength of spirit, and these suffice amply to create a most unlooked-for and grandiose aspect of beauty. Though the reader may encounter what is difficult and distasteful, it will not alter the easily verified fact that, if the author has sprinkled through his work a throng of touches at first sight prosaic, yet that in reality these touches contribute to the poetry of the *ensemble*. Take any of the great pieces haphazard, and remove such details as seem superfluous; you will perceive immediately that life and truth have vanished from the picture, and that it is now traversed only by great and monotonous sweeps of condor wings. . . . For, overcrowded and disorderly as it may be, if emotion and thought animate it, a work will always be of perfect beauty. But models fashioned of cinder and mud, though they be miracles of chiselling, will always remain cinder and mud.

VINCENT VAN GOGH

[1853–1890]

Letter to His Sister (1888)

HAVE YOU READ the American poems by *Whitman?* I am sure Theo has them, and I strongly advise you to read them, because to begin with they are really fine, and the English speak about them a good deal. He sees in the future, and even in the present, a world of healthy, carnal love, strong and frank—of friendship —of work—under the great starlit vault of heaven a something which after all one can only call God—and eternity in its place above this world. At first it makes you smile, it is all so candid and pure; but it sets you thinking for the same reason.

The "Prayer of Columbus" is very beautiful.

Reprinted by permission of New York Graphic Society Ltd. from *The Complete Letters of Vincent Van Gogh*, III, 445. Copyright of English translation, 1959, by New York Graphic Society.

JOHN ADDINGTON SYMONDS

[1 8 4 0 – 1 8 9 3]

The Love of Comrades (*1893*)

THE SECTION OF Whitman's works which deals with adhesiveness, or the love of comrades, is fully as important, and in some ways more difficult to deal with, than his "Children of Adam." He gave it the title "Calamus," from the root of a water-rush, adopted by him as the symbol of this love. Here the element of spirituality in passion, of romantic feeling, and of deep enduring sentiment, which was almost conspicuous by its absence from the section on sexual love, emerges into vivid prominence, and lends peculiar warmth of poetry to the artistic treatment. We had to expect so much from the poem quoted by me at the commencement of this disquisition. There Whitman described the love of man for woman as "fast-anchor'd, eternal"; the thought of the bride, the wife, as "more resistless than I can tell."[1] But for the love of man for man he finds quite a different class of descriptive phrases: "separate, disembodied, another born, ethereal, the last athletic reality, my consolation."[2] He hints that we have left the realm of sex and sense, and have ascended into a different and rarer atmosphere, where passion, though it has not lost its strength, is clarified. . . .

This emphatic treatment of an emotion which is usually talked about under the vague and formal term of friendship, gives peculiar importance to "Calamus." No man in the modern world has expressed so strong a conviction that "manly attach-

Reprinted from *Walt Whitman: A Study* (London, 1893), 67–85, abridged.

ment," "athletic love," "the high towering love of comrades," is a main factor in human life, a virtue upon which society will have to lay its firm foundations, and a passion equal in permanence, superior in spirituality, to the sexual affection. Whitman regards this emotion not only as the "consolation" of the individual, but also as a new and hitherto unapprehended force for stimulating national vitality.

There is no softness or sweetness in his treatment of this theme. His tone is sustained throughout at a high pitch of virile enthusiasm, which, at the same time, vibrates with acutest feeling, thrills with an undercurrent of the tenderest sensibility. Not only the sublimest thoughts and aspirations, but also the shyest, most shame-faced, yearnings are reserved for this love. . . .

These extracts[3] were necessary, because there is some misapprehension abroad regarding the precise nature of what Whitman meant by "Calamus." His method of treatment has, to a certain extent, exposed him to misconstruction. Still, as his friend and commentator, Mr. Burroughs, puts it: "The sentiment is primitive, athletic, taking form in all manner of large and homely out-of-door images, and springs, as any one may see, directly from the heart and experience of the poet."[4] The language has a passionate glow, a warmth of devotion, beyond anything to which the world is used in the celebration of friendship. At the same time the false note of insincerity or sensuousness is never heard. The melody is in the Dorian mood—recalling to our minds that fellowship in arms which flourished among the Dorian tribes, and formed the chivalry of pre-historic Hellas. . . .[5]

Like Plato, in the *Phædrus*,[6] Whitman describes an enthusiastic type of masculine emotion, leaving its private details to the moral sense and special inclination of the individuals concerned.

The poet himself appears to be not wholly unconscious that there are dangers and difficulties involved in the highly-pitched emotions he is praising. The whole tenor of two carefully-toned compositions, entitled "Whoever you are, Holding me now in hand," and "Trickle, Drops," suggest an underlying sense of spiritual conflict. . . .

It is clear then that, in his treatment of comradeship, or the impassioned love of man for man, Whitman has struck a keynote, to the emotional intensity of which the modern world is unaccustomed. It therefore becomes of much importance to discover the poet-prophet's *Stimmung*—his radical instinct with regard to the moral quality of the feeling he encourages. Studying his works by their own light, and by the light of their author's character, interpreting each part by reference to the whole and in the spirit of the whole, an impartial critic will, I think, be drawn to the conclusion that what he calls the "adhesiveness" of comradeship is meant to have no interblending with the "amativeness" of sexual love. Personally, it is undeniable that Whitman possessed a specially keen sense of the fine restraint and continence, the cleanliness and chastity, that are inseparable from the perfectly virile and physically complete nature of healthy manhood. Still we have the right to predicate the same ground-qualities in the early Dorians, those founders of the martial institution of Greek love; and yet it is notorious to students of Greek civilisation that the lofty sentiment of their masculine chivalry was intertwined with much that is repulsive to modern sentiment.

Whitman does not appear to have taken some of the phenomena of contemporary morals into due account, although he must have been aware of them. Else he would have foreseen that, human nature being what it is, we cannot expect to eliminate all sensual alloy from emotions raised to a high pitch of passionate intensity, and that permanent elements within the midst of our society will imperil the absolute purity of the ideal he attempts to establish. It is obvious that those unenviable mortals who are the inheritors of sexual anomalies, will recognise their own emotion in Whitman's "superb friendship, exaltè, previously unknown," which "waits, and has been always waiting, latent in all men,"[7] the "something fierce in me, eligible to burst forth,"[8] "ethereal comradeship," "the last athletic reality."[9] Had I not the strongest proof in Whitman's private correspondence with myself that he repudiated any such deductions from his "Calamus,"[10] I admit that I should have regarded them as justified; and I am not certain whether his own feelings

upon this delicate topic may not have altered since the time
when "Calamus" was first composed.

These considerations do not, however, affect the spiritual
quality of his ideal. After acknowledging, what Whitman omitted to perceive, that there are inevitable points of contact between sexual anomaly and his doctrine of comradeship, the
question now remains whether he has not suggested the way
whereby abnormal instincts may be moralised and raised to
higher value. In other words, are those exceptional instincts
provided in "Calamus" with the means of their salvation from
the filth and mire of brutal appetite? It is difficult to answer this
question; for the issue involved is nothing less momentous than
the possibility of evoking a new chivalrous enthusiasm, analogous to that of primitive Hellenic society, from emotions which
are at present classified among the turpitudes of human
nature. . . .

We may return from this analysis to the inquiry whether
anything like a new chivalry is to be expected from the doctrines
of "Calamus," which shall in the future utilise for noble purposes some of those unhappy instincts which at present run to
waste in vice and shame. It may be asked what these passions
have in common with the topic of Whitman's prophecy: They
have this in common with it. Whitman recognises among the
sacred emotions and social virtues, destined to regenerate political life and to cement nations, an intense, jealous, throbbing,
sensitive, expectant love of man for man: a love which yearns in
absence, droops under the sense of neglect, revives at the return
of the beloved: a love that finds honest delight in hand-touch,
meeting lips, hours of privacy, close personal contact. He proclaims this love to be not only a daily fact in the present, but also
a saving and ennobling aspiration. While he expressly repu-
diates, disowns, and brands as "damnable" all "morbid infer-
ences" which may be drawn by malevolence or vicious cunning
from his doctrine, he is prepared to extend the gospel of comradeship to the whole human race. He expects democracy, the
new social and political medium, the new religious ideal of
mankind, to develop and extend "that fervid comradeship," and
by its means to counterbalance and to spiritualise what is vulgar

and materialistic in the modern world. "Democracy," he maintains, "infers such loving comradeship, as its most inevitable twin or counterpart, without which it will be incomplete, in vain, and incapable of perpetuating itself."[11]

If this be not a dream, if he is right in believing that "threads of manly friendship, fond and loving, pure and sweet, strong and life-long, carried to degrees hitherto unknown," will penetrate the organism of society, "not only giving tone to individual character, and making it unprecedentedly emotional, muscular, heroic, and refined, but having deepest relations to general politics"—then are we perhaps justified in foreseeing here the advent of an enthusiasm which shall rehabilitate those outcast instincts, by giving them a spiritual atmosphere, an environment of recognised and healthy emotions, wherein to expand at liberty and purge away the grossness and the madness of their pariahdom?

This prospect, like all ideals, until they are realised in experience, may seem fantastically visionary. Moreover, the substance of human nature is so mixed that it would perhaps be fanatical to expect from Whitman's chivalry of "adhesiveness," a more immaculate purity than was attained by the mediæval chivalry of "amativeness." Nevertheless, that mediæval chivalry, the great emotional product of feudalism, though it fell short of its own aspiration, bequeathed incalculable good to modern society by refining and clarifying the crudest of male appetites. In like manner, this democratic chivalry, announced by Whitman, may be destined to absorb, control, and elevate those darker, more mysterious, apparently abnormal appetites, which we know to be widely diffused and ineradicable in the ground-work of human nature.

Returning from the dream, the vision of a future possibility, it will, at any rate, be conceded that Whitman has founded comradeship, the enthusiasm which binds man to man in fervent love, upon a natural basis. Eliminating classical associations of corruption, ignoring the perplexed questions of a guilty passion doomed by law and popular antipathy to failure, he begins anew with sound and primitive humanity. There he discovers "a superb friendship, exaltè, previously unknown." He perceives that "it waits, and has been always waiting, latent in all men."

His method of treatment, fearless, and uncowed by any thought of evil, his touch upon the matter, chaste and wholesome and aspiring, reveal the possibility of restoring in all innocence to human life a portion of its alienated or unclaimed moral birthright.

It were well to close upon this note. The half, as the Greeks said, is more than the whole; and the time has not yet come to raise the question whether the love of man for man shall be elevated through a hitherto unapprehended chivalry to nobler powers, even as the barbarous love of man for woman once was. This question at the present moment is deficient in actuality. The world cannot be invited to entertain it.

JOHN JAY CHAPMAN

[1 8 6 2 – 1 9 3 3]

Walt Whitman (1898)

WALT WHITMAN has given utterance to the soul of the tramp. A man of genius has passed sincerely and normally through this entire experience, himself unconscious of what he was, and has left a record of it to enlighten and bewilder the literary world.

In Whitman's works the elemental parts of a man's mind and the fragments of imperfect education may be seen merging together, floating and sinking in a sea of insensate egotism and rhapsody, repellent, divine, disgusting, extraordinary.

Included in *Emerson and Other Essays* (1898); the text used here was reprinted in *The Selected Writings of John Jay Chapman*, ed. Jacques Barzun (New York, 1957), 145–149. Wright Morris is greatly indebted to Chapman in his chapter on "The Open Road" in *The Territory Ahead* (New York, 1963), 51–66.

Our inability to place the man intellectually, and find a type and reason for his intellectual state, comes from this: that the revolt he represents is not an intellectual revolt. Ideas are not at the bottom of it. It is a revolt from drudgery. It is the revolt of laziness.

There is no intellectual coherence in his talk, but merely pathological coherence. Can the insulting jumble of ignorance and effrontery, of scientific phrase and French paraphrase, of slang and inspired adjective, which he puts forward with the pretence that it represents thought, be regarded, from any possible point of view, as a philosophy, or a system, or a belief? Is it individualism of any statable kind? Do the thoughts and phrases which float about in it have a meaning which bears any relation to the meaning they bear in the language of thinkers? Certainly not. Does all the patriotic talk, the talk about the United States and its future, have any significance as patriotism? Does it poetically represent the state of feeling of any class of American citizens towards their country? Or would you find the nearest equivalent to this emotion in the breast of the educated tramp of France, or Germany, or England? The speech of Whitman is English, and his metaphors and catchwords are apparently American, but the emotional content is cosmic. He put off patriotism when he took to the road.

The attraction exercised by his writings is due to their flashes of reality. Of course the man was a poseur, a most horrid mountebank and ego-maniac. His tawdry scraps of misused idea, of literary smartness, of dog-eared and greasy reminiscence, repel us. The world of men remained for him as his audience, and he did to civilized society the continuous compliment of an insane self-consciousness in its presence.

Perhaps this egotism and posturing is the revenge of a stilled conscience, and we ought to read in it the inversion of the social instincts. Perhaps all tramps are poseurs. But there is this to be said for Whitman, that whether or not his posing was an accident of a personal nature, or an organic result of his life, he was himself an authentic creature. He did not sit in a study and throw off his saga of balderdash, but he lived a life, and it is by his authenticity, and not by his poses, that he has survived.

The descriptions of nature, the visual observation of life, are first-hand and wonderful. It was no false light that led the Oxonians to call some of his phrases Homeric. The pundits were right in their curiosity over him; they went astray only in their attempt at classification.[1]

It is a pity that truth and beauty turn to cant on the second delivery, for it makes poetry, as a profession, impossible. The lyric poets have always spent most of their time in trying to write lyric poetry, and the very attempt disqualifies them.

A poet who discovers his mission is already half done for; and even Wordsworth, great genius though he was, succeeded in half drowning his talents in his parochial theories, in his own self-consciousness and self-conceit.

Walt Whitman thought he had a mission. He was a professional poet. He had purposes and theories about poetry which he started out to enforce and illustrate. He is as didactic as Wordsworth, and is thinking of himself the whole time. He belonged, moreover, to that class of professionals who are always particularly self-centred, autocratic, vain, and florid,—the class of quacks. There are, throughout society, men, and they are generally men of unusual natural powers, who, after gaining a little unassimilated education, launch out for themselves and set up as authorities on their own account. They are, perhaps, the successors of the old astrologers, in that what they seek to establish is some personal professorship or predominance. The old occultism and mystery was resorted to as the most obvious device for increasing the personal importance of the magician; and the chief difference today between a regular physician and a quack is, that the quack pretends to know it all.

Brigham Young and Joseph Smith were men of phenomenal capacity, who actually invented a religion and created a community by the apparent establishment of supernatural and occult powers. The phrenologists, the venders of patent medicine, the Christian Scientists, the single-taxers, and all who proclaim panaceas and nostrums make the same majestic and pontifical appeal to human nature. It is this mystical power, this religious element, which floats them, sells the drugs, cures the sick, and packs the meetings.

By temperament and education Walt Whitman was fitted to be a prophet of this kind. He became a quack poet, and hampered his talents by the imposition of a monstrous parade of rattletrap theories and professions. If he had not been endowed with a perfectly marvellous capacity, a wealth of nature beyond the reach and plumb of his rodomontade, he would have been ruined from the start. As it is, he has filled his work with grimace and vulgarity. He writes a few lines of epic directness and cyclopean vigor and naturalness, and then obtrudes himself and his mission.

He has the bad taste bred in the bone of all missionaries and palmists, the sign-manual of a true quack. This bad taste is nothing more than the offensive intrusion of himself and his mission into the matter in hand. As for his real merits and his true mission, too much can hardly be said in his favor. The field of his experience was narrow, and not in the least intellectual. It was narrow because of his isolation from human life. A poet like Browning, or Heine, or Alfred de Musset deals constantly with the problems and struggles that arise in civilized life out of the close relationships, the ties, the duties and desires of the human heart. He explains life on its social side. He gives us some more or less coherent view of an infinitely complicated matter. He is a guide-book or a notebook, a highly trained and intelligent companion.

Walt Whitman has no interest in any of these things. He was fortunately so very ignorant and untrained that his mind was utterly incoherent and unintellectual. His mind seems to be submerged and to have become almost a part of his body. The utter lack of concentration which resulted from living his whole life in the open air has left him spontaneous and unaccountable. And the great value of his work is, that it represents the spontaneous and unaccountable functioning of the mind and body in health.

It is doubtful whether a man ever enjoyed life more intensely than Walt Whitman, or expressed the physical joy of mere living more completely. He is robust, all tingling with health, and the sensations of health. All that is best in his poetry is the expression of bodily well-being.

A man who leaves his office and gets into a canoe on a Canadian river, sure of ten days' release from the cares of business and housekeeping, has a thrill of joy such as Walt

Whitman has here and there thrown into his poetry. One might say that to have done this is the greatest accomplishment in literature. Walt Whitman, in some of his lines, breaks the frame of poetry and gives us life in the throb.

It is the throb of the whole physical system of a man who breathes the open air and feels the sky over him. "When lilacs last in the dooryard bloomed" is a great lyric. Here is a whole poem without a trace of self-consciousness. It is little more than a description of nature. The allusions to Lincoln and to the funeral are but a word or two—merest suggestions of the tragedy. But grief, overwhelming grief, is in every line of it, the grief which has been transmuted into this sensitiveness to the landscape, to the song of the thrush, to the lilac's bloom, and the sunset.

Here is truth to life of the kind to be found in King Lear or Guy Mannering, in Æschylus or Burns.

Walt Whitman himself could not have told you why the poem was good. Had he had any intimation of the true reason, he would have spoiled the poem. The recurrence and antiphony of the thrush, the lilac, the thought of death, the beauty of nature, are in a balance and dream of natural symmetry such as no cunning could come at, no conscious art could do other than spoil.

It is ungrateful to note Whitman's limitations, his lack of human passion, the falseness of many of his notions about the American people. The man knew the world merely as an observer, he was never a living part of it, and no mere observer can understand the life about him. Even his work during the war was mainly the work of an observer, and his poems and notes upon the period are picturesque. As to his talk about comrades and Manhattanese car-drivers, and brass-founders displaying their brawny arms around each other's brawny necks, all this gush and sentiment in Whitman's poetry is false to life. It has a lyrical value, as representing Whitman's personal feelings, but no one else in the country was ever found who felt or acted like this.

In fact, in all that concerns the human relations Walt Whitman is as unreal as, let us say, William Morris, and the American mechanic would probably prefer Sigurd the Volsung, and understand it better than Whitman's poetry.

This falseness to the sentiment of the American is interwoven with such wonderful descriptions of American sights and scenery, of ferryboats, thoroughfares, cataracts, and machine-shops that it is not strange the foreigners should have accepted the gospel.

On the whole, Whitman, though he solves none of the problems of life and throws no light on American civilization, is a delightful appearance, and a strange creature to come out of our beehive. This man committed every unpardonable sin against our conventions, and his whole life was an outrage. He was neither chaste, nor industrious, nor religious. He patiently lived upon cold pie and tramped the earth in triumph.

He did really live the life he liked to live, in defiance of all men, and this is a great desert, a most stirring merit. And he gave, in his writings, a true picture of himself and of that life,—a picture which the world had never seen before, and which it is probable the world will not soon cease to wonder at.

BARRETT WENDELL

[1 8 5 5 – 1 9 2 1]

Walt Whitman (1900)

BEYOND QUESTION Whitman had remarkable individuality and power. Equally beyond question he was among the most eccentric individuals who ever put pen to paper. The natural result of this has been that his admirers have admired him intensely; while whoever has found his work repellent has found it irritating. Particularly abroad, however, he has attracted much criti-

Reprinted from *A Literary History of America* (New York, 1900), 466–479, abridged.

cal attention; and many critics have been disposed to maintain that his amorphous prophecies of democracy are deeply characteristic of America. The United States, they point out, are professedly the most democratic country in the world; Whitman is professedly the most democratic of American writers; consequently he must be the most typical. . . .

Now, Walt Whitman's gospel of democracy certainly included liberty and laid strong emphasis on fraternity. He liked to hail his fellow-citizens by the wild, queer name of "camerados," which, for some obscure reason of his own, he preferred to "comrades." The ideal which most appealed to him, however, was that of equality. Though he would hardly have assented to such orthodox terms, his creed seems to have been that, as God made everything, one thing is just as good as another. There are aspects in which such a proposition seems analogous to one which should maintain a bronze cent to be every whit as good as a gold eagle because both are issued by the same government from the same mint. At best, however, analogies are misleading arguments; and people who share Whitman's ideal are apt to disregard as superstitious any argument, however impressive, which should threaten to modify their faith in equality. It is a superstition, they would maintain, that some ways of doing things are decent and some not; one way is really just as good as another. It is a superstition that kings, nobles, and gentlemen are in any aspect lovelier than the mob. It is a superstition that men of learning are intellectually better than the untutored. It is a superstition which would hold a man who can make a chair unable consequently to make a constitution. It is a superstition that virtuous women are inherently better than street-walkers. It is a superstition that law is better than anarchy. There are things, to be sure, which are not superstitions. Evil and baseness and ugliness are real facts, to be supremely denounced and hated; and incidentally, we must admit, few arraignments of the vulgarity and materialism which have developed in the United States are more pitiless than those which appear in Whitman's "Democratic Vistas." The cause of these hurtful things, however, he is satisfied to find in the traces of our ancestral and superstitious devotion to outworn ideals of excellence. We can all find salvation in the new, life-saving ideal of equality. Let

America accept this ideal, and these faults will vanish into that limbo of the past to which he would gladly consign all superstitions. Among these, he logically, though reluctantly, includes a great part of the poetry of Shakspere; for Shakspere, undoubtedly a poet, was a poet of inequality, who represented the people as a mob. For all his genius, then, Shakspere was an apostle of the devil, another lying prophet of the superstition of excellence. . . .

Now, this dogma of equality clearly involves a trait which has not yet been generally characteristic of American thought or letters,—a complete confusion of values. In the early days of Renaissance in New England, to be sure, Emerson and the rest, dazzled by the splendours of that new world of art and literature which was at last thrown open, made small distinction between those aspects of it which are excellent and those which are only stimulating. At the same time they adhered as firmly as the Puritans themselves to the ideal of excellence; and among the things with which they were really familiar they pretty shrewdly distinguished those which were most valuable, either on earth or in heaven. With Walt Whitman, on the other hand, everything is confused. . . . . .

Here [Section 6 of "Song of Myself"] is perhaps his best-known phrase, "the beautiful uncut hair of graves." Here are other good phrases, like "the faint red roofs of mouths." Here, too, is undoubtedly tender feeling. Here, into the bargain, is such rubbish as "I guess it is the handkerchief of the Lord,"—who incidentally uses perfumery,—and such jargon as "Kanuck, Tuckahoe, Congressman, Cuff." In an inextricable hodge-podge you find at once beautiful phrases and silly gabble, tender imagination and insolent commonplace,—pretty much everything, in short, but humour. In America this literary anarchy, this complete confusion of values, is especially eccentric; for America has generally displayed instinctive common-sense, and common-sense implies some notion of what things are worth. One begins to see why Whitman has been so much more eagerly welcomed abroad than at home. His conception of equality, utterly ignoring values, is not that of American democracy, but rather that of European. His democracy, in short, is the least native which has ever found voice in his country. The saving grace of American democracy has been a tacit recognition that excellence is admirable.

In temper, then, Walt Whitman seems less American than any other of our conspicuous writers. It does not follow that in some aspects he is not very American indeed. Almost as certainly as Hawthorne, though very differently, he had the true artistic temperament; life moved him to moods which could find relief only in expression. Such a temperament would have expressed itself anywhere; and Whitman's would probably have found the most congenial material for expression in those European regions which have been most disturbed by French Revolutionary excess. He chanced, however, to be born, and to attain the maturity which he awaited before he began to publish, in unmingled American surroundings. As obviously as Hawthorne's experience was confined to New England, Whitman's was confined to that of the lower classes in those regions which were developing into modern New York. . . .

The eight preceding stanzas [of "Crossing Brooklyn Ferry"][1] are very like this,—confused, inarticulate, and surging in a mad kind of rhythm which sounds as if hexameters were trying to bubble through sewage. For all these faults, Whitman has here accomplished a wonder. Despite his eccentric insolence both of phrase and of temper you feel that in a region where another eye would have seen only unspeakable vileness, he has found impulses which prove it, like every other region on earth, a fragment of the divine eternities. The glories and beauties of the universe are really perceptible everywhere; and into what seemed utterly sordid Whitman has breathed ennobling imaginative fervour. Cultured and academic folk are disposed to shrink from what they call base, to ignore it, to sneer at it; looking closer, Whitman tells us that even amid base things you cannot wander so far as to lose sight of the heavens, with all their fountains of glorious emotion.

But what is this emotion? Just here Whitman seems to stop. With singular vividness, and with the unstinted sympathy of his fervent faith in equality, he tells what he sees. Though often his jargon is amorphously meaningless, his words are now and again so apt as to approach that inevitable union of thought and phrase which makes lasting poetry. When he has reported what he sees, however, utterly confusing its values, he has nothing more to say about it. At most he leaves you with a sense of new realities concerning which you must do your thinking for yourself. . . .

Even in bits like this,[2] however, which come so much nearer form than is usual with Whitman, one feels his perverse rudeness of style. Such eccentricity of manner is bound to affect different tempers in different ways. One kind of reader, naturally eager for individuality and fresh glimpses of truth, is disposed to identify oddity and originality. Another kind of reader distrusts literary eccentricity as instinctively as polite people distrust bad manners. In both of these instinctive reactions from such a method of address as Whitman's there is an element of truth. Beyond doubt, eccentric masters of the fine arts give rise to perverse eccentricity in imitators. Browning and Carlyle, to go no further, have bred in brains feebler than their own much nonsensical spawn; and so has Walt Whitman. But some artists of great power prove naturally unable to express themselves properly. Their trouble is like a muscular distortion which should compel lameness, or a vocal malformation which should make utterance hoarse or shrill. So there have been great men, and there will be more, whom fate compels either to express themselves uncouthly or else to stay dumb. Such a man, great or not, Whitman seems to have been. Such men, greater than he, were Carlyle and Browning. The critical temper which would hold them perverse, instead of unfortunate, is mistaken. . . .

In this decadent eccentricity of Whitman's style there is again something foreign to the spirit of this country. American men of letters have generally had deep artistic conscience. This trait has resulted, for one thing, in making the short story, an essentially organic form of composition, as characteristic of American literature as the straggling, inorganic three-volume novel is of English. Now and again, to be sure, American men of letters have chosen to express themselves in quite another manner. They have tried to reproduce the native dialects of the American people. This impulse has resulted in at least one masterpiece, that amazing Odyssey of the Mississippi to which Mark Twain gave the fantastic name of "Huckleberry Finn."

As we remarked of the "Biglow Papers," however, this "dialect" literature of America often proves on analysis more elaborately studied than orthodox work by the same writers. Neither the "Biglow Papers" nor "Huckleberry Finn" could have been produced without an artistic conscience as strenuous as Irving's, or Poe's, or Hawthorne's. The vagaries of Walt Whitman, on the other hand, are as far from literary conscience as the animals which he somewhere celebrates are from unhappiness or respectability. Whitman's style, then, is as little characteristic of America as his temper is of traditional American democracy. One can see why the decadent taste of modern Europe has welcomed him so much more ardently than he has ever been welcomed at home; in temper and in style he was an exotic member of that sterile brotherhood which eagerly greeted him abroad. In America his oddities were more eccentric than they would have been anywhere else.

On the other hand, there is an aspect in which he seems not only native but even promising. During the years when his observation was keenest, and his temper most alert, he lived in the environment from which our future America seems most likely to spring. He was born and grew up, he worked and lived, where on either side of the East River the old American towns of New York and Brooklyn were developing into the metropolis which is still too young to possess ripe traditions. In full maturity he devoted himself to army nursing,—the least picturesque or glorious, and the most humanely heroic, service which he could have rendered his country during its agony of civil war. In that Civil War the elder America perished; the new America which then arose is not yet mature enough for artistic record. Whitman's earthly experience, then, came throughout in chaotic times, when our past had faded and our future had not yet sprung into being. Bewildering confusion, fused by the accident of his lifetime into the seeming unity of a momentary whole, was the only aspect of human existence which could be afforded him by the native country which he so truly loved. For want of other surroundings he was content to seek the meaning of life amid New York slums and dingy suburban country, in the crossing of Brooklyn Ferry, or in the hospitals which strove to alleviate the drums and tramplings of civil war. His lifelong eagerness to find in life the stuff of which poetry is made has brought him, after all, the reward he would most have cared for. In one aspect he is thoroughly American. The spirit of his work is that of world-old anarchy; its form has all the perverse oddity of world-old abortive decadence; but the substance of which his poems are made —their imagery as distinguished from their form or their spirit —comes wholly from our native country.

In this aspect, then, though probably in no other, he may, after all, throw light on the future of literature in America. As has been said before, "He is uncouth, inarticulate, whatever you please that is least orthodox; yet, after all, he can make you feel for the moment how even the ferry-boats plying from New York to Brooklyn are fragments of God's eternities. Those of us who love the past are far from sharing his confidence in the future. Surely, however, that is no reason for denying the miracle that he has wrought by idealising the East River. The man who has done this is the only one who points out the stuff of which perhaps the new American literature of the future may in time be made."

RICHARD MAURICE BUCKE

[1 8 3 7 – 1 9 0 1]

Walt Whitman (*1901*)

WALT WHITMAN is the best, most perfect, example the world has so far had of the Cosmic Sense, first because he is the man in whom the new faculty has been, probably, most perfectly developed, and especially because he is, par excellence, the man who

Reprinted by permission of E. P. Dutton & Co., Inc., from *Cosmic Consciousness* (1923), 225–237. Copyright, 1901, 1923, by E. P. Dutton, Inc.

in modern times has written distinctly and at large from the point of view of Cosmic Consciousness, and who also has referred to its facts and phenomena more plainly and fully than any other writer either ancient or modern.

He tells us plainly, though not as fully as could be wished, of the moment when he attained illumination, and again towards the end of his life of its passing away. Not that it is to be supposed that he had the Cosmic Sense continuously, for years, but that it came less and less frequently as age advanced, probably lasted less and less long at a time, and decreased in vividness and intensity.

Moreover, in the case of Whitman, we have means of knowing the man thoroughly from youth till death—both before and after illumination—and so (better than in any other case, except, perhaps, that of Balzac) can compare the fully developed man with his earlier self. The line of demarcation (between the two Whitmans) is perfectly drawn.

On the one hand the Whitman of the forties, writing tales and essays (such as "Death in a School-room," 1841; "Wild Frank's Return," id.; "Bervance, or Father and Son," id.; "The Tomb Blossoms," 1842; "The Last of the Sacred Army," id.; "The Child Ghost, a Story of the Last Loyalist," id.; 'The Angel of Tears," id.; "Revenge and Requital,"[1] 1845; "A Dialogue," id.; etc.), which even his present splendid fame cannot galvanize into life; on the other the Whitman of the fifties, writing the first (1855) edition of the "Leaves."

We expect and always find a difference between the early and mature writings of the same man. What an interval, for instance, between Shelley's romances and the "Cenci"; between Macaulay's earliest essays and the history. But here is something quite apart from those and similar cases. . . . But in the case of Whitman (as in that of Balzac) writings of absolutely no value were *immediately* followed (and, at least in Whitman's case without practice or study) by pages across each of which in letters of ethereal fire are written the words ETERNAL LIFE; pages covered not only by a masterpiece but by such vital sentences as have not been written ten times in the history of the race. It is upon this instantaneous evolution of the *Titan* from the *Man*, this profound mystery of the attainment of the splendor and power of the kingdom of heaven, that this present volume seeks to throw light.

And it is interesting to remark here that Whitman seems to have had as little idea as had Gautama, Paul or Mohammed what it was that gave him the mental power, the moral elevation and the perennial joyousness which are among the characteristics of the state to which he attained and which seem to have been to him subjects of continual wonder. "Wandering amazed," he says, "at my own lightness and glee."[2]

Let us see, now, what Whitman says about this new sense which must have come to him in June, 1853 or 1854, at the age, that is, of thirty-four or thirty-five. The first direct mention of it is on page 15 of the 1855 edition of the "Leaves." That is to say, it is upon the third page of his first writing after this new faculty had come to him—for the long preface in this volume was written after the body of the book. The lines are found essentially unaltered in every subsequent edition.

As given here the quotation is from the 1855 edition, as it is important to get as near the man at the time of writing the words as possible. He says:

I believe in you my soul. . . . the other I am must not abase itself to you,
And you must not be abased to the other.
Loafe with me on the grass. . . . loose the stop from your throat,
Not words, not music or rhyme I want. . . . not custom or lecture, not even the best,
Only the lull I like, the hum of your valved voice.
I mind how we lay in June, such a transparent summer morning;
You settled your head athwart my hips and gently turned over upon me,
And parted the shirt from my bosom-bone, and plunged your tongue to my barestript heart,
And reached till you felt my beard, and reached till you held my feet.
Swiftly arose and spread around me the peace and joy and knowledge that pass all the art and argument of the earth;
And I know that the hand of God is the elderhand of my own,
And I know that the spirit of God is the eldest brother of my own,
And that all the men ever born are also my brothers. . . . and the women my sisters and lovers,
And that a kelson of the creation is love.[3]

Add now to this the following four lines, written at another time but certainly referring to the same or to a similar experience:

> As in a swoon, one instant,
> Another sun, ineffable full-dazzles me,
> And all the orbs I knew, and brighter, unknown orbs;
> One instant of the future land, Heaven's land.[4]

At the same time and in the same connection consider this passage:

Hast never come to thee an hour,
A sudden gleam divine, precipitating, bursting all these bubbles, fashions, wealth?
These eager business aims—books, politics, arts, amours,
To utter nothingness?[5]

For the purpose now of aiding to bring before the mind of the earnest reader (and any other has little business with this book) a hint, a suggestion (for what more is it possible to give here?) of what this Cosmic Consciousness is, it may be well to quote from a prose work of Whitman's certain passages that seem to throw light on the subject. Speaking of the people, he says: "The rare, cosmical, artist mind, lit with the infinite, alone confronts his manifold and oceanic qualities." Again: "There is yet, to whoever is eligible among us, the prophetic vision, the joy of being tossed in the brave turmoil of these times—the promulgation and the path, obedient, lowly reverent to the voice, the gesture of the god, or holy ghost, which others see not, hear not." Once more: "The thought of identity. . . . Miracle of miracles, beyond statement, most spiritual and vaguest of earth's dreams, yet hardest basic fact, and only entrance to all facts. In such devout hours, in the midst of the significant wonders of heaven and earth (significant only because of the *Me* in the centre), creeds, conventions, fall away and become of no account before this simple idea. Under the luminousness of real vision, it alone takes possession, takes value. Like the shadowy dwarf in the fable, once liberated and looked upon, it expands over the whole earth and spreads to the roof of heaven." Yet another: "I should say, indeed, that only in the perfect uncontamination and solitariness of individuality may the spirituality of religion positively come forth at all. Only here and on such terms, the meditation, the devout ecstasy, the soaring flight. Only here communion with the mysteries, the eternal problems, *whence? whither?* Alone and identity and the mood—and the soul emerges, and all statements, churches, sermons, melt away like vapors. Alone, and silent thought, and awe, and aspiration —and then the *interior consciousness*, like a hitherto unseen inscription, in magic ink, beams out its wondrous lines to the sense. Bibles may convey and priests expound, but it is exclusively for the noiseless operation of one's isolated *Self* to enter the pure ether of veneration, reach the divine levels, and commune with the unutterable." The next passage seems prophetical of the coming race: "A fitly born and bred race, growing up in right conditions of outdoor as much as indoor harmony, activity and development, would probably, from and in those conditions, find it enough merely *to live*—and would, in their relations to the sky, air, water, trees, etc., and to the countless common shows, and in the fact of *life* itself, discover and achieve happiness—with Being suffused night and day by wholesome ecstasy, surpassing all the pleasures that wealth, amusement, and even gratified intellect, erudition, or the sense of art, can give." And finally, and best of all, the following: "Lo! *Nature* (the only complete, actual poem) existing calmly in the divine scheme, containing all, content, careless of the criticisms of a day, or these endless and wordy chatterers. And lo! to the consciousness of the soul, the permanent identity, the thought, the something, before which the magnitude even of Democracy, art, literature, etc., dwindles, becomes partial, measurable— something that fully satisfies (which those do not). That something is the *All* and the idea of *All*, with the accompanying idea of eternity, and of itself, the soul, buoyant, indestructible, sailing Space forever, visiting every region, as a ship the sea. And again lo! the pulsations in all matter, all spirit, throbbing forever—the eternal beats, eternal systole and dyastole of life in things—wherefrom I feel and know that death is not the ending, as we thought, but rather the real beginning—and that nothing ever is or can be lost, nor even die, nor soul nor matter."[6] Here we have brought out strongly the consciousness of the Cosmos, its life and eternity—and the consciousness of the equal grandeur and eternity of the individual soul, the one balancing (equal to) the other. In a word, we have here the expression (as far, perhaps, as it can be expressed) of what is called in this volume Cosmic Consciousness. . . .

It may be that Walt Whitman is the first man who, having Cosmic Consciousness very fully developed, has deliberately set himself against being thus mastered by it, determining, on the contrary, to subdue it and make it the servant along with simple consciousness, self consciousness and the rest of the united, individual SELF. He saw, what neither Gautama nor Paul saw, what Jesus saw, though not so clearly as he, that though this faculty is truly Godlike, yet it is no more supernatural or preternatural than sight, hearing, taste, feeling, or any other, and he consequently refused to give it unlimited sway, and would not allow it to tyrannize over the rest. He believes in it, but he says the other self, the old self, must not abase itself to the new; neither must the new be encroached upon or limited by the old; he will see that they live as friendly co-workers together. And it may here be said that whoever does not realize this last clause will never fully understand the "Leaves."

The next reference made by Walt Whitman to Cosmic Consciousness, to be noted here, is in a poem called the "Prayer of Columbus," a few words on the history of which will be in order. It was written about 1874–5, when the condition of the poor, sick, neglected spiritual explorer was strikingly similar to that of the heroic geographical explorer shipwrecked on the Antillean island in 1503, at which time and place the prayer is supposed to be offered up. Walt Whitman—a very common trick with him—used this agreement of circumstance to put his own words (ostensibly) into the mouth of the other man. The prayer is in reality, of course, Walt Whitman's own and all the allusions in it are to his own life, work, fortunes—to himself. In it he refers specifically and pointedly to the present subject matter. Speaking to God, he says:

Thou knowest my manhood's solemn and visionary meditations.
. . . .
O I am sure they really came from Thee,
The urge, the ardor, the unconquerable will,
The potent, felt, interior command, stronger than words,

A message from the Heavens, whispering to me even in sleep,
These sped me on.

. . . .

One effort more, my altar this bleak sand;
That Thou O God my life hast lighted,
With ray of light, steady, ineffable, vouchsafed of Thee,
Light rare untellable, lighting the very light,
Beyond all signs, descriptions, languages;
For that O God, be it my latest word, here on my knees,
Old, poor, and paralyzed, I thank Thee.

. . . .

My hands, my limbs grew nerveless,
My brain feels rack'd, bewilder'd,
Let the old timbers part, I will not part,
I will cling fast to Thee O God, though the waves buffet me,
Thee, Thee at least I know.[7]

At the time of writing these lines Walt Whitman is fifty-five
or fifty-six years of age. For over twenty years he has been
guided by this (seeming) supernatural illumination. He has
yielded freely to it and obeyed its behests as being from God
Himself.

He has "loved the earth, sun, animals, despised riches, given
alms to every one that asked, stood up for the stupid and crazy,
devoted his income and labor to others," as commanded by the
divine voice and as impelled by the divine impulse, and now for
reward he is poor, sick, paralyzed, despised, neglected, dying.
His message to man, to the delivery of which he has devoted his
life, which has been dearer in his eyes (for man's sake) than
wife, children, life itself, is unread or scoffed and jeered at.
What shall he say to God? He says that God knows him through
and through, and that he is willing to leave himself in God's
hands. He says that he does not know men nor his own work,
and so does not judge what men may do with, or say to, the
"Leaves." But he says he does know God, and will cling to him
though the waves buffet him. Then about the inspiration, the
illumination, the potent, felt, interior command stronger than
words? He is sure that this comes from God. He has no doubt.
There can be no doubt of that.

He goes on to speak of the ray of light, steady, ineffable, with
which God has lighted his life, and says it is rare, untellable,
beyond all signs, descriptions, languages. And this (be it well

remembered) is not the utterance of wild enthusiasm, but of cold, hard fact by a worn-out old man on (as he supposed) his death-bed. . . .

The next direct allusion to Cosmic Consciousness to be noted is embodied in a poem called "Now Precedent Songs, Farewell," written in June, 1888, when he again, and with good reason, supposed himself dying. The poem was written as a hasty good-bye to the "Leaves." At the end of it he refers to his songs and their origin in these words:

O heaven! what flash and started endless train of all! compared
    indeed to that!
What wretched shred e'en at the best of all![8]

He says: Compared to the flash, the divine illumination from which they had their origin, how poor and worthless his poems are. And it must be borne in mind that Whitman never had a bad opinion of the "Leaves." He used to say (in a semi-jocular manner, but fully meaning it all the same) that none of the fellows (meaning out-and-out admirers), not even O'Connor, Burroughs or Bucke, thought as highly of them as he did. But thinking that way of them he could still exclaim how poor they were compared to the illumination from which they sprang. But he did not die at that time. He rallied, and again, it seems, from time to time the vision appeared and the voice whispered. Doubtless the vision grew more dim and the voice less distinct as time passed and the feebleness of age and sickness advanced upon him. At last, in 1891, at the age of seventy-two, the "Brahmic Splendor" finally departed, and in those mystic lines, "To the Sunset Breeze," which the Harpers returned to him as "a mere improvisation," he bids it farewell:

(Thou hast, O Nature! elements! utterance to my heart beyond the
    rest—and this is of them,) . . .
(For thou art spiritual, Godly, most of all known to my sense,)
Minister to speak to me, here and now, what word has never told,
    and cannot tell,
Art thou not universal concrete's distillation?[9]

As a man with Cosmic Consciousness *sees* the Cosmic order, and that, as Paul says, "all things work together for good," so every such man is what is called "an Optimist," and it may be freely stated that the *knowledge* of the friendliness of the universe to man is a distinctive mark of the class of men considered in this volume. That Whitman has this mark needs saying only to those who have not read him. Again and again in ever-varying words he says and repeats: "And I say there is in fact no evil." "Clear and sweet is my soul, and clear and sweet is all that is not my soul." "Is it lucky to be born?" he asks, and answers: "It is just as lucky to die."[10]

Summary

a. The subjective light appeared strongly to Whitman.

b. The moral elevation and

c. Intellectual illumination were extreme, and in his case stand out very clearly, since we know the man so well both before and after the oncoming of the Cosmic Sense.

d. In no other man who ever lived was the sense of eternal life so absolute.

e. Fear of death was absent. Neither in health nor in sickness did he show any sign of it, and there is every reason to believe he did not feel it.

f. He had no sense of sin. This must not be understood as meaning that he felt himself to be perfect. Whitman realized his own greatness as clearly and fully as did any of his admirers. He also realized how immeasurably he was below the ideal which he constantly set up before himself.

g. The change of the self conscious man into the Cosmic Conscious was instantaneous—occurring at a certain hour of a certain day.

h. It occurred at the characteristic age and at the characteristic time of the year.

i. The altered appearance of the man while in the Cosmic Conscious state was seen and noted.

WILLIAM JAMES

[1842–1910]

The Religion of Healthy-Mindedness (1902)

WALT WHITMAN owes his importance in literature to the systematic expulsion from his writings of all contractile elements. The only sentiments he allowed himself to express were of the expansive order; and he expressed these in the first person, not as your mere monstrously conceited individual might so express them, but vicariously for all men, so that a passionate and mystic ontological emotion suffuses his words, and ends by persuading the reader that men and women, life and death, and all things are divinely good.

Thus it has come about that many persons to-day regard Walt Whitman as the restorer of the eternal natural religion. He has infected them with his own love of comrades, with his own gladness that he and they exist. Societies are actually formed for his cult; a periodical organ exists for its propagation, in which the lines of orthodoxy and heterodoxy are already beginning to be drawn; hymns are written by others in his peculiar prosody; and he is even explicitly compared with the founder of the Christian religion, not altogether to the advantage of the latter.

Whitman is often spoken of as a "pagan." The word nowadays means sometimes the mere natural animal man without a sense of sin; sometimes it means a Greek or Roman with his own peculiar religious consciousness. In neither of these senses does

Reprinted from *The Varieties of Religious Experience* (Modern Library Edition), 84–86.

it fitly define this poet. He is more than your mere animal man who has not tasted of the tree of good and evil. He is aware enough of sin for a swagger to be present in his indifference towards it, a conscious pride in his freedom from flexions and contractions, which your genuine pagan in the first sense of the word would never show.

I could turn and live with animals, they are so placid and self-con-
    tain'd,
I stand and look at them long and long.

They do not sweat and whine about their condition,
They do not lie awake in the dark and weep for their sins,
. . . .
Not one is dissatisfied, not one is demented with the mania of
    owning things,
Not one kneels to another, nor to his kind that lived thousands of
    years ago,
Not one is respectable or unhappy over the whole earth.[1]

No natural pagan could have written these well-known lines. But on the other hand Whitman is less than a Greek or Roman; for their consciousness, even in Homeric times, was full to the brim of the sad mortality of this sunlit world, and such a consciousness Walt Whitman resolutely refuses to adopt. When, for example, Achilles, about to slay Lycaon, Priam's young son, hears him sue for mercy, he stops to say: —

> Ah, friend, thou too must die: why thus lamentest thou?
> Patroclos too is dead, who was better far than thou. . . . Over me
> too hang death and forceful fate. There cometh morn or eve or
> some noonday when my life too some man shall take in battle,
> whether with spear he smite, or arrow from the string.[2]

Then Achilles savagely severs the poor boy's neck with his sword, heaves him by the foot into the Scamander, and calls to the fishes of the river to eat the white fat of Lycaon. Just as here the cruelty and the sympathy each ring true, and do not mix or interfere with one another, so did the Greeks and Romans keep all their sadnesses and gladnesses unmingled and entire. Instinctive good they did not reckon sin; nor had they any such desire to save the credit of the universe as to make them insist, as so many of *us* insist, that what immediately appears as evil must be "good in the making," or something equally ingenious. Good was good, and bad just bad, for the earlier Greeks. They neither denied the ills of nature—Walt Whitman's verse, "What is called good is perfect, and what is called bad is just as perfect,"[3] would have been mere silliness to them—nor did they, in order to escape from those ills, invent "another and a better world" of the imagination, in which, along with the ills, the innocent goods of sense would also find no place. This integrity of the instinctive reactions, this freedom from all moral sophistry and strain, gives a pathetic dignity to ancient pagan feeling. And this quality Whitman's outpourings have not got. His optimism is too voluntary and defiant; his gospel has a touch of bravado and an affected twist, and this diminishes its effect on many readers who yet are well disposed towards optimism, and on the whole quite willing to admit that in important respects Whitman is of the genuine lineage of the prophets.

From TALKS TO TEACHERS ON PSYCHOLOGY (*1899*)

WALT WHITMAN, for instance, is accounted by many of us a contemporary prophet. He abolishes the usual human distinctions, brings all conventionalisms into solution, and loves and celebrates hardly any human attributes save those elementary ones common to all members of the race. For this he becomes a sort of ideal tramp, a rider on omnibus-tops and ferry-boats, and, considered either practically or academically, a worthless, unproductive being. His verses are but ejaculations—things mostly without subject or verb, a succession of interjections on an immense scale. He felt the human crowd as rapturously as Wordsworth felt the mountains, felt it as an overpoweringly significant presence, simply to absorb one's mind in which

Talks to Teachers on Psychology (New York, 1899); the text used here is the 1913 reprint, 248–254.

should be business sufficient and worthy to fill the days of a serious man. As he crosses Brooklyn ferry, this is what he feels. . . .[4]

And so on, through the rest of a divinely beautiful poem. And, if you wish to see what this hoary loafer considered the most worthy way of profiting by life's heaven-sent opportunities, read the delicious volume of his letters to a young car-conductor who had become his friend. . . . [James prints Whitman's letter to Peter Doyle, on October 9, 1868, in which he describes with exuberance a trip on a Broadway stage.][5]

Truly a futile way of passing the time, some of you may say, and not altogether creditable to a grown-up man. And yet, from the deepest point of view, who knows the more of truth, and who knows the less,—Whitman on his omnibus-top, full of the inner joy with which the spectacle inspires him, or you, full of the disdain which the futility of his occupation excites?

When your ordinary Brooklynite or New Yorker, leading a life replete with too much luxury, or tired and careworn about his personal affairs, crosses the ferry or goes up Broadway, *his* fancy does not thus 'soar away into the colors of the sunset' as did Whitman's, nor does he inwardly realize at all the indisputable fact that this world never did anywhere or at any time contain more of essential divinity, or of eternal meaning, than is embodied in the fields of vision over which his eyes so carelessly pass. There is life; and there, a step away, is death. There is the only kind of beauty there ever was. There is the old human struggle and its fruits together. There is the text and the sermon, the real and the ideal in one. But to the jaded and unquickened eye it is all dead and common, pure vulgarism, flatness, and disgust. "Hech! it is a sad sight!" says Carlyle, walking at night with some one who appeals to him to note the splendor of the stars. And that very repetition of the scene to new generations of men in *secula seculorum*, that eternal recurrence of the common order, which so fills a Whitman with mystic satisfaction, is to a Schopenhauer, with the emotional anæsthesia, the feeling of 'awful inner emptiness' from out of which he views it all, the chief ingredient of the tedium it instils. What is life on the largest scale, he asks, but the same recurrent inanities, the same dog barking, the same fly buzzing, forevermore? Yet of the kind of fibre of which such inanities consist is the material woven of all the excitements, joys, and meanings that ever were, or ever shall be, in this world.

To be rapt with satisfied attention, like Whitman, to the mere spectacle of the world's presence, is one way, and the most fundamental way, of confessing one's sense of its unfathomable significance and importance. . . .

EZRA POUND

[1 8 8 5 –   ]

What I Feel About Walt Whitman

(February 1, 1909)

FROM THIS SIDE of the Atlantic I am for the first time able to read Whitman, and from the vantage of my education and—if it be permitted a man of my scant years—my world citizenship: I see him America's poet. The only Poet before the artists of the Carmen-Hovey[1] [sic] period, or better, the only one of the conventionaly recognized "American Poets" who is worth reading. He *is* America. His crudity is an exceding great stench, but it

Reprinted by permission of Dorothy Pound, Committee for Ezra Pound, from Herbert Bergman's printing of Pound's previously unpublished manuscript "Ezra Pound and Walt Whitman" in *American Literature*, XXVII (Mar. 1955), 56–61. Copyright, 1955, by Ezra Pound. The manuscript is in the Yale University Library. For additional comment on Pound and Whitman, see the articles by Charles B. Willard in *Modern Langauge Notes*, LXXII (1957), 19–26, and *Studies in Philology*, LIV (1957), 573–581; and by Roy Harvey Pearce in *Modern Language Notes*, LXXIV (1959), 23–28. The erratic spelling is Pound's.

is America. He is the hollow place in the rock that echos with his time. He *does* "chant the crucial stage" and he is the 'voice triumphant.' He is disgusting. He is an excedingly nauseating pill, but he acomplishes his mission.

Entirely free from the renaissance humanist ideal of the complete man or from the Greek idealism, he is content to be what he is, and he is his time and his people. He is a genius because he has vision of what he is and of his function. He knows that he is a beginning and not a classicaly finished work.

I honor him for he prophesied me while I can only recognize him as a forebear of whom I ought to be proud.

In America there is much for the healing of the nations, but woe unto him of the cultured palate who attempts the dose.

As for Whitman, I read him (in many parts) with acute pain, but when I write of certain things I find myself using his rythms. The expression of certain things related to cosmic consciousness seems tainted with this maramis.

I am (in common with every educated man) an heir of the ages and I demand my birth-right. Yet if Whitman represented his time in language acceptable to one accustomed to my standard of intellectual-artistic living he would belie his time and nation. And yet I am but one of his "ages and ages' encrustations" or to be exact an encrustation of the next age. The vital part of my message, taken from the sap and fibre of America, is the same as his.

Mentaly I am a Walt Whitman who has learned to wear a colar and a dress shirt (although at times inimical to both). Personaly I might be very glad to conceal my relationship to my spiritual father and brag about my more congenial ancestry— Dante, Shakespeare, Theocritus, Villon, but the descent is a bit difficult to establish. And, to be frank, Whitman is to my fatherland (Patriam quam odi et amo for no uncertain reasons) what Dante is to Italy and I at my best can only be a strife for a renaissance in America of all the lost or temporarily mislaid beauty, truth, valor, glory of Greece, Italy, England and all the rest of it.

And yet if a man has written lines like Whitman's to the "Sunset breeze" one has to love him. I think we have not yet paid enough attention to the deliberate artistry of the man, not in details but in the large.

I am immortal even as he is, yet with a lesser vitality as I am the more in love with beauty (If I realy do love it more than he did). Like Dante he wrote in the 'vulgar tongue', in a new metric. The first great man to write in the language of his people.

Et ego Petrarca in lingua vetera scribo, and in a tongue my people understand not.

It seems to me I should like to drive Whitman into the old world. I sledge, he drill—and to scourge America with all the old beauty. (For Beauty *is* an accusation) and with a thousand thongs from Homer to Yeats, from Theocritus to Marcel Schwob.[2] This desire is because I am young and impatient, were I old and wise I should content myself in seeing and saying that these things will come. But now, since I am by no means sure it would be true prophecy, I am fain set my own hand to the labour.

It is a great thing, reading a man to know, not "His Tricks are not as yet my Tricks, but I can easily make them mine" but "His message is my message. We will see that men hear it."

GEORGE SANTAYANA

[1 8 6 3 – 1 9 5 2]

The Poetry of Barbarism (1911)

. . . [Robert Browning and Walt Whitman] are both analytic poets—poets who seek to reveal and express the elemental as opposed to the conventional; but the dissolution has progressed

Reprinted from *Interpretations of Poetry and Religion* (New York, 1911) 175–187.

much farther in Whitman than in Browning, doubtless because Whitman began at a much lower stage of moral and intellectual organization; for the good will to be radical was present in both. The elements to which Browning reduces experience are still passions, characters, persons; Whitman carries the disintegration further and knows nothing but moods and particular images. The world of Browning is a world of history with civilization for its setting and with the conventional passions for its motive forces. The world of Whitman is innocent of these things and contains only far simpler and more chaotic elements. In him the barbarism is much more pronounced; it is indeed, avowed, and the "barbaric yawp" is sent "over the roofs of the world" in full consciousness of its inarticulate character; but in Browning the barbarism is no less real though disguised by a literary and scientific language, since the passions of civilized life with which he deals are treated as so many "barbaric yawps," complex indeed in their conditions, puffings of an intricate engine, but aimless in their vehemence and mere ebullitions of lustiness in adventurous and profoundly ungoverned souls.

Irrationality on this level is viewed by Browning with the same satisfaction with which, on a lower level, it is viewed by Whitman; and the admirers of each hail it as the secret of a new poetry which pierces to the quick and awakens the imagination to a new and genuine vitality. It is in the rebellion against discipline, in the abandonment of the ideals of classic and Christian tradition, that this rejuvenation is found. Both poets represent, therefore, and are admired for representing, what may be called the poetry of barbarism in the most accurate and descriptive sense of this word. For the barbarian is the man who regards his passions as their own excuse for being; who does not domesticate them either by understanding their cause or by conceiving their ideal goal. He is the man who does not know his derivations nor perceive his tendencies, but who merely feels and acts, valuing in his life its force and its filling, but being careless of its purpose and its form. His delight is in abundance and vehemence; his art, like his life, shows an exclusive respect for quantity and splendour of materials. His scorn for what is poorer and weaker than himself is only surpassed by his ignorance of what is higher.

WALT WHITMAN

The works of Walt Whitman offer an extreme illustration of this phase of genius, both by their form and by their substance. It was the singularity of his literary form—the challenge it threw to the conventions of verse and of language—that first gave Whitman notoriety: but this notoriety has become fame, because those incapacities and solecisms which glare at us from his pages are only the obverse of a profound inspiration and of a genuine courage. Even the idiosyncrasies of his style have a side which is not mere perversity or affectation; the order of his words, the procession of his images, reproduce the method of a rich, spontaneous, absolutely lazy fancy. In most poets such a natural order is modified by various governing motives—the thought, the metrical form, the echo of other poems in the memory. By Walt Whitman these conventional influences are resolutely banished. We find the swarms of men and objects rendered as they might strike the retina in a sort of waking dream. It is the most sincere possible confession of the lowest—I mean the most primitive—type of perception. All ancient poets are sophisticated in comparison and give proof of longer intellectual and moral training. Walt Whitman has gone back to the innocent style of Adam, when the animals filed before him one by one and he called each of them by its name.

In fact, the influences to which Walt Whitman was subject were as favourable as possible to the imaginary experiment of beginning the world over again. Liberalism and transcendentalism both harboured some illusions on that score; and they were in the air which our poet breathed. Moreover he breathed this air in America, where the newness of the material environment made it easier to ignore the fatal antiquity of human nature. When he afterward became aware that there was or had been a world with a history, he studied that world with curiosity and spoke of it not without a certain shrewdness. But he still regarded it as a foreign world and imagined, as not a few Americans have done, that his own world was a fresh creation, not amenable to the same laws as the old. The difference in the conditions blinded him, in his merely sensuous apprehension, to the identity of the principles.

His parents were farmers in central Long Island and his early years were spent in that district. The family seems to have been not too prosperous and somewhat nomadic; Whitman himself drifted through boyhood without much guidance. We find him now at school, now helping the labourers at the farms, now wandering along the beaches of Long Island, finally at Brooklyn working in an apparently desultory way as a printer and sometimes as a writer for a local newspaper. He must have read or heard something, at this early period, of the English classics; his style often betrays the deep effect made upon him by the grandiloquence of the Bible, of Shakespeare, and of Milton. But his chief interest, if we may trust his account, was already in his own sensations. The aspects of Nature, the forms and habits of animals, the sights of cities, the movement and talk of common people, were his constant delight. His mind was flooded with these images, keenly felt and afterward to be vividly rendered with bold strokes of realism and imagination.

Many poets have had this faculty to seize the elementary aspects of things, but none has had it so exclusively; with Whitman the surface is absolutely all and the underlying structure is without interest and almost without existence. He had had no education and his natural delight in imbibing sensations had not been trained to the uses of practical or theoretical intelligence. He basked in the sunshine of perception and wallowed in the stream of his own sensibility, as later at Camden in the shallows of his favourite brook. Even during the civil war, when he heard the drum-taps so clearly, he could only gaze at the picturesque and terrible aspects of the struggle, and linger among the wounded day after day with a canine devotion; he could not be aroused either to clear thought or to positive action. So also in his poems; a multiplicity of images pass before him and he yields himself to each in turn with absolute passivity. The world has no inside; it is a phantasmagoria of continuous visions, vivid, impressive, but monotonous and hard to distinguish in memory, like the waves of the sea or the decorations of some barbarous temple, sublime only by the infinite aggregation of parts.

This abundance of detail without organization, this wealth of perception without intelligence and of imagination without taste, makes the singularity of Whitman's genius. Full of sympathy and receptivity, with a wonderful gift of graphic characterization and an occasional rare grandeur of diction, he fills us with a sense of the individuality and the universality of what he describes—it is a drop in itself yet a drop in the ocean. The absence of any principle of selection or of a sustained style enables him to render aspects of things and of emotion which would have eluded a trained writer. He is, therefore, interesting even where he is grotesque or perverse. He has accomplished, by the sacrifice of almost every other good quality, something never so well done before. He has approached common life without bringing in his mind any higher standard by which to criticise it; he has seen it, not in contrast with an ideal, but as the expression of forces more indeterminate and elementary than itself; and the vulgar, in this cosmic setting, has appeared to him sublime.

There is clearly some analogy between a mass of images without structure and the notion of an absolute democracy. Whitman, inclined by his genius and habits to see life without relief or organization, believed that his inclination in this respect corresponded with the spirit of his age and country, and that Nature and society, at least in the United States, were constituted after the fashion of his own mind. Being the poet of the average man, he wished all men to be specimens of that average, and being the poet of a fluid Nature, he believed that Nature was or should be a formless flux. This personal bias of Whitman's was further encouraged by the actual absence of distinction in his immediate environment. Surrounded by ugly things and common people, he felt himself happy, ecstatic, overflowing with a kind of patriarchal love. He accordingly came to think that there was a spirit of the New World which he embodied, and which was in complete opposition to that of the Old, and that a literature upon novel principles was needed to express and strengthen this American spirit.

Democracy was not to be merely a constitutional device for the better government of given nations, not merely a movement for the material improvement of the lot of the poorer classes. It was to be a social and a moral democracy and to involve an actual equality among all men. Whatever kept them apart and made it impossible for them to be messmates together was to be discarded. The literature of democracy was to ignore all extraordinary gifts of genius or virtue, all distinction drawn even from great passions or romantic adventures. In Whitman's works, in which this new literature is foreshadowed, there is accordingly not a single character nor a single story. His only hero is Myself, the "single separate person," endowed with the primary impulses, with health, and with sensitiveness to the elementary aspects of Nature. The perfect man of the future, the prolific begetter of other perfect men, is to work with his hands, chanting the poems of some future Walt, some ideally democratic bard. Women are to have as nearly as possible the same character as men: the emphasis is to pass from family life and local ties to the friendship of comrades and the general brotherhood of man. Men are to be vigorous, comfortable, sentimental, and irresponsible.

This dream is, of course, unrealized and unrealizable, in America as elsewhere. Undeniably there are in America many suggestions of such a society and such a national character. But the growing complexity and fixity of institutions necessarily tends to obscure these traits of a primitive and crude democracy. What Whitman seized upon as the promise of the future was in reality the survival of the past. He sings the song of pioneers, but it is in the nature of the pioneer that the greater his success the quicker must be his transformation into something different. When Whitman made the initial and amorphous phase of society his ideal, he became the prophet of a lost cause. That cause was lost, not merely when wealth and intelligence began to take shape in the American Commonwealth, but it was lost at the very foundation of the world, when those laws of evolution were established which Whitman, like Rousseau, failed to understand. If we may trust Mr. Herbert Spencer, these laws involve a passage from the homogeneous to the heterogeneous, and a constant progress at once in differentiation and in organization —all, in a word, that Whitman systematically deprecated or ignored. He is surely not the spokesman of the tendencies of his country, although he describes some aspects of its past and present condition: nor does he appeal to those whom he describes, but rather to the *dilettanti* he despises. He is regarded as representative chiefly by foreigners, who look for some grotesque expression of the genius of so young and prodigious a people.

Whitman, it is true, loved and comprehended men; but this love and comprehension had the same limits as his love and comprehension of Nature. He observed truly and responded to his observation with genuine and pervasive emotion. A great gregariousness, an innocent tolerance of moral weakness, a genuine admiration for bodily health and strength, made him bubble over with affection for the generic human creature. Incapable of an ideal passion, he was full of the milk of human kindness. Yet, for all his acquaintance with the ways and thoughts of the common man of his choice, he did not truly understand him. For to understand people is to go much deeper than they go themselves; to penetrate to their characters and disentangle their inmost ideals. Whitman's insight into man did not go beyond a sensuous sympathy; it consisted in a vicarious satisfaction in their pleasures, and an instinctive love of their persons. It never approached a scientific or imaginative knowledge of their hearts.

Therefore Whitman failed radically in his dearest ambition: he can never be a poet of the people. For the people, like the early races whose poetry was ideal, are natural believers in perfection. They have no doubts about the absolute desirability of wealth and learning and power, none about the worth of pure goodness and pure love. Their chosen poets, if they have any, will be always those who have known how to paint these ideals in lively even if in gaudy colours. Nothing is farther from the common people than the corrupt desire to be primitive. They instinctively look toward a more exalted life, which they imagine to be full of distinction and pleasure, and the idea of that brighter existence fills them with hope or with envy or with humble admiration.

If the people are ever won over to hostility to such ideals, it is only because they are cheated by demagogues who tell them that if all the flowers of civilization were destroyed its fruits would become more abundant. A greater share of happiness, people think, would fall to their lot could they destroy everything beyond their own possible possessions. But they are made thus envious and ignoble only by a deception: what they really desire is an ideal good for themselves which they are told they may secure by depriving others of their preëminence. Their hope is always to enjoy perfect satisfaction themselves; and therefore a poet who loves the picturesque aspects of labour and vagrancy will hardly be the poet of the poor. He may have described their figure and occupation, in neither of which they are much interested; he will not have read their souls. They will prefer to him any sentimental story-teller, any sensational dramatist, any moralizing poet; for they are hero-worshippers by temperament, and are too wise or too unfortunate to be much enamoured of themselves or of the conditions of their existence.

Fortunately, the political theory that makes Whitman's principle of literary prophecy and criticism does not always inspire his chants, nor is it presented, even in his prose works, quite bare and unadorned. In "Democratic Vistas" we find it clothed with something of the same poetic passion and lighted up with the same flashes of intuition which we admire in the poems. Even there the temperament is finer than the ideas and the poet wiser than the thinker. His ultimate appeal is really to something more primitive and general than any social aspirations, to something more elementary than an ideal of any kind. He speaks to those minds and to those moods in which sensuality is touched with mysticism. When the intellect is in abeyance, when we would "turn and live with the animals, they are so placid and self-contained," when we are weary of conscience and of ambition, and would yield ourselves for a while to the dream of sense, Walt Whitman is a welcome companion. The images he arouses in us, fresh, full of light and health and of a kind of frankness and beauty, are prized all the more at such a time because they are not choice, but drawn perhaps from a hideous and sordid environment. For this circumstance makes them a better means of escape from convention and from that fatigue and despair which lurk not far beneath the surface of conventional life. In casting off with self-assurance and a sense of fresh vitality the distinctions of tradition and reason a man may feel, as he sinks back comfortably to a lower level of sense and instinct, that he is returning to Nature or escaping into the infinite. Mysticism makes us proud and happy to renounce the work of intelligence, both in thought and in life, and persuades us that we become divine by remaining imperfectly human. Walt Whitman gives a new expression to this ancient and multiform tendency. He feels his own cosmic justification and he would lend the sanction of his inspiration to all loafers and holiday-makers. He would be the congenial patron of farmers and factory hands in their crude pleasures and pieties, as Pan was the patron of the shepherds of Arcadia: for he is sure that in spite of his hairiness and animality, the gods will acknowledge him as one of themselves and smile upon him from the serenity of Olympus.

BASIL DE SELINCOURT

[1 8 7 6 – 1 9 4 3]

The Form (*1914*)

OUR UNDERSTANDING OF Whitman's form is incomplete till we see what it excludes; for a thing has no positive if it has no negative qualities. Of course the idea of *Leaves of Grass* was to be all-inclusive; the poem was conceived in a spirit of universal hospitality, and such a spirit would be unfavourable to conscious method of any kind, would be likely to pride itself on having none. But this more or less inevitable pose must not bluff the critic. The form of a work which aims at impressing us with the spiritual coherence of all things may well share the elusiveness of its theme and be as inapprehensible as life itself. Yet unless

Reprinted from *Walt Whitman, a Critical Study* (London, 1914), 94–115, abridged.

some connecting thread, however fine, holds its divergences in a unity, the aim is unaccomplished.

Form in verse means, as a rule, metre. Whitman felt rightly that no metre or combination of metres could serve the peculiar purpose he had in view. At the same time he was not averse, as we have seen, to the introduction of metrical fragments here and there, and even shows a partiality for jingling effects. If we are right in thinking that he made a mistake in this, we have only to analyse the grounds on which our judgment rests, and we shall find the principle of exclusion which we are looking for.

But first let us note that the mistake itself was of secondary importance. The primary requisite for the form of *Leaves of Grass* was that its spaciousness should be recognised and that the composer should write to scale. No one afflicted with sensitiveness about the minor literary proprieties would have been likely to rise to the careless amplitude of manner necessary to the filling of so gigantic a mould. We recognise this easily enough if we compare the master with his followers, the originator with the mimics. The normal writer of Whitmanesque verse feels in every line the influence of the metre he has dispensed with and exhibits the affectations of a disdainful culture. But Whitman, like all who bring a revelation through art, is faithful to nature, and his method turns upon the discovery of nature in what had seemed unnatural. He aimed at being himself in his poetry, and this required him to stand out as poetry personified in solitary relief against the whole poetic achievement of the past. He seemed to ask less than others of the Muse. It devolved upon him to give more. Choosing informality, he chose in effect a form which permitted him no concealment, no breathing-space. We cannot wonder if he did not stay to consider what his ideals denied to him; his task was to be ready with what they exacted. Only the intrusion, the conspicuous and abiding presence of matter inconsistent with the common forms could justify his departure from them.

Yet if he rather transcends than refuses metre, it is not the less true that recognisably metrical lines are out of keeping with the spirit of his poetry. His lines are not metrical; what are they, then? We glanced earlier at an objection often taken to the form of *Leaves of Grass* to the effect that it has a spurious emotionality; that the line-system has the same relation to poetry as the habitual use of italics has to prose. The objection, we think, is inapplicable; but obviously the presentment of a composition in lines is meaningless and otiose, unless the lines have some common measure and are identities in nature as well as in name.

The identity of the lines in metrical poetry is an identity of pattern. The identity of the lines in *Leaves of Grass* is an identity of substance; and this is in effect by far the subtler and more exacting condition of the two. Tyrannous spontaneity allows the poet so little respite that every line must, as it were, contain his personality in the germ. Whitman himself never, I think, formulated this demand, and in the course of his work he frequently overrides it. But it is a natural deduction from his admitted principles. He looked upon each of his poems as the leaf or branch of a tree. The line is to the poem what the poem is to the work as a whole. To say this is to say that certain forms are excluded, that certain kinds of line will not do. . . .

It is to the junction in them of these two seemingly incompatible qualities, continuity and independence, that Whitman's mature lines owe their integrity, and it is this that dictates their behaviour in company, so to speak, explaining the shape of the poems, their formal development, and the difficulties and resources of the craftsman. The line is a personality, the poem is a battalion, the book is an army. To illustrate the point, let us quote a paragraph in full: —

Here is the efflux of the soul,
The efflux of the soul comes from within through embower'd gates,
    ever provoking questions,
These yearnings why are they? these thoughts in the darkness why
    are they?
Why are there men and women that while they are nigh me the
    sunlight expands my blood?
Why when they leave me do my pennants of joy sink flat and lank?
Why are there trees I never walk under but large and melodious
    thoughts descend upon me?
(I think they hang there winter and summer on those trees and
    always drop fruit as I pass;)
What is it I interchange so suddenly with strangers?
What with some driver as I ride on the seat by his side?
What with some fisherman drawing his seine by the shore as I walk
    by and pause?

What gives me to be free to a woman's and man's good-will? what
  gives them to be free to mine?[1]

The importance of continuity to the form is displayed at once
here in that *epanaphora*, that taking up of words or phrases,
which is a pronounced characteristic of the style of *Leaves of
Grass*. Each line hangs by a loop from the line before it. The
motion is like the motion of walking; we continually catch up
our foremost foot and take a half step beyond. It is of course the
substantial self-sufficiency of the lines that necessitates this in-
terlocking. And their equivalence turns upon their relation to a
progressive, an accumulating idea. For example, the repetition
of such a phrase as "the efflux of the soul," though it lengthens
the line in which it occurs, does nothing to help that line to take
us further; it has a different function; it joins the line more
closely to its predecessor than the pronoun "it" would do and,
by demanding less attention from the reader, decreases the
weight of the line, thus actually preserving the equivalence it
seems at first sight to impair.

In what sense, then, finally are the lines

> Here is the efflux of the soul

and

> The efflux of the soul comes from within through embower'd gates,
>   ever provoking questions,

equivalent lines? We have seen that their equivalence is in their
content; to say this is to say that it is in their context also—that it
depends upon their association together. They have not the
equivalence that two lines of blank verse have and which they
have equally whether they stand next to one another or not. The
second is equivalent to the first only as consequent upon it. In
the first, an image is, as it were, posited: the conception of the
soul as a radiating centre. In the second, the same image is
elaborated. Suppose then that for the second line, stumbled at
first sight by its length and complexity, we substitute

> The efflux of the soul comes from within through embower'd gates,

and stop there, we shall find, not only that the line has lost
poetry, but that it has lost equilibrium also. Why is this? Surely
because, in the line as Whitman wrote it, we take the phrase

> comes from within through embower'd gates

transitionally, and because it is when so taken that its true value appears. If we emphasise it, as would be necessary were it to stand alone, we lose its suggestiveness and go searching for some precise significance which we do not find. But if we pass by way of it to the words

> ever provoking questions

and look to them for the first purpose of the line, the phrase falls into its relative place with beautiful accuracy. Is it because the gates are embowered that the questions are provoked? This, or something like it, gives the line, no doubt, its coherence of idea. But the point is that a mystical and an everyday expression have been weighed together and that their effect is felt in their juxtaposition. We weigh them in this way together because they are placed before us as constituents of a single line; and, having so weighed them, we find that the momentum set up by

> Here is the efflux of the soul

is preserved and carried one stage further. The equivalence of the two lines is thus an equivalence of movement and of weight.

The problem of each succeeding line will be the same; to preserve the movement, to advance it by a stage and to maintain equilibrium in the advance. Reading to the end of the paragraph with this idea in view, we shall find that each line solves the problem in its own way. One has an element of surprise, another brings us into closer contact with the object, a third has its expanding generalisation, a fourth its illuminating detail; and the line in parenthesis is especially noticeable, niched there like some light obstacle in flowing water and revealing the current which it checks. To put the matter in general terms: the constitution of a line in *Leaves of Grass* is such that, taken in its context, the poetic idea to be conveyed by the words is only perfectly derivable from them when they are related to the line as a unit; and the equivalence of the lines is their equivalent appeal to our attention as contributors to the developing expression of the poetic idea of the whole.

Thus the progress of Whitman's verse has much in common with that of a musical composition. For we are carrying the sense of past effects along with us more closely and depending more intimately upon them than is possible in normal verse. What we can achieve at any point of our structure depends upon the trains of association we have set up, the number of balls we have kept spinning, the speed and quality of movement we have attacked or attained. And just as the context limits, so it also lays its claim upon us. For if no line can do more than maintain and add its unit to the general flow, none may do less. And just as in music, so here; it is impossible to lay down any rule for the maintenance of equivalence of effect, for the retaining of attention and accumulation of interest to the close. The condition of the effect that we are to produce now is the effect we have produced up to now; it lies with the modifications we have produced in our hearer's receptivity, the anticipations we have formed there. Here a *fortissimo* seems necessary; but its place is taken perhaps by a *pianissimo*, perhaps by a silence, and the effect is sustained. There we have a *diminuendo;* its point lies in the *crescendo* that preceded it; and behold! while the sound lessens, the meaning grows. Throughout, the test is whether the emotional pitch propounded is maintained, whether the piece continues to expand in significance as it expands in volume.

Perhaps it is because the significance of words accumulates faster than that of notes of music that frequent division into paragraphs becomes necessary, and also the frequent interpolation of parenthetical reflections. We go back and begin again where we began before in order, not that we may travel the same route a second time, but that we may travel to the same goal by a neighbouring route: —

Allons! whoever you are come travel with me!
Traveling with me you find what never tires.
The earth never tires,
The earth is rude, silent, incomprehensible at first, Nature is rude
    and incomprehensible at first.
Be not discouraged, keep on, there are divine things well envelop'd,
I swear to you there are divine things more beautiful than words can
    tell.

Allons! we must not stop here,
However sweet these laid-up stores, however convenient this dwell-
    ing we cannot remain here,

However shelter'd this port and however calm these waters we must
    not anchor here,
However welcome the hospitality that surrounds us we are permitted
    to receive it but a little while.[2]

These lines exhibit splendidly the alternating *crescendo* and
diminuendo spoken of above. In "Traveling with me you find
what never tires" we come immediately to a climax; there is no
carrying the idea further; we must have a line of silence and
start afresh. "The earth never tires" takes up the idea again,
and in a sense is an addition to it; but it is a concessive, an
explanatory addition; it is a concrete example and suggestion,
and, as such, is taken as platform for a new "flight into the
wordless." The poet soars, using a marked *crescendo*, which
comes freely because the theme is simple. The line "I swear to
you" is an easy and yet an enjoyable *fortissimo*. Again there is a
pause; and then a new theme develops (the transitoriness of life
on earth), needing tenderer handling; and so we have the deliberate and delicious *diminuendo* which brings the paragraph to a
close.

The use of parenthesis is a recurring feature of Whitman's
technique, and no explanation of his form can be adequate which
does not relate this peculiarity to the constructive principles of
the whole. He frequently begins a paragraph or ends one with a
bracketed sentence, or begins or ends some section of a poem
with a bracketed paragraph, sometimes even begins or ends a
poem parenthetically. Thus the *Song of the Exposition* opens
with the beautiful aside: —

> (Ah little recks the laborer,
> How near his work is holding him to God.
> The loving Laborer through space and time.)

and the last piece in *Calamus* significantly closes: —

Be it as if I were with you. (Be not too certain but I am now with
    you.)[3]

This persistent bracketing falls well into the scheme we have
laid down of independent units that serve an accumulating
effect. The bracket, one need not remark, secures a peculiar
detachment for its contents; it also, by placing them outside the
current and main flow of the sense, relates them to it in a

peculiar way. And although for the time being the flow is broken, it by no means follows, as we saw, that our sense of the flow is broken; on the contrary, it is probably enhanced. We look down upon the stream from a point of vantage and gauge its speed and direction. More precisely, the bracket opening a poem or paragraph gives us, of course, the idea which that whole poem or paragraph presupposes, while the closing bracket gives the idea by which what precedes is to be qualified and tempered. We have thus as it were a poem within a poem; or sometimes, when a series of brackets is used, we have a double stream of poetry, as in *By Blue Ontario's Shore* where the waters blend and yet remain discriminate, a deeper and more personal current of feeling persisting under the strength and buoyant onrush of the surface. All this carries out and amplifies the peculiar formal significance of *Leaves of Grass*, with its strange submission of words to unfamiliar musical associations. Continuity and independence being Whitman's opposing principles of composition, independence emerges in the bracket into relative prominence. The disjunctive spirit of language asserts itself; literature contemplates music.

But the analogy with music is still unexhausted. Not only is the method of progression similar, the means of progression have also much in common. The chief difference between musical and verbal expression, as a rule, is that words, carrying each their modicum of meaning, have done their part when they have delivered it, while notes, being meaningless except in combination, develop new meanings by presenting a single combination in varying contexts or with varying accompaniment. In fact, repetition, which the artist in language scrupulously avoids, is the foundation and substance of musical expression. Now Whitman, for reasons we have touched on, uses words and phrases more as if they were notes of music than any other writer. As we shall see elsewhere, it was to him part of the virtue and essence of life that its forms and processes were endlessly reduplicated; and poetry, which was delight in life, must somehow, he thought, mirror this elemental abundance. Language generally expects us, when an object has been mentioned, to hold that object in view until all that has to be said about it has been said. But the object, if it were actually before us, would continue to assert itself in a thousand ways, and its persistency—its refusal, as it were, to believe that it can be monotonous to us—is its reality, and if its reality, then surely its poetry also.

You have waited, you always wait, you dumb, beautiful ministers,
We receive you with free sense at last, and are insatiate hencefor-
    ward.[4]

Why should not words imitate things and keep up the same patient knocking at the mind's doors until we genuinely admit them?

The meaning of repetition lies of course in the fact that it is impossible to have the same experience twice. If there is to be value in the repeating over and over of some form of words, there must be something in them or in their varying contexts to enable the mind to pass from a first to a second impression of them, and from a second to a third and a fourth, feeling at each stage that more is added in discovery than is lost through the trouble of treading the old path. Words, we must recollect, are partly vehicles of truth, partly vehicles of emotion; they may exhibit a simple relation or suggest a complex one. Now the more complex the relation suggested, the more familiar we must be with the words that suggest it if we are to profit by every breath of suggestion they contain. We have only to grasp the sense of a geometrical proposition and we have done with the words of it; we have no disposition to say them over. But the words of a poem we often learn by heart and repeat them to ourselves as we might repeat a prayer. We are conscious that they proceed out of a certain state of feeling which we desire to enter into and to make our own; to enter into a state we must become familiar with it as an experience; and so we repeat the poem over and over to ourselves, at each repetition experiencing more intimately and more profoundly the spiritual state reflected in it. The poem thus becomes less and less a form of words to us and more and more a key to life. The reason is that the disposition of the words demands from the mind that is to understand them a corresponding disposition. They emanate from and represent a harmony into which we enter only by reproducing it in our own being.

What applies to our deliberate repetition of a poem to our-

selves can be applied to the handling of a poem by its composer
if he so chooses. His object is not to state truths but to convey
feelings; and the feeling with which we hear a certain form of
words may well depend precisely upon the fact that we are not
hearing it for the first time, the feeling itself changing and
developing as its occasion is repeated. Lyric poetry acknowledges the virtue of repetition in the refrain, which, though in the
main a concession to the forms of the musical accompaniment,
has its value in reviving and sustaining the implied emotional
mood.

But there is a further point. A truth necessarily continues
true. Of an emotion our chief test is the degree to which it
admits of constancy; feelings are habitually proved and established by a frequent reiteration of the expression of them. Now
poetry gives us this assurance as a rule by the elevation of
manner, the unified tone, the remoteness, which are in themselves evidences of sustained feeling, being unattainable without
it. Repetition (with certain exceptions irrelevant here) is thus
more otiose in poetry than in prose. For the web of expression is
more tightly woven, every word has full force, and a higher
concentration is demanded of the reader who is to assimilate the
mood. The poem does not so much rise to a certain altitude, as
exist there; and the danger is not that we may doubt the emotion, but that we may fail to recognise the objects to which it
attaches—a failing which sometimes extends beyond a poet's
readers to the poet himself.

Now the absence of recognised formalities which is characteristic of *Leaves of Grass* robs language of these high-pitched
associations, and obliges us to interpret it in accordance with the
dictates of mere common sense. When Whitman bids us

Behold this compost! behold it well![5]

we know that if we take up a handful of garden soil and turn it
over in our hands, we shall be quite in the spirit of his intention.
It was one of his ideals in poetry not to lose sight of these
everyday simplicities. Yet a form or style which begins from and
reverts to such simplicities must forge instruments of some kind
to carry it from the simplicities to the profundities. Poetic
exaltation is not the less necessary because it is not presupposed.

And of Whitman's instruments for obtaining it, repetition—repetition of forms, of phrases, of themes—is perhaps the chief. It is not only that it assists him, as we have seen, to carry out the principle of accumulating weight, his first law of construction. It is also that by it he brings home to us the increasing value for emotion of expressions the value of which, at first hearing, seemed to lie in their very divorce from it, in their cool substantiality. His most astonishing effects are thus often produced by means least compatible with ordinary poetry, the means, like the effects they serve, being peculiarly his own. *Crossing Brooklyn Ferry* is perhaps the greatest and boldest example of them: —

Flood-tide below me! I see you face to face!
Clouds of the west—sun there half an hour high—I see you also
     face to face.

Beginning thus with the common attitude to common objects, we find ourselves gradually, as it were, intermingled with them and caught up through the medium of the poet's interpretation into the sentiment and atmosphere they create: —

Ah, what can ever be more stately and admirable to me than
     mast-hemm'd Manhattan?
River and sunset and scallop-edg'd waves of flood-tide?

Without losing touch with our own experience, we make a passage from natural to impassioned vision. We do more than read poetry. We feel it in its process and formation; not lifted into another world, but acquainted with the deepening and extending vistas of the world we live in: —

Flow on, river! flow with the flood-tide, and ebb with the ebb-tide!
Frolic on, crested and scallop-edg'd waves!
Gorgeous clouds of the sunset! drench with your splendor me, or the
     men and women generations after me!
Cross from shore to shore, countless crowds of passengers!
Stand up, tall masts of Mannahatta! stand up, beautiful hills of
     Brooklyn! . . .
You have waited, you always wait, you dumb, beautiful ministers,
We receive you with free sense at last, and are insatiate henceforward,
Not you any more shall be able to foil us, or withhold yourselves
     from us,
We use you, and do not cast you aside—we plant you permanently
     within us,

We fathom you not—we love you—there is perfection in you also,
You furnish your parts toward eternity,
Great or small, you furnish your parts toward the soul.[6]

There is in this a living presentment of the condition out of
which all poetry springs. It is sometimes made a criticism of
Whitman that, instead of writing poetry, he writes about it and
tries to explain what it is. Often he does so; but often when he
seems to be doing so, he is in reality doing much more. He is
communicating not merely a poem, an example of poetry, but
the spiritual attitude, which if we can assimilate it, will make us
according to our measure poets ourselves. No process of explanation serves here. It is work for the greatest of poets in their
moments of greatest inspiration. *Crossing Brooklyn Ferry* is
such a 'poem of poetry'; it summarises experience, offers a new
key to that dark door, would endow us with a new experiencing
faculty. A purpose so sublime may well have demanded this
strange blend of the ecstasies of music, the exactitudes of
speech.

JOHN COWPER POWYS

[1 8 7 2 – 1 9 6 3]

Walt Whitman (1915)

I WANT TO APPROACH this great Soothsayer from the angle
least of all profaned by popular verdicts. I mean from the angle
of his poetry. We all know what a splendid heroic Anarchist he

Reprinted from *Visions and Revisions* (New York, 1915), 281–289.

was. We all know with what rude zest he gave himself up to that "Cosmic Emotion," to which in these days the world does respectful, if distant, reverence. We know his mania for the word "en masse," for the words "ensemble," "democracy" and "libertad." We know his defiant celebrations of Sex, of amorousness, of maternity; of that Love of Comrades which "passeth the love of women." We know the world-shaking effort he made—and to have made it at all, quite apart from its success, marks him a unique genius!—to write poetry about every mortal thing that exists, and to bring the whole breathing palpable world into his Gargantuan Catalogues. It is absurd to grumble at these Inventories of the Round Earth. They may not all move to Dorian flutes, but they form a background—like the lists of the kings in the Bible and the lists of the ships in Homer—against which, as against the great blank spaces of Life itself, "the writing upon the wall" may make itself visible.

What seems much less universally realized is the extraordinary genius for sheer "poetry" which this prophet of optimism possessed. I agree that Walt Whitman's optimism is the only kind, of that sort of thing, that one can submit to without a blush. At least it is not indecent, bourgeois, and ill-bred, like the fourth-hand Protestantism that Browning dishes up, for the delectation of Ethical Societies. It is the optimism of a person who has seen the American Civil War. It is the optimism of a man who knows "the Bowery," and "the road," and has had queer friends in his mortal pilgrimage.

It is an interesting psychological point, this difference between the "marching breast-forward" of Mrs. Browning's energetic husband, and the "taking to the open road" of Whitman. In some curious way the former gets upon one's nerves where the latter does not. Perhaps it is that the boisterous animal-spirits which one appreciates in the open air become vulgar and irritating when they are practised within the walls of a house. A satyr who stretches his hairy shanks in the open forest is a pleasant thing to see; but a gentleman, with lavender-coloured gloves, putting his feet on the chimney-piece is not so appealing. No doubt it is precisely for these Domestic Exercises that Mr. Chesterton, let us say, would have us love Browning. Well! It is a matter of taste.

But it is not of Walt Whitman's optimism that I want to speak; it is of his poetry.

To grasp the full importance of what this great man did in this sphere one has only to read modern "free verse." After Walt Whitman, Paul Fort,[1] for instance, seems simply an eloquent prose writer. And none of them can get the trick of it. None of them! Somewhere, once, I heard a voice that approached it; a voice murmuring of

> Those that sleep upon the wind,
> And those that lie along the rain,
> Cursing Egypt—

But that voice went its way; and for the rest—what banalities! What ineptitudes! They make the mistake, our modern free-versifiers, of thinking that Art can be founded on the negation of form. Art can be founded on every other negation. But not on that one—never on that one! Certainly they have a right to experiment; to invent—if they can—new forms. But they must invent them. They must not just arrange their lines *to look like poetry*, and leave it at that.

Walt Whitman's new form of verse was, as all such things must be, as Mr. Hardy's strange poetry, for instance, is, a deliberate and laborious struggle—ending in what is a struggle no more—to express his own personality in a unique and recognizable manner. This is the secret of all "style" in poetry. And it is the absence of this labour, of this premeditated concentration, which leads to the curious result we see on all sides of us, the fact, namely, that all young modern poets *write alike*. They write alike, and they *are* alike—just as all men are like all other men, and all women like all other women, when, without the "art" of clothing, or the "art" of flesh and blood, they lie down side by side in the free cemetery. The old poetic forms will always have their place. They can never grow old-fashioned; any more than Pisanello, or El Greco, or Botticelli, or Scopas,[2] or any ancient Chinese painter, can grow old-fashioned. But when a modern artist or poet sets to work to create a new form, let him remember what he is doing! It is not the pastime of an hour, this. It is not the casual gesture of a mad iconoclast breaking classic statues into mud, out of which to make goblins.

It is the fierce, tenacious, patient, constructive work of a life-time, based upon a tremendous and overpowering Vision. Such a vision Walt Whitman had, and to such constant inspired labour he gave his life—notwithstanding his talk about "loafing and inviting his soul."

The "free" poetry of Walt Whitman obeys inflexible, occult laws, the laws commanded unto it by his own creative instinct. We need, as Nietzsche says, to learn the art of "commands" of this kind. Transvaluers of old values do not spend all their time sipping absinthe. Is it a secret still, then, the magical unity of rhythm, which Walt Whitman has conveyed to the words he uses? Those long, plangent, wailing lines, broken by little gurgling gasps and sobs; those sudden thrilling apostrophes and recognitions; those far-drawn flute-notes; those resounding sea-trumpets; all such effects have their place in the great orchestral symphony he conducts!

Take that little poem—quite spoiled before the end by a horrible bit of democratic vulgarity—which begins:

> Come, I will build a Continent indissoluble,
> I will make the most splendid race the sun ever shone upon—[3]

Is it possible to miss the hidden spheric law which governs such a challenge? Take the poem which begins:

> In the growth by the margins of pond-waters—[4]

Do you not divine, delicate reader, the peculiar subtlety of that reference to the rank, rain-drenched *anonymous weeds*, which every day we pass in our walks inland? A botanical name would have driven the magic of it quite away.

Walt Whitman, more than anyone, is able to convey to us that sense of the unclassified pell-mell, of weeds and stones and rubble and wreckage, of vast, desolate spaces, and spaces full of débris and litter, which is most of all characteristic of the melancholy American landscape, but which those who love England know where to find, even among our trim gardens. No one like Walt Whitman can convey to us the magical *ugliness* of certain aspects of Nature—the bleak, stunted, God-forsaken things; the murky pools where the grey leaves fall; the dead reeds where the wind whistles no sweet fairy tunes; the unspeakable margins of murderous floods; the tangled seadrift, scurfed with scum; the black sea-winrow of broken shells and dead fishes' scales; the roots of willow trees in moonlit places crying out for demon-lovers; the long, moaning grass that grows outside the walls of prisons; the leprous mosses that cover paupers' graves; the mountainous wastes and blighted marshlands which only unknown wild-birds ever touch with their flying wings, and of which madmen dream—these are the things, the ugly, terrible things, that this great optimist turns into poetry. "Yo honk!"⁵ cries the wild goose, as it crosses the midnight sky. Others may miss that mad-tossed shadow, that heartbreaking defiance—but from amid the drift of leaves by the roadside, this bearded Fakir of Outcasts has caught its meaning; has heard, and given it its answer.

Ah, gentle and tender reader; thou whose heart, it may be has never cried all night for what it must not name, did you think Swinburne or Byron were the poets of "love"? Perhaps you do not know that the only "short story" on the title-page of which Guy de Maupassant found it in him to write *that word* is a story about the wild things we go out to kill?

Walt Whitman, too, does not confine his notions of love to normal human coquetries. The most devastating love-cry ever uttered, except that of King David over his friend, is the cry this American poet dares to put into the heart of "a wild-bird from Alabama"⁶ that has lost its mate. I wonder if critics have done justice to the incredible genius of this man who can find words for that aching of the soul we do not confess even to our dearest? The sudden words he makes use of, in certain connections, awe us, hush us, confound us, take our breath,—as some of Shakespeare's do—with their mysterious congruity. Has my reader ever read the little poem called "Tears"? And what *purity* in the truest, deepest sense, lies behind his pity for such tragic craving; his understanding of what love-stricken, banished ones feel. I do not speak now of his happily amorous verses. They have their place. I speak of those desperate lines that come, here and there, throughout his work, where, with his huge, Titanic back set against the world-wall, and his wild-tossed beard streaming in the wind, he seems *to hold open* by main, gigantic force that door of hope which Fate and God and Man and the Laws of

Nature are all endeavoring to close. *And he holds it open!* And it is open still. It is for this reason—let the profane hold their peace!—that I do not hesitate to understand very clearly why he addresses a certain poem to the Lord Christ.[7] Whether it be true or not that the Pure in Heart see God, it is certainly true that they have a power of saving us from God's Law of Cause and Effect. According to this Law, we all "have our reward" and reap what we have sown. But sometimes, like a deep-sea murmur, there rises from the poetry of Walt Whitman a Protest that *must* be heard! Then it is that the tetrarchs of science forbid in vain "that one should raise the Dead." For the Dead are raised up, and come forth, even in the likeness wherein we loved them! If words, my friends; if the use of words in poetry can convey such intimations as these to such a generation as ours, can anyone deny that Walt Whitman is a great poet?

Deny it, who may or will. There will always gather round him—as he predicted—out of City-Tenements and Artist-Studios and Factory-Shops and Ware-Houses and Bordelloes—aye! and, it may be, out of the purlieus of Palaces themselves—a strange, mad, heart-broken company of life-defeated derelicts, who come, not for Cosmic Emotion or Democracy or Anarchy or Amorousness, or even "Comradeship," but for that touch, that whisper, that word, that hand outstretched in the darkness, which makes them *know*—against reason and argument and all evidence—that they may hope still—*for the Impossible is true!*

D. H. LAWRENCE

[1885–1930]

Whitman (1921)

WHITMAN is the greatest of the Americans. One of the greatest poets of the world, in him an element of falsity troubles us still. Something is wrong; we cannot be quite at ease in his greatness.

This may be our own fault. But we sincerely feel that something is overdone in Whitman; there is something that is too much. Let us get over our quarrel with him first.

All the Americans, when they have trodden new ground, seem to have been conscious of making a breach in the established order. They have been self-conscious about it. They have felt that they were trespassing, transgressing, or going very far, and this has given a certain stridency, or portentousness, or luridness to their manner. Perhaps that is because the steps were taken so rapidly. From Franklin to Whitman is a hundred years. It might be a thousand.

The Americans have finished in haste, with a certain violence and violation, that which Europe began two thousand years ago or more. Rapidly they have returned to lay open the secrets which the Christian epoch has taken two thousand years to close up.

Reprinted from *The Nation & The Athenæum* (July 23, 1921), 616–619. This earlier version of Lawrence's remarks on Whitman is less eccentric and flamboyant than the revision included in *Studies in Classic American Literature*. Reprinted by permission of the Viking Press, Inc., Laurence Pollinger Limited, and the Estate of Mrs. Frieda Lawrence. *Studies in Classic American Literature* copyright, 1923, 1951, by Frieda Lawrence. All rights reserved.

With the Greeks started the great passion for the ideal, the passion for translating all consciousness into terms of spirit and ideal or idea. They did this in reaction from the vast old world which was dying in Egypt. But the Greeks, though they set out to conquer the animal or sensual being in man, did not set out to annihilate it. This was left for the Christians.

The Christians, phase by phase, set out actually to *annihilate* the sensual being in man. They insisted that man was in his reality *pure spirit*, and that he was perfectible as such. And this was their business, to achieve such a perfection.

They worked from a profound inward impulse, the Christian religious impulse. But their proceeding was the same, in living extension, as that of the Greek esoterics, such as John the Evangel or Socrates. They proceeded, by will and by exaltation, to overcome *all* the passions and all the appetites and prides.

Now, so far, in Europe, the conquest of the lower self has been objective. That is, man has moved from a great impulse within himself, unconscious. But once the conquest has been effected, there is a temptation for the conscious mind to return and finger and explore, just as tourists now explore battlefields. This self-conscious *mental* provoking of sensation and reaction in the great affective centres is what we call sentimentalism or sensationalism. The mind returns upon the affective centres, and sets up in them a deliberate reaction.

And this is what all the Americans do, beginning with Crèvecœur, Hawthorne, Poe, all the transcendentalists, Melville, Prescott, Wendell Holmes, Whitman, they are all guilty of this provoking of mental reactions in the physical self, passions exploited by the mind. In Europe, men like Balzac and Dickens, Tolstoi and Hardy, still act direct from the passional motive, and not inversely, from mental provocation. But the æsthetes and symbolists, from Baudelaire and Maeterlinck and Oscar Wilde onwards, and nearly all later Russian, French, and English novelists set up their reactions in the mind and reflect them by a secondary process down into the body. This makes a vicious living and a spurious art. It is one of the last and most fatal effects of idealism. Everything becomes self-conscious and spurious, to the pitch of madness. It is the madness of the world of to-day. Europe and America are all alike; all the nations self-consciously provoking their own passional reactions from the mind, and *nothing* spontaneous.

And this is our accusation against Whitman, as against the others. Too often he deliberately, self-consciously *affects* himself. It puts us off, it makes us dislike him. But since such self-conscious secondariness is a concomitant of all American art, and yet not sufficiently so to prevent that art from being of rare quality, we must get over it. The excuse is that the Americans have had to perform in a century a curve which it will take Europe much longer to finish, if ever she finishes it.

Whitman has gone further, in actual living expression, than any man, it seems to me. Dostoevsky has burrowed underground into the decomposing psyche. But Whitman has gone forward in life-knowledge. It is he who surmounts the grand climacteric of our civilization.

Whitman enters on the last phase of spiritual triumph. He really arrives at that stage of infinity which the seers sought. By subjecting the *deepest centres* of the lower self, he attains the maximum consciousness in the higher self: a degree of extensive consciousness greater, perhaps, than any man in the modern world.

We have seen Dana and Melville, the two adventurers, setting out to conquer the last vast *element*, with the spirit. We have seen Melville touching at last the far end of the immemorial, prehistoric Pacific civilization, in "Typee." We have seen his terrific cruise into universality.

Now we must remember that the way, even towards a state of infinite comprehension, is through the externals towards the quick. And the vast elements, the cosmos, the big things, the universals, these are always the externals. These are met first and conquered first. That is why science is so much easier than art. The quick is the living being, the quick of quicks is the individual soul. And it is here, at the quick, that Whitman proceeds to find the experience of infinitude, his vast extension, or concentrated intensification into Allness. He carries the conquest to its end.

If we read his pæans, his chants of praise and deliverance and accession, what do we find? All-embracing, indiscriminate, passional acceptance; surges of chaotic vehemence of invitation and embrace, catalogues, lists, enumerations. "Whoever you are, to you endless announcements! . . ." "And of these one and all I weave the song of myself." "Lovers, endless lovers."[1]

Continually the one cry: I am everything and everything is me. I accept everything in my consciousness; nothing is rejected: —

I am he that aches with amorous love;
Does the earth gravitate? does not all matter, aching, attract all
    matter?
So the body of me to all I meet or know.[2]

At last everything is conquered. At last the lower centres are conquered. At last the lowest plane is submitted to the highest. At last there is nothing more to conquer. At last all is one, all is love, even hate is love, even flesh is spirit. The great oneness, the experience of infinity, the triumph of the living spirit, which at last includes everything, is here accomplished.

It is man's accession into wholeness, his knowledge in full. Now he is united with everything. Now he embraces everything into himself in a oneness. Whitman is drunk with the new wine of this new great experience, really drunk with the strange wine of infinitude. So he pours forth his words, his chants of praise and acclamation. It is man's maximum state of consciousness, his highest state of spiritual being. Supreme spiritual consciousness, and the divine drunkenness of supreme consciousness. It is reached through embracing love. "And whoever walks a furlong without sympathy walks to his own funeral dresst in his shroud."[3] And this supreme state, once reached, shows us the One Identity in everything, Whitman's cryptic *One Identity*.

Thus Whitman becomes in his own person the whole world, the whole universe, the whole eternity of time. Nothing is rejected. Because nothing opposes him. All adds up to one in him. Item by item he identifies himself with the universe, and this accumulative identity he calls Democracy, En Masse, One Identity, and so on.

But this is the last and final truth, the last truth is at the quick. And the quick is the single individual soul, which is never more than itself, though it embrace eternity and infinity, and never *other* than itself, though it include all men. Each vivid soul is unique, and though one soul embrace another, and include it, still it cannot *become* that other soul, or livingly dispossess that other soul. In extending himself, Whitman still remains himself; he does not become the other man, or the other woman, or the tree, or the universe: in spite of Plato.

Which is the maximum truth, though it appears so small in contrast to all these infinites, and En Masses, and Democracies, and Almightynesses. The essential truth is that a man is himself, and only himself, throughout all his greatnesses and extensions and intensifications.

The second truth which we must bring as a charge against Whitman is the one we brought before, namely, that his Allness, his One Identity, his En Masse, his Democracy, is only a half-truth—an enormous half-truth. The other half is Jehovah, and Egypt, and Sennacherib: the other form of Allness, terrible and grand, even as in the Psalms.

Now Whitman's way to Allness, he tells us, is through endless sympathy, merging. But in merging you must merge away from something, as well as towards something, and in sympathy you must depart from one point to arrive at another. Whitman lays down this law of sympathy as the one law, the direction of merging as the one direction. Which is obviously wrong. Why not a right-about-turn? Why not turn slap back to the point from which you started to merge? Why not *that* direction, the reverse of merging, back to the single and overweening self? Why not, instead of endless dilation of sympathy, the retraction into isolation and pride?

Why not? The heart has its systole diastole, the shuttle comes and goes, even the sun rises and sets. We know, as a matter of fact, that all life lies between two poles. The direction is twofold. Whitman's *one direction* becomes a hideous tyranny once he has attained his goal of Allness. His One Identity is a prison of horror, once realized. For identities are manifold and each jewel-like, different as a sapphire from an opal. And the motion of merging becomes at last a vice, a nasty degeneration, as when tissue breaks down into a mucous slime. There must be the sharp retraction from isolation, following the expansion into unification, otherwise the integral being is overstrained and will break, break down like disintegrating tissue into slime, imbecility, epilepsy, vice, like Dostoevsky.

And one word more. Even if you reach the state of infinity, you can't sit down there. You just physically can't. You either have to strain still further into universality and become vaporish, or slimy: or you have to hold your toes and sit tight and practise Nirvana; or you have to come back to common dimensions, eat your pudding and blow your nose and be just yourself; or die and have done with it. A grand experience is a grand experience. It brings a man to his maximum. But even at his maximum a man is not more than himself. When he is infinite he is still himself. He still has a nose to wipe. The state of infinity is *only* a state, even if it be the supreme one.

But in achieving this state Whitman opened a new field of living. He drives on to the very centre of life and sublimates even this into consciousness. Melville hunts the remote white whale of the deepest passional body, tracks it down. But it is Whitman who captures the whale. The pure sensual body of man, at its deepest remoteness and intensity, this is the White Whale. And this is what Whitman captures.

He seeks his consummation through one continual ecstacy: the ecstacy of *giving himself*, and of being taken. The ecstacy of his own reaping and merging with another, with others; the sword-cut of sensual death. Whitman's motion is always the motion of *giving himself:* This is my body—take, and eat. It is the great sacrament. He knows nothing of the other sacrament, the sacrament in pride, where the communicant envelops the victim and host in a flame of ecstatic consuming, sensual gratification, and triumph.

But he is concerned with others beside himself: with woman, for example. But what is woman to Whitman? Not much? She is a great function—no more. Whitman's "athletic mothers of these States"[4] are depressing. Muscles and wombs: functional creatures—no more.

As I see my soul reflected in Nature,
As I see through a mist, One with inexpressible completeness,
    sanity, beauty,
See the bent head and arms folded over the breast, the Female I see.[5]

That is all. The woman is reduced, really, to a submissive function. She is no longer an individual being with a living soul.

She must fold her arms and bend her head and submit to her functioning capacity. Function of sex, function of birth.

This the nucleus—after the child is born of woman, man is born of woman,
This the bath of birth, this the merge of small and large, and the outlet again—[6]

Acting from the last and profoundest centres, man acts womanless. It is no longer a question of race continuance. It is a question of sheer, ultimate being, the perfection of life, nearest to death. Acting from these centres, man is an extreme being, the unthinkable warrior, creator, mover, and maker.

And the polarity is between man and man. Whitman alone of all moderns has known this positively. Others have known it negatively, *pour épater les bourgeois.* But Whitman knew it positively, in its tremendous knowledge, knew the extremity, the perfectness, and the fatality.

Even Whitman becomes grave, tremulous, before the last dynamic truth of life. In *Calamus* he does not shout. He hesitates: he is reluctant, wistful. But none the less he goes on. And he tells the mystery of manly love, the love of comrades. Continually he tells us the same truth: the new world will be built upon the love of comrades, the new great dynamic of life will be manly love. Out of this inspiration the creation of the future.

⌐ The strange Calamus has its pink-tinged root by the pond, and it sends up its leaves of comradeship, comrades at one root, without the intervention of woman, the female. This comradeship is to be the final cohering principle of the new world, the new Democracy.[7] It is the cohering principle of perfect soldiery, as he tells in "Drum Taps." It is the cohering principle of final *unison* in creative activity. And it is extreme and alone, touching the confines of death. It is something terrible to bear, terrible to be responsible for. It is the soul's last and most vivid responsibility, the responsibility for the circuit of final friendship, comradeship, manly love.

Yet you are beautiful to me you faint-tinged roots, you make me think of death,
Death is beautiful from you, (what indeed is finally beautiful except death and love?)

O I think it is not for life I am chanting here my chant of lovers, I
    think it must be for death.
For how calm, how solemn it grows to ascend to the atmosphere of
    lovers,
Death or life I am then indifferent, my soul declines to prefer,
(I am not sure but the high soul of lovers welcomes death most,)
Indeed O death, I think now these leaves mean precisely the same as
    you mean—[8]

Here we have the deepest, finest Whitman, the Whitman who
knows the extremity of life, and of the soul's responsibility. He
has come near now to death, in his creative life. But creative life
must come near to death, to link up the mystic circuit. The pure
warriors must stand on the brink of death. So must the men of a
pure creative nation. We shall have no beauty, no dignity, no
essential freedom otherwise./ And so it is from Sea-Drift, where
the male bird sings the lost female: not that she is lost, but lost
to him who has had to go beyond her, to sing on the edge of the
great sea, in the night. It is the last voice on the shore.

Whereto answering, the sea,
Delaying not, hurrying not,
Whisper'd to me through the night, and very plainly before day-
    break,
Lisp'd to me the low and delicious word death,
And again death, death, death, death,
Hissing melodious, neither like the bird nor like my arous'd child's
    heart,
But edging near as privately for me rustling at my feet,
Creeping thence steadily up to my ears and laving me softly all over,
Death, death, death, death, death—[9]

What a great poet Whitman is: great like a great Greek. For
him the last enclosures have fallen, he finds himself on the shore
of the last sea. The extreme of life: so near to death. It is a
hushed, deep responsibility. And what is the responsibility? It is
for the new great era of mankind. And upon what is this new
era established? On the perfect circuits of vital flow between
human beings. First, the great sexless normal relation between
individuals, simple sexless friendships, unison of family, and
clan, and nation, and group. Next, the powerful sex relation
between man and woman, culminating in the eternal orbit of
marriage. And, finally, the sheer friendship, the love between

comrades, the manly love which alone can create a new era of life.

The one state, however, does not annul the other: it fulfils the other. Marriage is the great step beyond friendship, and family, and nationality, but it does not supersede these. Marriage should only give repose and perfection to the great previous bonds and relationships. A wife or husband who sets about to annul the old, pre-marriage affections and connections ruins the foundations of marriage. And so with the last, extremest love, the love of comrades. The ultimate comradeship which sets about to destroy marriage destroys its own *raison d'être*. The ultimate comradeship is the final progression from marriage; it is the last seedless flower of pure beauty, beyond purpose. But if it destroys marriage it makes itself purely deathly. In its beauty, the ultimate comradeship flowers on the brink of death. But it flowers from the root of all life upon the blossoming tree of life.

The life-circuit now depends entirely upon the sex-unison of marriage. This circuit must never be broken. But it must be still surpassed. We cannot help the laws of life.

If marriage is sacred, the ultimate comradeship is utterly sacred, since it has no ulterior motive whatever, like procreation. If marriage is eternal, the great bond of life, how much more is this bond eternal, being the great life-circuit which borders on death in all its round. The new, extreme, the sacred relationship of comrades awaits us, and the future of mankind depends on the way in which this relation is entered upon by us. It is a relation between fearless, honorable, self-responsible men, a balance in perfect polarity.

The last phase is entered upon, shakily, by Whitman. It will take us an epoch to establish the new, perfect circuit of our being. It will take an epoch to establish the love of comrades, as marriage is really established now. For fear of going on, forwards, we turn round and destroy, or try to destroy, what lies behind. We are trying to destroy marriage, because we have not the courage to go forward from marriage to the new issue. Marriage must never be wantonly attacked. *True* marriage is eternal; in it we have our consummation and being. But the final consummation lies in that which is beyond marriage.

And when the bond, or circuit of perfect comrades is established, what then, when we are on the brink of death, fulfilled in the vastness of life? Then, at last, we shall know a starry maturity.

Whitman put us on the track years ago. Why has no one gone on from him? The great poet, why does no one accept his greatest word? The Americans are not worthy of their Whitman. They take him like a cocktail, for fun. Miracle that they have not annihilated every word of him. But these miracles happen.

The greatest modern poet! Whitman, at his best, is purely himself. His verse springs sheer from the spontaneous sources of his being. Hence its lovely, lovely form and rhythm: at the best. It is sheer, perfect, *human* spontaneity, spontaneous as a nightingale throbbing, but still controlled, the highest loveliness of human spontaneity, undecorated, unclothed. The whole being is there, sensually throbbing, spiritually quivering, mentally, ideally speaking. It is not, like Swinburne, an exaggeration of the one part of being. It is perfect and whole. The whole soul speaks at once, and is too pure for mechanical assistance of rhyme and measure. The perfect utterance of a concentrated, spontaneous soul. The unforgettable loveliness of Whitman's lines:

Out of the cradle endlessly rocking.

Ave America!

T. S. ELIOT

[1 8 8 8 – 1 9 6 5]

Observations on Walt Whitman (1926, 1928)

I DO NOT MEAN TO SUGGEST that all discontent is divine, or that all self-righteousness is loathesome. On the contrary, both Tennyson and Whitman made satisfaction almost magnificent. It is not the best aspect of their verse; if neither of them had more, neither of them would be still a great poet. But Whitman succeeds in making America as it was, just as Tennyson made England as it was, into something grand and significant. You cannot quite say that either was deceived, and you cannot at all say that either was insincere, or the victim of popular cant. They had the faculty—Whitman perhaps more prodigiously than Tennyson—of transmuting the real into an ideal. Whitman had the ordinary desires of the flesh; for him there was no chasm between the real and the ideal, such as opened before the horrified eyes of Baudelaire. But this, and the "frankness" about sex for which he is either extolled or mildly reproved did not spring from any particular honesty or clearness of vision: it sprang from what may be called either "idealisation" or a faculty for make-believe, according as we are disposed. There is, fundamentally, no difference between the Whitman frankness and the Tennyson delicacy, except in its relation to public opinion of the time. And Tennyson liked monarchs, and Whitman liked presidents. Both were conservative, rather than reactionary or revolu-

Reprinted by permission of Mrs. Valerie Eliot and Faber and Faber Ltd. from Eliot's review of Emory Holloway's biography in *The Nation & The Athenæum*, XL (Dec. 18, 1926), 426. Copyright by Mrs. Valerie Eliot.

tionary; that is to say, they believed explicitly in progress, and believed implicitly that progress consists in things remaining much as they are.

If this were all there is to Whitman, it would still be a great deal; he would remain a great representative of America, but emphatically of an America which no longer exists. It is not the America of Mr. Scott Fitzgerald, or Mr. Dos Passos, or Mr. Hemingway—to name some of the more interesting of contemporary American writers. If I may draw still one more comparison, it is with Hugo. Beneath all the declamations there is another tone, and behind all the illusions there is another vision. When Whitman speaks of the lilacs or of the mocking-bird, his theories and beliefs drop away like a needless pretext.

From Introduction to
Ezra Pound's SELECTED POEMS (*1928*)

Now POUND'S ORIGINALITY IS genuine in that his versification is a *logical* development of the verse of his English predecessors. Whitman's originality is both genuine and spurious. It is genuine in so far as it is a *logical* development of certain English prose; Whitman was a great prose writer. It is spurious in so far as Whitman wrote in a way that asserted that his great prose was a new form of verse. (And I am ignoring in this connexion the large part of clap-trap in Whitman's content.) The word 'revolutionary' has no meaning, for this reason: we confound under the same name those who are revolutionary because they develop logically, and those who are 'revolutionary' because they innovate illogically. It is *very* difficult, at any moment, to discriminate between the two.

Reprinted by permission of Mrs. Valerie Eliot and Faber and Faber Ltd. from Eliot's introduction to Ezra Pound's *Selected Poems* (London, 1928), xi. Copyright by Mrs. Valerie Eliot.

VERNON LOUIS PARRINGTON

[1871–1929]

The Afterglow of the Enlightenment— Walt Whitman (1929?)

IN HIS SOMEWHAT TRUCULENT POSE of democratic undress Whitman was a singular figure for a poet, and especially an American poet. The amplitude and frankness and sincerity of his rich nature were an affront to every polite convention of the day. Endowed with abundant sensuousness and catholic sympathies, he took impressions as sharply as wax from the etcher's hand; and those impressions he transcribed with the careful impartiality of the modern expressionist. His sensitive reactions to experience were emotional rather than intellectual. A pagan, a romantic, a transcendentalist, a mystic—a child of the Enlightenment yet heeding the lessons of science and regarding himself as a realist who honored the physical as the repository of the spiritual—to an amazing degree he was an unconscious embodiment of American aspiration in the days when the romantic revolution was at flood tide. His buoyant nature floated easily on the turbulent stream of national being, and his songs were defiant chants in praise of life—strong, abundant, procreative— flowing through the veins of America.

Oracular and discursive, Whitman lived and moved in a world of sensuous imagery. His imagination was Gothic in its

Reprinted by permission of Harcourt, Brace & World, Inc., from *Main Currents in American Thought* (New York, 1927–1930), III, 69–86, abridged. Copyright, 1930, by Harcourt, Brace & World, Inc. Copyright, 1958, by Vernon L. Parrington, Jr., Louise P. Tucker, Elizabeth P. Thomas.

vast reaches. Thronging troops of pictures passed before him, vivid, vital, transcripts of reality, the sharp impress of some experience or fleeting observation—his own and no one's else, and therefore authentic. Delighting in the cosmos he saw reflecting its myriad phases in the mirror of his own ego, he sank into experience joyously like a strong swimmer idling in the salt waves. Borne up by the caressing waters, repressing nothing, rejecting nothing, he found life good in all its manifestations. As an Emersonian he was content to receive his sanctions from within, and as he yielded to the stimulus of the environing present his imagination expanded, his spirits rose to earth's jubilee, his speech fell into lyric cadences, and from the exalted abandon of egoistic experience there issued a strong rich note of the universal. His like had not before appeared in our literature for the reason that the childlike pagan had not before appeared. Emerson with his serene intelligence almost disencumbered of the flesh, and Hawthorne with his dessicating skepticisms that left him afraid of sex, were the fruits of a Hebraized culture that Puritan America understood; but Walt Whitman the caresser of life, the lover who found no sweeter fat than stuck to his own bones, was incomprehensible, and not being understood, it was inevitable that he should be inexorably damned. The most deeply religious soul that American literature knows, the friend and lover of all the world, the poet of the democratic ideal to which, presumably, America was dedicated, Whitman was flung into outer darkness by the moral custodians of an age that knew morality only from the precepts of the fathers. . . .[1]

So it was as a revolutionary that Whitman began his work; and a revolutionary he remained to the end, although in his last years he chose to call himself an evolutionist. A born rebel, he was always preaching the gospel of rebellion. "I am a radical of radicals," he said late in life, "but I don't belong to any school." It was this revolutionary spirit that made him the friend of all rebellious souls past and present. "My heart is with all you rebels—all of you, today, always, wherever: your flag is my flag," he said to a Russian anarchist; and it was this sympathy that enabled him to understand Fanny Wright and Tom Paine and Priestley, who "have never had justice done them."[2] "The future belongs to the radical," and so *Leaves of Grass*—he says in "Starting from Paumanok"—"beat the gong of revolt." Conventional law and order he frankly despised and those individuals who sought their own law and followed it awoke his admiration. Thoreau's "lawlessness" delighted him—"his going his own absolute road let hell blaze all it chooses." It is a coward and a poltroon who accepts his law from others—as true of communities as it is true of individuals. He was a good Jeffersonian in his fear of Federalistic consolidation that must put an end to local rights and freedoms. . . .

As such lyric chants fell on Whitman's ears, they must have quickened the ferment of thought that was eventually to clarify for him the ideal of democracy, exalting it by making it warm and human and social. The old Jacksonian leveling had been negative; its freedoms had been individual, its anarchism selfish and unsocial. The great ideal of the fellowship had been lost in the scramble for rights. Even transcendental democracy had narrowed its contacts. The hermit Thoreau in his cabin at Walden Pond was no symbol of a generous democratic future. In the struggle for liberty and equality the conception of fraternity had been denied and the golden trinity of the Enlightenment dismembered. It was this idea of fraternity, made human and hearty by his warm love of men and women, that Whitman got from the expansive fifties and built into his thinking. The conception of solidarity, then entering the realm of proletarian thought through the labors of Friedrich Engels and Karl Marx, was his response to the new times—a response that infused his democratic faith with a glowing humanism. Democracy spiritualized by Channing and Emerson and Parker had suffered limitations from their lingering Hebraisms—the Puritan passion for righteousness had imposed strict ethical bounds on the democratic will. In Thoreau it had been subjected to caustic skepticisms—the transcendental individualist quizzically asked, "What *is* your people?" and refused to subject himself to the mass. But in Whitman all limitations and skepticisms were swept away by the feeling of comradeship. Flesh is kin to flesh, and out of the great reserves of life is born the average man "with his excellent good manliness." Not in distinction but in oneness with the whole is found the good life, for in fellowship is love and in the whole is freedom; and love and freedom are the law and the prophets. The disintegrations of the earlier individualism must be succeeded by a new integration; fear and hate and jealousy and pride have held men apart hitherto, but love will draw them together. After all solidarity—the children of America merging in the fellowship, sympathetic, responsive, manlike yet divine, of which the poet should be the prophet and literature provide the sermons.

It was a noble conception—washing away all the meanness that befouled Jacksonian individualism—and it somewhat slowly found its way to parity with his first master conception, the universal ego, and settled into place in those latter opening lines of *Leaves of Grass:*

> One's-self I sing, a simple separate person,
> Yet utter the word Democratic, the word En-Masse. . . .

But this new religion of the mystical Whitman, in harmony with post-transcendental thought, was deeply impregnated with the spirit of science. He was in the very fullness of his powers when the conception of evolution came to him and he greeted it gladly, weaving it into all his thinking and discovering in it a confirmation of his idealistic philosophy. It was the evolution of Herbert Spencer, it must be remembered, that Whitman accepted—teleological, buoyantly optimistic, dominated by the conception of progress, shot through with the spirit of the Enlightenment; and such an evolution was a confirmation and not a denial of his transcendental premises. It supplemented rather than contradicted the tenets of his faith. Like Emerson as he saw the bounds of the material universe slowly pushed back by science he discovered amidst the constant change the presence of growth, development, the natural passage from the simple to the complex; and like Theodore Parker he felt that this slow unfolding was no other than the unfolding of God, making Himself evident and unmistakable to man. Evolution was God's great plan. "The law over all, the law of laws, is the law of successions,"[3] he was persuaded; "for what is the present after all but a growth out of the past?" But noble as is the evidence of God's work discoverable by science, the soul is not content to rest with such evidence; it must seek out the reality behind the manifestation; and for this work the poet alone is fitted. The poet must complete the work of the scientist. The noble "Passage to India" is a lovely chant of human progress, the adventurous soul conquering the earth; but it must not pause there; it must seek God through the universe until it finds Him, and "Nature and Man shall be disjoin'd and diffused no more," and "All these hearts as of fretted children shall be sooth'd."

> Bathe me O God in thee, mounting to thee,
> I and my soul to range in range of thee. . . .[4]

Equipped with such a philosophy and supported by such a faith Whitman accepted the twin duties laid upon him: to make clear to America her present failure in the great adventure—how far she had fallen short hitherto of any adequate democratic reality; and to mark out afresh the path to the Canaan of democratic hopes—reviving the early hopes of the Enlightenment and drawing in lovelier colors the democratic Utopia dreamed of for a hundred years. To be both critic and prophet —that he conceived to be his mission, a mission that he was faithful to for upwards of forty years. For the first duty he was admirably equipped. No other knew this America so intimately or so broadly—had penetrated so lovingly to the common heart and read so clearly its secret hopes and fears. That America was not yet a democracy—was very far indeed from a democracy— that it was a somewhat shoddy *bourgeois* capitalistic society shot through with cant and hypocrisy and every meanness, he saw with calm, searching eyes. No contemporary critic, not Godkin, not Emerson, saw more clearly the unlovely reality or dealt with it more scathingly, not only in *Leaves of Grass* but especially in his prose writings and in casual talk. . . .

As a realist Whitman granted the worst charges of the critics of democracy, but he probed deeper and brought other facts to light that modified the equation. It was the difficult question the old Federalists had posed and that Carlyle had lately revived— the question, is not this meanness inseparable from democracy? is not your people in fact a great beast, requiring the lash and the curb? It was the crux of the long debate over democracy and to it Whitman gave anxious and frequent consideration. In fighting the battle of 1790 over again, like Jefferson he rested his case on the native integrity and measureless potentiality of the "bulk-people"—they are the deep soil from which spring the abundant fruits and flowers of civilization. Gentle-nurtured folk do not understand this—they do not like the rank qualities of vital being. Matthew Arnold "always gives you the notion that he hates to touch the dirt—the dirt is so dirty! But everything comes out of the dirt—everything: everything comes out of the people . . . not university people, not F.F.V. people: people, people, just people!" In the rude, vital, natural man is the inexhaustible wellspring of good and evil; "He's got it all . . . not only the cruel, beastly, hoggish, cheating, bedbug qualities, but also the spiritual—the noble—the high-born"; in "some ways" he is a "devil of a fellow," but he is not "all devil or even chiefly devil." . . .[5]

Individualism, solidarity—on such strong bases he erected his ideal democracy, and the heaven-reaching temple will be overlaid with the rich arts and graces of a civilization worthy at last of the name. Such was the Enlightenment as it came to flower in the passionate idealism of Walt Whitman—a dream that was mocked and flouted and nullified by the Drews and Fisks and Goulds—the "hoggish, cheating, bedbug qualities" of a generation that scorned him for a beast. Even his stout faith was shaken at times by the infidelities of the Gilded Age. He was troubled by the gap that opened between the free individual and the perfect State. "I seem to be reaching for a new politics—for a new economy," he confessed in 1888; "I don't quite know what, but for something." Although he protested, "The older I grow . . . the more I am confirmed in my optimism, my democracy," he projected his hopes farther into the future. He sympathized with the socialists but he was not one of them. His revolutionary ardor abated and he preferred in later years to call himself an evolutionist. "Be radical—be radical," he said to Traubel, "be not too damned radical." With his catholic sympathies that refused all bitterness he could not be a partisan—"after the best the partisan will say something better will be said by the man."[6]

So in the twilight of the romantic revolution Whitman quietly slipped away. The great hopes on which he fed have been belied by after events—so his critics say; as the great hopes of the Enlightenment have been belied. Certainly in this welter of

today, with science become the drab and slut of war and indus-
trialism, with sterile money-slaves instead of men, Whitman's
expansive hopes seem grotesque enough. Democracy may indeed be only a euphemism for the rulership of fools. Yet in a
time of huge infidelities, in the dun breakdown and disintegration of all faiths, it is not wholly useless to recall the large
proportions of Walt Whitman, his tenderness, his heartiness,
his faith, his hope. There was in him no weak evasion, no
sniveling over the shards of the goodly vessel broken at the well,
but even when "old, alone, sick, weak-down, melted-worn with
sweat,"[7] a free and joyous acceptance of life.

Thanks in old age—thanks ere I go,
For health, the midday sun, the impalpable air—for life, mere life,
. . . .
For all my days—not those of peace alone—the days of war the
    same,
For gentle words, caressess, gifts from foreign lands,
For shelter, wine and meat—for sweet appreciation,
. . . .
For beings, groups, love, deeds, words, books—for colors, forms,
For all the brave strong men—devoted, hardy, men—who've for-
    ward sprung in freedom's help, all years, all lands,
For braver, stronger, more devoted men—(a special laurel ere I go,
    to life's war's chosen ones,
The cannoneers of song and thought—the great artillerists—the
    foremost leaders, captains of the soul:)
As soldier from an ended war return'd—As traveler out of myriads,
    to the long procession retrospective,
Thanks—joyful thanks!—a soldier's, traveler's thanks.[8]

A great figure, the greatest assuredly in our literature—yet
perhaps only a great child—summing up and transmitting into
poetry all the passionate aspirations of an America that had
passed through the romantic revolution, the poet of selfhood and
the prophet of brotherhood, the virile man and the catholic lover
—how shall Walt Whitman become dumb or cease to speak to
men unless the children of those who are now half-devil and
half-God shall prove to be wholly devil—or wholly moron?

JAMES JOYCE

[1882-1941]

Two Excerpts from FINNEGANS WAKE (*1939*)

. . . And old Whiteman self, the blighty blotchy, beyond the bays, hope of ostrogothic and ottomanic faith converters, despair of Pandemia's post-wartem plastic surgeons? But is was all so long ago.

. . . I foredreamed for thee and more than full-maked: I prevened for thee in the haunts that joybelled frail light-a-leaves for sturdy traemen: *pelves ad hombres sumus:* I said to the shiftless prostitute; let me be your fodder; and to rodies and prater brothers; Chau, Camerade!: evangel of good tidings, omnient as the Healer's word, for the lost, loathsome and whomsoever will: who, in regimentation through liberal donation in coordination for organisation of their installation and augmentation plus some annexation and amplification without precipitation towards the culmination in latification of what was formerly their utter privation, competence, cheerfulness, usefulness and the meed, shall, in their second adams, all be made alive: my tow tugs sterred down canal grand, my lighters lay longside on Regalia Water.

F. O. MATTHIESSEN

[1902–1950]

Only a Language Experiment (1941)

ONE ASPECT OF Whitman's work that has not yet received its due attention is outlined in *An American Primer*, notes for a lecture that he seems to have collected mainly between 1855 and 1860, using the paper covers of the unbound copies of the first edition of *Leaves of Grass* for his improvised sheets. This lecture, which, as he says, 'does not suggest the invention but describes the growth of an American English enjoying a distinct identity,' remained, like most of Whitman's lectures, undelivered and unpublished at his death. But he often talked to Traubel about it in the late eighteen-eighties, telling him that he never quite got its subject out of his mind, that he had long thought of making it into a book, and adding: 'I sometimes think the *Leaves* is only a language experiment.' It will be interesting, therefore, to begin by seeing how much we can learn about Whitman just by examining his diction.

He understood that language was not 'an abstract construction' made by the learned, but that it had arisen out of the work and needs, the joys and struggles and desires of long generations of humanity, and that it had 'its bases broad and low, close to the ground.' Words were not arbitrary inventions, but the

Reprinted by permission of Oxford University Press, Inc., from *American Renaissance: Art and Expression in the Age of Emerson and Whitman* (New York, 1941), 517–532, abridged. Original footnotes omitted. Copyright, 1941, by Oxford University Press, Inc. *An American Primer* appeared in 1904.

product of human events and customs, the progeny of folkways. Consequently he believed that the fresh opportunities for the English tongue in America were immense, offering themselves in the whole range of American facts. His poems, by cleaving to these facts, could thereby release 'new potentialities' of expression for our native character. When he started to develop his conviction that 'a perfect user of words uses things,' and to mention some of the things, he unconsciously dilated into the loose beats of his poetry: 'they exude in power and beauty from him—miracles from his hands—miracles from his mouth . . . things, whirled like chain-shot rocks, defiance, compulsion, houses, iron, locomotives, the oak, the pine, the keen eye, the hairy breast, the Texan ranger, the Boston truckman, the woman that arouses a man, the man that arouses a woman.'

He there reveals the joy of the child or the primitive poet just in naming things. This was the quality in Coleridge that made Whitman speak of him as being 'like Adam in Paradise, and almost as free from artificiality'—though Whitman's own joy is far more naïve and relaxed than anything in Coleridge. Whitman's excitement carries weight because he realized that a man cannot use words so unless he has experienced the facts that they express, unless he has grasped them with his senses. This kind of realization was generally obscured in the nineteenth century, partly by its tendency to divorce education of the mind from the body and to treat language as something to be learned from a dictionary. Such division of the individual's wholeness, intensified by the specializations of a mechanized society, has become a chief cause of the neurotic strain oppressing present-day man, for whom the words that pour into him from headlines so infrequently correspond to a concrete actuality that he has touched at first hand. For Whitman it was axiomatic that the speakers of such words are merely juggling helplessly with a foreign tongue. He was already convinced by 1847—as he recorded in the earliest of his manuscript notebooks that has been preserved—that 'a man only is interested in anything when he identifies himself with it.' When he came to observe in the *Primer* that 'a perfect writer would make words sing, dance, kiss . . . or do any thing that man or woman or the natural powers can do,' he believed that such a writer must have realized the full resources of his physical life, and have been immersed in the evolving social experience of his own time. . . .

Feeling that he had discovered the real America that had been hidden behind the diction of a superficial culture which hardly touched native life, Whitman exclaimed with delight: 'Monongahela—it rolls with venison richness upon the palate.' He pursued the subject of how 'words become vitaliz'd, and stand for things' in an essay in his late *November Boughs* called 'Slang in America' (1885). He grasped there the truth that language is the 'universal absorber and combiner,' the best index we have to the history of civilization. In the *Primer* his cognizance that English had assimilated contributions from every stock, that it had become an amalgamation from all races, rejecting none, had led him to declare that he would never allude to this tongue 'without exultation.' In the few pages of his printed essay there is more exultation than clarity, particularly in his conception of slang. His starting point is straightforward enough, the statement that 'slang, profoundly consider'd, is the lawless germinal element, below all words and sentences, and behind all poetry, and proves a certain perennial rankness and protestantism in speech.'[1] But when he equates slang with 'indirection, an attempt of common humanity to escape from bald literalism, and express itself illimitably,' we are reminded of Emerson's use of the term 'indirection' and need recourse to other passages in Whitman for the elusive connotations that he associated with this word.

When he said in his 1855 preface that the expression of the American poet was to be 'transcendent and new,' 'indirect and not direct or descriptive or epic,' he had just been enumerating the kinds of things the poet must incarnate if he was to be commensurate with his people: the continent's geography and history, the fluid movement of the population, the life of its factories and commerce and of the southern plantations. He appears to have thought that the expression of this surging newness must be 'indirect' in the sense that it could not find its voice through any of the conventional modes, but must wait for the poet who 'sees the solid and beautiful forms of the future where there are now no solid forms.' Here Whitman's belief in the way in which the organic style is called into being is seen to converge with his similar understanding of the origin of words. He might have had in mind either or both in his account of the creative process, in another early notebook: 'All truths lie waiting in all things.—They neither urge the opening of themselves nor resist it. For their birth you need not the obstetric forceps of the surgeon. They unfold to you and emit themselves more fragrant than roses from living buds, whenever you fetch the spring sunshine moistened with summer rain.—But it must be in yourself.—It shall come from your soul.—It shall be love.'

Living speech could come to a man only through his absorption in the life surrounding him. He must learn that the final decisions of language are not made by dictionary makers but 'by the masses, people nearest the concrete, having most to do with actual land and sea.' By such a route, illogical as it may be, Whitman came to think of slang as indirection, as the power to embody in a vibrant word or phrase 'the deep silent mysterious never to be examined, never to be told quality of life itself.' When he tried to make his meaning plainer by giving examples of how many 'of the oldest and solidest words we use, were originally generated from the daring and license of slang,' he showed that what he was really thinking of was something very like Emerson's first proposition about language—that words are signs of natural facts. Whitman's examples are almost identical with those in *Nature:* 'Thus the term *right* means literally only straight. *Wrong* primarily meant twisted, distorted. *Integrity* meant oneness. *Spirit* meant breath, or flame. A *supercilious* person was one who rais'd his eyebrows. To *insult* was to leap against. If you *influenc'd* a man, you but flow'd into him.' Moreover, as Whitman continued, he expanded into Emerson's next proposition—that natural facts are symbols of spiritual facts—by launching from the word 'prophesy' into an enunciation of the transcendental view of the poet: 'The Hebrew word which is translated *prophesy* meant to bubble up and pour forth as a fountain. The enthusiast bubbles up from the Spirit of God within him, and it pours forth from him like a fountain. The word prophecy is misunderstood. Many suppose that it is limited to mere prediction; that is but the lesser portion of prophecy. The greater work is to reveal God. Every true religious enthusiast is a prophet.'

In such a passage you come up against one of the most confusing aspects of Whitman, the easy-hearted way he could shuttle back and forth from materialism to idealism without troubling himself about any inconsistency. Thinking of *Children of Adam* or of what Lawrence cared for in Whitman, 'the sheer appreciation of the instant moment, life surging itself at its very wellhead,' we tend to deny that his bond with transcendentalism could have been strong. But it is significant that his earliest quotation from one of Emerson's 'inimitable lectures,' in a notice for *The Brooklyn Eagle* in 1847, is from 'Spiritual Laws' and begins, 'When the act of reflection takes place in the mind, when we look at ourselves in the light of thought, we discover that our life is embosomed in beauty.' Whitman's response to this kind of idealism was more than fleeting, as we may judge from his marginal note on an unidentified essay on 'Imagination and Fact,' which Bucke dated to the early fifties. The sentence that struck the poet reads: 'The mountains, rivers, forests and the elements that gird them round about would be only blank conditions of matter if the mind did not fling its own divinity around them.' Whitman commented: 'This I think is one of the most indicative sentences I ever read.'

The idealistic strain also runs through his conception of language. Although he asks in his 'Song of the Banner at Daybreak':

Words! book-words! what are you?

and affirms in 'A Song of the Rolling Earth':

The substantial words are in the ground and sea,

nevertheless he proclaims on the first page of his *Primer:* 'All words are spiritual—nothing is more spiritual than words.' This is the Whitman who could say, 'The words of my book nothing, the drift of it every thing,'[2] the Whitman so concerned with the idea rather than the form that he could take flight into the vaguest undifferentiated generalizations about 'Democracy, ma femme,' or could write on occasion even of 'the body electric' with no sensuous touch of his material:

O for you whoever you are your correlative body! O it, more than all else, you delighting![3]

This is the Whitman who has seemed to linguists as though he was trying to get beyond the limits of language altogether. . . .

It is not hard to find, for what they are worth, passages in Whitman running parallel to most of Emerson's major convictions about the nature of art. But it would always be salutary to head them with these two from 'Self-Reliance' and 'Song of Myself': 'Suppose you should contradict yourself; what then? . . . With consistency a great soul has simply nothing to do'; and

> Do I contradict myself?
> Very well then I contradict myself,
> (I am large, I contain multitudes.)

At the end of a long paragraph of appreciation of Emerson that Bucke places around eighteen-fifty, Whitman had already observed that 'there is hardly a proposition in Emerson's poems or prose which you cannot find the opposite of in some other place.' Nevertheless, the main contours of Emerson's doctrine of expression, as we have seen it develop, are unmistakable, and unmistakably Whitman's as well. They can both compress it into headlines: Emerson, 'By God, it is in me, and must come forth of me'; Whitman, 'Walt you contain enough, why don't you let it out then?' Again, whole essays of Emerson's, notably that on 'The Poet,' speak eloquently about the very things from which Whitman made his poetry. The two share the same view of the poet as inspired seer, of his dependence for his utterance upon his moments of inner illumination. Yet looking back over forty years, though Whitman reaffirmed that his last word would be 'loyal, loyal,' he admitted that Emerson's work had latterly seemed to him 'pretty thin,' 'always a *make*, never an unconscious *growth*,' and 'some ways short of earth.'

Whitman's language is more earthy because he was aware, in a way that distinguished him not merely from Emerson but from every other writer of the day, of the power of sex. In affirming natural passion to be 'the enclosing basis of everything,' he spoke of its sanity, of the sacredness of the human body, using specifically religious terms: 'we were all lost without redemption, except we retain the sexual fibre of things.' In defending his insistence on this element in his poems (1856), he made clear his understanding of its immediate bearing upon a living speech: 'To the lack of an avowed, empowered, unabashed development of sex, (the only salvation for the same,) and to the fact of speakers and writers fraudulently assuming as always dead what every one knows to be always alive, is attributable the remarkable non-personality and indistinctness of modern productions in books.' Continuing in this vein he made almost the same observations about conventional society as were later to be expressed by Henry Adams, who, incidentally, found Whitman to be the only American writer who had drawn upon the dynamic force of sex 'as every classic had always done.' Both were agreed, though the phrasing here is Whitman's, that particularly among the so-called cultivated class the neuter gender prevailed, and that 'if the dresses were changed, the men might easily pass for women and the women for men.'[4]

Emerson never gave up deploring the want of male principle in our literature, but one reason why it remained remote from his own pages is contained in his pronouncement (1834): 'I believe in the existence of the material world as the expression of the spiritual or real.' The continuation of his thought reveals the difference of his emphasis from that of the poet of 'Crossing Brooklyn Ferry': 'and so look with a quite comic and condescending interest upon the show of Broadway with the air of an old gentleman when he says, "Sir, I knew your father." Is it not forever the aim and endeavor of the real to embody itself in the phenomenal?' No matter how happily inconsistent Emerson might be on other matters, this basic position of the idealist was one from which he never departed. Whitman was far less consistent in his consideration of the relation between body and soul. He was impressed by a line of John Sterling's, which was also a favorite of Emerson's, 'Still lives the song tho' Regnar dies.' Whitman added this gloss to it: 'The word is become flesh.'[5] Just what he implied in talking about language as incarnation, and how he diverged from Emerson, can be followed most briefly in his own words.

In the manuscript draft for the opening section of 'Song of Myself,' he announced the equalitarian inclusiveness that was destined always to be part of his desire:

> And I say that the soul is not greater than the body,
> And I say that the body is not greater than the soul.

However, that arbitrary equilibrium between the two is far less characteristic of his accents of most intimate discovery than his exultant reckless feeling in *Children of Adam* that the body 'includes and is the soul,'

> And if the body were not the soul, what is the soul?[6]

But in different moods, as in 'A Song of Joys,' he veers towards the other pole and seems loosely to approximate Blake in saying that the real life of his senses transcends his senses and flesh, that it is not his material eyes that finally see, or his material body that finally loves. However, he does not pursue this strain very long, and says more usually that the soul achieves its 'identity' through the act of observing, loving, and absorbing concrete objects:

> We realize the soul only by you, you faithful solids and fluids.

This particular kind of material ideality, suggestive in general of Fichte's, remains his dominant thought, so it is worth observing how he formulated it in one of his notebooks: 'Most writers have disclaimed the physical world and they have not over-estimated the other, or soul, but have under-estimated the corporeal. How shall my eye separate the beauty of the blossoming buckwheat field from the stalks and heads of tangible matter? How shall I know what the life is except as I see it in the flesh? I will not praise one without the other or any more than the other.'

In commenting on the mixture of his heritage, Whitman once remarked that 'like the Quakers, the Dutch are very practical and materialistic . . . but are terribly transcendental and cloudy too.' That mixture confronts and tantalizes you throughout his poetry. He is at his firmest when he says that 'imagination and actuality must be united.' But in spite of his enthusiasm for the natural sciences as well as for every other manifestation of progress, he never came very close to a scientific realism. When he enunciated, in the eighteen-seventies, that 'body and mind are one,' he had then been led into this thought by his reading of—or about—the German metaphysicians. And he declared that 'only Hegel is fit for America,' since in his system 'the human soul stands in the centre, and all the universes minister to it.'[7] Following the Civil War, and increasingly during the last twenty years of his life, he kept saying that in his *Leaves*, 'One deep purpose underlay the others—and that has been the Religious purpose.'[8] He often posed variants of the question, 'If the spiritual is not behind the material, to what purpose is the material?' Yet, even then, his most natural way of reconciling the dichotomy between the two elements, 'fused though antagonistic,' was to reaffirm his earlier analogy: 'The Soul of the Universe is the Male and genital master and the impregnating and animating spirit—Physical matter is Female and Mother and waits. . . .'

No arrangement or rearrangement of Whitman's thoughts on this or any other subject can resolve the paradoxes or discover in them a fully coherent pattern. He was incapable of sustained logic, but that should not blind the reader into impatient rejection of the ebb and flow of his antitheses. They possess a loose dialectic of their own, and a clue of how to find it is provided by Engels' discussion of Feuerbach: 'One knows that these antitheses have only a relative validity; that that which is recognized now as true has also its latent false side which will later manifest itself, just as that which is now regarded as false has also its true side by virtue of which it could previously have been regarded as true.' Whitman's ability to make a synthesis in his poems of the contrasting elements that he calls body and soul may serve as a measure of his stature as a poet. When his words adhere to concrete experience and yet are bathed in imagination, his statements become broadly representative of humanity:

> I am she who adorn'd herself and folded her hair expectantly,
> My truant lover has come, and it is dark.[9]

When he fails to make that synthesis, his language can break into the extremes noted by Emerson when he called it 'a remarkable mixture of the *Bhagvat-Geeta* and the *New York Herald*.' The incongruous lengths to which Whitman was frequently carried in each direction shows how hard a task he undertook. On the one hand, his desire to grasp American facts could lead him beyond slang into the rawest jargon, the journalese of the day. On the other, his attempts to pass beyond the restrictions of language into the atmosphere it could suggest often produced only the barest formulas. His inordinate and grotesque failures in both directions throw into clearer light his rare successes, and the fusion upon which they depend.

The slang that he relished as providing more fun than 'the books of all "the American humorists" ' was what he heard in the ordinary talk of 'a gang of laborers, rail-road men, miners, drivers, or boatmen,' in their tendency 'to approach a meaning not directly and squarely' but by the circuitous routes of lively fancy. This tendency expressed itself in their fondness for nick-names like Old Hickory, or Wolverines, or Suckers, or Buck-eyes. Their inventiveness had sowed the frontier with many a Shirttail Bend and Toenail Lake. Current evasions of the literal transformed a horsecar conductor into a 'snatcher,' straight whisky into 'barefoot,' and codfish balls into 'sleeve buttons.' But even though Whitman held such slang to be the source of all that was poetical in human utterance, he was aware that its fermentation was often hasty and frothy, and, except for occasional friendly regional epithets like Hoosiers or Kanucks, he used it only sparingly in his poems. Indeed, in some notes during the period of the gestation of his first *Leaves*, he advised himself to use 'common idioms and phrases—Yankeeisms and vulgarisms—cant expressions, when very pat only.' In consequence, the diction of his poetry is seldom as unconventional as that in the advice he gave himself for an essay on contemporary writing: 'Bring in a sockdolager on the Dickens-fawners.' He gave examples of 'fierce words' in the *Primer*—'skulk,' 'shyster,' 'doughface,' 'mean cuss,' 'backslider,' 'lickspittle'—and some-times cut loose in the talk that Traubel reported. But only on the rare occasions when he felt scorn did he introduce into his poems any expressions as savagely untrammelled as

> This now is too lamentable a face for a man,
> Some abject louse asking leave to be, cringing for it,
> Some milk-nosed maggot blessing what lets it wrig to its hole.[10]

By contrast his most characteristic colloquialisms are easy and relaxed, as when he said 'howdy' to Traubel and told him that he felt 'flirty' or 'hunkydory,' or fell into slang with no self-consciousness, but with the careless aplomb of a man speaking the language most natural to him:

> I reckon I am their boss and they make me a pet besides.

> And will go gallivant with the light and air myself.

> Shoulder your duds dear son, and I will mine.

> Earth! you seem to look for something at my hands,
> Say, old top-knot, what do you want?[11]

One of Whitman's demands in the *Primer* was that words should be brought into literature from factories and farms and trades, for he knew that 'around the markets, among the fish-smacks, along the wharves, you hear a thousand words, never yet printed in the repertoire of any lexicon.' What resulted was sometimes as mechanical as the long lists in 'A Song for Occupations,' but his resolve for inclusiveness also produced dozens of snap-shot impressions as accurate as

> The butcher-boy puts off his killing-clothes, or sharpens his knife at
>   the stall in the market,
> I loiter enjoying his repartee and his shuffle and break-down.

Watching men in action called out of him some of his most fluid phrases, which seem to bathe and surround the objects they describe—as this, of the blacksmiths:

> The *lithe sheer* of their waists plays even with their massive arms.

Or this,

> The negro holds firmly the reins of his four horses, the block *swags
>   underneath* on its tied-over chain.

Or a line that is itself a description of the very process by which he enfolds such movement:

> In me the caresser of life wherever moving, backward as well as
>   forward *sluing*.

At times he produced suggestive coinages of his own:

> The blab of the pave, tires of carts, sluff of boot-soles, talk of the
>   promenaders.[12]

Yet he is making various approaches to language even in that one line. 'Blab' and 'sluff' have risen from his desire to suggest actual sounds, but 'promenaders,' which also sounds well, has clearly been employed for that reason alone since it does not belong to the talk of any American folk. 'Pave' instead of 'pavement' is the kind of bastard word that, to use another, Whitman liked to 'promulge.' Sometimes it is hard to tell whether such words sprang from intention or ignorance, particularly in view of the appearance of 'semitic' in place of 'seminal' ('semitic muscle,' 'semitic milk') in both the 1855 preface and the first printing of 'A Woman Waits for Me.' Most frequently his hybrids take the form of the free substitution of one part of speech for another—sometimes quite effectively ('the soothe of the waves'), sometimes less so (she that 'birth'd him').

Although it has been estimated that Whitman had a vocabulary of more than thirteen thousand words, of which slightly over half were used by him only once,[13] the number of his authentic coinages is not very large. Probably the largest group is composed of his agent-nouns, which is not surprising for a poet who was so occupied with types and classes of men and women. Unfortunately these also furnish some of the ugliest-sounding words in his pages, 'originatress,' 'revoltress,' 'dispensatress,' which have hardly been surpassed even in the age of the realtor and the beautician. He was luckier with an occasional abstract noun like 'presidentiad,' though this is offset by a needless monstrosity like 'savantism.' The one kind of coinage where his ear was listening sensitively is in such compounds as 'the transparent green-shine' of the water around the naked swimmer in 'I Sing the Body Electric,' or that evoking the apples hanging 'indolent-ripe' in 'Halcyon Days.'

His belief in the need to speak not merely for Americans but for the workers of all lands seems to have given the impetus for his odd habit of introducing random words from other languages, to the point of talking about 'the ouvrier class'! He took from the Italian chiefly the terms of the opera, also 'viva,' 'romanza,' and even 'ambulanza.' From the Spanish he was pleased to borrow the orotund way of naming his countrymen 'Americanos,' while the occasional circulation of Mexican dollars in the States during the eighteen-forties may have given him his word 'Libertad.' His favorite 'camerado,' an archaic English version of the Spanish 'camarada,' seems most likely to have come to him from the pages of the Waverley novels, of which he had been an enthusiastic reader in his youth. But the smattering of French which he picked up on his trip to New Orleans, and which constituted the most extensive knowledge that he ever was to have of another tongue, furnished him with the majority of his borrowings. It allowed him to talk of his 'amour' and his 'eleves,' of a 'soiree' or an 'accoucheur,' of 'trottoirs' and 'feuillage' and 'delicatesse'; to say that his were not 'the songs of an ennuyeed person,' or to shout, 'Allons! from all formules! . . . Allons! the road is before us!'[14] Frequently he was speaking no language, as when he proclaimed himself 'no dainty dolce affettuoso.'[15] But he could go much farther than that into a foreign jargon in his desire to 'eclaircise the myths Asiatic' in his 'Passage to India,' or to fulfil 'the rapt promises and luminè of seers.' He could address God, with ecstatic and monumental tastelessness, as 'thou reservoir.'

Many of these are samples of the confused American effort to talk big by using high-sounding terms with only the vaguest notion of their original meaning. The resultant fantastic transformations have enlivened every stage of our history, from the frontiersman's determination to twist his tongue around the syllables of the French settlement at Chemincouvert, Ark., which ended up with the name being turned into Smackover, down to Ring Lardner's dumb nurse who thought people were calling her 'a mormon or something.' In Whitman's case, the fact that he was a reader and so could depend upon letters as well as upon sounds overheard kept him from drifting to such gorgeous lengths. His transformations retain some battered semblance of the original word, which, with the happy pride of the half-educated in the learned term, he then deployed grandly for purposes of his own. Often the attraction for him in the French words ran counter to the identification he usually desired between the word and the thing, since it sprang from intoxication with the mere sound. You can observe the same tendency in some of the jotted lists of his notebooks, 'Cantaloupe. Muskmelon. Cantabile. Cacique City,' or in his shaping such a generalized description of the earth as 'O vast rondure swimming in space.' When caught up by the desire to include the whole universe in his embrace, he could be swept far into the intense inane, chanting in 'Night on the Prairies' of 'immortality and peace':

How plenteous! how spiritual! how resumé!

The two diverging strains in his use of language were with him to the end, for he never outgrew his tendency to lapse from specific images into undifferentiated and lifeless abstractions, as in the closing phrase of this description of his grandfather: 'jovial, red, stout, with sonorous voice and characteristic physiognomy.' In some of his latest poems, *Sands at Seventy*, he could still be satisfied with the merest rhetoric:

Of ye, O God, Life, Nature, Freedom, Poetry.[16]

In his fondness for all his *Leaves*, he seems never to have perceived what we can note in the two halves of a single line,

I concentrate toward them that are nigh, I wait on the door-slab,[17]

—the contrast between the clumsy stilted opening and the simple close. The total pattern of his speech is, therefore, difficult to chart, since it is formed both by the improviser's carelessness about words and by the kind of attention to them indicated in his telling Burroughs that he had been 'searching for twenty-five years for the word to express what the twilight note of the robin meant to him.' He also engaged in endless minute revisions of his poems, the purpose of which is often baffling. Although sometimes serving to fuse the syllables into an ampler rhythm, as in the transformation of

Out of the rocked cradle

into one of his most memorable opening lines; they seem almost as likely to add up to nothing more than the dozens of minor substitutions in 'Salut au Monde,' which leave it the flat and formless catalogue that it was in the beginning.

In a warm appreciation of Burns in *November Boughs*, Whitman said that 'his brightest hit is his use of the Scotch patois, so full of terms flavor'd like wild fruits or berries.' Thinking not only of Burns he relished a special charm in 'the very neglect, unfinish, careless nudity,' which were not to be found in more polished language and verse. But his suggested comparison between the Scotch poet and himself would bring out at once the important difference that Whitman is not using anything like a folk-speech. Indeed, his phrasing is generally remote from any customary locutions of the sort that he jotted down as notes for one unwritten poem. This was to have been based on a free rendering of local native calls, such as 'Here goes your fine fat oysters—Rock Point oysters—here they go.' When put beside such natural words and cadences, Whitman's usual diction is clearly not that of a countryman but of what he called himself, 'a jour printer.' In its curious amalgamation of homely and simple usage with half-remembered terms he read once somewhere, and with casual inventions of the moment, he often gives the impression of using a language not quite his own. In his determination to strike up for a new world, he deliberately rid himself of foreign models. But, so far as his speech is concerned, this was only very partially possible, and consequently Whitman reveals the peculiarly American combination of a childish freshness with a mechanical and desiccated repetition of book terms that had had significance for the more complex civilization in which they had had their roots and growth. The freshness has come, as it did to Huck Finn, through instinctive rejection of the authority of those terms, in Whitman's reaction against what he called Emerson's cold intellectuality: 'Suppose his books becoming absorb'd, the permanent chyle of American general and particular character—what a well-wash'd and grammatical, but bloodless and helpless race we should turn out!'

Yet the broken chrysalis of the old restrictions still hangs about Whitman. Every page betrays that his language is deeply ingrained with the educational habits of a middle-class people who put a fierce emphasis on the importance of the written word. His speech did not spring primarily from contact with the soil, for though his father was a descendant of Long Island farmers, he was also a citizen of the age of reason, an acquaintance and admirer of Tom Paine. Nor did Whitman himself develop his diction as Thoreau did, by the slow absorption through every pore of the folkways of a single spot of earth. He was attracted by the wider sweep of the city, and though his language is a natural product, it is the natural product of a

Brooklyn journalist of the eighteen-forties who had previously
been a country schoolteacher and a carpenter's helper, and who
had finally felt an irresistible impulse to be a poet.

MURIEL RUKEYSER

[1 9 1 3 –   ]

Backgrounds and Sources (*1949*)

IT HAS BEEN SAID, and there are lines in the poems to prove it,
that Walt Whitman could not discriminate between good and
evil, that indeed with his inclusive benevolence Whitman dismissed the problem of evil altogether. But it is not proved. As
the critics add to their quotations, one thing comes through:
Whitman from the beginning felt himself to be deeply evil and
good. Within that conflict—again like the conflict of his culture
—there was a *problem* of good. It was no matter of simple
recognition, with direct action to follow. How was it possible to
search for the good, find it, and use it? Whitman's answer was
"Identify."

But, before Whitman could be, in his own words, likened and
restored, he must deal completely with himself; and I think
there has been no conflict deeper than the nature of that self ever
solved in poetry. . . .

This awareness of Whitman's is a process, lifelong, and
whatever acceptance was finally reached expressed itself in an

Reprinted by permission of Muriel Rukeyser from *The Life of Poetry*
(New York, 1949), 73–85, abridged. *The Life of Poetry* was reprinted
in 1968 by the Kraus-Thomson Organization Ltd.

identification with America as a people, multitudinous and full
of contradictions.

But, first, Whitman needed to accept himself. In the testimony of the poems, this most decisive step was the most difficult.
Every trap was ready, just here. His idealized image was far
from what he knew he was, in the late 1840s. Deeper than the
acts of his living or the image-making of himself, his conflicts
tore him: truth and reality were both at stake, and unless he
could find them both, he would be lost to himself. His struggle
was a struggle for identity.

He faced, not only good, but the *problem* of good.

Among his many faces, how was he to reach and insist on the
good? How was he to be enough for himself, and take the
terrible forms of earth also to be his own? How was he to
identify, to talk of the expression of love for men and women,
and see flashing that America—with its power, war, Congress,
weapons, testimony, and endless gestation? America is what he
identified with: not only the "you" in his lifelong singing of love
and identification, but "me" also.

It was harder for Whitman to identify with himself than with
the "you" of the poems.

To discover his nature as a poet and to make his nature by
knowing it is the task before every poet. But to Walt Whitman,
crowded with contradictions, the fifteen-year-old large as a man,
the conventional verse-maker who learned his own rhythms at
the sea-edge, the discovery of his nature was a continual crisis.
He speaks of himself as ill-assorted, contradictory. His readers
reacted violently from the beginning to his writing about sex—
and of course it is not writing *about* sex, it is that physical
rhythms are the base of every clear line, and that the avowals
and the secrecy are both part of the life of a person who is,
himself, a battleground of forces. . . .

In the short conventional meter of *After the Pleasure Party*,
Melville's bitter pain at

The human integral clove asunder

makes its cry. Melville, however, was speaking of a couple—of
himself as half, needing to mate with the "co-relative," and
crying out for the power to free sex by setting free the sexless

essential man, or by remaking himself. Whitman, also used these terms of need; but the "halves" he fought to bring together were in himself, and he chose, early in his life as a poet, not to allow himself the concept of a central sexless man, but to take the other way: to remake himself.

It is in the remaking of himself that Whitman speaks for the general conflict in our culture. For, in the poems, his discovery of himself is a discovery of America; he is able to give it to anyone who reaches his lines.

Apparent again and again are the relationships with himself, the people, and the "you" of any of the poems. From these relationships, we may derive the fact of his physical split with himself and the heroic quality of his struggle to achieve strength from that conflict. . . . I venture to suggest that the inclusive personality which Whitman created from his own conflict is heroic proof of a life in which apparent antagonisms have been reconciled and purified into art. If this is true, the definitions of good and evil, in relation to Whitman and his sense of possibility, may be re-explored.

The effort to make a balance must have been intense. When Whitman, in an early poem, speaks of the threat of being

> lost to myself, ill-assorted, contradictory,[1]

He shows us the beginning of a long and conscious work performed according to the challenges before a mythical hero. He wrote of the terrible doubt of appearances, and of himself among the shows of the day and night. He spoke of

> the sense of what is real, the thought if
> after all it should prove unreal . . .[2]

This struggle was not a struggle for conformity in the "normal," but for the most intense reality which the individual can achieve, a struggle of process and hope and possibility which we all make when we desire to include our farthest range and then extend the newly-created self into the new again, when we base our desire in the belief that the most real is the most subtle, in art and in life.

It was Whitman's acceptance of his entire nature that made the work possible. The line of a man full of doubt is

I never doubt whether that is really me. . . .[3]

Will went into this work on the self, and there are signs of the achievements here as well as the scars. Whitman is accused by many of showing too much will, and we know how unlikely it is for the efforts of will to lead alone to form. The form of Whitman does not arrive as a product of will, line by line. Each poem follows the curves of its own life in passion; it stands or falls, dies or grows, by that. The form is there, but it is a form of details. For the large work is a double work, and we must seek form in its two expressions: the entire collection of *Leaves of Grass*, and the life-image of Whitman as he made himself, able to identify at last with both the people in their contradictions and himself in his. Able to identify—and this is his inner achievement—with his own spirit, of which his body, his life, his poems are the language.

For Whitman grew to be able to say, out of his own fears,

Be not afraid of my body,[4]

and, out of his own scattering,

I am a dance.[5]

He remembered his body as other poets of his time remembered English verse. Out of his own body, and its relation to itself and the sea, he drew his basic rhythms. They are not the rhythms, as has been asserted, of work and love-making; but rather of the relation of our breathing to our heartbeat, and these measured against an ideal of water at the shore, not beginning nor ending, but endlessly drawing in, making forever its forms of massing and falling among the breakers, seething in the white recessions of its surf, never finishing, always making a meeting-place.

Not out of English prosody but the fluids of organism, not so much from the feet and the footbeat except as they too derive from the rhythms of pulse and lung, Whitman made his music signify. Rarely, in the sweep of lines, is the breath harshened and interrupted. The tension of Hopkins is nearer to activity: it is activity, muscular, violent, and formal. Emily Dickinson's strictness, sometimes almost a slang of strictness, speaks with an intellectually active, stimulated quick music. But Whitman offers us the rhythms of resolved physical conflict. When he says, "I have found the law of my own poems," he celebrates that victory. . . .

Whitman is a "bad influence"; that is, he cannot be imitated. He can, in hilarious or very dull burlesques, be parodied; but anyone who has come under his rhythms to the extent of trying to use them knows how great a folly is there. He cannot be extended; it is as if his own curse on "poems distill'd from poems"[6] were still effective (as it forever is); but what is always possible is to go deeper into one's own sources, the body and the ancient religious poetry, and go on with the work he began.

As for the "cataloguing" lines: it seems to me that they stand in a very clear light, not only among his poems entire, but also in regard to present techniques.

There has been a good deal of regret over the printed poem, since first the press was used; and recently, with the mourning over a supposed breakdown in communication, I have heard simple people and college presidents complain that the function of the poet is past, that the bard is gone. Now it is true that a poem heard does enter very vividly into the consciousness; but, with the habit of reading as widespread as it now is, many prefer to see the poem, at least to see it before hearing it, and this is apart from that number who can imagine better when they read than when they listen. For those who care more for the hearing of poetry, there is the stage and the radio, mediums allowing very little verse to make itself heard, except in such ways as I propose later to show. But, whether a poem is approached through the eyes in a book, or through the ears, the eyes within the eyes, the visual imagination, are reached; and this in itself is a way of reaching the total imagination. This visual summoning may be made often or very seldom, depending on your poet; if the occurrence is well prepared, the impact is unforgettably strong. The visual imagination may be spoken of as including the eyes. The imaginative function includes the senses. It includes, perhaps most easily, a kind of seeing; we are perhaps most used to having sight invoked in the telling of stories and poems.

Whitman draws on this continually, sometimes with a word at a time—

The birth, the hasting after the physician, the beggar's tramp, the
   drunkard's stagger, the laughing party of mechanics,
The escaped youth, the rich person's carriage, the fop, the eloping
   couple,
The early market-man, the hearse, the moving of furniture into the
   town, the return back from the town,
They pass, I also pass—[7]

sometimes these visual summonings are accomplished in a procession of short phrases:

> Passage to more than India!
> O secret of the earth and sky!
> Of you O waters of the sea! O winding creeks and rivers!
> Of you O woods and fields! of you strong mountains of my
>   land!
> Of you O prairies! of you gray rocks!
> O morning red! O clouds! O rain and snows!
> O day and night, passage to you![8]

sometimes they follow each other line after line:

With the fresh sweet herbage under foot, and the pale green leaves
   of the trees prolific,
In the distance the flowing glaze, the breast of the river, with a
   wind-dapple here and there,
With ranging hills on the banks, with many a line against the sky,
   and shadows,
And the city at hand with dwellings so dense, and stacks of chim-
   neys,
And all the scenes of life and the workshops, and the workmen
   homeward returning.[9]

These successions are not to be called catalogues. That name
has thrown readers off; it is misleading. What we are confronted
with here, each time, is not a list, but a sequence with its own
direction. It is visual; it is close to another form, and its purpose
is the same as the purpose which drives this passage:

And Sutter, on his way home—
—passes through the prosperous landscapes of a happy countryside.
Wealth, fertility and contentment can be sensed everywhere.
The rain has ceased . . . Myriads of raindrops shimmer in the
   sunshine.
Suddenly, he meets a group of working people with picks, and pans
   for gold-washing.

Astonished, Sutter follows them with his eyes, then turns his horse
and gallops towards the fort.
The store-keeper from near the fort comes up to Sutter to show him
gold dust in the palm of his hand.
He asks Sutter if this is really gold or not.
Sutter nods slowly.

That sequence describes a key action; in the next few lines,

The dams are taut with their heavy loads, the canal locks are
shattered, and the waters rush through their old courses.

You will recognize the form of that passage, if you imagine it
with your eyes. It is typical, and it is very like Whitman. But it
is a fragment of the script of a movie called *Sutter's Gold*.

Whitman, writing years before the invention of the moving
picture camera, has in his poems given to us sequence after
sequence that might be the detailed instructions, not to the
director and cameramen only, but to the film editor as well. The
rhythm of these sequences is film rhythm, the form is montage;
and movies could easily be made of these poems, in which the
lines in the longer, more sustained speech rhythms would serve
as sound track, while these seemingly broken and choppy descriptive lines would serve well as image track.[10]

HENRY MILLER
[1 8 9 1 –   ]

Letter to Pierre Lesdain (1950)

. . . Let us compare two men who ought really not to be
compared, since one was a novelist and the other a poet: I mean
Dostoievsky and Whitman. I choose them arbitrarily because

for me they represent the peaks in modern literature. Dostoievsky was infinitely more than a novelist, of course, just as Whitman was greater than a poet. But the difference between the two, in my eyes at least, is that Whitman, though the lesser artist, though not as profound, saw bigger than Dostoievsky. He had the cosmic sweep, yes. We speak of him as "the great democrat." Now that particular appelation could never be given Dostoievsky—not because of his religious, political and social beliefs but because Dostoievsky was more and less than a "democrat." (I hope it is understood that when I use the word "democrat" I mean to signify a unique self-sufficient type of individual whose allegiance no government has yet arisen big enough, wise enough, tolerant enough, to include as citizen.) No, Dostoievsky was human in that "all too human" sense of Nietzsche. He wrings our withers when he unrolls his scroll of life. Whitman is impersonal by comparison; he takes in the crowd, the masses, the great swarms of humanity. His eyes are constantly fixed on the potential, the divine potential, in man. He talks brotherhood; Dostoievsky talks fellowship. Dostoievsky stirs us to the depths, causes us to shudder and grimace, to wince, to close our eyes at times. Not Whitman. Whitman has the faculty of looking at everything, divine or demonic, as part of the ceaseless Heraclitean stream. No end, no beginning. A lofty, sturdy wind blows through his poems. There is a healing quality to his vision.

We know that the great problem with Dostoievsky was God. God was no problem for Whitman ever. He was with God, just as the Word was with God, from the very beginning. Dostoievsky had virtually to create God—and what a Herculean task that was! Dostoievsky rose from the depths and, reaching the summit, retained something of the depths about him still. With Whitman I have the image of a man tossing like a cork in a turbulent stream; he is submerged now and then but there is never any danger of his going down for good. The very substance of him prevented that. One may say, of course, that our natures are God-given. We may also say that the Russia of Dostoievsky's day was a far different world from the one Whitman grew up in. But, after acknowledging and giving due emphasis to all the factors which determine the development of character as well as the temperament of an artist, I come back to the question of vision. Both had the prophetic strain; both were imbued with a message for the world. And both saw the world clearly! Both mingled with the world too, let us not forget. From Whitman there exudes a largesse which is godlike; in Dostoievsky there is an intensity and acuity almost superhuman. But the one emphasized the future and the other the present. Dostoievsky, like so many of the Nineteenth Century Russians, is eschatological: he has the Messianic strain. Whitman, anchored firmly in the eternal now, in the flux, is almost indifferent to the fate of the world. He has a hearty, boisterous, good-natured hail-fellow-well-met tone often. He knows au fond that all's well with the world. He knows more. He knows that if there is anything wrong with it, no tinkering on his part will mend it. He knows that the only way to put it to rights, if we must use the expression, is for every living individual to first put himself to rights. His love and compassion for the whore, the beggar, the outcast, the afflicted, delivers him from inspection and examination of social problems. He preaches no dogma, celebrates no Church, recognizes no mediator. He lives outdoors, circulating with the wind, observing the seasons and the revolutions of the heavens. His worship is implicit, and that is why he can do nothing better than sing hosanna the whole day long. He had problems, I know. He had his sore moments, his trials and tribulations. He had his moments of doubt too, perhaps. But they never obtrude in his work. He remains not so much the great democrat as the hail and hearty cosmocrator. He has abundant health and vitality. *There* perhaps I have put my finger on it. (Not that I mean to compare the two physically— the epileptic versus the man of the outdoors. No.) I am talking of the health and vitality which exudes from his language, which reflects, therefore, his inner state of being. Stressing this, I mean to indicate that freedom from cultural cares, the lack of concern for the exacerbating problems of culture, probably had a great deal to do with this tonic quality of his poetry. It spared him those inroads which most European men of culture are at one time or another subject to. Whitman seems almost impervious to the ills of the day. He was not living in the times but in a condition of spiritual fullness. A European has much more difficulty maintaining such a "condition" when he attains it. He is beleaguered on all sides. He must be for or against. He must participate. It is almost impossible for him to be "a world citizen": at the most he can be "a good European." Here too it is getting to be difficult to be above the mêlée, but not impossible. There is the element of chance here which in Europe seems altogether eliminated.

I wonder if I have made clear what I meant to bring out? I was speaking of the fullness of life as it is reflected in literature. It is really the fullness of the world I am concerned with. Whitman is closer to the Upanishads, Dostoievsky to the New Testament. The rich cultural stew of Europe is one kind of fullness, the heavy ore of everyday American life another. Compared to Dostoievsky, Whitman is in a sense empty. It is not the emptiness of the abstract, either. It is rather a divine emptiness. It is the quality of the nameless void out of which sprang chaos. It is the emptiness which precedes creation. Dostoievsky is chaos and fecundity. Humanity, with him, is but a vortex in the bubbling maelstrom. He had it in him to give birth to many orders of humanity. In order to prescribe some livable order he had, one might almost say, to create a God. For himself? Yes. But for all other men and women too. And for the children of this world. Dostoievsky could not live alone, no matter how perfect his life or the life of the world. Whitman could, we feel. And it is Whitman who is called the great democrat. He was that, to be sure. He was because he had achieved self-sufficiency . . . What speculations this thought opens up! Whitman arrived, Dostoievsky still winging his way heavenward. But there is no question of precedence here, no superior or inferior. One is a sun, if you like, the other a star. Lawrence spoke somewhere of Dostoievsky striving to reach the moon of his being. A typical Lawrencian image. Behind it lay a thesis which Lawrence was endeavoring to support. I have no axe to grind: I accept them both, Dostoievsky and Whitman, in essence and in utterance. I have put these two luminaries side by side merely to bring out certain differences. The one seems to me to glow with a human light, and he is thought of as a fanatic, as a demonic being; the other radiates a cool cosmic light, and he is thought of as the brother of all men, as the man in the midst of life. They both *gave* light, that is the important thing. Dostoievsky is all passion, Whitman compassion. A difference in voltage, if you like. In Dostoievsky's work one has the feeling that the angel and the devil walk hand in hand; they understand one another and they are tolerant of one another. Whitman's work is devoid of such entities: there is humanity in the rough, there is Nature grandiose and eternal, and there is the breath of the great Spirit. . . .

In summarizing his pages on Whitman, Bucke makes, among others, the following statements:

> In no man who ever lived was the sense of eternal life so absolute.
> Fear of death was absent. Neither in health nor in sickness did he show any sign of it, and there is every reason to believe he did not feel it.
> He had no sense of sin.[1]

And what of Evil? Suddenly it is Dostoievsky's voice I hear. If there be evil, there can be no God. Was that not the thought which plagued Dostoievsky? Whoever knows Dostoievsky knows the torments he endured because of this conflict. But the rebel and doubter is silenced towards the end, silenced by a magnificent affirmation. . . .

> Love all God's creation and every grain of sand in it. Love every leaf, every ray of God's light. If you love everything, you will preserve the divine mystery of things. (Father Zosima, alias the real Dostoievsky.)

And what of Evil?
Whitman answered thus, not once, but again and again: "And I say there is in fact no evil.". . .

When some pages back I referred to that veiled and distant look in Whitman's eyes, it was not, I hope, to give the impression that I think of him as cold, indifferent, aloof, a man living apart in "Brahmic splendor," and deigning, when the mood seizes him, to mingle with the crowd! The record of his years on the battlefield and in the hospitals should be enough to erase any such suspicion. What greater sacrifice, what greater renouncement of self, could any man have made? He emerged from that experience shattered to the core. He had witnessed more than is humanly demanded of a man. It was not the inroads upon his health that were so cruel, though a great tribulation, but rather the ordeal of too close communion. Much is related of his inexhaustible sympathy. *Empathy* is more nearly the word for it. But the word to describe this enlarged state of feeling is lacking in our tongue.

This experience, which, I repeat, must be compared with Dostoievsky's ordeal in Siberia, incites endless speculation. In both instances it was a Calvary. The inborn brotherly feeling of Dostoievsky, the natural comradely spirit in Whitman, were tested in the fiery crucible by command of Fate. No matter how great the humanity in them, neither would have *elected* for such an experience. (I do not make this remark idly. There have been glorious instances in man's history where individuals did elect to undergo some awesome trial or test. I think of Jesus and Joan of Arc immediately.) Whitman did not rush headlong to volunteer his services as a soldier of the Republic. Dostoievsky did not fling himself into the "movement" in order to prove his capacity for martyrdom. In both instances the situation was thrust upon them. But there, after all, is the test of a man—how he meets the blows of Fate! It was in exile that Dostoievsky really became acquainted with the teachings of Jesus. It was on the battlefield, among the dead and wounded, that Whitman discovered the meaning of abnegation, or better, of service without thought of reward. Only heroic men could have survived such ordeals. Only illuminated men could have transformed these experiences into great messages of love and benediction.

Whitman had seen the light, had received his illumination, some few years before this crucial period in his life. Not so with Dostoievsky. Both had a lesson to learn, and they learned it in the midst of suffering, sickness and death. That insouciant spirit of Whitman underwent a change, a deepening. His "camaraderie" developed into a more passionate acceptance of his fellowman. That look of 1854, the look of a man who is a bit stunned by the vision he has had, changes to a broader and deeper gleam which embraces the whole universe of sentient beings—and the inanimate world as well. His expression is no longer that of one coming from afar but of one who is in the thick of it, who accepts his lot completely, who rejoices in it, come what may. There may be less of the divine in it, but there is more of the purely human. Whitman had need of this humanization. If, as I firmly believe, there took place in him an expansion of consciousness (in 1854 or '55), there had also to take place, unless he were to go mad, a revaluation of all human values. Whitman had to live as a man, not as a god. We know, in Dostoievsky's case, how (via Solovyev probably) this obsession with the idea of a "man-god" persisted. Dostoievsky, illumined from the depths, had to humanize the god in him. Whitman, receiving his illumination from beyond, sought to divinize the man in him. This fecundation of god and man—the man in god, the god in man—had far-reaching effects in both instances. Today it is common to hear that the prophecies of these two great figures have come to nought. Both Russia and America have become thoroughly mechanized, autocratic, tyrannical, materialistic and power mad. But wait! History must run its course. The negative aspect always precedes the positive.

Biographers and critics often take these crucial periods in the life of a subject and, dwelling on "brotherhood" and "universality of spirit," give the impression that it was the mere proximity to suffering and death which developed these attributes in their subjects. But what affected Whitman and Dostoievsky, if I read their characters rightly, was the ceaseless unbaring of the soul which they were made to witness. They were affected, *wounded* is the word, in their souls. Dostoievsky did not go to prison as a social worker, nor Whitman to the battlefield as nurse, doctor, or priest. Dostoievsky was obliged to live the lives of each one of his fellow prisoners because of utter lack of privacy: he lived like a beast, as we know from the records. Whitman had to become nurse, doctor, priest all in one, because there was no one else about who combined these rare gifts. His temperament would never have led him to choose any of these pursuits. But that same animal magnetism—or that same divinity in each— forced these two individuals, under similar stress, to go beyond themselves. An ordinary man, after release from such a situation, might well devote himself for the rest of his days to the care of the unfortunate; he might well conceive it to be his "mission" to thus dedicate his life. But Whitman and Dostoievsky go back to their writing. If they have a mission it will be incorporated in their "message."

If I have not made it clear already, let me say that it was

precisely because they were artists first and foremost that these two men created the special conditions relating to their cruel experience, *and* conditioned themselves to transmute and ennoble the experience. Not all great men are capable of supporting the naked meeting of soul with soul, as was the case with these two. To witness not once, but again and again, the spectacle of a man unbaring his soul is almost beyond human endurance. We do not come forward with our souls ordinarily. A man may lay his heart bare, but not his soul. When a man does expose himself to another in this way there is demanded a response which few men, apparently, are capable of. In some ways I think that Dostoievsky's situation was even more trying than Whitman's. Performing for his fellow-sufferers all the services that Whitman did, he was nevertheless always regarded as one of them, that is, a criminal. Naturally he thought no more of "reward" than Whitman, but his dignity as a human being was ever deprived him. In another sense, of course, it could be said that this very fact made it easier for him to act the "ministering angel." It nullified all thought of *being* an angel. He could see himself as a victim and a sufferer because in fact he was one.

But the important point—let me not lose it!—is that, whether the rôles they assumed were deliberate or forced upon them, it was to these two beings that the anguished souls about them turned instinctively and unerringly. Acting as mediators between God and man, or if not mediators then intercessors, they surpassed the "experts" whose calling they had assumed. The one quality which they had strongly in common was their inability to reject *any* experience. It was their utter humanness which made them capable of accepting the great "responsibility" of suffering. They embraced more than their share because it was a "privilege," not because it was their duty or their mission in life. Thus, all that passed between them and their fellow sufferers went beyond the gamut of ordinary experience. Men saw into their souls and they saw into men's souls. The little self, in each instance, was burned away. When it was over they could not do other than resume their private tasks. They were no longer "men of letters," no, not even artists any more, but deliverers. We know only too well how their respective messages burst the frames of the old vehicles. How could it be otherwise? The revolutionizing of art which they helped bring about, which they initiated to an extent we are not yet properly aware of, was part and parcel of the greater task of transvaluating all human values. Their concern with art was of a different order from that of other celebrated revolutionaries. It was a movement from the center of man's being outward, and the repercussions from that outer sphere (which is still veiled to us) we have yet to hear. But let us not for one moment believe that it was a vain or lost irruption of the spirit. Dostoievsky plunged deeper than any man before letting fly his arrows; Whitman soared higher than any before tuning in to our antennae.

From "Walt Whitman"

I HAVE NEVER UNDERSTOOD why he should be called "the good gray poet." The color of his language, his temperament, his whole being is electric blue. I hardly think of him as poet. Bard, yes. The bard of the future.

America has never really understood Whitman, or accepted him. America has exalted Lincoln, a lesser figure. . . .

The poet in Whitman interests me far less than the seer. Perhaps the only poet with whom he can be compared is Dante. More than any other single figure, Dante symbolizes the medieval world. Whitman is the incarnation of the modern man, of whom thus far we have only had intimations. Modern life has not yet begun. Here and there men have arisen who have given us glimpses of this world to come. Whitman not only voiced the keynote of this new life in process of creation but behaved as if it already existed. The wonder is that he was not crucified. But

Reprinted by permission of New Directions Publishing Corporation from *Stand Still Like a Hummingbird* (New York, 1962), 107–110. These extracts were taken from the chapter on Whitman. Copyright, 1962, by Henry Miller.

here we touch the mystery which shrouds his seemingly open life. . . .

I maintain most stoutly that Whitman's outlook is not American, any more than it is Chinese, Hindu or European. It is the unique view of an emancipated individual, expressed in the broadest American idiom, understandable to men of all languages. The flavor of his language, though altogether American, is a rare one. It has never been captured again. It probably never will. Its universality springs from its uniqueness. In this sense it has all tradition behind it. Yet, I repeat, Whitman had no respect for tradition; that he forged a new language is due entirely to the singularity of his vision, to the fact that he felt himself to be a new being. Between the early Whitman and the "awakened" Whitman there is no resemblance whatever. No one, scanning his early writings, could possibly detect the germ of the future genius. Whitman remade himself from head to foot. . . .

He has been called a pantheist. Many have referred to him as the great democrat. Some have asserted that he possessed a cosmic consciousness. All attempts to label and categorize him eventually break down. Why not accept him as a pure phenomenon? Why not admit that he is without a peer? I am not attempting to divinize him. How could I, since he was so strikingly human? If I insist on the uniqueness of his being, is it not to suggest the clue which will unravel the mysterious claims of democracy?

GUSTAV BYCHOWSKI

[1 8 9 5 –   ]

Walt Whitman—A Study in Sublimation (*1951*)

WALT WHITMAN was not only the greatest American poet but
certainly one of the great poets of our times. He revealed his
innermost feelings and ideas not only in his poetry, but discussed them in his prose and left abundant autobiographic material in the form of diaries and letters. He offers, therefore, a
unique opportunity for the study of artistic expression and sublimation and he is a great temptation to an analyst fascinated by
the problem of artistic creation. He provides an excellent illustration of the power of the creative ego to deal with its difficulties, to make use of the most disturbing elemental forces. To
establish the connection between such primitive elements and
sublime operations of the creative mind offers an unusual insight
into the intricate ways of sublimation.

   Whitman's poetic production gives us some information
about the early struggles of his ego and about his attitude
toward reality. In a poem entitled "There Was a Child Went
Forth Every Day," he describes with unusual lucidity the processes of early introjection and identification.

And the first object he look'd upon, that object he became,
And that object became part of him for the day or a certain part of
      the day,
Or for many years or stretching cycles of years.

Reprinted by permission of International Universities Press, Inc., from
Psychoanalysis and the Social Sciences, 3 (1951), 223–261, abridged. I
have corrected Bychowski's errors in transcription.

This process then applies more specifically to his parents.

His own parents, he that had father'd him, and she that had
    conceiv'd him in her womb and birth'd him,
They gave this child more of themselves than that,
They gave him afterward every day, they became part of him.

Strangely enough what we learn about the attitude of young
Walt toward reality indicates very early and very acute feelings
of depersonalization.

    In the above-quoted poem we read:

The family usages, the language, the company, the furniture, the
    yearning and swelling heart,
Affection that will not be gainsay'd, the sense of what is real, the
    thought if after all it should prove unreal,
The doubts of day-time and the doubts of night-time, the curious
    whether and how,
Whether that which appears so is so, or is it all flashes and specks?
Men and women crowding fast in the streets, if they are not flashes
    and specks what are they? . . .[1]

    This early anguish about outward reality and about his own
ego was closely interwoven with the anguish of love. One of
Whitman's most moving poems contains an eloquent testimony
of those early sufferings and at the same time a clear indication
as to their eventual outcome in the evolution of the poet. It may
seem almost sacrilegious to analyze the gem of tender poetry,
called "Out Of The Cradle Endlessly Rocking." I take it that
every reader knows it or will refresh his memory by reading it
again. This poem taps the deep unconscious sources so as to
convey to the reader the world of early emotions, well-nigh the
beginnings of individual self-awareness, the birth of the ego,
born in pain of love.

    The unhappy male bird bereaved by the loss of his mate and
mourning her in a song unleashes in the boy, Walt—that is in
the "outsetting bard"—"the love in the heart long pent, now
loose, now at last tumultuously bursting." The future poet
identifies himself with this unfortunate lover:

O you singer solitary, singing by yourself, projecting me,
O solitary me listening, never more shall I cease perpetuating you,
Never more shall I escape, never more the reverberations,
Never more the cries of unsatisfied love be absent from me,

Never again leave me to be the peaceful child I was before what
    there in the night,
By the sea under the yellow and sagging moon,
The messenger there arous'd, the fire, the sweet hell within,
The unknown want, the destiny of me.

However, it seems as though the future poet would identify
himself not only with the unhappy lover but also with his lost
companion.

Demon or bird (said the boy's soul,)
Is it indeed toward your mate you sing, or is it really to me?[2]

The "clew" for which the poet asks, "the word final, superior to
all" is revealed to him by the sea, the "old mother." It is she,
who, while closing the song by the same initial theme of infancy
("Or like some old crone rocking the cradle, swathed in sweet
garments, bending aside") whispers the word "Death," "the
key, the word up from the waves, / The word of the sweetest
song and all songs, / That strong and delicious word . . ."

When we reduce the poignant beauty of this poem to its
unconscious core, we see the first separation of infancy, the first
anguish of infantile love underlying all the future pain of love.
Sweet death emerges then as the great benefactor, as a supreme
salvation, since it promises a reunion with the beloved mother,
earth, sea, and maybe the universe. . . .

We may assume that fear of death, which we have pointed
out in Whitman's poems, was a reaction of his ego to this early
yearning. It was the fright of annihilation for which it was
secretly longing, as a way of restoring the lost dual unity with
his mother. The ultimate overcoming of this fear seems to be the
acceptance of Death as most convincingly acclaimed in some
poems written in the period of decline and assembled under the
significant title: "Whispers of Heavenly Death." In "Assurances," death is being affirmed as "purport of life," in "Night
on the Prairies," death appears as a way of achieving ultimate
knowledge, understanding of the last truth which was beyond
reach when the greed of life was at its peak—a truly mystic-reli-
gious insight with an obvious, although unconscious motivation.

O, I see now that life cannot exhibit all to me, as the day cannot,
I see that I am to wait for what will be exhibited by death.[3]

With Whitman's early longing for a return to mother, it is easy to understand that not only outward reality must have appeared as something vague but the same must have been true for his ego, never completely freed from its prenatal fixation. Therefore, since the boundaries of his ego were unusually fleeting, it was either yearning for and actually merging with its place of origin or in self-defense and compensation trying to assert itself in glory and importance. These attempts at reassertion could not help, as a true defense mechanism, swinging the ego to the other extremes, namely to reaffirmation of primary narcissism and early megalomania. . . .

After this we are well prepared for the hymn to the body in "I Sing the Body Electric." John Burroughs traces the poems of both groups—"Children of Adam" and "Calamus"—to this period of body erotism.

We pause a while to consider the veiled confessions of the former "sinner" laboring under the feeling of guilt and shame.

Was it doubted that those who corrupt their own bodies conceal themselves?
And if those who defile the living are as bad as they who defile the dead?
And if the body does not do fully as much as the soul?
And if the body were not the soul, what is the soul?

And later again:

Have you seen the fool that corrupted his own live body? or the fool that corrupted her own live body?
For they do not conceal themselves, and cannot conceal themselves.[4]

And then comes a praise of the body and all its parts, a true enumeration of limbs and organs. This enumeration reminds us of a general characteristic of some of Walt Whitman's poems which a malevolent critic once characterized as a catalogue. In connection with our previous remarks, I would venture the suggestion that this feature is an expression of elation originating in the rediscovery of objects outside and inside the limits of ego boundaries, it is the joy of Adam, the first man, naming the objects of creation. . . .

However, the most important gateway of both introjection and projection,[5] the most libidinized sensual perception, seems to be to our poet, the sense of touch. He recreates his craving for a love companion through the sense of touch.

As if a phantom caress'd me,
I thought I was not alone walking here by the shore;
But the one I thought was with me as now I walk by the shore, the one I loved that caress'd me,
As I lean and look through the glimmering light, that one has utterly disappear'd,
And those appear that are hateful to me and mock.[6]

In his all-pervading, supreme desire to embrace reality, the poet speaks of touch as of the most important way of achieving this goal:

The atmosphere is not a perfume, it has no taste of the distillation, it is odorless,
It is for my mouth forever, I am in love with it,
I will go to the bank by the wood and become undisguised and naked,
I am mad for it to be in contact with me.[7]

("Song of Myself")

This extremely sensitive poignant tactile perception helps the poet to maintain the contact with reality for which he hungers with all his soul, yet the libidinization is so strong that the ego—in danger of being completely submerged—has to defend itself.

Mine is no callous shell,
I have instant conductors all over me whether I pass or stop
They seize every object and lead it harmlessly through me

I merely stir, press, feel with my fingers, and am happy,
To touch my person to some one else's is about as much as I can stand.

Is this then a touch? quivering me to a new identity,
Flames and ether making a rush for my veins,
Treacherous tip of me reaching and crowding to help them,
My flesh and blood playing out lightning to strike what is hardly different from myself.

You villain touch! what are you doing? my breath is tight in its throat,
Unclench your floodgates, you are too much for me.

Blind loving wrestling touch, sheath'd hooded sharp-tooth'd touch!
Did it make you ache so, leaving me?[8]

And finally in a revealing notebook poem Whitman tells us how
submerged he became by the sense of touch—an all-absorbing,
delightfully painful sensation, culminating in sexual ecstasy
and, at the same time, opening the gates for the absorption of
total reality.

They have left me to touch, and taken their place on a headland.
The sentries have deserted every part of me
They have left me helpless to the torrent of touch
They have all come to the headland to witness and assist against me.

There is in these lines a poignant, almost pathetic description of
the submission of the ego which became overwhelmed by libidinal sensation and surrendered to them with a characteristic
passive-masochistic delight. Here the autoerotic element struggles with the imperative desire to transcend the boundaries of
the ego, since the ego is unable to contain so much delight: "I
did not think I was big enough for so much ecstasy / Or that a
touch could take it all out of me."[9]

With floods of libido pent up and held back by dams of
repression and secondarily increased autoerotism Whitman attempts to produce his love objects in fantasy instead of finding
them in the outside world. The reaffirmation of his bodily and
mental ego, the soul, helps him in this process and prepares him
for the final extraversion of libido—extraversion which, however, will never deny its narcissistic origin.

Stanza 5 of the "Song of Myself" is extremely revealing of
those never-terminated processes. [Bychowski quotes the famous lines, 87–98.] It seems as though the understanding of
these lines might provide the key for insight into the core of the
processes of sublimation. The borderline between the narcissistic and object libido begins to be transcended. The feeling of
guilt attached to sex is lifted and libido is recognized as a
general force pervading the universe. From here, then, the path
leads toward the overcoming of original inhibitions, loneliness
and isolation; the path also leads to mystico-philosophical ideas
of identity which reaffirm unity and overcome separation
anxiety. . . .

Tied up in his narcissism, Whitman cannot get away from his mother fixation. Toward her, he still feels the same attachment of a dependent child, full of boundless admiration, and her death in his fifty-fourth year comes as a great shock and leaves him deeply disturbed and perplexed.

Throughout his adult existence Whitman identified himself with his beloved mother. This identification manifested itself in a double way. On the one hand, his affection for young men was full of maternity, as apparent, e.g., from his correspondence with Peter Doyle. He inquires about Peter's health with truly maternal solicitude and upon learning about a cold from which the boy, Pete, as he calls him, suffers, Whitman assures him that he is "already sick himself." "Everything is very complete and correct here—but O, I need your dear loving face and hand and voice." He orders some shirts for his "dear boy," the same shirts he has himself and he explains: "I like mine so well, I have had yours made like them." He suffers from their separation, but it is a great comfort to him that his feelings are shared by his friend. "I never dreamed that you made so much of having me with you, nor that you could feel so downcast at losing me. I foolishly thought it was all on the other side." And in a pathetic letter written as an afterthought, after Peter had confessed to him that he was thinking of suicide, he assures him: "My love for you is indestructible, and since that night and morning has returned more than before. Dear Peter, dear son, my darling boy, my young and loving brother, don't let the devil put such thoughts in your head again—wickedness unspeakable—death and disgrace here, and hell's agonies hereafter—then what would it be afterward to the mother, what to me?"[10]

This attitude blossomed in its full during his charitable services in the Civil War. Whitman loved the sick and wounded soldiers as a devoted mother (as ascertained by witnesses), which to a great extent explains his magnetic influence upon them. He is quoted (by Mrs. Ellen M. Calder)[11] as saying that he did not envy men their wives but that he did envy them their children. He was full of praise for mothers, and what he found most glorious, he said, was to be a woman and a mother.

. . . Out of this feminine identification sprang his fervent admiration for manifestations of virility in other men and his constant craving for contact with their maleness. In other words, here we put our finger on one of the essential sources of Whitman's homoerotism. It would fill pages to quote all the exclamations in which Whitman sings his admiration of virility. At times it seems as though he felt a truly feminine cult of manliness and of the phallos. . . .[12] In the terms of his studies on homosexuality, the writer can also describe this development as follows: Because of his prenatal, narcissistic and maternal fixation, Whitman's masculine ego never fully developed. In his incessant desire to build it up, to replenish it, he was searching for other, truly "manly" men. To substantiate this point by quotations would be simple enough. Not satisfied with their "manliness," Whitman wants his men rude, "low," as if in self-defense against his own feminine delicate sensitivity! . . .[13] This exultation and this ever-burning desire of virility find their climax in the fantasy of himself as "the begetter of splendid men."[14] The latter appear, then, as an expression of his narcissistic projection. In his fantasy he creates men only to make them objects of his love. This consideration sheds more additional light on the structure of his homosexuality. Real men to him were a screen on which to project his own imaginary narcissistic concept of virility, and he was bound to adore those figures of his own creation and to consume himself in such eternal longing:

Behold me well-clothed going gayly or returning in the afternoon,
    my brood of tough boys accompanying me,
My brood of grown and part-grown boys, who love to be with no one
    else so well as they love to be with me,
By day to work with me, and by night to sleep with me.[15]

It becomes clear that in his immense longing for "manly love" Whitman blended into one powerful drive, his desire to build up his own, never fully developed, virility and his narcissistic love for his own infantile image, upon which he bestowed all the emanation of his maternal love.

It took him some time before he could praise this love as a happy and fulfilled one. Before he could reach this paradise, he had to go through a purgatory of unrequited longing, resulting in feelings of loneliness and dejection. Many steps had to be taken before he could reach this stage of happy fulfillment. He had to free himself from the feeling of guilt and shame originating in his bisexuality and autoerotism with additional oedipal and inverted oedipal implications. Thus after sex and libido received their full recognition, the ego was cleansed from guilt and could give way to libidinal strivings without castigations from the superego. A veritable *tour de force* was performed when the poet proclaimed his "effusion of egotism,"[16] that is, when he succeeded in overcoming the gap between his immense narcissism and his desire for universal love. . . .

Whitman's identification with God has little in common with the humility of a true mystic. It is rather an identification with the all-powerful father, and as such, a reaction meant to overcome old feelings of inferiority and oedipal guilt. At last Whitman can proudly declare: "I never yet knew how it felt to think I stood in the presence of my superior,"[17] as it was only natural for a poet who "avowedly chanted the great pride of man in himself."[18] However, in this reaction he obviously swings to the opposite extreme and revives old sources of primary narcissism, so much so, that his megalomania seems to merge in a fantastic paraphrenia. . . .

This opens the question of the relations between the poet and his father. We have very little direct material for our construction on this subject, since, in contrast to his mother, Whitman mentions his father quite rarely. However, both references to Whitman senior that this writer was able to notice, are quite eloquent when confronted with the general blackout. . . .[19]

If we confront all these data with the consuming desire and longing for love of strong men exuding from Whitman's poems, then it will seem probable that this deep wish may be at least partly due to his early feeling of disappointment in fatherly love. It is a matter of pure conjecture as to what extent this disappointment was due to the attitude of Whitman senior who must have felt irritated by this son, so different from his own sober practical stock, and how much it was a result of deep and violent oedipal conflicts raging in the young Walt.

As in so many of our clinical observations, these conflicts might have ended deep hostility for the father. However, the positive frustrated component of this deeply ambivalent relationship became transferred to other men who in Walt's fantasy would act as true substitutes for the beloved and hated parent. At first they seemed out of reach, in perfect analogy to the distant and yet deeply craved-for father. "All this diseased, feverish disproportionate adhesiveness" for which the poet admonishes himself in his Notebook, would then appear as a derivative of this deeply frustrated early filial love.

It was only in the mystical identification with God, that the poet could at last achieve a sublimated fulfillment of his frustrated longing for his father. . . .

. . . The purpose of this long quotation is[20] to indicate the way by which he achieved a salvation from a potential paraphrenia. In his poetic creation, the poet could sublimate his primary narcissism and could gratify his megalomania, without the psychotic denial of reality. Of this, he was fully aware as he was of the sources of his poetic sublimation. In his prefaces to the various editions of *Leaves* in his "Democratic Vista" and finally in such poems as e.g., "By Blue Ontario's Shore," he not only claims full compensation for all the gloomy years of weakness and inadequacy but grandiloquently exults his poetic and prophetic role. On the magnificent setting of growing American democracy, object of his pride and admiration, he sees in shining light his own magnificent role. . . .[21] It seems quite clear that by his poetic creation, Whitman did not only regain faith in himself, but also found gratification for his narcissism. Moreover, this fulfillment was of such a nature as to help him transcend the limitations of his own ego and, in so doing, escape what might have been a psychotic overcathexis. His poetic creation was to him a powerful instrument for integrating his ego into the expanding Whole of young American democracy. From autoerotic solitude on the shores of Paumanok he boldly leaped into the world of other human beings, no longer fearing rejection but with a growing feeling of acceptance and spiritual leadership. . . .

It is because of those vicissitudes of his unrequited love that the poet felt more and more compelled to widen the scope of his libido and to shift from the desire of individual and direct gratification to the longing for universal love with, by and large, spiritual attributes. In other words, we can see here the process of sublimation. Moreover, along with this achievement, the growing faith in himself and in his great mission could definitely take the place of former melancholic dejection.

This double achievement is perhaps most poignantly expressed in the "Passage to India," ostensibly an occasional poem celebrating the almost simultaneous completion of the Suez waterway to the East and the transcontinental railway to the West, but in reality a poem which he declared contained more of his real spiritual autobiography than any other he ever wrote. Here Whitman was identifying himself with the true Son of God and was making true the wonderful hopes and self-praise he had expressed in his self-written reviews. Manly love became sublimated to the all-embracing brotherhood of man which transcended limits of time and space and thus was rapidly acquiring a mystical swing.

> O soul, repressless, I with thee and thou with me,
> Thy circumnavigation of the world begin,
> Of man, the voyage of his mind's return,
> To reason's early paradise,
> Back, back to wisdom's birth, to innocent intuition,
> Again with fair creation.

Yet, despite all the veil of sublimation, the poet embarking on the voyage of spiritual liberation takes up an old image which at some earlier time was unmistakably sexual and which now reappears in a highly purified form:

O, we can wait no longer,
We too take ship O soul,
Joyous we too launch out on trackless seas,
Fearless for unknown shores on waves of ecstasy to sail,
Amid the wafting winds, (thou pressing me to thee, I thee to me, O
    soul,)
Caroling free, singing our songs of God,
Chanting our chant of pleasant exploration.[22]

Of this process of mystical sublimation, a particularly illuminating illustration should be noted. "There was in a note-book of 1862–3 a poem of the Calamus type comparing the spider throwing out experimental anchors of silk to the individual soldier seeking his proper comrade and lover. But when the poem was perfected in structure and published among the 'Whispers of Heavenly Death' in 1871 it contained but one note

—that of religious mysticism, the soul's outreaching for reality."
. . .[23] In these peaks of mysticism and spiritual liberation the
chant of death seems to be strikingly close to the praise of life.
Even if this motive had appeared in Whitman's poetry at an
earlier time, it seems as though with progressing sublimation,
the *motif* of death had gained a powerful ascendance. Was this
apparent triumph of the death instinct a premonition of approaching decline of vitality or should we consider it, rather, as
a necessary prerequisite for such a highly advanced sublimation? . . .

Thus democracy really means—at least for Whitman—the
brotherhood of men. "And topping democracy, this most allur-
ing record that it alone can bind, and ever seeks to bind, all
nations, all men, of however various and distant lands, into a
brotherhood, a family." Whitman knew only too well the pain
of narcissistic isolation. However, there is "not that half only,
individualism, which isolates. There is another half, which is
adhesiveness or love that fuses, ties and aggregates, making the
race comrades, and fraternizing all."[24] What then about that
other half, "individualism that isolates"? It seems as though the
proud proclamation and happy acceptance of "adhesiveness" as
the general principle of ideal society, were the necessary prerequisite for a final recognition paid by Whitman, without any
feeling of guilt, to the principle of individuality as the great
underlying principle of democracy. This acceptance is obviously
impossible as long as an aggressive, stern, intolerant, fanatical
superego prevails and with rare self-awareness the poet is able
to articulate the liberation from this kind of conscience not only
for himself but for the democratic society at large. In so doing,
he certainly most strikingly anticipates the discoveries of psychoanalysis.

I am reminded as I write that out of this very conscience, or
idea of conscience of intense moral right, and in its name and
strain'd construction, the worst fanaticisms, wars, persecutions,
murders, etc. have yet in all lands, in the past been broach'd and
have come to their devilish fruition. . . . Conscience, too, isolated from all else, and from the emotional nature, may but
attain the beauty and purity of glacial, snowy ice.

After these preliminaries the way is paved for a simultaneous recognition of both essential principles of democracy, that is of society based on brotherhood of men and the recognition of the sacred rights of the individual. What Whitman has proclaimed in his poems, becomes at last verbalized in a more systematic and clear way; the respect of the individual, any individual, not only the leading and the important "Me." Having been able to identify himself with the "felons and with assassins, with the weak and miserable, sufferers on this earth," he cannot condemn them, since he cannot condemn himself. Therefore he is far from showering exaggerated praise on people as such, a development so characteristic of revolutionary fanaticism from Robespierre to Communism. "We do not, (at any rate I do not,) put it either on the ground that the People, the masses, even the best of them, are, in their latent or exhibited qualities, essentially sensible and good—nor on the ground of their rights; but that good or bad, rights or no rights, the democratic formula is the only safe and preservative one for coming times."[25]

However, identification with and recognition of other individuals permits the poet to proclaim the right of the individual being, to assert himself and thus to emphasize the individuality as the other great principle of democracy.

This sublimated, I should say, this tame, narcissism (egotism in Whitman's terminology), received its higher praise from a poet who, at last, succeeded in solving the great dilemma of his spiritual life: "There is, in sanest hours, a consciousness, a thought that rises, independent, lifted out from all else, calm, like the stars, shining eternal. This is the thought of identity—yours for you, whoever you are, as mine for me."[26]

Thus at last Whitman completely overcame his narcissistic isolation. Blending himself with the splendidly growing young American democracy, he found a screen of tremendous magnitude on which to project his own dearest desires and ideas. In this reunion, he could at last achieve happiness. He could find and reassert his own ego, but also his origins from the oceanic and maternal cradle, the original unity with his mother. He could love others with all the implications of his love hungry heart and he could love them without ever stopping to love himself. He could effuse "egotism" and yet proclaim the religion of brotherhood and true humanity.

[215

RANDALL JARRELL

[1914–1965]

Some Lines from Whitman (1953)

WHITMAN, Dickinson, and Melville seem to me the best poets of the 19th Century here in America. Melville's poetry has been grotesquely underestimated, but of course it is only in the last four or five years that it has been much read; in the long run, in spite of the awkwardness and amateurishness of so much of it, it will surely be thought well of. (In the short run it will probably be thought entirely too well of. Melville is a great poet only in the prose of *Moby Dick.*) Dickinson's poetry has been thoroughly read, and well though undifferentiatingly loved—after a few decades or centuries almost everybody will be able to see through Dickinson to her poems. But something odd has happened to the living changing part of Whitman's reputation: nowadays it is people who are not particularly interested in poetry, people who say that they read a poem for what it says, not for how it says it, who admire Whitman most. Whitman is often written about, either approvingly or disapprovingly, as if he were the Thomas Wolfe of 19th Century democracy, the hero of a de Mille movie about Walt Whitman. (People even talk about a war in which Walt Whitman and Henry James chose up sides, to begin with, and in which you and I will go on

Reprinted by permission of Alfred A. Knopf, Inc., from *Poetry and the Age* (New York, 1953), 101–120. Copyright, 1952, 1953, by Randall Jarrell. The essay appeared earlier as "Walt Whitman: He Had His Nerve," *Kenyon Review*, XIV (Winter 1952), 63–71, and with the later title in *Perspectives*, no. 2 (Winter 1953), 61–77.

fighting till the day we die.) All this sort of thing, and all the bad poetry that there of course is in Whitman—for any poet has written enough bad poetry to scare away anybody—has helped to scare away from Whitman most "serious readers of modern poetry." They do not talk of his poems, as a rule, with any real liking or knowledge. Serious readers, people who are ashamed of not knowing all Hopkins by heart, are not at all ashamed to say, "I don't really know Whitman very well." This may harm Whitman in your eyes, they know, but that is a chance that poets have to take. Yet "their" Hopkins, that good critic and great poet, wrote about Whitman, after seeing five or six of his poems in a newspaper review: "I may as well say what I should not otherwise have said, that I always knew in my heart Walt Whitman's mind to be more like my own than any other man's living. As he is a very great scoundrel this is not a very pleasant confession."[1] And Henry James, the leader of "their" side in that awful imaginary war of which I spoke, once read Whitman to Edith Wharton (much as Mozart used to imitate, on the piano, the organ) with such power and solemnity that both sat shaken and silent; it was after this reading that James expressed his regret at Whitman's "too extensive acquaintance with the foreign languages."[2] Almost all the most "original and advanced" poets and critics and readers of the last part of the 19th Century thought Whitman as original and advanced as themselves, in manner as well as in matter. Can Whitman really be a sort of Thomas Wolfe or Carl Sandburg or Robinson Jeffers or Henry Miller—or a sort of Balzac of poetry, whose every part is crude but whose whole is somehow great? He is not, nor could he be; a poem, like Pope's spider, "lives along the line," and all the dead lines in the world will not make one live poem. As Blake says, "all sublimity is founded on minute discrimination," and it is in these "minute particulars" of Blake's that any poem has its primary existence.

To show Whitman for what he is one does not need to praise or explain or argue, one needs simply to quote. He himself said, "I and mine do not convince by arguments, similes, rhymes,/ We convince by our presence."[3] Even a few of his phrases are enough to show us that Whitman was no sweeping rhetorician, but a poet of the greatest and oddest delicacy and originality and sensitivity, so far as words are concerned. This is, after all, the poet who said, "Blind loving wrestling touch, sheath'd hooded sharp-tooth'd touch"; who said, "Smartly attired, countenance smiling, form upright, death under the breast-bones, hell under the skull-bones"; who said, "Agonies are one of my changes of garments"; who saw grass as the "flag of my disposition," saw "the sharp-peak'd farm house, with its scallop'd scum and slender shoots from the gutters," heard a plane's "wild ascending lisp," and saw and heard how at the amputation "what is removed drops horribly in a pail."[4] This is the poet for whom the sea was "howler and scooper of storms," reaching out to us with "crooked inviting fingers"; who went "leaping chasms with a pike-pointed staff, clinging to topples of brittle and blue"; who, a run-away slave, saw how "my gore dribs, thinn'd with the ooze of my skin"; who went "lithographing Kronos . . . buying drafts of Osiris"; who stared out at the "little plentiful manikins skipping around in collars and tail'd coat,/ I am aware who they are, (they are positively not worms or fleas)."[5] For he is, at his best, beautifully witty: he says gravely, "I find I incorporate gneiss, coals, long-threaded moss, fruits, grains, esculent roots,/ And am stucco'd with quadrupeds and birds all over"; and of these quadrupeds and birds "not one is respectable or unhappy over the whole earth."[6] He calls advice: "Unscrew the locks from the doors!/ Unscrew the doors themselves from their jambs!"[7] He publishes the results of research: "Having pried through the strata, analyzed to a hair, counsel'd with doctors and calculated close,/ I find no sweeter fat than sticks to my own bones."[8] Everybody remembers how he told the Muse to "cross out please those immensely overpaid accounts,/ That matter of Troy and Achilles' wrath, and Æneas', Odysseus' wanderings," but his account of the arrival of the "illustrious emigré" here in the New World is even better: "Bluff'd not a bit by drain-pipe, gasometers, artificial fertilizers,/ Smiling and pleas'd with palpable intent to stay,/ She's here, install'd amid the kitchen ware."[9] Or he sees, like another Breughel, "the mechanic's wife with her babe at her nipple interceding for every person born,/ Three scythes at harvest whizzing in a row from three lusty angels with shirts bagg'd out at their waists,/ The snag-tooth'd hostler with red hair redeeming sins past and to come"[10]—the passage has enough wit not only (in Johnson's phrase) to keep it sweet, but enough to make it believable. He says:

> I project my hat, sit shame-faced, and beg.
>
> Enough! enough! enough!
> Somehow I have been stunn'd. Stand back!
> Give me a little time beyond my cuff'd head, slumbers,
>   dreams, gaping,
> I discover myself on the verge of a usual mistake.[11]

There is in such changes of tone as these the essence of wit. And Whitman is even more far-fetched than he is witty; he can say about Doubters, in the most improbable and explosive of juxtapositions: "I know every one of you, I know the sea of torment, doubt, despair and unbelief./ How the flukes splash!/ How they contort rapid as lightning, with spasms and spouts of blood!"[12] Who else would have said about God: "As the hugging and loving bed-fellow sleeps at my side through the night, and withdraws at the peep of the day with stealthy tread,/ Leaving me baskets cover'd with white towels swelling the house with their plenty"?[13]—the Psalmist himself, his cup running over, would have looked at Whitman with dazzled eyes. (Whitman was persuaded by friends to hide the fact that it was God he was talking about.) He says, "Flaunt of the sunshine I need not your bask—lie over!"[14] This unusual employment of verbs is usual enough in participle-loving Whitman, who also asks you to "look in my face while I snuff the sidle of evening," or tells you, "I effuse my flesh in eddies, and drift it in lacy jags."[15] Here are some typical beginnings of poems: "City of orgies, walks, and joys. . . . Not heaving from my ribb'd breast only. . . . O take my hand Walt Whitman! Such gliding wonders! Such sights and sounds! Such join'd unended links. . . ." He says to the objects of the world, "You have waited, you always wait, you dumb, beautiful ministers"; sees "the sun and stars that float in the open air,/ The apple-shaped earth"; says, "O suns— O grass of graves— O perpetual transfers and promotions,/ If you do not say any thing how can I say any thing?"[16] Not many poets have written better, in queerer and more convincing and more individual language, about the

world's *gliding wonders:* the phrase seems particularly right for
Whitman. He speaks of those "circling rivers the breath," of
the "savage old mother incessantly crying,/ To the boy's soul's
questions sullenly timing, some drown'd secret hissing"—ends a
poem, once, "We have voided all but freedom and all but our
own joy."[17] How can one quote enough? If the reader thinks that
all this is like Thomas Wolfe he *is* Thomas Wolfe; nothing else
could explain it. Poetry like this is as far as possible from the
work of any ordinary rhetorician, whose phrases cascade over us
like suds of the oldest and most-advertised detergent.

The interesting thing about Whitman's worst language (for,
just as few poets have ever written better, few poets have ever
written worse) is how unusually absurd, how really ingeniously
bad, such language is. I will quote none of the most famous
examples; but even a line like *O culpable! I acknowledge—I
exposé!*[18] is not anything that you and I could do—only a man
with the most extraordinary feel for language, or none whatsoever, could have cooked up Whitman's worst messes. For
instance: what other man in all the history of this planet would
have said, "I am a habitan of Vienna"?[19] (One has an immediate
vision of him as a sort of French-Canadian halfbreed to whom
the Viennese are offering, with trepidation, through the bars of
a zoological garden, little mounds of whipped cream.) And
enclaircise—why, it's as bad as *explicate!* We are right to resent
his having made up his own horrors, instead of sticking to the
ones that we ourselves employ. But when Whitman says, "I
dote on myself, there is that lot of me and all so luscious,"[20] we
should realize that we are not the only ones who are amused.
And the queerly bad and merely queer and queerly good will
often change into one another without warning: "Hefts of the
moving world at innocent gambols silently rising freshly
exuding,/ Scooting obliquely high and low"—not good, but
queer!—suddenly becomes, "Something I cannot see puts upward libidinous prongs,/ Seas of bright juice suffuse heaven,"[21]
and it is sunrise.

But it is not in individual lines and phrases, but in passages of
some length, that Whitman is at his best. In the following
quotation Whitman has something difficult to express, something that there are many formulas, all bad, for expressing; he

expresses it with complete success, in language of the most dazzling originality:

The orchestra whirls me wider than Uranus flies,
It wrenches such ardors from me I did not know I possess'd them,
It sails me, I dab with bare feet, they are lick'd by the indolent waves,
I am cut by bitter and angry hail, I lose my breath,
Steep'd amid honey'd morphine, my windpipe throttled in fakes of death,
At length let up again to feel the puzzle of puzzles,
And that we call Being.[22]

One hardly knows what to point at—everything works. But *wrenches* and *did not know I possess'd them;* the incredible *it sails me, I dab with bare feet; lick'd by the indolent; steep'd amid honey'd morphine; my windpipe throttled in fakes of death* —no wonder Crane admired Whitman! This originality, as absolute in its way as that of Berlioz' orchestration, is often at Whitman's command:

I am a dance—play up there! the fit is whirling me fast!
I am the ever-laughing—it is new moon and twilight,
I see the hiding of douceurs, I see nimble ghosts whichever way I look,
Cache and cache again deep in the ground and sea, and where it is neither ground nor sea.
Well do they do their jobs those journeymen divine,
Only from me can they hide nothing, and would not if they could,
I reckon I am their boss and they make me a pet besides,
And surround me and lead me and run ahead when I walk,
To lift their cunning covers to signify me with stretch'd arms, and resume the way;
Onward we move, a gay gang of blackguards! with mirth-shouting music and wild-flapping pennants of joy![23]

If you did not believe Hopkins' remark about Whitman, that *gay gang of blackguards* ought to shake you. Whitman shares Hopkins' passion for "dappled" effects, but he slides in and out of them with ambiguous swiftness. And he has at his command a language of the calmest and most prosaic reality, one that seems to do no more than present:

The little one sleeps in its cradle.
I lift the gauze and look a long time, and silently brush away flies with my hand.

The youngster and the red-faced girl turn aside up the bushy hill,
I peeringly view them from the top.

The suicide sprawls on the bloody floor of the bedroom.
I witness the corpse with its dabbled hair, I note where the pistol has
fallen.[24]

It is like magic: that is, something has been done to us without
our knowing how it was done; but if we look at the lines again
we see the *gauze, silently, youngster, red-faced, bushy, peeringly, dabbled*—not that this is all we see. "Present! present!"
said James; these are presented, put down side by side to form a
little "view of life," from the cradle to the last bloody floor of
the bedroom. Very often the things presented form nothing but
a list:

The pure contralto sings in the organ loft,
The carpenter dresses his plank, the tongue of his foreplane whistles
    its wild ascending lisp,
The married and unmarried children ride home to their Thanksgiv-
    ing dinner,
The pilot seizes the king-pin, he heaves down with a strong arm,
The mate stands braced in the whale-boat, lance and harpoon are
    ready,
The duck-shooter walks by silent and cautious stretches,
The deacons are ordain'd with cross'd hands at the altar,
The spinning-girl retreats and advances to the hum of the big wheel,
The farmer stops by the bars as he walks on a First-day loafe and
    looks at the oats and rye,
The lunatic is carried at last to the asylum a confirm'd case,
(He will never sleep any more as he did in the cot in his mother's
    bed-room;)
The jour printer with gray head and gaunt jaws works at his case,
He turns his quid of tobacco while his eyes blurr with the manu-
    script;
The malform'd limbs are tied to the surgeon's table,
What is removed drops horribly in a pail; . . .

It is only a list—but what a list! And how delicately, in what
different ways—likeness and opposition and continuation and
climax and anticlimax—the transitions are managed, whenever
Whitman wants to manage them. Notice them in the next
quotation, another "mere list":

The bride unrumples her white dress, the minute-hand of the clock
    moves slowly,

The opium-eater reclines with rigid head and just-open'd lips,
The prostitute draggles her shawl, her bonnet bobs on her tipsy and
    pimpled neck. . . .

The first line is joined to the third by *unrumples* and *draggles,*
white dress and *shawl;* the second to the third by *rigid head,*
bobs, tipsy, neck; the first to the second by slowly, *just-open'd,*
and the slowing-down of time in both states. And occasionally
one of these lists is metamorphosed into something we have no
name for; the man who would call the next quotation a mere list
—anybody will feel this—would boil his babies up for soap:

Ever the hard unsunk ground,
Ever the eaters and drinkers, ever the upward and downward sun,
    ever the air and the ceaseless tides,
Ever myself and my neighbors, refreshing, wicked, real,
Ever the old inexplicable query, ever that thorn'd thumb, that breath
    of itches and thirsts,
Ever the vexer's *hoot! hoot!* till we find where the sly one hides and
    bring him forth,
Ever love, ever the sobbing liquid of life,
Ever the bandage under the chin, ever the trestles of death.[25]

Sometimes Whitman will take what would generally be considered an unpromising subject (in this case, a woman peeping
at men in bathing naked) and treat it with such tenderness and
subtlety and understanding that we are ashamed of ourselves for
having thought it unpromising, and murmur that Chekhov himself couldn't have treated it better. [Jarrell quotes Section 11 of
"Song of Myself" in entirety.]

And in the same poem (that "Song of Myself" in which one
finds half his best work) the writer can say of a sea-fight:

Stretch'd and still lies the midnight,
Two great hulls motionless on the breast of the darkness,
Our vessel riddled and slowly sinking, preparations to pass to the
    one we have conquer'd,
The captain on the quarter-deck coldly giving his orders through a
    countenance white as a sheet,
Near by the corpse of the child that serv'd in the cabin,
The dead face of an old salt with long white hair and carefully curl'd
    whiskers,
The flames spite of all that can be done flickering aloft and below,
The husky voices of the two or three officers yet fit for duty,

Formless stacks of bodies and bodies by themselves, dabs of flesh
    upon the masts and spars,
Cut of cordage, dangle of rigging, slight shock of the soothe of
    waves,
Black and impassive guns, litter of powder-parcels, strong scent,
A few large stars overhead, silent and mournful shining,
Delicate sniffs of sea-breeze, smells of sedgy grass and fields by the
    shore, death-messages given in charge to survivors,
The hiss of the surgeon's knife, the gnawing teeth of his saw,
Wheeze, cluck, swash of falling blood, short wild scream, and long,
    dull, tapering groan,
These so, these irretrievable.[26]

There are faults in this passage, and they *do not matter:* the
serious truth, the complete realization of these last lines make us
remember that few poets have shown more of the tears of
things, and the joy of things, and of the reality beneath either
tears or joy. Even Whitman's most general or political statements sometimes are good: everybody knows his "When liberty
goes out of a place it is not the first to go, nor the second or third
to go,/ It waits for all the rest to go, it is the last";[27] these
sentences about the United States just before the Civil War may
be less familiar:

Are those really Congressmen? are those the great Judges? is that
    the President?
Then I will sleep awhile yet, for I see that these States sleep, for
    reasons;
(With gathering murk, with muttering thunder and lambent shoots
    we all duly awake,
South, North, East, West, inland and seaboard, we will surely
    awake.)[28]

How well, with what firmness and dignity and command, Whitman does such passages! And Whitman's doubts that he has
done them or anything else well—ah, there is nothing he does
better:

The best I had done seem'd to me blank and suspicious,
My great thoughts as I supposed them, were they not in reality
    meagre?
   .   .   .   .
I am he who knew what it was to be evil,
I too knitted the old knot of contrariety,
   .   .   .   .

Saw many I loved in the street or ferry-boat or public assembly, yet
    never told them a word,
Lived the same life with the rest, the same old laughing, gnawing,
    sleeping,
Play'd the part that still looks back on the actor or actress,
The same old role, the role that is what we make it . . .[29]

Whitman says once that the "look of the bay mare shames
silliness out of me."[30] This is true—sometimes it is true; but
more often the silliness and affection and cant and exaggeration
are there shamelessly, the Old Adam that was in Whitman from
the beginning and the awful new one that he created to keep it
company. But as he says, "I know perfectly well my own
egotism,/ Know my omnivorous lines and must not write any
less."[31] He says over and over that there are in him good and
bad, wise and foolish, anything at all and its antonym, and he is
telling the truth; there is in him almost everything in the world,
so that one responds to him, willingly or unwillingly, almost as
one does to the world, that world which makes the hairs of one's
flesh stand up, which seems both evil beyond any rejection and
wonderful beyond any acceptance. We cannot help seeing that
there is something absurd about any judgment we make of its
whole—for there is no "point of view" at which we can stand to
make the judgment, and the moral categories that mean most to
us seem no more to apply to its whole than our spatial or
temporal or causal categories seem to apply to its beginning or
its end. (But we need no arguments to make our judgments
seem absurd—we feel their absurdity without argument.) In
some like sense Whitman is a world, a waste with, here and
there, systems blazing at random out of the darkness. Only an
innocent and rigidly methodical mind will reject it for this
disorganization, particularly since there are in it, here and there,
little systems as beautifully and astonishingly organized as the
rings and statellites of Saturn:

I understand the large hearts of heroes,
The courage of present times and all times,
How the skipper saw the crowded and rudderless wreck of the
    steam-ship, and Death chasing it up and down the storm,
How he knuckled tight and gave not back an inch, and was faithful
    of days and faithful of nights,

And chalk'd in large letters on a board, *Be of good cheer, we will not desert you;*
How he follow'd with them and tack'd with them three days and would not give it up,
How he saved the drifting company at last,
How the lank loose-gown'd women look'd when boated from the side of their prepared graves,
How the silent old-faced infants and the lifted sick, and the sharp-lipp'd unshaved men;
All this I swallow, it tastes good, I like it well, it becomes mine,
I am the man, I suffer'd, I was there.[32]

In the last lines of this quotation Whitman has reached—as great writers always reach—a point at which criticism seems not only unnecessary but absurd: these lines are so good that even admiration feels like insolence, and one is ashamed of anything that one can find to say about them. How anyone can dismiss or accept patronizingly the man who wrote them, I do not understand.

The enormous and apparent advantages of form, of omission and selection, of the highest degree of organization, are accompanied by important disadvantages—and there are far greater works than *Leaves of Grass* to make us realize this. But if we compare Whitman with that very beautiful poet Alfred Tennyson, the most skillful of all Whitman's contemporaries, we are at once aware of how limiting Tennyson's forms have been, of how much Tennyson has had to leave out, even in those discursive poems where he is trying to put everything in. Whitman's poems *represent* his world and himself much more satisfactorily than Tennyson's do his. In the past a few poets have both formed and represented, each in the highest degree; but in modern times what controlling, organizing, selecting poet has created a world with as much in it as Whitman's, a world that so plainly *is* the world? Of all modern poets he has, quantitatively speaking, "the most comprehensive soul"—and, qualitatively, a most comprehensive and comprehending one, with charities and concessions and qualifications that are rare in any time.

"Do I contradict myself? Very well then I contradict myself," wrote Whitman, as everybody remembers, and this is not naive, or something he got from Emerson, or a complacent pose. When you organize one of the contradictory elements out of your work of art, you are getting rid not just of it, but of the contradiction of which it was a part; and it is the contradictions in works of art which make them able to represent to us—as logical and methodical generalizations cannot—our world and our selves, which are also full of contradictions. In Whitman we do not get the controlled, compressed, seemingly concordant contradictions of the great lyric poets, of a poem like, say, Hardy's "During Wind and Rain"; Whitman's contradictions are sometimes announced openly, but are more often scattered at random throughout the poems. For instance: Whitman specializes in ways of saying that there is in some sense (a very Hegelian one, generally) no evil—he says a hundred times that evil is not Real; but he also specializes in making lists of the evil of the world, lists of an unarguable reality. After his minister has recounted "the rounded catalogue divine complete," Whitman comes home and puts down what has been left out: "the countless (nineteen-twentieths) low and evil, crude and savage . . ./ The barren soil, the evil men, the slag and hideous rot."[33] He ends another such catalogue with the plain unexcusing "All these— all the meanness and agony without end I sitting look out upon,/ See, hear, and am silent."[34] Whitman offered himself to everybody, and said brilliantly and at length what a good thing he was offering:

Sure as the most certain sure, plumb in the uprights, well entretied,
        braced in the beams,
Stout as a horse, affectionate, haughty, electrical,
I and this mystery here we stand.[35]

Just for oddness, characteristicalness, differentness, what more could you ask in a letter of recommendation? (Whitman sounds as if he were recommending a house—haunted, but what foundations!) But after a few pages he is oddly different:

Apart from the pulling and hauling stands what I am,
Stands amused, complacent, compassionating, idle, unitary,
Looks down, is erect, or bends an arm on an impalpable certain rest
Looking with side-curved head curious what will come next,
Both in and out of the game and watching and wondering at it.[36]

Tamburlaine is already beginning to sound like Hamlet: the employer feels uneasily, "Why, I might as well hire myself. . . ." And, a few pages later, Whitman puts down in ordinary-sized type, in the middle of the page, this warning to any *new person drawn toward me:*

Do you think I am trusty and faithful?
Do you see no further than this façade, this smooth and tolerant manner of me?
Do you suppose yourself advancing on real ground toward a real heroic man?
Have you no thought O dreamer that it may be all maya, illusion?[37]

Having wonderful dreams, telling wonderful lies, was a temptation Whitman could never resist; but telling the truth was a temptation he could never resist, either. When you buy him you know what you are buying. And only an innocent and solemn and systematic mind will condemn him for his contradictions: Whitman's catalogues of evils represent realities, and his denials of their reality represent other realities, of feeling and intuition and desire. If he is faithless to logic, to Reality As It Is—whatever that is—he is faithful to the feel of things, to reality as it seems; this is all that a poet has to be faithful to, and philosophers have been known to leave logic and Reality for it.

Whitman is more coordinate and parallel than anybody, is *the* poet of parallel present participles, of twenty verbs joined by a single subject: all this helps to give his work its feeling of raw hypnotic reality, of being that world which also streams over us joined only by *ands*, until we supply the subordinating conjunctions; and since as children we see the *ands* and not the *becauses*, this method helps to give Whitman some of the freshness of childhood. How inexhaustibly interesting the world is in Whitman! Arnold all his life kept wishing that he could see the world "with a plainness as near, as flashing" as that with which Moses and Rebekah and the Argonauts saw it. He asked with elegiac nostalgia, "Who can see the green earth any more/ As she was by the sources of Time?"—and all the time there was somebody alive who saw it so, as plain and near and flashing, and with a kind of calm, pastoral, Biblical dignity and elegance as well, sometimes. The *thereness* and *suchness* of the world are incarnate in Whitman as they are in few other writers.

They might have put on his tombstone WALT WHITMAN: HE HAD HIS NERVE. He is the rashest, the most inexplicable and unlikely—the most impossible, one wants to say—of poets. He somehow *is* in a class by himself, so that one compares him with other poets about as readily as one compares *Alice* with other books. (Even his free verse has a completely different effect from anybody else's.) Who would think of comparing him with Tennyson or Browning or Arnold or Baudelaire?—it is Homer, or the sagas, or something far away and long ago, that comes to one's mind only to be dismissed; for sometimes Whitman *is* epic, just as *Moby Dick* is, and it surprises us to be able to use truthfully this word that we have misused so many times. Whitman *is* grand, and elevated, and comprehensive, and real with an astonishing reality, and many other things—the critic points at his qualities in despair and wonder, all method failing, and simply calls them by their names. And the range of these qualities is the most extraordinary thing of all. We can surely say about him, "He was a man, take him for all in all. I shall not look upon his like again"—and wish that people had seen this and not tried to be his like: one Whitman is miracle enough, and when he comes again it will be the end of the world.

I have said so little about Whitman's faults because they are so plain: baby critics who have barely learned to complain of the lack of ambiguity in *Peter Rabbit* can tell you all that is wrong with *Leaves of Grass*. But a good many of my readers must have felt that it is ridiculous to write an essay about the obvious fact that Whitman is a great poet. It is ridiculous—just as, in 1851, it would have been ridiculous for anyone to write an essay about the obvious fact that Pope was no "classic of our prose" but a great poet. Critics have to spend half their time reiterating whatever ridiculously obvious things their age or the critics of their age have found it necessary to forget: they say despairingly, at parties, that Wordsworth is a great poet, and *won't* bore you, and tell Mr. Leavis that Milton is a great poet whose deposition *hasn't* been accomplished with astonishing ease by a few words from Eliot. . . . There is something essentially ridiculous about critics, anyway: what is good is good without our saying so, and beneath all our majesty we know this.

Let me finish by mentioning another quality of Whitman's—a

quality, delightful to me, that I have said nothing of. If someday a tourist notices, among the ruins of New York City, a copy of *Leaves of Grass*, and stops and picks it up and reads some lines in it, she will be able to say to herself: "How very American! If he and his country had not existed, it would have been impossible to imagine them."

WALLACE STEVENS

[1879-1955]

Letter to Joseph Bennett (February 8, 1955)

. . . In order to comment on Walt Whitman conscientiously, I ought to re-read him and this is more than I have the time to do at the moment. Last Sunday I read him for several hours and if a few offhand remarks as a result of that reading would be of any interest to you, here they are.

I can well believe that he remains highly vital for many people. The poems in which he collects large numbers of concrete things, particularly things each of which is poetic in itself or as part of the collection, have a validity which, for many people, must be enough and must seem to them all opulence and elan.

For others, I imagine that what was once opulent begins to look a little threadbare and the collections seem substitutes for opulence even though they remain gatherings-together of precious Americana, certain to remain precious but not certain to remain poetry. The typical elan survives in many things.

It seems to me, then, that Whitman is distintegrating as the world, of which he made himself a part, disintegrates. *Crossing Brooklyn Ferry* exhibits this disintegration.

The elan of the essential Whitman is still deeply moving in the things in which he was himself deeply moved. These would have to be picked out from compilations like *Song of the Broad-Axe*, *Song of the Exposition*.

It is useless to treat everything in Whitman as of equal merit. A great deal of it exhibits little or none of his specific power. He seems often to have driven himself to write like himself. The good things, the superbly beautiful and moving things, are those that he wrote naturally, with an extemporaneousness and irrepressible vehemence of emotion.

I am sorry not to be able to spend more time on this.

MALCOLM COWLEY

[1 8 9 8 –   ]

"Song of Myself" and Indian Philosophy (1959)

ONE REASON AMONG OTHERS why "Song of Myself" has been widely misprized and misinterpreted, especially by scholars, is that they have paid a disproportionate share of attention to its

Reprinted by permission of The Viking Press, Inc., and Laurence Pollinger Limited from Introduction of *Leaves of Grass—The First (1855) Edition* (New York, 1959), x–xxvi. Copyright, 1959, by The Viking Press, Inc. The quotations are from the first edition. V. K. Chari attempts to offer substantiation for Cowley's general references to Indian philosophy in *Whitman in the Light of Vedantic Mysticism* (Lincoln, Neb., 1964). For Chari's analysis of "Song of Myself," see 124–126.

sources in contemporary culture. Besides noting many parallels with Emerson, they have found that it reflected a number of popular works and spectacles. Among these are Italian opera (notably as sung at the Astor Place Theatre in the great season of 1852–1853, when "Alboni's great self" paid her long and only visit to New York); George Sand's novel, *The Countess of Rudolstadt*, which presented the figure of a wandering bard and prophet (as well as another of her novels, *The Journeyman Joiner*, in which the hero was a carpenter and a proletarian saint); Frances Wright's then famous defense of Epicurean philosophy, *A Few Days in Athens;* the Count de Volney's *Ruins*, predicting the final union of all religions; Dr. Abbott's Egyptian Museum, on Broadway; O. M. Mitchel's book, *A Course of Six Lectures on Astronomy*, as well as other writings on the subject; and a number of essays clipped from the English quarterly reviews, of which the poet seems to have been a faithful reader. All these works and shows had a discernible influence on Whitman, but when they are listed with others and discussed at length they lead to one of the misconceptions that are the professional weakness of scholars. They tempt us to conclude that "Song of Myself" was merely a journalist's report, inspired but uneven, of popular culture in the 1850s. It was something more than that, and something vastly different from any of its literary sources.

I might suggest that the real nature of the poem becomes clearer when it is considered in relation to quite another list of works, even though Whitman had probably read none of them in 1855. Most of them he could not have read, because they were not yet written, or not published, or not translated into English. That other list might include the *Bhagavad-Gita*, the *Upanishads*, Christopher Smart's long crazy inspired poem *Jubilate Agno*, Blake's prophetic books (not forgetting *The Marriage of Heaven and Hell*), Rimbaud's *Illuminations*, *The Chants of Maldoror*, and Nietzsche's *Thus Spake Zarathustra*, as well as *The Gospel of Sri Ramakrishna* and a compendious handbook, *The Philosophies of India*, by Heinrich Zimmer (New York, 1951). I am offering what might seem to be a curious list of titles, but its double purpose is easy to explain. "Song of Myself" should be judged, I think, as one of the great inspired (and sometimes insane) prophetic works that have appeared at intervals in the Western world, like *Jubilate Agno* (which is written in a biblical style sometimes suggesting Whitman's), like the *Illuminations*, like *Thus Spake Zarathustra*. But the system of doctrine suggested by the poem is more Eastern than Western, it includes notions like metempsychosis and karma, and it might almost be one of those *Philosophies of India* that Zimmer expounds at length.

What is extraordinary about this Eastern element is that Whitman, when he was writing the poems of the first edition, seems to have known little or nothing about Indian philosophy. It is more than doubtful that he had even read the *Bhagavad-Gita*, one of the few Indian works then available in translation. He does not refer to it in his notebooks of the early 1850s, where he mentions most of the books he was poring over. A year after the first edition was published, Thoreau went to see him in Brooklyn and told him that *Leaves of Grass* was "Wonderfully like the Orientals." Had Whitman read them? he asked. The poet answered, "No: tell me about them." He seems to have taken advantage of Thoreau's reading list, since words from the Sanskrit (notably "Maya" and "sudra") are used correctly in some of the poems written after 1858. They do not appear in "Song of Myself," in spite of the recognizably Indian ideas expressed in the poem, and I would hazard the guess that the ideas are not of literary derivation. It is true that they were vaguely in the air of the time and that Whitman may have breathed them in from the Transcendentalists or even from some of the English quarterly reviewers. It also seems possible, however, that he reinvented them for himself, after an experience similar to the one for which the Sanskrit word is samadhi, or absorption.

What it must have been was a mystical experience in the proper sense of the term. Dr. Richard Maurice Bucke, the most acute of Whitman's immediate disciples, believed that it took place on a June morning in 1853 or 1854.[1] He also believed that it was repeated on other occasions, but neither these nor the original experience can be dated from Whitman's papers. On the other hand, his notebooks and manuscripts of the early 1850s are full of sidelong references to such an experience, and they suggest that it was essentially the same as the illuminations or ecstasies of earlier bards and prophets. Such ecstasies consist in a rapt feeling of union or identity with God (or the Soul, or Mankind, or the Cosmos), a sense of ineffable joy leading to the conviction that the seer has been released from the limitations of space and time and has been granted a direct vision of truths impossible to express. As Whitman says in the famous fifth chant of "Song of Myself":

Swiftly arose and spread around me the peace and joy and knowl-
edge that pass all the art and argument of the earth;
And I know that the hand of God is the elderhand of my own,
And I know that the spirit of God is the eldest brother of my own,
And that all the men ever born are also my brothers . . . . and the
women my sisters and lovers.

It is to be noted that there is no argument about the real occurrence of such ecstasies. They have been reported, sometimes in sharp detail, by men and women of many different nations, at many historical periods, and each report seems to bear a family resemblance to the others. Part of the resemblance is a feeling universally expressed by mystics that they have acquired a special sort of knowledge not learned from others, but directly revealed to the inner eye. This supposed knowledge has given independent rise to many systems of philosophy or cosmology, once again in many different cultures, and once again there is or should be no argument about one feature of almost all the systems or bodies of teaching: that they too have a family resemblance, like the experiences on which they are based. Indeed, they hold so many principles in common that it is possible for Aldous Huxley and others to group them all together as "the perennial philosophy."

The arguments, which will never end, are first about the nature of the mystical state—is it a form of self-hypnosis, is it a pathological condition to be induced by fasting, vigils, drugs, and other means of abusing the physical organism, or is it, as Whitman believed, the result of superabundant health and energy?—and then about the source and value of the philosophical notions to which it gives rise. Do these merely express the unconscious desires of the individual, and chiefly his sexual desires? Or, as Jungian psychologists like to suggest, are they derived from a racial or universally human unconscious? Are they revelations or hallucinations? Are they supreme doctrines, or are they heretical, false, and even satanic? They belong in the orthodox tradition of Indian philosophy. In Western Christianity, as also in Mohammedanism, the pure and self-consistent forms of mysticism are usually regarded as heresies, with the result that several of the medieval mystics were burned at the stake (though Theresa of Avila and John of the Cross found an orthodox interpretation for their visions and became saints).

Whitman cannot be called a Christian heretic, for the simple reason that he was not a Christian at any stage of his career, early or late.[2] In some of the poems written after the Civil War, and in revisions of older poems made at the same time, he approached the Christian notion of a personal God, whom he invoked as the Elder Brother or the great Camerado. But then he insisted—in another poem of the same period, "Chanting the Square Deific"—that God was not a trinity but a quaternity, and that one of his faces was the "sudra face" of Satan. In "Song of Myself" as originally written, God is neither a person nor, in the strict sense, even a being; God is an abstract principle of energy that is manifested in every living creature, as well as in "the grass that grows wherever the land is and the water is." In some ways this God of the first edition resembles Emerson's Oversoul, but he seems much closer to the Brahman of the *Upanishads*, the absolute, unchanging, all-enfolding Consciousness, the Divine Ground from which all things emanate and to which all living things may hope to return. And this Divine Ground is by no means the only conception that Whitman shared with Indian philosophers, in the days when he was writing "Song of Myself."

The poem is hardly at all concerned with American nationalism, political democracy, contemporary progress, or other social themes that are commonly associated with Whitman's work. The "incomparable things" that Emerson found in it are philosophical and religious principles. Its subject is a state of illumination induced by two (or three) separate moments of ecstasy. In more or less narrative sequence it describes those moments, their sequels in life, and the doctrines to which they give rise.

The doctrines are not expounded by logical steps or supported by arguments; instead they are presented dramatically, that is, as the new convictions of a hero, and they are revealed by successive unfoldings of his states of mind.

The hero as pictured in the frontispiece—this hero named "I" or "Walt Whitman" in the text—should not be confused with the Whitman of daily life. He is, as I said, a dramatized or idealized figure, and he is put forward as a representative American workingman, but one who prefers to loaf and invite his soul. Thus, he is rough, sunburned, bearded; he cocks his hat as he pleases, indoors or out; but in the text of the first edition he has no local or family background, and he is deprived of strictly individual characteristics, with the exception of curiosity, boastfulness, and an abnormally developed sense of touch. His really distinguishing feature is that he has been granted a vision, as a result of which he has realized the potentialities latent in every American and indeed, he says, in every living person, even "the brutish koboo, called the ordure of humanity." This dramatization of the hero makes it possible for the living Whitman to exalt him—as he would not have ventured, at the time, to exalt himself—but also to poke mild fun at the hero for his gab and loitering, for his tall talk or "omnivorous words," and for sounding his barbaric yawp over the roofs of the world. The religious feeling in "Song of Myself" is counterpoised by a humor that takes the form of slangy and mischievous impudence or drawling Yankee self-ridicule.[3]

There has been a good deal of discussion about the structure of the poem. In spite of revealing analyses made by a few Whitman scholars, notably Carl F. Strauch and James E. Miller, Jr.,[4] a feeling still seems to prevail that it has no structure properly speaking; that it is inspired but uneven, repetitive, and especially weak in its transitions from one theme to another. I suspect that much of this feeling may be due to Whitman's later changes in the text, including his arbitrary scheme, first introduced in the 1867 edition, of dividing the poem into fifty-two numbered paragraphs or chants. One is tempted to read the chants as if they were separate poems, thus overlooking the unity and flow of the work as a whole. It may also be, however, that most of the scholars have been looking for a geometrical pattern, such as can be found and diagramed in some of the later poems. If there is no such pattern in "Song of Myself," that is because the poem was written on a different principle, one much closer to the spirit of the Symbolists or even the Surrealists.

The true structure of the poem is not primarily logical but psychological, and is not a geometrical figure but a musical progression. As music "Song of Myself" is not a symphony with contrasting movements, nor is it an operatic work like "Out of the Cradle Endlessly Rocking," with an overture, arias, recitatives, and a finale. It comes closer to being a rhapsody or tone poem, one that modulates from theme to theme, often changing in key and tempo, falling into reveries and rising toward moments of climax, but always preserving its unity of feeling as it moves onward in a wavelike flow. It is a poem that bears the marks of having been conceived as a whole and written in one prolonged burst of inspiration, but its unity is also the result of conscious art, as can be seen from Whitman's corrections in the early manuscripts. He did not recognize all the bad lines, some of which survive in the printed text, but there is no line in the first edition that seems false to a single prevailing tone. There are passages weaker than others, but none without a place in the general scheme. The repetitions are always musical variations and amplifications. Some of the transitions seem abrupt when the poem is read as if it were an essay, but Whitman was not working in terms of "therefore" and "however." He preferred to let one image suggest another image, which in turn suggests a new statement of mood or doctrine. His themes modulate into one another by pure association, as in a waking dream, with the result that all his transitions seem instinctively right.

In spite of these oneiric elements, the form of the poem is something more than a forward movement in rising and subsiding waves of emotion. There is also a firm narrative structure, one that becomes easier to grasp when we start by dividing the poem into a number of parts or sequences. I think there are nine of these, but the exact number is not important; another critic might say there were seven (as Professor Miller does),[5] or eight or ten. Some of the transitions are gradual, and in such cases it is hard to determine the exact line that ends one sequence and starts another. The essential point is that the parts, however

defined, follow one another in irreversible order, like the beginning, middle, and end of any good narrative. My own outline,
not necessarily final, would run as follows:

First sequence (chants 1–4): the poet or hero introduced to
his audience. Leaning and loafing at his ease, "observing a spear
of summer grass," he presents himself as a man who lives
outdoors and worships his own naked body, not the least part of
which is vile. He is also in love with his deeper self or soul, but
explains that it is not to be confused with his mere personality.
His joyful contentment can be shared by you, the listener, "For
every atom belonging to me as good belongs to you."

Second sequence (chant 5): the ecstasy. This consists in the
rapt union of the poet and his soul, and it is described—figuratively, on the present occasion—in terms of sexual union. The
poet now has a sense of loving brotherhood with God and with
all mankind. His eyes being truly open for the first time, he sees
that even the humblest objects contain the infinite universe—

And limitless are leaves stiff or drooping in the fields,
And brown ants in the little wells beneath them,
And mossy scabs of the wormfence, and heaped stones, and elder
    and mullen and pokeweed.

Third sequence (chants 6–19): the grass. Chant 6 starts
with one of Whitman's brilliant transitions. A child comes with
both hands full of those same leaves from the fields. "What is
the grass?" the child asks—and suddenly we are presented with
the central image of the poem, that is, the grass as symbolizing
the miracle of common things and the divinity (which implies
both the equality and the immortality) of ordinary persons.[6]
During the remainder of the sequence, the poet observes men
and women—and animals too—at their daily occupations. He is
part of this life, he says, and even his thoughts are those of all
men in all ages and lands. There are two things to be noted
about the sequence, which contains some of Whitman's freshest
lyrics. First, the people with a few exceptions (such as the
trapper and his bride) are those whom Whitman has known all
his life, while the scenes described at length are Manhattan
streets and Long Island beaches or countryside. Second, the poet
merely roams, watches, and listens, like a sort of Tiresias. The

keynote of the sequence—as Professor Strauch was the first to explain—is the two words "I observe."

Fourth sequence (chants 20–25): the poet in person. "Hankering, gross, mystical, nude," he venerates himself as august and immortal, but so, he says, is everyone else. He is the poet of the body and of the soul, of night, earth, and sea, and of vice and feebleness as well as virtue, so that "many long dumb voices" speak through his lips, including those of slaves, prostitutes, even beetles rolling balls of dung. All life to him is such a miracle of beauty that the sunrise would kill him if he could not find expression for it—"If I could not now and always send sunrise out of me." The sequence ends with a dialogue between the poet and his power of speech, during which the poet insists that his deeper self—"the best I am"—is beyond expression.

Fifth sequence (chants 26–29): ecstasy through the senses. Beginning with chant 26, the poem sets out in a new direction. The poet decides to be completely passive: "I think I will do nothing for a long time but listen." What he hears at first are quiet familiar sounds like the gossip of flames on the hearth and the bustle of growing wheat; but the sounds rise quickly to a higher pitch, becoming the matchless voice of a trained soprano, and he is plunged into an ecstasy of hearing, or rather of Being. Then he starts over again, still passively, with the sense of touch, and finds himself rising to the ecstasy of sexual union. This time the union is actual, not figurative, as can be seen from the much longer version of chant 29 preserved in an early notebook.[7]

Sixth sequence (chants 30–38): the power of identification. After his first ecstasy, as presented in chant 5, the poet had acquired a sort of microscopic vision that enabled him to find infinite wonders in the smallest and most familiar things. The second ecstasy (or pair of ecstasies) has an entirely different effect, conferring as it does a sort of vision that is both telescopic and spiritual. The poet sees far into space and time; "afoot with my vision" he ranges over the continent and goes speeding through the heavens among tailed meteors. His secret is the power of identification. Since everything emanates from the universal soul, and since his own soul is of the same essence, he can identify himself with every object and with every person living or dead, heroic or criminal. Thus, he is massacred with the Texans at Goliad, he fights on the *Bonhomme Richard*, he dies on the cross, and he rises again as "one of an average unending procession." Whereas the keynote of the third sequence was "I observe," here it becomes "I am"—"I am a free companion"—"My voice is the wife's voice, the screech by the rail of the stairs"—"I am the man. . . . I suffered. . . . I was there."

Seventh sequence (chants 39–41): the superman. When Indian sages emerge from the state of samadhi or absorption, they often have the feeling of being omnipotent. It is so with the poet, who now feels gifted with superhuman powers. He is the universally beloved Answerer (chant 39), then the Healer, raising men from their deathbeds (40), and then the Prophet (41) of a new religion that outbids "the old cautious hucksters" by announcing that men are divine and will eventually be gods.

Eighth sequence (chants 42–50): the sermon. "A call in the midst of the crowd" is the poet's voice, "orotund sweeping and final." He is about to offer a statement of the doctrines implied by the narrative (but note that his statement comes at the right point psychologically and plays its part in the narrative sequence). As strangers listen, he proclaims that society is full of injustice, but that the reality beneath it is deathless persons (chant 42); that he accepts and practices all religions, but looks beyond them to "what is untried and afterward" (43); that he and his listeners are the fruit of ages, and the seed of untold ages to be (44); that our final goal is appointed: "God will be there and wait till we come" (45); that he tramps a perpetual journey and longs for companions, to whom he will reveal a new world by washing the gum from their eyes—but each must then continue the journey alone (46); that he is the teacher of men who work in the open air (47); that he is not curious about God, but sees God everywhere, at every moment (48); that we shall all be reborn in different forms ("No doubt I have died myself ten thousand times before"); and that the evil in the world is like moonlight, a mere reflection of the sun (49). The end of the sermon (chant 50) is the hardest passage to interpret in the whole poem. I think, though I cannot be certain, that the poet is harking back to the period after one of his ten thousand deaths, when he slept and slept long before his next awakening. He seems to remember vague shapes, and he beseeches these Outlines, as he calls them, to let him reveal the "word unsaid." Then turning back to his audience, "It is not chaos or death," he says. "It is form and union and plan. . . . it is eternal life. . . . it is happiness."

Ninth sequence (chants 51–52): the poet's farewell. Having finished his sermon, the poet gets ready to depart, that is, to die and wait for another incarnation or "fold of the future," while still inviting others to follow. At the beginning of the poem he had been leaning and loafing at ease in the summer grass. Now, having rounded the circle, he bequeaths himself to the dirt "to grow from the grass I love." I do not see how any careful reader, unless blinded with preconceptions, could overlook the unity of the poem in tone and image and direction.

It is in the eighth sequence, which is a sermon, that Whitman gives us most of the doctrines suggested by his mystical experience, but they are also implied in the rest of the poem and indeed in the whole text of the first edition. Almost always he expresses them in the figurative and paradoxical language that prophets have used from the beginning. Now I should like to state them explicitly, even at the cost of some repetition.

Whitman believed when he was writing "Song of Myself"— and at later periods too, but with many changes in emphasis— that there is a distinction between one's mere personality and the deeper Self (or between ego and soul). He believed that the Self (or atman, to use a Sanskrit word) is of the same essence as the universal spirit (though he did not quite say it *is* the universal spirit, as Indian philosophers do in the phrase "Atman is Brahman"). He believed that true knowledge is to be acquired not through the senses or the intellect, but through union with the Self. At such moments of union (or "merge," as Whitman called it) the gum is washed from one's eyes (that is his own phrase), and one can read an infinite lesson in common things, discovering that a mouse, for example, "is miracle enough to stagger sextillions of infidels." This true knowledge is available to every man and woman, since each conceals a divine Self. Moreover, the divinity of all implies the perfect equality of all, the immortality of all, and the universal duty of loving one another.

Immortality for Whitman took the form of metempsychosis, and he believed that every individual will be reborn, usually but not always in a higher form. He had also worked out for himself something approaching the Indian notion of karma, which is the doctrine that actions performed during one incarnation determine the nature and fate of the individual during his next incarnation; the doctrine is emphatically if somewhat unclearly stated in a passage of his prose introduction that was later rewritten as a poem, "Song of Prudence." By means of metempsychosis and karma, we are all involved in a process of spiritual evolution that might be compared to natural evolution. Even the latter process, however, was not regarded by Whitman as strictly natural or material. He believed that animals have a rudimentary sort of soul ("They bring me tokens of myself"), and he hinted or surmised, without directly saying, that rocks, trees, and planets possess an identity, or "eidólon," that persists as they rise to higher states of being. The double process of evolution, natural and spiritual, can be traced for ages into the past, and he believed that it will continue for ages beyond ages. Still, it is not an eternal process, since it has an ultimate goal, which appears to be the reabsorption of all things into the Divine Ground.

Most of Whitman's doctrines, though by no means all of them, belong to the mainstream of Indian philosophy. In some respects he went against the stream. Unlike most of the Indian sages, for example, he was not a thoroughgoing idealist. He did not believe that the whole world of the senses, of desires, of birth and death, was only maya, illusion, nor did he hold that it was a sort of purgatory; instead he praised the world as real and joyful. He did not despise the body, but proclaimed that it was as miraculous as the soul. He was too good a citizen of the nineteenth century to surrender his faith in material progress as the necessary counterpart of spiritual progress. Although he yearned for ecstatic union with the soul or Oversoul, he did not try to achieve it by subjugating the senses, as advised by yogis and Buddhists alike; on the contrary, he thought the "merge" could also be achieved (as in chants 26–29) by a total surrender to the senses. These are important differences, but it must be remembered that Indian philosophy or theology is not such a unified structure as it appears to us from a distance. Whitman might have found Indian sages or gurus and even whole sects that agreed with one or another of his heterodoxies (perhaps excepting his belief in material progress). One is tempted to say that instead of being a Christian heretic, he was an Indian rebel and sectarian.

Sometimes he seems to be a Mahayana Buddhist, promising nirvana for all after countless reincarnations, and also sharing the belief of some Mahayana sects that the sexual act can serve as one of the sacraments. At other times he might be an older brother of Sri Ramakrishna (1836–1886), the nineteenth-century apostle of Tantric Brahmanism and of joyous affirmation. Although this priest of Kali, the Mother Goddess, refused to learn English, one finds him delivering some of Whitman's messages in—what is more surprising—the same tone of voice. Read, for example, this fairly typical passage from *The Gospel of Sri Ramakrishna*, while remembering that "Consciousness" is to be taken here as a synonym for Divinity:

> The Divine Mother revealed to me in the Kali temple that it was She who had become everything. She showed me that everything was full of Consciousness. The Image was Consciousness, the altar was Consciousness, the water-vessels were Consciousness, the door-sill was Consciousness, the marble floor was Consciousness—all was Consciousness. . . . I saw a wicked man in front of the Kali temple; but in him I saw the Power of the Divine Mother vibrating. That was why I fed a cat with the food that was to be offered to the Divine Mother.

Whitman expresses the same idea at the end of chant 48, and in the same half-playful fashion:

Why should I wish to see God better than this day?
I see something of God each hour of the twenty-four, and each
    moment then,
In the faces of men and women I see God, and in my own face in the
    glass;
I find letters from God dropped in the street, and every one is signed
    by God's name,
And I leave them where they are, for I know that others will
    punctually come forever and ever.

Such parallels—and there are dozens that might be quoted—are more than accidental. They reveal a kinship in thinking and experience that can be of practical value to students of Whitman. Since the Indian mystical philosophies are elaborate structures, based on conceptions that have been shaped and defined by centuries of discussion, they help to explain Whitman's ideas at points in the first edition where he seems at first glance to be vague or self-contradictory. There is, for example, his unusual combination of realism—sometimes brutal realism—and serene optimism. Today he is usually praised for the first, blamed for the second (optimism being out of fashion), and blamed still more for the inconsistency he showed in denying the existence of evil. The usual jibe is that Whitman thought the universe was perfect and was getting better every day.

It is obvious, however, that he never meant to deny the existence of evil in himself or his era or his nation. He knew that it existed in his own family, where one of his brothers was a congenital idiot, another was a drunkard married to a streetwalker, and still another, who had caught "the bad disorder," later died of general paresis in an insane asylum. Whitman's doctrine implied that each of them would have an opportunity to avoid those misfortunes or punishments in another incarnation, where each would be rewarded for his good actions. The universe was an eternal becoming for Whitman, a process not a structure, and it had to be judged from the standpoint of eternity. After his mystical experience, which seemed to offer a vision of eternity, he had become convinced that evil existed only as part of a universally perfect design. That explains his combination of realism and optimism, which seems unusual only in our Western world.[8] In India, Henrich Zimmer says, "Philosophic theory, religious belief, and intuitive experience support each other . . . in the basic insight that, fundamentally, all is well. A supreme optimism prevails everywhere, in spite of the unromantic recognition that the universe of man's affairs is in the most imperfect state imaginable, one amounting practically to chaos."

Another point explained by Indian conceptions is the sort of democracy Whitman was preaching in "Song of Myself." There is no doubt that he was always a democrat politically—

which is to say a Jacksonian Democrat, a Barnburner writing editorials against the Hunkers, a Free Soiler in sympathy, and then a liberal but not a radical Republican. He remained faithful to what he called "the good old cause" of liberty, equality, and fraternity, and he wrote two moving elegies for the European rebels of 1848. In "Song of Myself," however, he is not advocating rebellion or even reform. "To a drudge of the cotton-fields," he says, "or emptier of privies I lean. . . . on his right cheek I put the family kiss"; but he offers nothing more than a kiss and an implied promise. What he preaches throughout the poem is not political but religious democracy, such as was practiced by the early Christians. Today it is practiced, at least in theory, by the Tantric sect, and we read in *Philosophies of India:*

> All beings and things are members of a single mystic family (*kula*). There is therefore no thought of caste within the Tantric holy "circles" (*cakra*). . . . Women as well as men are eligible not only to receive the highest initiation but also to confer it in the role of guru. . . . However, it must not be supposed that this indifference to the rules of caste implies any idea of revolution within the social sphere, as distinguished from the sphere of spiritual progress. The initiate returns to his post in society; for there too is the manifestation of Sakti. The world is affirmed, just as it is—neither renounced, as by an ascetic, nor corrected, as by a social reformer.

The promise that Whitman offers to the drudge of the cotton-fields, the emptier of privies, and the prostitute draggling her shawl is that they too can set out with him on his perpetual journey—perhaps not in their present incarnations, but at least in some future life. And that leads to another footnote offered by the Indian philosophies: they explain what the poet meant by the Open Road. It starts as an actual road that winds through fields and cities, but Whitman is doing more than inviting us to shoulder our duds and go hiking along it. The real journey is toward spiritual vision, toward reunion with the Divine Ground; and thus the Open Road becomes Whitman's equivalent for all the other roads and paths and ways that appear in mystical teachings. It reminds us of the Noble Eightfold Path of the Buddhists, and the Taoist Way; it suggests both the *bhakti-marga* or "path of devotion" and the *karma-marga* or "path of sacrifice"; while it comes closer to being the "big ferry" of the Mahayana sect, in which there is room for every soul to cross to the farther shore. Whitman's conception, however, was even broader. He said one should know "the universe itself as a road, as many roads, as roads for traveling souls."[9]

I am not pleading for the acceptance of Whitman's ideas or for any other form of mysticism, Eastern or Western. I am only suggesting that his ideas as expressed in "Song of Myself" were bolder and more coherent than is generally supposed, and philosophically a great deal more respectable.

RICHARD CHASE

[1 9 1 4 – 1 9 6 2]

"Song of Myself": Comic drama of the self (1955)

THE MAIN ITEM of the 1855 edition of *Leaves of Grass* was, of course, "Song of Myself," the profound and lovely comic drama of the self which is Whitman's best poem and contains in essence nearly all, yet not quite all, there is to *Leaves of Grass*. The comic spirit of the poem is of the characteristic American sort, providing expression for a realism at once naturalistic and transcendental, for the wit, gaiety, and festive energy of all good comedy, and also for meditative soliloquy, at once intensely personal and strongly generic.

One circumstance that contributes to the general spontaneity of "Song of Myself" is, in fact, Whitman's unsuccessful at-

Reprinted by permission of William Morrow & Company, Inc., from *Walt Whitman Reconsidered* (New York, 1955), 58–82, abridged.

tempt to be an Emersonian or Wordsworthian moralist. In his preface, he wrote that "of all mankind the great poet is the equable man. Not in him but off from him things are grotesque or eccentric or fail of their sanity . . . He is the arbiter of the diverse and he is the key. He is the equalizer of his age and land." Whitman tries, indeed, to install himself in his poem on this high moral ground: he will, he says, first regenerate himself by leaving the fallacious artificialities of modern life and getting back to fundamentals; then, having perfected himself as the norm, he will summon all the world to him to be freed of its abnormalities. But although in the poem the self remains pretty much at the center of things, Whitman finds it impossible to accept the idea that it is a norm. To the sententious prophet who "promulges" the normative self, the comic poet and ironic realist keep introducing other, disconcertingly eccentric selves.

Who goes there? hankering, gross, mystical, nude. . . .[1]

Whoever he is, he is not in a position to utter morality. The self in this poem *is* (to use Lawrence's phrase) "tricksy-tricksy"; it does "shy all sorts of ways" and is finally, as the poet says, "not a bit tamed," for "I too am untranslatable." So that as in all true, or high, comedy, the sententious, the too overtly insisted-on morality (if any) plays a losing game with ironical realism. In the social comedy of Molière, Congreve, or Jane Austen, moral sententiousness, like other deformities of comportment or personality, is corrected by society. But this attitude is, of course, foreign to Whitman, who has already wished to invite society to correct itself by comparing itself with him and who, furthermore, cannot even sustain this democratic inversion of an aristocratic idea. Whitman's comic poetry deflates pretensions and chides moral rigidity by opposing to them a diverse, vital, indeterminate reality.

"I resist any thing better than my own diversity," says Whitman, and this is the characteristic note of "Song of Myself." Not that by referring to "Song of Myself" as a "comic" poem I wish too narrowly to limit the scope of discussion—nor do I suggest in using the term a special theory of Whitman or of American literature. I simply respond to my sense that "Song of Myself" is on the whole comic in tone and that although the poem's comic effects are of universal significance, they often take the specific form of American humor. If one finds "Song of Myself" enjoyable at all, it is because one is conscious of how much of the poem, though the feeling in many of its passages need not perhaps have been comic at all, nevertheless appeals to one, first and last, in its comic aspect. The poem is full of odd gestures and whimsical acts; it is written by a neo-Ovidian poet for whom self-metamorphosis is almost as free as free association, who can write "I am an old artillerist" or "I will go to the bank by the wood and become undisguised and naked" as easily as he can write:

> Askers embody themselves in me and I am embodied in them,
> I project my hat, sit shame-faced, and beg.

The sense of incongruous diversity is very strong in "Song of Myself," and although one does not know how the sly beggar projecting his hat or the martial patriot is transformed into the "acme of things accomplish'd," and "encloser of things to be" who suddenly says:

I find I incorporate gneiss, coal, long-threaded moss, fruits, grains,
    esculent roots,
And am stucco'd with quadrupeds and birds all over,

one is nevertheless charmed with the transformation.

Whitman conceives of the self, one might say, as James conceives of Christopher Newman in *The American*—as having the "look of being committed to nothing in particular, of standing in an attitude of general hospitality to the chances of life." In other words, the "self" who is the protagonist of Whitman's poem is a character portrayed in a recognizable American way; it illustrates the fluid, unformed personality exulting alternately in its provisional attempts to define itself and in its sense that it has no definition. The chief difference between "Song of Myself" and *The American* is, of course, the difference between the stages on which Whitman and James allow the self to act, James confining the action to his international scene and Whitman opening his stage out into an eventful universe which is a contradictory but witty collocation of the natural and the transcendent, the imperfect and the utopian, the personal and the generic—a dialectic world out of whose "dimness opposite equals advance" and in which there is "always a knot of identity" but "always distinction.". . .

As every poet does, Whitman asks us provisionally to accept the imagined world of his poem. It is a fantastic world in which it is presumed that the self can become identical with all other selves in the universe, regardless of time and space. Not without precedent in Hindu poetry, this central metaphor is, as an artistic device, unique in American literature, as is the extraordinary collection of small imagist poems, versified short stories, realistic urban and rural genre paintings, inventories, homilies, philosophizings, farcical episodes, confessions, and lyric musings it encompasses in "Song of Myself." Yet as heavily taxing our powers of provisional credence, as inventing a highly idiosyncratic and illusory world, "Song of Myself" invites comparison with other curious works of the American imagination— *Moby Dick*, let us say, and *The Scarlet Letter* and *The Wings of the Dove*. It is of the first importance at any rate to see that Whitman's relation of the self to the rest of the universe is a successful aesthetic or compositional device, whatever we may think of it as a moral assertion.

If we look at Whitman's implicit metaphor more closely, we see that it consists in the paradox of "identity." The opening words of *Leaves of Grass*, placed there in 1867, state the paradox:

> One's-Self I sing, a simple separate person,
> Yet utter the word Democratic, the word En-Masse.

In more general terms the opening lines of "Song of Myself" state the same paradox:

> I celebrate myself, and sing myself,
> And what I assume you shall assume,
> For every atom belonging to me as good belongs to you.

Both politically and by nature man has "identity," in two senses of the word: on the one hand, he is integral in himself, unique, and separate; on the other hand, he is equal to, or even the same as, everyone else. Like the Concord transcendentalists, Whitman was easily led in prophetic moods to generalize the second term of the paradox of identity beyond the merely human world and with his ruthless equalitarianism to conceive the All, a vast cosmic democracy, placid, without episode, separation or conflict, though suffused, perhaps, with a bland illumination. More than anything else, it is this latter tendency which finally ruined Whitman as a poet, submerging as it did, his chief forte and glory—his entirely original, vividly realistic presentation of the comedy and pathos of "the simple separate person."

What finally happens is that Whitman loses his sense that his metaphor of self vs. en-masse is a *paradox*, that self and en-masse are in dialectic opposition. When this sense is lost the spontaneously eventful, flowing, and largely indeterminate universe of "Song of Myself" is replaced by a universe that is both mechanical and vaguely abstract. Whatever, in this universe, is in a state of becoming is moving toward the All, and the self becomes merely the vehicle by which the journey is made.

In some of his best as well as in some of his worst poems, Whitman actually conceives of the self as making a journey— for example, "Song of the Open Road," "Crossing Brooklyn Ferry," and "Passage to India." In others the self journeys, as it were, not forward and outward but backward and inward, back to the roots of its being, and discovers there a final mystery, or love, comradeship, or death—for example, the *Calamus* and *Sea Drift* poems. (Notably among the latter are "Out of the Cradle Endlessly Rocking" and "As I Ebb'd with the Ocean of Life".) In "Song of Myself," however, the self is not felt to be incomplete; it has no questing odyssey to make. It stands aggressively at the center of things, "Sure as the most certain sure, plumb in the uprights, well entretied, braced in the beams." It summons the universe, "syphons" universal experience through its dilating pores, calls "anything back again when I desire it." Or the self imagines itself to be infinitely expandable and contractible (like the web of the spider in Whitman's little poem called "A Noiseless Patient Spider"), so that there is no place where at any moment it may not be, no thing or person with whom it may not merge, no act in which it may not participate. Of great importance is the fact that most of "Song of Myself" has to do not with the self searching for a final identity but with the self escaping a series of identities which threaten to destroy its lively and various spontaneity. This combination of attitudes is what gives "Song of Myself" the alternately ecstatic and gravely musing, pastoral-godlike stability one feels at the center, around which, however, the poet is able to weave the most astonishing embellishments of wit and lyric song.

This is perhaps a valid way of feeling the shifting modes of sensibility in the poem. Yet it would be wrong to attribute any clear cut structure to "Song of Myself." "The United States themselves are essentially the greatest poem," wrote Whitman in his preface. A Jacksonian Democrat, Whitman was not an admirer of federal unity, either in a nation or a poem. He was content to make his poem a loose congeries of states and half-settled territories. He was content that his poem should mirror that "freshness and candor of . . . physiognomy," that "picturesque looseness of carriage," and that "deathless attachment to freedom" which, in his preface, he attributed to his countrymen. His style would be organic; he would "speak in literature with the perfect rectitude and insouciance" of animals and growing things. Although capable of finely pictorial images, Whitman composed more by ear than by eye, and his ear being attuned to music of the looser, more variable sort, such as the Italian operas, he strung his poems together on a free melodic line and by means of motifs, voices, recapitulations, recitatives, rests, *crescendi* and *diminuendi*.

The motif of "Song of Myself" is the self taking on a bewildering variety of identities and with a truly virtuoso agility extricating itself from each one. The poem begins with the exhortation to leave the "rooms . . . full of perfume," the "creeds and schools." Apart from conventions,

> Apart from the pulling and hauling stands what I am,
> Stands amused, complacent, compassionating, idle, unitary.

Having put society and convention behind, "What I am" finds itself in an Edenlike, early-morning world, wherein one easily observes the portentous dialectics of the universe:

Urge and urge and urge,
Always the procreant urge of the world.
Out of the dimness opposite equals advance, always substance and
    increase, always sex,
Always a knit of identity, always distinction, always a breed of life.

[2 5 1

of more importance is the fact that in this idyllic world the
is lifted from the jaundiced eye, the cramped sensibility is
set free, the senses and pores of the body receive the joyful
intelligences dispatched to them by a friendly and providential
nature. The self appears to be the offspring of a happy union of
body and soul; sublime and delightful thoughts issue from the
mind in the same miraculous way as the grass from the ground.
Death itself is seen to be "lucky." And, in short, "what I am"
can well afford to be complacent, to be certain that it is "unitary." Nor is the feeling of power denied to the self. It derives
power from nature, as does the horse—"affectionate, haughty,
electrical"—with which the poet compares himself. It derives
power, too, from identification with others—the "runaway
slave," "the butcher-boy," the "blacksmiths," "the boatmen
and clam-diggers," the "trapper," the "red girl"—and finally
with America itself.

In me the caresser of life wherever moving, backward as well as
    forward sluing,
To niches aside and junior bending, not a person or object missing,
Absorbing all to myself and for this song.

Sections 24–28, though in places rather obscure, contain the
essence of Whitman's drama of identity. The poet begins by
proclaiming himself a Kosmos, and commanding us to "unscrew the locks from the doors! / Unscrew the doors themselves
from their jambs!" so that the universe may flow through him—
"through me the current and index" (that is, the undifferentiated flux and the "identities" that emerge therefrom). This
proclamation announces not only the unshakable status and
palpable reality but also the redemptive powers of the self. In a
world which has been created by banishing social sanctions and
social intelligence, what will keep man from being lost in idiocy,
crime, squalor? What of that underground realm inhabited by

    . . . the deform'd, trivial, flat, foolish, despised,
    Fog in the air, beetles rolling balls of dung?

The threat of madness, crime, and obscenity is to be allayed
by the curative powers of that Adamic world where wisdom
consists in uttering "the pass-word primeval," "the sign of
democracy." Siphoned through the haughty, electrical self or

discussed frankly by persons not inhibited by prudery (the discourses seem perilously interchangeable), the crimes and obscenities will be redeemed:

> Voices indecent by me clarified and transfigur'd.

The poet then records a dreamlike idyl of auto-erotic experience, in which the parts of the body merge mysteriously with natural objects, and a great deal of diffuse and wistful love is generated. And, when dawn comes, the redemption is symbolized in these astonishing metaphors:

> Hefts of the moving world at innocent gambols silently rising freshly exuding,
> Scooting obliquely high and low.
> Something I cannot see puts upward libidinous prongs,
> Seas of bright juice suffuse heaven.

The poem then speaks anew of how the self may be distorted or destroyed. The poet's "identity" is said to be assailed and warped into other "identities" by agents referred to as "traitors," "wasters," and "marauders." Somewhat elusive in particular, these appear to have in common a quality of aggressiveness and imperiousness. They act as a radical individualist conceives society to act. They break down the self, they swagger, they assert convention, responsibility and reason, they dominate and impose passivity and furtiveness on the individual.

The beautiful, diffuse, kindly dawn is succeeded by a more formidable, a more imperious, apparition. The "dazzling and tremendous" sun leaps over the horizon and cries, "See then whether you shall be master!" The poet replies to this challenge by saying that the sunrise would indeed "kill me / If I could not now and always send sun-rise out of me." The power with which the poet defeats what seeks to destroy him is asserted to be "my vision" and "my voice."

> My voice goes after what my eyes cannot reach,
> With the twirl of my tongue I encompass worlds. . . .

In Section 28 there occurs the famous auto-erotic pastoral dream in which "prurient provokers," like nibbling cows, "graze at the edges of me." The "provokers," conceived as symbolic of the sense of touch, arouse and madden the dreaming poet and then they all unite "to stand on a headland and worry me." After touch has "quivered" him "to a new identity"—has left him confused, vexed, self-reproachful, and isolated—he proceeds in the following sections to resume a "true," "real," or "divine" identity. This act of restoration is accomplished through love, natural piety, pastoral and cosmic meditations, symbolic fusions of self with America, allegations of the "deific" nature of democratic man, ritual celebrations, and fatherly preachments, and finally, in the last Section, by the assertion that death is also merely an extrication of the self from an identity.

Everyone has noticed that the large, bland exterior of Walt Whitman concealed a Dionysus or Pan—one of the first was Moncure Conway, who visited Walt in Brooklyn in the summer of 1857,[2] found him basking in the sun on a hill near the Whitman house, and later noticed that the only decorations in the poet's room were two engravings, "one of Silenus and the other of Bacchus." And surely no one can read "Song of Myself" without seeing that Whitman recreates there something of the spirit of the Greek cults out of which comedy evolved. Does he not summon us, his boon companions, to the outdoor revel, to "dance, laugh, sing," to celebrate the phallic god? Are not masks donned and removed, "identities" concealed and exchanged? Do we not have a ritual celebration of "Nature without check with original energy," of the cycle of death and rebirth, the *agon*, sacrifice, and *gamos* of the protagonist, i.e. the self? Do we not have in Whitman's image of the diffusion of the self in nature a religious feeling akin to that engendered in the Dionysian mysteries by the dismemberment and assimilation of the sacrificial victim?

To be sure, the "mysticism" we ordinarily associate with Whitman is less akin to Dionysian than to Oriental and Quaker religion. His mode of religious contemplation, taking it by and large, tends toward passivity and quietism. There is much of this quietism even in "Song of Myself." But the poem as a whole takes its tone from something more vital, indeterminate, violent, and primitive. And it is only to find the most appropriate name for this that one hits on the word "Dionysian." The ritual submovement of comedy asserts itself with a brilliant if spasmodic energy in "Song of Myself." It provides a metaphorical foundation for even the most elaborately artificial of verbal fancies such as "I recline by the sills of the exquisite flexible doors" or "I depart as air, I shake my white locks at the runaway sun"—lines which in point of rococo refinement rival anything that Congreve's Millamant might say to Mirabell.

Historically, Whitman's "American humor" is indeed related, however remotely, to the Restoration comedy. Broadly speaking, there have been in English since 1660 three manifestations of the comic spirit: the aristocratic high comedy of Congreve, the bourgeois sentimental or genteel comedy (by far the most pervasive and influential sort ever since the Restoration), and that American humor which has been practiced in one way or another and at one time or another by nearly all of our best writers. This is not the place to attempt a history of comedy or an analysis of American humor—the latter has been done exquisitely, if a little impressionistically, by Constance Rourke. One may merely venture the idea that, historically, American humor is a radical modification of sentimental comedy. At its best—in Mark Twain, Melville, Thoreau, or Whitman—it retains the capacity of sentimental comedy for pathos but escapes its sentimentality and its hypocrisy. It achieved this by rejecting the cardinal ethical values of bourgeois comedy—money and domestic fidelity. American humor is contemptuous of, or at least feels remote from, the family and money as ethical norms. In this respect and in its tendency toward cruelty and sheer verbal brilliance it is akin to high comedy.

Considered as a comic poem, "Song of Myself" combines Dionysian gaiety and an impulse toward verbal artificiality with the tone and cultural presuppositions of American humor—a striking feat of hybridization certainly, yet no more so than that which produced *Moby Dick*. The intention here is not to deny the justice of Emerson's remark that Whitman's poem was "a remarkable mixture of the *Bhagvatgeeta* and the *New York Herald*" or of the voluminous but one-sided academic scholarship which, following Emerson's remark, has regarded "Song of Myself" as an amalgam of Oriental philosophy and American realism. The intention is rather to shift the ground of discourse toward a more strictly literary view—the view which Emerson also adumbrated in his remark that the first edition of *Leaves of Grass* was an "extraordinary piece of wit & wisdom."

In 1889 Whitman said to his Camden friends, "I pride myself on being a real humorist underneath everything else" and when it was suggested that he might after all go down in history as a "comedian" he replied that one "might easily end up worse." He will certainly not go down in history as, purely and simply, a comedian. But humor was always a strong part of his sensibility, and it is difficult to see how it ever came to be a cliché about Whitman that "he had no sense of humor." There is substantial evidence that in his early life his mind turned naturally toward comic writing. Much of his newspaper work, particularly the "Sun-Down Papers From the Desk of a School-master," which he wrote for the *Long Island Democrat* and the sketches he did for the New Orleans *Crescent* (1848) show that he had mastered at least the easier tricks of the native folk humor. At various times during the 1840's Whitman expressed in newspaper articles his partiality to Dickens and Carlyle—Dickens whom "I love and esteem . . . for what he has taught me through his writings"; Carlyle, whose *Sartor Resartus* exhibits in abundance the author's "strange wild way." From these two writers Whitman seems to have learned that a great book might be eloquent, crotchety, full of curious events and observations, or a humorous compound of realism, philosophy, and sentiment. He surely learned this even more directly from Emerson's essays. If indeed there are so many parallels between "Song of Myself" and "Self-Reliance" that we almost think the poem a versification of the essay, it is nevertheless true that the parallels are not confined to the philosophic or moral message. There is a good deal of humor in Emerson's essay of the spontaneous, odd, yeasty sort noticed by Santayana, who said that Emerson "was like a young god making experiments in creation: he botched the work and always began on a new and better plan. Every day he said, 'Let there be light,' and every day the light was new." More specifically, what Whitman may have sensed in "Self-Reliance" is the humorous touch-and-go between the self and the author, which underlies the elaborate web of portentous epigram. . . .

But aside from the question of literary influences there is the more fundamental question of cultural influence. Whitman emulated our democratic American ideals to an extent unexampled among our great writers, and there can be no doubt that many of his moral utterances and even his poetic effects are produced by the sublime literalness of the democratic assumptions which were so faithfully registered on his plastic mind and temperament. Tocqueville . . . based a part of his discussion of language and literature in the United States upon his observation that

> In democratic communities each citizen is habitually engaged in the contemplation of a very puny object, namely, himself. If he ever raises his looks higher, he then perceives nothing but the immense form of society at large, or the still more imposing aspect of mankind. His ideas are all either extremely minute and clear, or extremely general and vague; what lies between is an open void.

This habit of mind has induced in American writing a style capable of very great and sudden extremes and has drawn from such writers as Melville, Emerson, Thoreau, and Emily Dickinson their idiosyncratic styles—the common denominator among them being a tendency of the language to shift rapidly from the homely and the colloquial to a rhetoric at once highly self-conscious, highly abstract, and highly elaborate. Since such shifts of ground between incongruous extremes are of the essence of wit, it is proper to speak of wit, or as we say, of "American humor," as a central problem in any exact investigation of the language of American literature—so long as we keep in mind how very pervasive an attitude is American humor. For indeed this form of wit is not confined to rural hoe-downs, minstrel shows, or tall tales about Paul Bunyan. It is a style, a habit of thought which allows for the different combinations of the native vernacular and traditional English created by the American authors, as well as their common habit of shifting with such brilliant effect from the particular to the general, from the small to the great, from the concrete to the transcendent. To encompass such effects a language must be highly flexible, capable not of subtle and sustained modulations, as is the prose of Edmund Burke or the poetry of Shakespeare, but—as Selincourt observed in writing about Whitman's language—of rapid transpositions, rapid shifts of language and of levels of discourse. And if these remarks are generally true of all American authors, they seem more literally true of Whitman than of anyone else. . . .

One had better hasten to admit that a good deal of caution is called for in arguments which adduce the culture a poet lives in to explain his aesthetics. For one thing, it is of course impossible to say just what American culture is or to be sure that one traces aright its manifold influences on poetry. Then, again, no culture is perfectly unique. France has had democratic poets, there are moments in Rabelais and Kafka which seem indistinguishable from "American humor," Heine and Arnold wrote relatively "free verse," Whitman's own ideals were not only national but international. Yet the fact remains that we do have an observable national culture as well as an inherited European one, and that a truly historical critique of Whitman's poetry must begin with a view of the spoken and unspoken assumptions, the myths and habits of mind, the manners and "sentiments," of the culture the poet lived in. . . .

Granted, these are not qualities which excite our age, which is very much an age of moral gloom. Granted, too, that Whitman's moral vision is dubious and contradictory. One must admit, furthermore, that although it has its own virtues, Whitman's utopian version of the American pastoral myth has so far proved less artistically dependable, less suggestive of imaginative possibility than the myth as conceived by the other classic authors. And despite Whitman's much asserted Americanism, theirs seems just at present to be historically the more influential myth. As I have suggested before, Whitman achieved the remarkable feat of being an eccentric by taking more literally and mythicizing more simply and directly than anyone else the expressed intentions and ideals of our democracy. He is, in "Song of Myself," the only really "free" American. He is, or seems to be, beyond good and evil, beyond the compulsion to pit his ideals against history and social reality. Cooper, Melville, Mark Twain are never so transcendently free; their dreams are troubled and their having dreams makes them sad and guilty; they impose upon us the weary task of moral judgment and upon themselves a willed and rhetorical self-justification. And if Whitman affords a welcome contrast to our American moralists, he also floods the ego with a vital gaiety of a special quality unknown to Europe—unless, indeed, the note was struck by Nietzsche, who complains of the thinkers and scholars of his time because "thinking itself is regarded by them as something slow and hesitating, almost as a trouble, and often enough as 'worthy of the sweat of the noble'—not at all as something easy and divine, closely related to dancing and exuberance!" In "Song of Myself" there is none of that straining desperation, that gloomy, willful, grammatical Romanticism which always threatens to take the joy out of the egotism of Byron, Carlyle, and sometimes of Nietzsche himself, no sense of the fated will of the European nineteenth century urging itself toward its melodramatic suicide. And so it is possible sometimes to prefer Whitman's comic vision to the social melodrama of the European writers and the moral idyls of Whitman's compatriots, to value it separately and for what it is—a great releasing and regenerative force.

One may even suppose that future readers may find Whitman more relevant to their vital concerns than the tragic moralists among our American writers. Of these tragic moralists, with their pastoral legend, Cooper may seem the first and Hemingway the last. Yet Whitman may be regarded as more modern than Hemingway. For was it not Whitman who first sought out the grounds on which in the midst of our urban modernization the individual with all his dilemmas and aspirations can exist, whereas Hemingway still clings to a version of nineteenth-century romanticism which in Melville and Mark Twain was already nostalgic? The future reader may not think it an extreme case if someone should remark to him that Whitman's utopian rejection of society is under modern conditions the necessary first step toward the preservation of what is vital in society and the revitalization of what is not, and, furthermore, that despite his intellectual shortcomings, despite even the final disappearance of his idealism into the All, Whitman knew more of the homely root facts of the life of modern society than did Melville or Mark Twain, and that at his best his vision stubbornly began and ended with these root facts.

EDWIN HAVILAND MILLER

[1 9 1 8 –   ]

The doubts of daytime and . . . nighttime:
"The Sleepers" (1968)

"THE SLEEPERS," that strange, haunting, and in places baffling poem which until recently has been neglected and misunderstood, is not only a confession, one of Whitman's most personal revelations, but, more important, a reenactment of ancient puberty rites. The landscape, in which obscure symbols disguise the latent content and the universal taboos, and in which the protagonist undergoes sudden and seemingly inexplicable personal and sexual transformations, is dreamlike, even surrealistic at times, because it evokes vague memories of almost forgotten rites of cultures which provided meaningful communal ceremonies to celebrate the individual's journey to adulthood, as a modern industrial society does not. Unlike a dream, the poem does not end inconclusively, but as in a rite of adolescence the protagonist experiences the terrors of anticipated initiation, with its physical pain, as well as the attendant joys of entrance into manhood and into society—except that the drama in Whitman's poem, of necessity, is played out in the protagonist's consciousness, and that the conclusion is sublimation.

At the beginning of the poem the "I" is wandering "confused . . . . lost to myself," as "with open eyes" he observes the

Reprinted by permission of Houghton Mifflin Company from *Walt Whitman's Poetry: A Psychological Journey* (Boston, 1968), 72–84. All quotations from "The Sleepers" are from the 1855 edition.

sleepers: the wretched who have destroyed themselves, "the gashed bodies on battlefields," the fulfilled lovers, the unrequited lovers. In his bewilderment he sees only the waste of human life, the loneliness of those destined to isolation. Overcome with despair, he stands "with drooping eyes," between wakefulness and sleep, between an oppressive reality and a vision of what may be called a truer reality. Quietly, almost unnoticed, he passes his "hands soothingly to and fro a few inches from" the unhappy people. Almost at once a magical transformation takes place:

The earth recedes from me into the night,
I saw that it was beautiful . . . . and I see that what is not the
    earth is beautiful.

I go from bedside to bedside . . . . I sleep close with the other
    sleepers, each in turn;
I dream in my dream all the dreams of the other dreamers,
And I become the other dreamers.

I am a dance . . . . Play up there! the fit is whirling me fast.

I am the everlaughing . . . . it is new moon and twilight,
I see the hiding of douceurs . . . . I see nimble ghosts whichever
    way I look,
Cache and cache again deep in the ground and sea, and where it is
    neither ground or sea.

With the mind's eye the protagonist sees only superficially and at a distance. With the intuitive eye and with physical contact he enters empathetically into the pangs and joys of the sleepers. For like a child he "sees" through all the senses, particularly the tactile sense. When he is metamorphosed into the "everlaughing," not only is he a child who has abandoned Apollonian reason and cultural repression but also, in his uninhibited dance, a Dionysian in the realm of irrationality, undirected eroticism, and sensuous freedom.

The movement of the hand is pivotal in the development of the poem as well as characteristic of the tactility present in Whitman's poetry. The hand at various times is linked with the mother soothing a child, the father conferring a blessing upon a son, or with autoerotic gratification. The hand brings comfort in "To One Shortly to Die": "Softly I lay my right hand upon

you"; and again in "The Wound-Dresser" in *Drum-Taps:* "The
hurt and the wounded I pacify with soothing hand." In his
idealization of the poet, Whitman endows him with a hand like
that of Michelangelo's Jehovah as he reaches toward Adam.
"Salut Au Monde!" begins, "O take my hand, Walt Whitman!" and concludes like a benediction: "I raise high the
perpendicular hand—I make the signal." The poet in "Starting
from Paumanok" has "a flowing mouth and indicative hand,"
and his power, in "Song of Prudence," is in "the shaping of his
great hands." In "By Blue Ontario's Shore" Whitman declares,
"I lead the present with friendly hand." In place of the chilled
separateness of contemporary America, he foresees, in "For
You O Democracy," "There shall be countless linked hands."
(Gatsby, in a later age, when the "green light" is almost
blacked out, futilely raises his "right hand" to confer futile
blessings.) The hand is also linked with adolescent sexual explo-
rations. The "journeymen divine" in "The Sleepers" accept the
protagonist amorously "with stretched arms." At the conclusion
of an autoerotic dream, "My hands are spread forth . . . I pass
them in all directions," a passage paralleled by one in "Spontaneous Me": ". . . the hot hand seeking to repress what would
master him." Of his beloved he concludes in "Of the Terrible
Doubt of Appearances": "He ahold of my hand has completely
satisfied me." Or in "I Sing the Body Electric" (1860 version): "The curious sympathy one feels, when feeling with the
hand the naked meat of his own body, or another person's
body."

The hand, then, is directly linked with the three roles the "I"
in "The Sleepers" will play in his frequent physical and sexual
metamorphoses—mother, father, and adolescent. It is also vis-
ually expressive of his deepest emotional needs; he seeks the
soothing, protective hand of the mother, sometimes in oedipal
rivalry and eventually in a return to the womb; he craves the
guidance of a father, the symbolic "laying on of hands," which
will free him from dependency and permit him to enter adult
sexuality; and, finally, as a young man entering puberty and
genital awareness he is baffled by his strange reactions to his
parents but elated by the excitement his hands contribute to his
sexual awakening.

Immediately in his night journey the "hero" begins a series of transformations which express his emotional needs and his sexual confusion—in short, the trauma of every adolescent. At first he appears to be "the everlaughing," an aggressive over-man or "boss" of "those journeymen divine," a dominant masculine role which he assumes for a moment as he moves at the head of this "gay gang of blackguards" with "wildflapping pennants of joy"—in unrestrained phallic splendor. But since he has presumed to be the initiator rather than the initiate of the rites, he simultaneously retreats to the role of a dependent youth protected by adults:

> they make me a pet besides,
> And surround me, and lead me and run ahead when I walk,
> And lift their cunning covers and signify me with stretched arms,
>   and resume the way. . . .

The "blackguards"—the term is used affectionately by one emulous of the "roughs"—coax their "pet" to abandon his self-consciousness and adolescent fears of sexuality and "uncover" in order to enter man's estate.

Before the protagonist can assume a masculine role, however, he must reexperience the bisexual desires of adolescence and relive the oedipal conflict. Upon the disappearance of the "blackguards," he declares: "I am the actor and the actress" and "the wellformed person . . . the wasted or feeble person"; and in the first extended dream, beginning with line 46, he plays all the parts in a three-character drama: the amorous woman who "folded her hair expectantly," her "truant love," and the erotic "darkness."

Double yourself and receive me darkness,
Receive me and my lover too . . . . he will not let me go without
   him.

I roll myself upon you as upon a bed . . . . I resign myself to the
   dusk.

He whom I call answers me and takes the place of my lover,
He rises with me silently from the bed.
Darkness you are gentler than my lover . . . . his flesh was sweaty
   and panting,
I feel the hot moisture yet that he left me.

My hands are spread forth . . . I pass them in all directions,
I would sound up the shadowy shore to which you are journeying.

The drama has the confused aspects of a sexual dream in which
the dreamer achieves yet fails of the consummation he craves
because the craving springs from deep-rooted but forbidden
desires which a cultural inhibition decrees must be played out in
shadows. The protagonist is both "the actor and the actress,"
the father as well as the mother. The action represents both
sides of the oedipal ambivalence: the "I" is the woman receiving her "lover," the father, and is the "darkness" that is "gentler than my lover" and replaces the father; thus he is the
father's rival for the mother, and at the same time he substitutes
for the mother in the primal act.

The woman fades away, and the "I" awakens from this
descent into the ambivalences of the human drama—"O hot-
cheeked and blushing! O foolish hectic!" "Where shall I run?" he
asks. He blushes because he dimly perceives, although he dare
not verbalize them, his secret desires, and his guilt again compels him to seek protection. This time he wants to run to the
"Pier that I saw dimly last night when I looked from the win-
dows." Obviously, but "dimly" to the troubled youth, the pier
represents the security of a child-adult relationship, and is apparently like the flag in "Delicate Cluster," a bisexual symbol
—"Pier out from the main, let me catch myself with you and
stay. . . . I will not chafe you." "Chafe" suggests some kind of
physical involvement. If the pier is construed as a male symbol,
at least two interpretations are possible: the "I" seeks again the
relationship he has enjoyed as the "pet" of the "blackguards"
—"chafe" suggesting muscular and sexual overtones—and the
flight may represent the guilty boy's search for the father. If, on
the other hand, the pier is to be linked with feminine water
imagery, then "chafe" may refer to the child at the mother's
breast or to the fetus in the amniotic waters. The latter construction is supported by the last line in the preceding erotic dream of
the woman—"I would sound up the shadowy shore to which you
are journeying"—and by the womblike state depicted in the
concluding lines of the poem.

Both constructions are valid and applicable in view of the
previously noted sexual transformations and the oedipal ambi-

valences. At the same time the young man is, literally, awakening from an erotic dream and is perplexed and frightened by his aroused sexuality:

I feel ashamed to go naked about the world,
And am curious to know where my feet stand . . . . and what is
    this flooding me, childhood or manhood . . . . and the hunger
    that crosses the bridge between.

Here with sensitive insight Whitman recreates a young man's feeling of shame, about which Erik Erikson has written most perceptively:

Shame is an infantile emotion insufficiently studied. . . . Shame supposes that one is completely exposed and conscious of being looked at: in one word, self-conscious. One is visible and not ready to be visible; which is why we dream of shame as a situation in which we are stared at in a condition of incomplete dress, in night attire, "with one's pants down." Shame is early expressed in an impulse to bury one's face, or to sink, right then and there, into the ground.[1]

For the protagonist, since he is alone, only imagines his public exposure, and reveals, as in his earlier retreat into the arms of the "blackguards," that he is not ready to be seen as a man. (Perhaps it is oversubtle to point out what appear to be unconscious associations of "pier" and "peer," both in terms of sight and relationships.)

The involuntary orgasmic spasm, which duplicates the involuntary movement of the hand at the beginning of the night journey, introduces the second crucial symbol—"the bridge." The sexual context in which the word appears reveals that it is more than simply a means of crossing from childhood to manhood, and seems better explained by Marie Bonaparte's psychoanalytic commentary: a bridge is "a representation of the penis which the male infant cannot and the male adult must not use as a means of sexual intercourse with the mother, but also a symbol of the 'extroverted mother . . .' or vagina dentata."[2] The obscurities of the following stanza become more comprehensible when we recognize the bisexual fantasy and what may be traces of the ancient puberty rites which Bruno Bettelheim analyzes in *Symbolic Wounds*.

The cloth laps a first sweet eating and drinking,
Laps life-swelling yolks . . . . laps ear of rose-corn, milky and just
    ripened:
The white teeth stay, and the boss-tooth advances in darkness,
And liquor is spilled on lips and bosoms by touching glasses, and the
    best liquor afterward.

It is, of course, obvious and significant that the "I" visualizes genitals and sexuality in oral images—that, in other words, the protagonist, according to Bettelheim's description of an ancient ceremony, "may also be mastering great fear of or desire for the vagina through oral incorporation."[3] At the same time the passage reveals the boy's misunderstanding of the female genitals, when Whitman employs the (now) classic symbol of "white teeth." ("Boss-tooth" recalls the earlier reference to "boss.") The youth's conception of coitus retains the infantile association of sexuality and physical assault, just as the earlier line, "Double yourself and receive me darkness," is more reminiscent of masturbation than of mature sexuality. And the last line in this extraordinary passage is a strange combination of masturbatory and sexual imagery which at the same time suggests that the child is still at the mother's breast.

Despite Whitman's evocation of psychic depths, artistically he is in firm control of his material, since this first poetic climax corresponds with the autoerotic climax, which, in turn, fuses the tactile imagery ("touching glasses"), the phallicism, and the regressive sexual fantasies. The movement of the poem, like the orgiastic crescendoes and decrescendoes in the music of Richard Wagner, captures the protagonist's sexual tensions and anxieties, the release or autoerotic gratification, and the relaxation of the sexual afterglow ("and the best liquor afterward"). Only with this sexual expenditure is the protagonist at peace with himself and the universe: "I descend my western course . . . . my sinews are flaccid." The disturbing subterranean excitement in some of Whitman's best poems comes in large part from this orgiastic movement.

With seeming serenity the protagonist now continues his quest in order to make the choice between "childhood or manhood," but since the choice has already been made—in his retreat among the "blackguards" and in his search for the protection of the "pier"—the quest is basically illusory. New situations are only variations upon earlier situations, and the "I" invariably retreats to the protected position of the child or of the fetus. The destination is indicated in his transformations into a grandmother darning "my grandson's stockings" and into "the sleepless widow"—the one looks after the child and the other mourns her husband, whose role the "I" immediately assumes. At the conclusion of the brief second section the "I," significantly, is in the "coffin" and is enjoying the warm protectiveness of the "dark grave." (Here we have the linkage of the cradle and the coffin which is to be elaborated later in "Out of the Cradle Endlessly Rocking.") That the sexual bed in the preceding scene becomes the death bed is inevitable: "Sinews . . . flaccid" with sexual satiety find their ultimate place of rest, and the veiled oedipal desire has no resolution except in death. For in this episode the "I" is the widow and the shroud, husband and wife, father and mother—the grave is the "solution" for the boy who wishes the father dead, and wishes himself dead for having the wish. In death there is release from guilt and torment: "it is not evil or pain here . . . . it is blank here, for reasons."

In the third section the "I" is on the shore observing "a beautiful gigantic swimmer" "in the prime of his middle age" —a figure that immediately calls to mind the middle-aged poet himself who, as we have noted, "dotes" upon the beauties of his body. The swimmer, we are told, has "courageous arms" which, however, cannot save him from the "swift-running eddies." His vigorous muscular movements are as futile as the protagonist's verbalization of his hatred for the "ruffianly red-trickled waves." In fact, the swimmer's struggles are as fruitless as the "I's" erotic wishes, and end in the same way, in death: "Swiftly and out of sight is borne the brave swimmer." The insistent use of water imagery to suggest sexuality further links the middle-aged athlete and the protagonist: "the shadowy shore" in the scene with the expectant woman, the pier to which the boy flees, the description of orgasm in terms of "flooding" and "spilled" liquor. The death of the swimmer appears to be an elaboration of the image of the "white teeth," the emblem of destructive feminine sexuality.

If the sea, as customarily in Whitman's poetry, is the female principle—the use of the word "ruffianly" tends to make the waves human—then once again we are witnesses of a trio. This time the helpless boy on the shore watches the destruction of man by woman. Similarly, in the next scene he observes as the sea destroys a ship and spews the bodies of men on the shore. The hands which bring rest to the restless in the opening section and which lead to autoerotic gratification in the second section are now as impotent as the swimmer's "courageous arms": "I cannot aid with my wringing fingers." These two scenes, then, appear to depict the sexually aggressive woman (or mother), the destruction of virile men by a superior force, and the "I" as a passive spectator or helpless child—or, to put it in psychological terms, one half of the oedipal ambivalence. At the same time the episodes suggest, although undoubtedly their author had no such conscious intention, Whitman's fear of heterosexuality and his evasion of "manhood." Yet this is not quite the whole story, for when the body of the swimmer is "borne" away by the sea, it disappears only to be "born" again.

Abruptly in Section 5 the poem shifts from its sequence of events occurring in the timeless vacuum of dreams to incidents in historical time. At first sight the transition appears to be sudden and perhaps even contrived, but actually the episode involving George Washington and the tale allegedly told to the poet by his mother are elaborations of themes present in the preceding action of the poem. For the "I's" feeling of inadequacy as he witnesses the deaths of the swimmer and then of the ship's crew parallels a similar feeling on the part of General Washington, who "cannot repress the weeping drops" when "he sees the slaughter of the southern braves confided to him by their parents." After "the defeat at Brooklyn" we see Washington, now about to become the father of his country, saying farewell to his officers: "He kisses lightly the wet cheeks one after another." Like the "fish-shaped island" in "As I Ebb'd with the Ocean of Life," Washington is a benevolent father-figure who can give affection and weep in pity but who is powerless to check the slaughter of young men; and he reappears in "The Centenarian's Story," one of the poems in *Drum-Taps:*

I saw the moisture gather in drops on the face of the
General;
I saw how he wrung his hands in anguish.

Interestingly, Whitman chooses, although other choices were
possible, to describe "the defeat at Brooklyn," the scene of a
major historical defeat but also of a personal one. And it can
scarcely be overlooked that the poem is in one sense a chronicle
of the deaths of men, the husband in the coffin, the middle-aged
swimmer, the sailors, and now the Revolutionary War soldiers.

The tale Whitman tells in the following section of an event in
his mother's early life also centers upon loss. In her childhood a
beautiful Indian squaw had come to her home one day selling
"rushes for rushbottoming chairs." At once Mrs. Whitman fell
in love with the Indian: "The more she looked upon her she
loved her." Later in the day the Indian went on her way, but
"All the week she thought of her . . . . she watched for her
many a month." This tale of a young girl's infatuation with the
squaw leads to an outburst of rage:

Now Lucifer was not dead . . . . or if he was I am his sorrowful
    terrible heir;
I have been wronged . . . . I am oppressed . . . . I hate him that
    oppresses me,
I will either destroy him, or he shall release me.

Damn him! how he does defile me,
How he informs against my brother and sister and takes pay for
    their blood,
How he laughs when I look down the bend after the steamboat that
    carries away my woman.

The protagonist's sudden fury is not related directly to the
encounter between his mother and the Indian woman, which
occurred before he was born, but to unconscious associations
which, though disguised in the tale, are related to an unresolved
personal conflict.

The squaw's disappearance is a betrayal and rejection of a
child's love by an older woman. Like the merciless sea she is
another destructive maternal figure. Unconsciously the "I" is
recording a young man's feeling of maternal betrayal by projecting the betrayal upon the Indian, since he does not dare to

indict the mother directly. At the same time the squaw, like his father, is his rival since she has stolen his mother's affections. Thus it is that when he is ready to "destroy" his rival, he suddenly shifts to the masculine pronoun, and at once makes clear, as Richard Chase has observed, that he is voicing his oedipal murderous tendencies. He invokes the mythic arch-traitor, Lucifer, who serves a complex function in the poem. Lucifer, of course, had rebelled against the Father, as the "I" does in his oedipal rivalry. The fallen angel had also deprived Adam and Eve of their idyllic happiness in Eden, as a father deprives the son who wants to maintain his possessive relationship with his mother. At the same time there are still traces in the passage of an earlier version in which "Black Lucifer" is an enraged slave whose master begets children by the Negro's "woman" and then sells mother and children down the river. On a mythic and social level, then, the "I" identifies himself with people as dispossessed as he is. In addition, the Indian squaw and Lucifer, both of whom are aliens, as is the Negro, are lawless and treacherous, and so too is the protagonist's frenzy for vengeance.

The journey that begins with "mirthshouting music" reaches its climax with the "I's" expression of murderous fury. But the rage is merely verbalized, not acted upon. Once more the protagonist is wringing his hands. When he exclaims, "how he does defile me," he voices his feelings of impotency, as in that fearful earlier line, "I feel ashamed to go naked about the world." The disappearance of the woman "down the bend" recalls the line in the dream sequence, "I would sound up the shadowy shore to which you [the woman] are journeying." The protagonist attributes a perhaps imaginary mirth to the man (the father) who "laughs when I look down the bend after the steamboat that carries away my woman." "My woman" is, ambiguously, a wife or, more precisely, a mother.

The verbal outburst, like the earlier orgasm, provides release for pent-up tension and anxiety. As the cyclical pattern of the poem is repeated, once again the protagonist retreats—first to the protective custody of the Dionysians, then to the "pier" after the autoerotic scene which is dominated by regressive oral imagery, and now, in a brilliant metamorphosis not without its humorous aspects, to the role of a gigantic but phlegmatic whale.

Now the vast dusk bulk that is the whale's bulk . . . . it seems mine,
Warily, sportsman! though I lie so sleepy and sluggish, my tap is death.

The whale (in color here not unreminiscent of Lucifer, or at least "Black Lucifer"), in myth and in *Moby-Dick*, plays a bisexual role not unrelated to the protagonist's confused bisexuality. The "I" momentarily fancies that "my tap is death," as he pictures himself in an aggressively masculine role. But "pennants of joy" again prove too much for him, and despite his latent power he lies "sleepy and sluggish" in the feminine sea. The final visual effect is of a fetus lying safely and securely in the womb. Again "my sinews are flaccid." The "sportsman" need not fear the child or rival: he will not—indeed, he cannot —cross the "bridge." He has returned home.

And so too, as the catalogue beginning at line 142 makes clear, the tormented, unrequited people who appear early in the poem are now sailing home. The atmosphere magically changes to reflect the "I's" new mood: there is "A show of summer softness," and the moon is no longer "floundering" because the "I" has found himself. Although there is still another trio—the light, the air, and the "I"—the eroticism is playful rather than anxiety-producing: "And have an unseen something to be in contact with them also." The "tap" is now a child's harmless and innocent sexual play. Even the "myth of heaven" which "indicates the soul" is transformed, somewhat miraculously, by the childlike, narcissistic perspective from which it is viewed:

It comes from its embowered garden and looks pleasantly on itself and encloses the world;
Perfect and clean the genitals previously jetting, and perfect and clean the womb cohering,
The head wellgrown and proportioned and plumb, and the bowels and joints proportioned and plumb.

With this birth, "every thing is in its place." The agitated music characteristic of a young man's erotic and oedipal torment gives way to the music of the waves of the sea, not dashing

white bodies against the rocks, but serene and regular and
unceasing, as the sleepers, like children, "flow hand in hand
over the whole earth from east to west." What an extraordinary
line this is, so wondrously evocative, so natural and unobtrusive
in its diction—and Whitman is alleged to be a careless artist!
Almost unnoticed, the water imagery culminates in the word
"flow"; "hand in hand" quietly reintroduces this pivotal motif
and at the same time establishes a tactile bond where before
there was only separateness; and the simple, childlike language
is not only a statement of affirmation but also preparation for the
completion of the circular journey.

I too pass from the night;
I stay awhile away O night, but I return to you again and love you;
Why should I be afraid to trust myself to you?
I am not afraid . . . . I have been well brought forward by you;
I love the rich running day, but I do not desert her in whom I lay so
    long:
I know not how I came of you, and I know not where I go with you
    . . . . but I know I came well and shall go well.

From what is in one sense an evasive perspective since it is a
kind of death wish for an edenic home, the final retreat, but in
another sense an acceptance of, or faith in, the meaningfulness
of life despite painful evidence to the contrary, the "I" sees
himself as part of an eternal cycle which is dominated not by a
destructive maternal figure but by a goddess of fertility:

I will duly pass the day O my mother and duly return to you;
Not you will yield forth the dawn again more surely than you will
    yield forth me again,
Not the womb yields the babe in its time more surely than I shall be
    yielded from you in my time.

How different yet similar the conclusion of *Moby-Dick* is. While
Whitman sings "a constant sacrament of praise" (to borrow
Wallace Stevens' lovely phrase), and moves beyond tragedy to
what, of course, may be only illusory security, Melville records
the frightful destruction of the Pequod—"then all collapsed, and
the great shroud of the sea rolled on as it rolled five thousand
years ago"—only to correct this tragic perspective in an epilogue
in which Ishmael's words and invocation of the eternal mother
resemble Whitman's:

Buoyed up by that coffin, for almost one whole day and night, I floated on a soft and dirge-like main. The unharming sharks, they glided by as if with padlocks on their mouths; the savage sea-hawks sailed with sheathed beaks. On the second day, a sail drew near, nearer, and picked me up at last. It was the devious-cruising Rachel, that in her retracing search after her missing children, only found another orphan.

LEO SPITZER

[1887–1960]

EXPLICATION DE TEXTE *Applied to Walt Whitman's Poem "Out of the Cradle Endlessly Rocking" (1949)*

AFTER THIS RAPID and over-simplified survey it should have become clear that in the poem "Out of the Cradle" Whitman has offered a powerful original synthesis of motifs which have been elaborated through a period of 1500 years of Occidental poetry. The poems I have mentioned are not necessarily his immediate material sources; but I am convinced that his "bird or demon" is a descendant of Shelley's "Sprite bird," that the brother mocking-bird is one of Saint Francis' brother creatures, that his "feathered guests from Alabama" is a derivate from Arnold's "wanderer from a Grecian shore," that the conception of "a thousand singers, a thousand songs . . . a thousand echoes" all present in the poet is a re-elaboration of Victor Hugo's "âme aux mille voix" and "écho sonore."[1] Be this as it

Reprinted by permission of Princeton University Press from *Essays on English and American Literature*, ed. by Anna Hatcher (Princeton, 1962), 21–36, abridged; reprinted from *Journal of English Literary History*, XVI (1949). I have omitted Spitzer's notes, which, while interesting, are not necessary for the explication.

may, the basic motifs in which the idea of world harmony has taken shape in Europe must be in our mind when we read Whitman's poem, which becomes greater to the degree that it can be shown as ranking with, and sometimes excelling, the great parallel poems of world literature.

Our poem is organized in three parts: a *procemium* (ll. 1–22), the tale of the bird (ll. 23–143), and the conclusion in which the influence of the bird on the "outsetting bard" is stated (l. 144 to the end). Parts one and three correspond to each other and occasionally offer parallel wording.

The proem, composed in the epic style of "arma virumque cano," not only defines the theme of the whole poem clearly but translates this definition into poetry. The proem consists of one long, "oceanic" sentence which symbolizes by its structure the poetic victory achieved by the poet: "Out of the Cradle . . . down . . . up . . . out . . . from . . . I, chanter of pains and joys, uniter of here and hereafter . . . A reminiscence sing." Out of the maze of the world, symbolized by those numerous parallel phrases, introduced by contrasting prepositions, which invite the inner eye of the reader to look in manifold directions, though *out of* and *from* predominate—out of the maze of the world emerges the powerful Ego, the "I" of the poet, who has extricated himself from the labyrinth (his victory being as it were sealed by the clipped last line "a reminiscence sing").

The longer the sentence, the longer the reader must wait for its subject, the more we sense the feeling of triumph once this subject is reached: the Ego of the poet that dominates the cosmos. It is well known that this is the basic attitude of Walt Whitman toward the world. "Walt Whitman am I, a kosmos, of mighty Manhattan the son! turbulent, fleshy, and sensual . . . ," he says in the "Song of Myself" (24). He felt himself to be a microcosm reflecting the macrocosm. He shares with Dante the conviction that the Here and the Hereafter collaborate toward his poetry, and as with Dante this attitude is not one of boastfulness. Dante felt impelled to include his own human self (with all his faults) because in his poem his Ego is necessary as a representative of Christendom on its voyage to the Beyond. Walt Whitman felt impelled to include in his poetry his own self (with all his faults) as the representative of American democracy undertaking this worldly voyage of exploration. "And I say to mankind, Be not curious about God . . . I see something of God each hour of the twenty-four, . . . In the faces of men and women I see God, and in my own face in the glass." "I am of old and young, of the foolish as much as the wise, . . . one of the Nation of many nations . . . A Southerner soon as a Northerner . . . Of every hue and caste am I, of every rank and religion."[2] But in contrast to Dante, who knew of an eternal order in this world as in the Beyond, Whitman finds himself faced with an earthly reality whose increasing complexity made correspondingly more difficult his achievement of poetic mastery. Therefore Whitman must emphasize more his personal triumph. The complexity of the modern world finds its usual expression with Whitman in the endless catalogues, so rarely understood by commentators: in what I have called his "chaotic enumeration" . . . , a device, much imitated after him by Rubén Darío, Claudel, and Werfel. This poetic device consists of lumping together things spiritual and physical, as the raw material of our rich, but unordered modern civilization which is made to resemble an oriental bazaar. In this poem it is only one specific situation whose material and spiritual ingredients Whitman enumerates: the natural scene (Paumanok beach at night), the birds, the sea, the thousand responses of the heart of the boy-poet, and his "myriad thence-arous'd words"—they are all on one plane in this poem, no one subordinated to another, because this arrangement corresponds to Whitman's chaotic experience. Similarly the two temporal planes, the moment when the boy felt the "myriad words" aroused in him on Paumanok beach, and the other when the mature poet feels the rise of "the words such as now start the scene revisiting," are made to coincide because, at the time of the composition of the poem, they are felt as one chaotic but finally mastered experience: the boy who observed the birds now has become the poet. When defining his creative role here in the poem, Whitman does not indulge in chaotic enumeration of his qualities as he does in the passage from the "Song of Myself" in which he appears as a Protean demigod. Now he presents himself simply and succinctly as: "I, chanter of pains and joys, uniter of here and hereafter." Out of hydra-like anarchy he has created unity;

and, as we see, he has gained not only an emotional, but an intellectual triumph; he represents himself as "taking all hints, but swiftly leaping beyond them" like a master philologian or medieval glossator (later he will insist on his role as cautious "translator of the birds' cry," lines 31 and 69). Whitman takes care to impress upon us the intellectual side of the synthesis he has achieved, a claim that is not unjustified and an aspect that should be stressed more in a poet in whose work generally only the sensuous and chaotic aspect is emphasized.

His "uniting" powers have been revealed to us in his first stanza, in fact in the first line of the poem which gives it its title. With its rocking rhythm, the line suggests the cradle of the infinite sea from which later, at the end of the poem, *death* will emerge. At this stage, however, death is already a part of the situation. It is present in the phrase "From the word stronger and more delicious than any," which the reader is not yet able to understand. Now we can visualize only the ocean, the main instrument in the concert of world harmony with which the song of the bird and the thousand responses of the poet fuse. Whitman restores the Ambrosian fullness and the unity of *Stimmung* of the world concert of love, music, and ocean (but obviously without Ambrose's theism).[3] There will be no dainty *Vogelkonzert* in a German romantic nook, no dolorous dialogue between a soul estranged from nature and a bird-sprite in an English countryside; the American ocean, "the savage old mother," will provide the background and the undertone to the whole poem. In this Ambrosian concert of world harmony we may distinguish also the Hugoian voice of the poet consisting of a thousand voices; but the insistent repetitions "a thousand singers, a thousand echoes" give rather the effect of a struggle on the poet's part, a struggle with the infinite, than that of a complacent equation ("I am the universe!") such as we find in Hugo.

After the organ- and tuba-notes that resound in the proem, the tone changes entirely in the main part, which is devoted to the reminiscence proper, to the singing of the mocking-birds and the listening of the boy. Here we find a straightforward narrative interrupted by the lyrical songs or "arias" of the birds. Given the setting of nature within which the boy and the bird meet, the term *aria* (ll. 130, 138) with its operatic, theatrical connotation as well as the musicological term *trio* (l. 140) that immediately follows (applied to the ears, the tears, and the soul of the boy), may seem too *précieux*. In "Song of Myself," we recall, Whitman speaks of the tree-toad as "a *chef-d'œuvre* for the highest."[4] But we must also remember that Whitman's world-embracing vision is able to contain in itself opposite aspects of the world at once together. In this vision the man-made or artificial has its genuine place near the product of nature and may even be only another aspect of the natural. The song of the mocking-bird, so naturally sweet, is an artifact of nature that teaches the human artist Whitman.

To return to our narrative, this offers us a development in time of the theme that had been compressed to one plane in the proem: the boy become poet. In such a development, we would expect, according to conventional syntax, to find the historical flow of events expressed by verbs. But to the contrary, this narrative section offers throughout an almost exclusively nominal style, that is, the coupling of nouns with adjectives or participles, without benefit of finite verbs or copulas. This is an impressionistic device known in French as *écriture artiste*, which was introduced by the Goncourts in their diary in the 1850's; for example, "Dans la rue. Tête de femme aux cheveux retroussés en arrière, dégageant le bossuage d'un front étroit, les sourcils remontés vers les tempes. . . ; un type physique curieux de l'énergie et de la volonté féminines" (*Journal des Goncourt*, 1856, 1, 134). This we call impressionistic because with the suppression of the verb the concatenation and development of happenings give way to the listing of unconnected ingredients, or, in pictorial terms, to touches of color irrespective of the units to which the colored objects belong. Accordingly, we find with Whitman: "Once Paumanok . . . two feather'd guests . . . and their nest . . . and every day the he-bird to and fro . . . and every day . . . I . . . cautiously peering . . . ," a procedure that is brought to a high point of perfection in that masterpiece of the last stanza of the second part: "The aria sinking, all else continuing, the stars shining. . . . The boy ecstatic. . . . The love in the heart long pent. . . ." I see in these participles nervous notations of the moment which serve not to re-enact actions, but to perpetuate the momentary impressions which these have made on the boy when he was perceiving them. When the boy sensed that the melancholy song was subsiding, he jotted down in the book of memory the words: "Aria sinking," and we the readers may still perceive that first nervous reaction. The development of the boy is then given the style appropriate to a "reminiscence." The style here chosen is such as to impress upon us the fragmentary nature of the naked "reminiscence." Because of the non-finite form of the participles, single moments are forever arrested, but, owing to the verbal nature of these forms, the moment is one of movement, of movement crystallized. Of course, such vivid rendering of a reminiscence is possible only in languages, such as English or Spanish, that possess the progressive form, of which the simple participle may represent the elliptical variant.

Now, from line 138 on, while the initial rhythm of the stanza seems to continue, there appear strange inversions such as "The aria's meaning, the ears, the soul, swiftly depositing" (for "the ears, the soul swiftly depositing the aria's meaning" and similarly in lines 139 and 140), inversions quite unusual in English, even jarring upon the English *Sprachgefühl*. We must evidently suppose that the *extasis* (l. 136) of the boy is working in an effort comparable to travail toward an intellectual achievement. It is "the aria's *meaning*" that is now being found by him and the jarring construction is the "impressionistic" rendering of the difficulty with which this inner event is made to happen. It has already been noted that the activities here reflected by the sequence of participles and other modifiers are all of equal weight. We have not yet stressed the extent to which the "enumerative" procedure has been carried out in our stanza, which indeed consists only of detached phrases of the type "the . . . . . . -ing (-ed)." The chaotic enumeration offered us here is intended to show the collaboration of the whole world ("all else," "the stars," "the winds," "the fierce old mother," "the yellow half-moon," "the boy ecstatic," "the love," "the ears, the soul," "the strange tears," "the colloquy, the trio," and "the undertone of the sea") toward that unique event—the birth of a poet out of a child who has grasped the meaning of the world. The nervous, impressionistic enumeration is symbolic of the travail of this birth. On the other hand, the repetition in this whole stanza of the atonic rhyme *-ing*, an ending that had already appeared in the first line with the suggestion of *rocking*, evokes the all-embracing rhythm and permanent undertone or counterpoint of the sea, whether fiercely howling or softly rocking, as it comes to drown out the chamber-music, the *trio* of ears, soul, and tears in the boy. The rhyme in *-ing* is a *leitmotif* that orchestrates the arias of boy and bird and gives the poem a Wagnerian musical density of texture.

As for the songs of the birds, let us note first that Whitman has chosen to replace the hackneyed literary nightingale by a domestic bird of America, the mocking-bird, compared to which, Jefferson once declared, the European nightingale is a third-rate singer. The manner in which Whitman has "translated," to use his modest expression, the song of the mocking-bird into words deserves boundless admiration. I know of no other poem in which we find such a heart-rending impersonation of a bird by a poet, such a welding of bird's voice and human word, such an empathy for the joy and pain expressed by nature's singers. The European poets we have listed above have accurately defined or admiringly praised the musical tone of the bird-notes issuing from tiny throats, but no one attempted to choose just those human articulate words which would correspond to birds' song if these creatures had possessed the faculty of speech . . . : the simple, over and over repeated exclamations of a helpless being haunted by pain, which, while monotonously repeating the same *oh!* or giving in to the automatism that is characteristic of overwhelming emotion ("my love, my love"), call upon all elements to bring back the mate. Thus in one common purpose the whole creation is united by the bird in the manner of Saint Francis, but this time in a dirge that associates the creation ("Oh night"—"Low-hanging moon," "Land, land, land," "Oh rising stars," "Oh darkness") with the mourner, with his elemental body and his elemental desires: "Oh throat," . . . "Oh throbbing heart," . . . "Oh past," "Oh happy life," "O songs of joy." The mournful bird shakes out "reckless despairing carols," songs of *world disharmony* in which love and death are felt as irreconcilable enemies ("carols of lonesome love"—"death's carols"). The long-drawn-out refrains of despair ("soothe soothe soothe," "land land land," "loved loved loved . . .") alternate with everyday speech whose minimum of expressivity becomes a maximum in a moment of tribulation that is beyond words ("so faint, I must be still, be still to listen, but not altogether still, for then she might not come immediately to me," or "O darkness! O in vain! O I am very sick and sorrowful"). The most dynamic American poet has here become the gentlest. We remember Musset's lines quoted above;[5] Whitman's bird's song is a *pur sanglot*.

We may surmise that this lyric section (within a lyric poem) has been somewhat influenced by Matthew Arnold's "Forsaken Merman" ("Come dear children, let us away, down and always below. / Come dear children, come away down, call no more . . ."). But Arnold's merman is one of the last offsprings of that futile masquerade of elementary spirits revived by the Romantics, a pagan demon who is presented as *defeated* by Christianity instead of a figure dangerously seductive to Christians. But Whitman's mocking-bird, the spirit become human, who symbolizes all earthly loveliness subject to grief and death, will live forever. It is one of those historical miracles we cannot explain that in the age of machines and capitalism there should arise a poet who feels himself to be a brother to nature as naturally as did Saint Francis, but who at the same time was enough of an intellectual to know the uniqueness of his gift. To *him* the bird poured forth the "meanings which I of all men know, Yes my brother I know, the rest might not." This is again no boasting; this is the simple truth, a perspicacious self-definition of one who has a primeval genius of empathy for nature.

Now let us turn to the last part of the poem which begins with the words "demon *or* bird" (I, 144), an expression followed later (175) by my "dusky demon *and* brother." The Shelleyan ambiguity disappears here. This marks the end of the parabola that began with "the two feather'd guests from Alabama" (26) and was continued sadly with "the solitary guest from Alabama" (51) and "the lone singer wonderful" (58). While the mood of the bird develops from careless rapture to "dusky" melancholy, a contrary change takes place in the sea. "The fierce old mother incessantly moaning" (133), the "savage old mother incessantly crying" (141) becomes the "old crone rocking the cradle," "hissing melodious," "laving me softly all over." The two opposite developments must be seen in connection. To the degree that the bird is crushed by fate, the sea develops its soothing qualities; to the degree that beauty fades away, wisdom becomes manifest. The sea represents the sweet wisdom of death. The forces of nature are thus ambivalent, Janus-like. Nature wills sorrow and joy, life and death, and it may be that death will become or foster life. "Out of the cradle endlessly rocking," that is (we understand it now), out of the cradle of *death*, the poet will sing life. By presenting, in the beginning, the sea only as a cradle gently rocking, there was suggested the idea of birth and life; but now, the gently rocking cradle is seen as the symbol of recurring death and re-birth. A poet is born by the death of the bird who is a brother and a demon. A brother because he teaches the boy love; a demon, because he "projects" the poet, anticipates, and heralds him, stirs up in him those creative faculties which must partake of the frightening and of the daemonic. But while the bird was destined to teach the boy love ("death" being a reality the bird was not able to reconcile with love), the sea, wiser than the bird and the "arous'd child's heart," has another message to bring to the boy: "Death, death, death, death, death" (173). This line is the counterpart of the mocking-bird's "loved! loved! loved! loved! loved!" and it is couched in the same exclamational style, as though it were the organic continuation thereof. The word *death* is "the word final, superior to all," "the key," "the clew" which awakes in the boy the thousand responses, songs, echoes, and the myriad words; and once he has discovered this *meaning* of life, which is death, he is no longer the boy of the beginning ("never again leave me to be the peaceful child I was before"). He has become the poet, the "uniter of here and hereafter," able to fuse the voices of the *musica mundana* into one symphony, and we the readers can now understand his words in their full depth. In the conclusion we recognize certain lines of the proem textually repeated but now clarified and deepened by the key-word; we understand at last the symphonic value of "that strong and delicious word" alluded to in the proem. The liquid fusion

suggested by the sea of death is symbolized by the fluid syntax
of the last three stanzas; the relative constructions which we find
in l. 165 "Whereto answering, the sea . . ." and l. 174
"Which I do not forget" weld the three stanzas together into
one stream or chain which comprehends the question of the boy,
the answer of the sea, and his choice of avocation, into one
melody in which inspiration flows uninterruptedly from the
watery element to the poet. The bird and the poet have been
given their respective solos in the symphony. The bird's solo is
the *aria* and the boy's the *trio* of ears, soul, and tears; the
endless counterpoint and contrabasso of the sea has accompanied their detached musical pieces. Now all voices blend in an
unendliche Melodie, an infinite melody, the unfixed form of
nineteenth-century pantheism, with Wagnerian orchestration.
"But fuse the song of my dusky demon and brother . . . with
the thousand responsive songs, at random, my own songs . . .
and with them the key, the word up from the waves." The last
word in the poem, however, is the personal pronoun *me*.
Though placed inconspicuously in an unstressed position in the
short line "the sea whisper'd me," this personal word nevertheless represents a (modest) climax. It is to Whitman that has
been revealed the musical meaning of the world, the chord
formed by Eros and Thanatos, the infinite cosmos created from
infinite chaos, and, finally, his own microcosmic role in the
creation. It is the knowledge of death that will make him the
poet of life, of this world, *not* of the Hereafter. The promise in
the beginning to sing of the Here and Hereafter can be said to
have been fulfilled only if the Hereafter is understood as comprised in the Here. We will note that no reference is made in
Whitman's poem to the world harmony of the Christian Beyond
in the manner of Milton. The fullness of life of which Whitman
sings can come to an end only in the sealike, endlessly-rocking
embrace of nothingness, an end that is sweet and sensuous
("delicious" is Whitman's epithet), and, indeed, he appears
sensuously to enjoy the sound of the word *death* that he so often
repeats. We may pause at this point to remember that in 1860,
one year after our lyric was written, Whitman gives expression
to the same feeling in the poem "Scented herbage of my
breast":

You [the leaves] make me think of death,
Death is beautiful from you, (what indeed is finally beautiful except
death and love?)
Oh I think it is not for life I am chanting here my chant of lovers, I
think it must be for death, . . .
Death or life I am then indifferent, my soul declines to prefer,
(I am not sure but the high soul of lovers welcomes death
most,) . . .[6]

The same feeling for the voluptuousness of death and the death-
like quality of love we find not only in Wagner's *Tristan und
Isolde* (1857), in which we hear the same words applied to the
love-scene and to the death-scene, *unbewusst—höchste* (*Liebes-*)
Lust. There is also the same motif in Baudelaire's *Invitation*
of 1857, in which the "invitation" is the lure of death, described
as voluptuous hashish and scented lotus. Perhaps powerful per-
sonalities crave death as a liberation from the burden of their
own individuality, and sensuous poets wish to have a sensuous
death. Perhaps also the concurrence in one motif of three poets
not in direct contact with each other means that their subtle
sensitivity instinctively anticipated the death-germs implanted in
a luxuriant, sensuous, worldly civilization of "Enrichissez-
vous," of Victorianism, and the Second Empire. This was long
before the *fin de siècle* generation of D'Annunzio, Barrès, Hof-
mannsthal, and Thomas Mann, when the theme of love-death,
inherited from Baudelaire and Wagner, finally became the
theme par excellence. But Whitman, unlike his two sickly European contemporary confrères, will remain for us not the poet of
death (although the idea of death may have perturbed him more
than once), but the unique poet of American *optimism* and love
of life, who has been able, naturally and naïvely, to unite what
in other contemporary poets tends to fall apart, the life of man
and that of nature.

A last question arises. To what sub-genre does our lyrical
poem belong? It is obviously an *ode*, the genre made famous by
Pindar, Horace, Milton, and Hölderlin, if the ode may be defined as a solemn, lengthy, lyric-epic poem that celebrates an
event significant for the community, such as, with Pindar, the
victory of a champion in the Olympic games. . . . Whitman
has acclimated the ode on American soil and democratized it.
The lyric-epic texture, the solemn basic tone and the stylistic

variation, the whimsical word-coinages and the chaotic fragmentariness are preserved. The latter feature has even found a modern justification in the complexity of the modern world. For the rhymeless Greek verse, Whitman by a bold intuition found an equivalent in the Bible verset, but he used this meter in order to express a creed diametrically opposed to that of the Bible. Theoretically, he could have borrowed expressions of his pantheistic beliefs from the mythology of the Greeks, but in reality he did away with *all* mythology, pagan as well as Christian. He replaces the pagan Pantheon by the deified eternal forces of nature to which any American of today may feel close. The Ocean is the old savage mother, not Neptune with the trident (a mother, a primeval chthonian goddess), and the bird is not Philomela, but the mocking-bird who is a demon of fertility (only in the phrase "feathered guests of Alabama" do we find a faint reminiscence of Homeric expression, the *epitheton constans*). The Neo-Catholic poet Paul Claudel who, as recently as the last decades, gave the French for the first time a true ode and was able to do so only by a detour through America, by imitating Whitman (even the metric form of his free verse), found it necessary to discard Whitman's pantheistic naturalism and to replace it by the *merveilleux chrétien* which a hundred years ago Chateaubriand had introduced into French prose. But it cannot be denied that Whitman's ode can reach a wider range of modern readers than can Claudel's orthodox Catholic *grande ode*. As for the solemn event significant for the community which the ode must by its nature celebrate—this we have in the consecration of Walt Whitman as a poet, the glorification, not of a Greek aristocratic athlete born of Gods, but of a nameless American boy, a solitary listener and singer on a little-known Long Island shore who, having met with nature and with his own heart, becomes the American national poet, the democratic and priestly *vates Americanus*.

STEPHEN E. WHICHER

[1915-1961]

Whitman's Awakening to Death—Toward a Biographical Reading of "Out of the Cradle Endlessly Rocking" (1960)

IT IS STILL too little realized that, with the possible but not obvious exception of Melville, no American author has ever engaged in a more daring or eventful voyage of the mind than Whitman. In his later years Whitman himself for some reason attempted to hide its extent, retouched and toned down his most revealing poems and ingeniously fitted them together into a structure toward which he claimed he had been working all the time. This jerry-built monument to the aging Whitman, which remains to this day the basis of nearly all anthologies of his work and is still reverently toured by uncritical guides, is actually a major obstacle to the recognition of his true stature. Fortunately a strong critical tradition has now for many years been working to lay bare for us the real structure of Whitman's work, the spiritual biography that emerges from a comparative reading of all the editions of his *Leaves*. In this paper 1 wish to re-examine some part of this story as it emerges from certain key poems of the 1855 and 1860 editions, in particular "Out of the Cradle.". . .¹

This paper was read before the English Institute in 1960 and published in *Studies in Romanticism* (Boston University), I (1961), 9–10, 22–28; also included in *The Presence of Walt Whitman*, ed. R. W. B. Lewis (New York, 1962). Reprinted by permission of Columbia University Press.

In "Out of the Cradle" Whitman has contrived to tell his whole story and even to go beyond it. The long one-sentence "pre-verse" is intended to establish the basic fiction of the poem. The poet will tell us of something long past, he suggests, which now for some reason comes over his memory. By this distancing device he contrives to win some artistic and personal control over his material. In most versions the distinction of the poet that is and the boy that was is made sharp and distinct:

> I, chanter of pains and joys, uniter of here and hereafter . . .
> A reminiscence sing.

Such a bardic line implies firm poetic control, emotion recollected in tranquillity. But neither this line nor the following one is in the 1859 version, where the poet therefore seems much more under the spell of the memories that have seized him:

> A man—yet by these tears a little boy again,
> Throwing myself on the sand, I,
> Confronting the waves, sing.

What has actually seized him, of course, is the meaning *now* to him of these images, so much so that in the first version he has a hard time keeping the presentness of his feelings from bursting through and destroying his narrative fiction.

Nevertheless, the reminiscent mode of the poem greatly enlarges its range by permitting him to bring his whole life to bear on it. As a poem of loss and awakening it goes back even to his very earliest loss and awakening, the "primal" separation of the child from the mother.[2] Though this theme is stressed at once by the poet, especially in the original version, one must avoid reductiveness here. This layer of the poem underlies the whole and already predicts its shape, but it is not the complete structure. From it comes, however, a powerful metaphor for the awakening that is the main subject.

The boy, leaving his bed, finds himself wandering in a strange dark world like something out of Blake, a haunted borderland between shore and sea, here and hereafter, conscious and unconscious. In its troubled restlessness it resembles the moonlit swamp that is glimpsed for a moment in "Song of Myself,"[3] or some of the dream-scenes in "The Sleepers." We sense here, especially in the 1859 version, which is more dark and troubled throughout than the final one, the same dumb, unassuageable grief as in "As I Ebb'd." It also is a wounded world, impotently twining and twisting with the pain of some obscure fatality. Here there is even less visible occasion for such agony, since the chief actor is not a broken poet but a curious child. The poem is heavy with the man's foreknowledge of what the child, now born, must go through. Like the star in "When Lilacs Last," however, the scene also has something to tell, some "drowned secret" which it is struggling to utter. It does not merely mourn a loss, like the seascape in "As I Ebb'd," but also hints of something to be found.

What has drawn the boy from his infantile security into this parturient midnight is a bird. In a flashback the poet tells of the brief May idyll of Two Together, the sudden loss of the she-bird, and the wonderful song of woe that followed, drawing the boy back night after night to listen until the night came when he awakened to its meaning. Then it seemed to him that the bird was a messenger, an interpreter, singing on behalf of the new world he had entered to tell him its secret. This secret is really two secrets, that the meaning of life is love and that he is to be its poet. The song releases the love and the songs of love in his own heart, which he now realizes has long been ready and waiting for this moment; he awakes and ecstatically dedicates himself to this service.

Yet, bewilderingly, this discovery of what life means and what he is for at once plunges him into new trouble and doubt; he finds himself once more groping for something unknown, and is not released until the voice of the sea whispers him a very different secret, the word death. This *double* awakening provides criticism with its chief problem in this poem. It is true that the boy's spiritual development is dramatically consistent and requires no explanation from outside the poem, but it is complex and rapid, an extreme example of dramatic foreshortening. Since it is also intensely personal, the biographical framework I have sketched helps to make its meaning clear.

To put the matter summarily, in the boy's awakening Whitman has fused all his own awakenings together, with the result that his poem moves in one night over a distance which he had taken forty years of life to cover. The emotional foreground, of course, is occupied by the tragic awakening of 1859, the discovery of love not merely as a passion for one particular being rather than an appetite for everything in general, but also as inherently unsatisfied. Love and grief are one. The bird's story is Whitman's story, distanced and disguised, but it is also man's. The outsetting bard of love will be the bard of unsatisfied love because there is no other kind.

But here we encounter a difficulty, for in many of the other poems of 1859 Whitman had suggested that his awakening to love had stopped his poems and ended his poetic career. Of course he could hardly have overlooked the fact that his crisis did arouse him to new poems and to some of his best. Certainly he was proud of this poem, immediately printed it and followed it with one of his self-written reviews announcing that he would not be mute any more. Perhaps we may read a special meaning into his selection of this poem as the first public evidence of his return to song. In this "reminiscence" of the birth of his poetic vocation he is actually celebrating its recovery. The process of relieving his pain in song has now proceeded so far, past "death's outlet" songs like "Hours Continuing Long"[4] and "As I Ebb'd," past a poem of first recognition like "Scented Herbage," that he can now begin to see that the deathblow to his old "arrogant poems" is proving to be a lifeblow to new and better if more sorrowful ones, and so for the first time, in the guise of a reminiscence, he can make not just his grief, but its transmutation into the relief of song the subject of his singing.

In the measure that he recovers his poetic future he also recovers his past. His sense of returning powers naturally picks up and blends with his memories of that other awakening, whenever and whatever it was, that led to the poems of 1855. In the boy's joy he draws on and echoes his first awakening, the ecstatic union of self and soul celebrated in "Song of Myself," when he *had* felt a thousand songs starting to life within him in response to the "song of Two Together." Overlaid on that is his second dark awakening to the truth of "two together no more" which had at first appeared to end his singing. If we thus provisionally disentangle the strands that Whitman has woven together we can understand better why the song of the bird must plunge the boy almost simultaneously into ecstasy and despair.

The steps of this process are obscured for us in the final version by Whitman's deletion of a crucial stanza that explains why the boy needs a word from the sea when he already has so much from the bird. After the lines

O give me some clue!
O if I am to have so much, let me have more!

the original version continued as follows:

O a word! O what is my destination?
O I fear it is henceforth chaos!
O how joys, dreads, convolutions, human shapes, and all shapes,
   spring as from graves around me!
O phantoms! You cover all the land and all the sea!
O I cannot see in the dimness whether you smile or frown upon me!
O vapor, a look, a word! O well-beloved!
O you dear women's and men's phantoms!

This stanza or something similar appears in all editions of "Out of the Cradle" until the last version of 1881, when Whitman was twenty years away from his poem. Perhaps he dropped it then because he felt it spoke too plainly from the emotions of 1859 and was not in keeping with what his poem had become. That it was not necessary to the success of the poem is proved by the success the poem has had without it, yet its omission greatly changes the total effect. The quality of the boy's need is lightened to a more usual adolescent distress and the sea's answer becomes the kind of grave reassurance characteristic of the later Whitman. In the original version the boy is not just distressed, he is desperate with the desperation of the man of 1859. The first act of his awakened poet's vision has been to abort and produce a frightening chaos. Instead of the triumphant vision of Life which Whitman himself had known, when the whole world smiled on its conquering lover, nothing rises now before the outsetting bard but a dim phantasmagoria of death-shapes. It is almost impossible not to read this passage as coming from the poet himself rather than from the boy—indeed, Whitman was right to cut it, it *is* out of keeping—for these "dear women's and men's phantoms" are surely dear because they are those of the men and women and the whole world that had *already* started to life for him in his poems, their life the eddying of his living soul, but are now strengthless ghosts, like the power of vision from which their life had come. This is the "terrible doubt of appearances" that had plagued him from the beginning, now revived and confirmed by his new crisis. Whitman here openly transfers to the boy the man's despair.

With this background it should not be hard to see that the answer the sea gives to the despair characteristic of 1859 is the answer characteristic of 1859. Its essential quality is the same tragic acceptance as in "Scented Herbage," a knowledge of death not as consolation or promise, still less as mere appearance, but as reality, the "real reality" that completes the reality of love in the only way in which it can be completed. In the language of Thoreau, the sea is a "realometer" that says, "this is, and no mistake." The lift her answer brings is like that of "Scented Herbage," the lift of naming the whole truth and so passing beyond illusion to a consent to fate. A sign that this is so is the sea's taciturnity. The thrush's beautiful song of death in 1865, weaving a veil of life-illusion over the same hard truth and so easing it for us, is not present here; simply the word, the thing itself. In this stark directness, again, the kinship is to "Scented Herbage" rather than to "When Lilacs Last."

Yet certainly the fact that this word also, like the bird's song of love and the boy's despair, is ascribed to a dramatic character makes a profound difference. The sea as dramatic character in this poem has two phases. In the earlier part, before the boy turns to her for his answer, she is a background voice blending with the drama of bird and boy but essentially not a part of it. She has an ancient sorrow of her own which leaves her no grief to spare for this small incident on her shores. She does not share the egocentric fallacy of boy and bird, in which even moon, wind, and shadows join in futile sympathy. In this part of the poem she is the same sea as in "As I Ebb'd," the "fierce old mother" who "endlessly cries for her castaways"—all her castaways, not just these—the deep ocean of life and death that rolls through all things.

Of course, behind every detail of the poem, including this one, we feel the poet's shaping power, creating a symbolical language for the life of his own mind. In this kind of subjective drama the author is all the characters; bird, boy, and sea are one and join in a grief that is at bottom the same because it is his own. But Whitman has now seen through the Emersonian illusion that the power of the poet prophesies a victory for the man. Where "Song of Myself" had dramatized the omnipotence of bardic vision, "Out of the Cradle" dramatizes the discovery that the power of the bard is only to sing his own limits. Like the bird in Marianne Moore's poem, his singing is mighty because he is caged. As a dramatic character, then, the sea is the Not-Me, Fate, Karma, that-which-cannot-be-changed. As such she dominates the scene, which is all, as Kenneth Burke would say, under her aegis, but she does not share in its temporal passions.

At the end, however, she condescends to reveal herself and changes from the ground of the question to the answer. The change is not so much in the sea as in the boy. As before, he hears when he is ready to listen; the sea has been speaking all the time. Even the bird, in the early version, heard her and responded with continued song. Before he can hear her the boy must finish his egocentric cycle and pass from his hybristic promise to sing "clearer, louder, and more sorrowful" songs than the bird's to his despairing recognition that there is no good in him. The sign that he is ready is the question itself. Then the sea approaches and whispers as privately for him, revealing the secret which will release him from passion to perception. What she shows him is, I have suggested, no consoling revelation but simply reality. Yet the fact that this answer is now felt to come from the sea, from the heart of the Not-Me that has defeated Whitman's arrogant demands for another Me, suggests that the division between him and his world is not final after all, that the separation both have suffered can still be healed. The elemental forces of "As I Ebb'd" have fused with the perception of reality in "Scented Herbage" to form a new Thou, in Buber's language—no longer the tousled mistress Whitman had ordered around in "Song of Myself," certainly, but a goddess who will speak to him when he is ready to accept her on her own terms. Then he can hear in the voice of the sea the voice of a mother, a figure as we know "always near and always divine" to him. The real reality of "Scented Herbage" has acquired a local habitation and a name, has gathered around itself life and numenosity, and Whitman is well on his way by this dark path to replace the Comrade who had deserted him on the open road.

KENNETH BURKE

[1897-   ]

"When Lilacs Last in the Dooryard Bloom'd" (1955)

HAVING CONSIDERED Whitman's political philosophy in general, and the general way in which he personalized his outlook by translation into the rapt editorializing of his verse, we would here narrow our concerns to a close look at one poem, his very moving dirge, "When Lilacs Last in the Dooryard Bloom'd," perhaps the poem of his in which policies and personalizations came most nearly perfectly together.

The programmatic zestfulness that marks Whitman's verse as strongly as Emerson's essays encountered two challenges for which it had not been originally "promulged": the Civil War, and the valetudinarianism forced upon him by his partial paralytic stroke in 1873.

Before these developments, his stylistics of "spiritualization"

Reprinted by permission of Stanford University Press from "Policy Made Personal—Whitman's Verse and Prose-Salient Traits," *Leaves of Grass One Hundred Years After*, ed. Milton Hindus (Stanford, 1955), 74–108. Copyright, 1955, by the Board of Trustees of the Leland Stanford Junior University. Only the section on "When Lilacs Last in the Dooryard Bloom'd" (97–106) is reprinted here.

had provided him with a categorical solution for the problem of evil as he saw it. Except for the outlaw moment of "Respondez! Respondez!"[1] (or its much briefer form, "Reversals") his futuristic idealizing could readily transform all apprehensions into promises, and could discern a unitary democratic spirit behind any aggregate of natural or man-made places or things that added up to national power and prowess. This same principle was embodied in the random samplings that made up his poetic surveys and catalogues (which do impart a note of exhilaration to his text, even though one inclines to skim through them somewhat as when running the eye down the column of a telephone directory). And whatever guilt was left unresolved by his code could be canceled by the accents of perfervid evangelism (notably in his celebrating of "adhesiveness").

But since the entire scheme was based upon an ideal of all-pervasive and almost promiscuous Union, the motives of secession that culminated in the Civil War necessarily filled him with anguish. And even many of the inferior poems in *Drum-Taps* become urgent and poignant, if read as the diary of a man whose views necessarily made him most sensitive to the dread of national dismemberment. Here, above all, was the development in history itself which ran harshly counter to the basic promises in which his poetry had invested. He reproaches not himself but "America": "Long, too long . . . / you learn'd from joys and prosperity only." And, in slightly wavering syntax, he says the need is henceforth "to learn from crises of anguish."[2]

Yet in one notable respect, his doctrines had prepared him for this trial. In contrast with the crudity of mutual revilement and incrimination that marks so many contemporary battles between the advocates of Rightist and Leftist politics, Whitman retained some of the spontaneous gallantry toward the enemy that sometimes (as in *Chevy-Chase*) gives the old English-Scottish border ballads their enlightening moral nobility. And whatever problematical ingredients there may have been in his code of love as celebrated in the *Calamus* poems, these motives were sacrificially transformed in his work and thoughts as wound-dresser ("I have nourish'd the wounded and sooth'd many a dying soldier" . . . "Upon this breast has many a dying soldier lean'd to breathe his last" . . . "Many a soldier's loving arms about this neck have cross'd and rested, / Many a soldier's kiss dwells on these bearded lips").[3]

Similarly, when ill health beset him, though it went badly with one who had made a particular point of celebrating the body at the height of its physical powers, here too he had a reserve to draw upon. For his cult of death as a kind of all-mother (like the sea) did allow him a place in his system for infirmities. Further, since death was that condition toward which all life *tends*, he could write of old age, "I see in you the estuary that enlarges and spreads itself grandly as it pours in the great sea"[4] —and though this is nearly his briefest poem, it is surely as *expansionist* a view as he ever proclaimed in his times of broad-axe vigor. We have already mentioned his new-found sympathy with the fallen redwood tree.[5] Other identifications of this sort are imagined in his lines about an ox tamer, and about a locomotive in winter (he now wrote "recitatives").

As for the lament on the death of Lincoln: here surely was a kind of Grand Resolution, done at the height of his powers. Embodied in it, there is a notable trinity of sensory images, since the three major interwoven symbolic elements—evening star, singing bird, and lilac—compose a threeness of sight, sound, and scent respectively. Also, perhaps they make a threeness of paternal, filial, and maternal respectively. Clearly, the star stands for the dead hero; and the "hermit" bird, "warbling a song," just as clearly stands for the author's poetizing self. But whereas vicarious aspects of star and bird are thus defined within the poem itself, we believe that the role of the lilac is better understood if approached through an inquiry into the subject of scent in general, as it figures in Whitman's idiom.

In the section on *Vistas*, we put much store by the passage where, after referring to "that indescribable perfume of genuine womanhood," Whitman next speaks of his mother, then proceeds to describe an elderly lady, a "resplendent person, down on Long Island."[6] We consider this set of steps strongly indicative, particularly in so far as many other passages can be assembled which point in the same direction. And though Whitman's associations with scent radiate beyond the orbit of the feminine, maternal, and grandmotherly, we believe that his terms for scent have their strongest motivational jurisdiction in this area, with the *Calamus* motive next.

In this Lincoln poem, the lilac is explicitly called "the perfume strong I love." The sprigs from the lilac bushes ("to perfume the grave of him I love") are not just for this one coffin, but for "coffins all." And the Death figured in such lilac-covered coffins is called a "Dark Mother." In "Out of the Cradle Endlessly Rocking," where there is the same identification of the maternal and the deathy, the development is built about the account of a solitary "he-bird . . . warbling" for his lost mate, quite as with the mournful warbling of the hermit thrush—and the incident is said to have taken place "When the lilac-scent was in the air and Fifth-month grass was growing."

The cedars and pines in the "recesses" of the swamp where the hermit thrush is singing are also explicitly included in the realm of scent, as evidenced by the lines: "From the fragrant cedars and the ghostly pines"; "Clear in the freshness moist and the swamp-perfume"; "There in the fragrant pines and the cedars dusk and dim." See also, in *Starting from Paumanok*, that poem of his origins and of his femme Democracy: having heard "the hermit thrush from the swamp-cedars, / Solitary, singing in the West, I strike up for a New World."⁷ But it is the lilac that holds the poet "with mastering odor," as he says in the Lincoln poem.

In another poem, *A Broadway Pageant* (and one should think also of broad-axe and broad breast), there is a passage that clearly brings out the identification between scent and the maternal, though in this case the usage is somewhat ambiguous in attitude, whereas by far the great majority of references to scent in Whitman are decidedly on the favorable side: "The Originatress comes, / The nest of languages, the bequeather of poems, the race of eld, / Florid with blood, pensive, rapt with musings, hot with passion, / Sultry with perfume."⁸ (His word "florid" here could be correlated with a reference to "Florida perfumes," in a poem on Columbia, "the Mother of All.")⁹ In this same poem, near the end, there is a passage about "the all-mother" and "the long-off mother" which develops from the line: "The box-lid is but perceptibly open'd, nevertheless the perfume pours copiously out of the whole box." Psychoanalytically, the point about identification here could be buttressed by the standard psychoanalytic interpretation of "box," and thus perhaps by extending the same idea to the coffin—but we would prefer to stress merely the sequence of steps in this passage itself, while noting that the terms for derivation ("out of") take us once again back to the "Cradle" poem.

Consider also this passage, near the windup of *Song of Myself*:

> The past and present wilt—I have fill'd them, emptied them,
> And proceed to fill my next fold of the future.
>
> Listener up there! what have you to confide to me?
> Look in my face while I snuff the sidle of evening . . .[10]

Does not "snuff the sidle" here suggest the picture of a youngster nosing against the side of the evening, as were the evening an adult, with a child pressing his face against its breast? In any case, "fold" is a notable word in Whitman, with its maternal connotations obvious in the line where the syllable is repeated almost like an *idée fixe*: "Unfolded out of the folds of the woman man comes unfolded,"[11] an expression that also has the "out of" construction. Another reference, "Endless unfolding of words of ages," leads into talk of acceptance ("I accept Reality and dare not question it, / Materialism first and last imbuing")[12]—and two lines later he speaks of "cedar and branches of lilac." Recall also the traditional association of the feminine with matter (as in Aristotle). In the "Lilacs" poem, immediately before the words "dark mother," death is called "cool-enfolding."

In one of the *Calamus* poems, a reference to "perfume" follows immediately after the line, "Buds to be unfolded on the old terms,"[13] and there are other lines that extend the area of the perfume beyond the feminine and maternal to the realm of manly adhesiveness, and to his poetic development in general, as in "In Cabin'd Ships at Sea": "Bear forth to them folded my love, (dear mariners, for you I fold it here in every leaf)."

There are many other references, direct and indirect, which we could offer to establish the maternal as a major element in the lilac theme. But we believe that these should be enough to prove the point.

Imagine, then, a situation of this sort:

A poet has worked out a scheme for identifying his art with the ideal of a democratic "empire" that he thinks of as a matrix, an All-Mother, a principle of unity bestowing its sanctions upon a strong love of man for man, an "adhesiveness" generally "spiritual," but also made concrete in imagery of "athletic" physical attachment. Quite as God is conceived as both efficient cause and final cause, so this poet's unitary principle is identified with both a source from which he was "unfolded" (the maternal origins "out of" which his art derived) and an end toward which he "ever-tended" (death, that will receive him by "enfolding" him, thus completing the state of "manifold ensemble" through which he had continually "passed," by repeatedly "coming" and "departing"). A beloved democratic hero has died—and the lyric commemoration of this tragic death will be the occasion of the poem.

How then would he proceed, within the regular bounds of his methods and terminology, to endow this occasion with the personal and impersonal *dimensions* that give it scope and resonance? (For a good poem will be not just one strand, but the interweaving of strands.)

Note, first, that the poem involves several situations. There is the commemorated situation, the death of the hero, as made specific in the journey of the coffin on its last journey. There is the immediate situation of the commemorating poet, among a set of sensory perceptions that he associates, for us, with the hero's death. There is the national scene that he can review, after the fashion of his catalogues, when charting the journey of the coffin (and when radiating into other details loosely connected with this). Near the end, a national scene that had *preceded* the hero's death will be recalled (the time of civil war, or intestine strife, that had accounted historically for the tragic sacrifice). And in the offing, "over-arching" all, there is the notion of an ultimate scene (life, death, eternity, and a possibility of interrelationships in terms of which immediate sensory images can seem to take on an element of the marvelous, or transcendent, through standing for correspondences beyond their nature as sheerly physical objects). The reader shifts back and forth spontaneously, almost unawares, among these different scenes, with their different orders of motivation, the interpenetration of which adds subtlety and variety to the poem's easy simplicity.

The three major *sensory* images are star, bird, and bush (each with its own special surroundings: the darkening Western sky for the "drooping" star, the "recesses" of the swamp for the "hermit" bird, the dooryard for the lilac, with its loved strong perfume—and for all three, the evening in "ever-returning spring"). As regards their correspondences with things beyond their nature as sheerly sensory images: the star stands for the dead loved hero (in a scheme that, as with so much of the Wagnerian nineteenth century, readily equates love and death). The bird crosses over, to a realm beyond its sheerly sensuous self, by standing for the poet who mourns, or celebrates, the dead hero (while also ambiguously mourning or celebrating himself).

And what of the third image, the scent of lilac? It fits the occasion in the obvious sense that it blooms in the springtime and is a proper offering for coffins. And though it is from a realm more material, more earthy, than sight or sound, it has a strong claim to "spirit" as well, since scent is *breathed*. (Passages elsewhere in Whitman, such as "sweet-breath'd," "inhaling the ripe breath of autumn," and "the shelves are crowded with perfumes, / I breathe the fragrance,"[14] remind us that references to breathing can be secondarily in the scent orbit, and often are in Whitman's idiom.)

Though, in the lore of the Trinity, the Father is equated with power, the Son with wisdom, and the Holy Spirit with love, it is also said that these marks of the three persons overlap. And similarly, in this trinity (of star, bird, and bush) there are confusions atop the distinctions. In so far as the bird stands for the poet whose art (according to the *Vistas*) was to teach us lessons, the bird would correspond to the son, and wisdom. The star, in standing for the dead Lincoln, would surely be an equivalent of the father, implying power in so far as Lincoln had been a national democratic leader. Yet the nearest explicit attribution of power, the adjective "strong," is applied only in connection with the *lilac*, which would be analogous to the third person of the trinity, the holy spirit (with the notable exception that we would treat it as *maternal*, whereas the Sanctus Spiritus is, *grammatically* at least, imagined after the analogy of the masculine, though often surrounded by imagery that suggests maternal, quasi-Mariolatrous connotations).

The relation of lilac to love is in the reference to "heart-shaped leaves." Since the evening star is unquestionably Venus, the love theme is implicitly figured, though ambiguously, in so far as Venus is feminine, but is here the sign of a dead *man*. As for the "solitary" thrush, who sings "death's outlet song of life," his "carol of death" is a love song at least secondarily, in so far as love and death are convertible terms. Also, in so far as the bird song is explicitly said to be a "tallying chant" that matches the poet's own "thought of him I love," the love motif is connected with it by this route.

But the words, "song of the bleeding throat," remind us of another motive here, more *autistic*, intrinsic to the self, as might be expected of a "hermit" singer. Implicit in the singing of the thrush, there is the theme most clearly expressed perhaps in these earlier lines, from *Calamus*:

Trickle drops! my blue veins leaving!
O drops of me! trickle, slow drops,
Candid from me falling, drip, bleeding drops,
From wounds made to free you whence you were prison'd,
From my face, from my forehead and lips,
From my breast, from within where I was conceal'd, press forth red
    drops, confession drops,
Stain every page, stain every song I sing, every word I say, bloody
    drops,
Let them know your scarlet heat, let them glisten,
Saturate them with yourself all ashamed and wet,
Glow upon all I have written or shall write, bleeding drops,
Let it all be seen in your light, blushing drops.

Do we not here find the theme of utterance proclaimed in and for itself, yet after the analogy of violence done upon the self?

Regrettably, we cannot pause to appreciate the "Lilacs" poem in detail. But a few terministic considerations might be mentioned. There is the interesting set of modulations, for instance, in the series: night, black murk, gray debris, dark-brown fields, great cloud darkening the land, draped in black, crepe-veiled, dim-lit, netherward black of the night, gray smoke, gray-brown bird out of the dusk, long black trail, swamp in the dimness, shadowy cedars, dark mother, dusk and dim—all in contrast with the "lustrous" star. (If you will turn to *Song of Myself*, section 6, you will find the "dark mother" theme interestingly foreshadowed in the "dark . . . darker . . . dark" stanza that serves as a transition from "mothers' laps" to "uttering tongues.")[15] And noting the absence of Whitman's distance-blue, we find that he has moved into the more solemn area of lilac, purple, and violet. Note also the spring-sprig modulation.

There are many devices for merging the components. At times, for instance, the swampy "recesses" where the bird is singing are described in terms of scent. Or sight and scent are intermingled when "fragrant cedars" are matched with "ghostly pines" at one point, and "fragrant pines" are matched with "cedars dusk and dim" at another. And of course, there is the notable closing merger, "Lilac and star and bird twined with the chant of my soul," a revision of his "trinity" in the opening stanzas, where the bird does not figure at all, the third of the three being the poet's "thought of him I love."

Prophesying after the event, of course, we could say that the bird had figured *implicitly* from the very first, since the bird duplicates the poet, though this duplex element will not begin to emerge until section 4, where the bird is first mentioned. But once the bird has been introduced, much effectiveness derives from the poem's return, at intervals, to this theme, which is thus astutely released and developed. One gets the feel of an almost frenzied or orgiastic outpouring, that has never stopped for one moment, and somehow even now goes unendingly on.

One gets no such clear sense of progression in the poem as when, say, reading *Lycidas*. But if pressed, we could offer grounds for contending that section 13 (the mathematical center of the poem) is the point of maximum internality. For instance, whereas in sections 4 and 9, the thrush is "warbling" *in* the swamp, here the song is said to come *from* the swamps, *from* the bushes, *out of* the dusk, *out of* the cedars and pines (a prepositional form which we, of course, associate with the maternal connotations it has in the opening stanzas of "Out of the Cradle Endlessly Rocking"). Thus, one might argue that there is a crucial change of direction shaping up here. Also, whereas section 4 had featured the sound of the bird's song, and section 9 had added the star along with talk of the bird's song, in section 13 we have bird, star, and lilac, all three (plus a paradox which we may ascribe at least in part to the accidental limitations of English—for whereas we feel positive in associating lilac with the feminine or maternal, the poet writes of the "mastering" odor with which the lilac holds him).

We could say that the theme of the cradle song, or "Death Carol" (that follows, after a brief catalogue passage) had been implicitly introduced in the "from's" and "out of's" that characterize the first stanza of section 13. But in any case, a clear change of direction follows this movement, with its theme of death as "dark mother." And since we would make much of this point, let us pause to get the steps clear:

As regards the purely sensory imagination, the theme (of the "Death Carol" as cradle song) is developed in the spirit of such words as soothe, serenely, undulate, delicate, soft, floating, loved, laved. And whereas there is no sensory experience suggested in the words "praise! praise! praise!" surely they belong here wholly because of the poet's desire to use whatever associations suggest total relaxation, and because of the perfect freedom that goes with the act of genuine, unstinted praise, when given without ulterior purpose, from sheer spontaneous delight.

What next, then, after this moment of farthest yielding? Either the poem must end there (as it doesn't), or it must find some proper aftermath. The remaining stanzas, as we interpret them, have it in their favor that they offer a solution of this problem.

As we see it, a notable duality of adjustment takes place here (along lines somewhat analogous to the biologists' notion of the correspondence between ontogenetic and phylogenetic evolution, with regard to the stages that the individual foetus passes through, in the course of its development).

In brief, there are certain matters of recapitulation to be treated, purely within the conditions of the poem; but if these are to be wholly vital, there must be a kind of *new act* here, even thus late in the poem, so far as the momentum of the poet is concerned. And we believe that something of the following sort takes place:

In imagining death as maternal, the poet has imagined a state of ideal infantile or intra-uterine bliss. Hence, anything experienced *after* that stage will be like the emergence of the child from its state of Eden into the world of conflict. Accordingly, after the "Death Carol," the poet works up to a recital in terms of armies, battle flags, the "torn and bloody," "debris," etc. Strictly within the conditions of the poem, all these details figure as recollections of the Civil War, with its conditions of strife which accounted historically for the hero's death. But from the standpoint of this section's place *after* the imagining of infantile contentment, all such imagery of discord is, in effect, the recapitulation of a human being's emergence into the intestine turmoils of childhood and adolescence.

After this review of discord, there is a recapitulation designed to bring about the final mergings, fittingly introduced by the repetition of Whitman's password, "passing." There had been much merging already. Now, in the gathering of the clan, there is a final assertion of merger, made as strong and comprehensive as possible. The "hermit song" is explicitly related to the "tallying song" of the poet's "own soul." The "gray-brown bird" is subtly matched by the "silver face" of the star. Our previous notion about the possible pun in "leaves" (as noun and verb) comes as near to substantiation as could be, in the line: "Passing I leave thee lilac with heart-shaped leaves." There is a comradely holding of hands.

So, with the thought of the hero's death, all is joined: "the holders holding my hand"; "lilac and star and bird twined with the chant of my soul"; "and this for his dear sake," a sacrifice that ends on the line, "The fragrant pines and cedars dusk and dim"—nor should we forget that the sounds issuing from there came from the "recesses" of the "swamp-perfume."

JAMES E. MILLER, JR.

[1920-   ]

"Calamus": The Leaf and the Root (1957)

NO SECTION IN *Leaves of Grass* has received so much close attention and been the center of so much discussion and controversy as "Calamus." Friends of Whitman, particularly the "hot little prophet[s],"[1] have indignantly defended the section against the charge of "indecency," usually by raising the opposite cry, "purity," and by citing Whitman's own saintlike, spiritual life as proof that the poems could not be unwholesome. William Sloane Kennedy calls "Calamus" "Whitman's beautiful democratic poems of friendship" and adds, "A genuine lover speaks in the Calamus pieces: a great and generous heart there pours forth its secret. Set side by side with these glowing confessions, other writings on friendship seem frigid and calculating."[2] At the opposite extreme is Mark Van Doren's recent judgment, which has been widely influential: "His [Whitman's] democratic dogmas—of what validity are they when we consider that they base themselves upon the sentiment of 'manly love,' and that manly love is neither more nor less than an abnormal and deficient love?"[3] To the serious reader of "Calamus," the "manly love" that recurs both as a term and as an idea is of such genuine poetic complexity as to render it a good deal more than "abnormal" and considerably less than "deficient."

Reprinted by permission of University of Chicago Press from *A Critical Guide to Leaves of Grass* (Chicago, 1957), 52–79, abridged.

[*303*

It is indeed strange that the very element in Whitman's poetry that gained him nineteenth-century praise for his "purity" should bring him twentieth-century condemnation for his "immorality." It is worthwhile examining "Calamus" in detail in order to test the validity of the prevailing belief that in it Whitman gave stammering utterance to a doctrine whose implications he did not fully comprehend. I would first like to glance briefly at data external to the poems that might shed light on their meaning; next I would like to search through Whitman's revisions of the poems; then I shall turn attention to the major themes in "Calamus"; and finally I shall explore Whitman's poetic technique, particularly the recurring leaf-root metaphor, for any illumination it might afford in interpretation.

I. *External Evidence* . . .

The figure of Walt Whitman as alien to his own book is not so strange in an age of criticism that frequently asserts that the poet includes in his poems more than he knows, or in an age of Freud that is continually revealing that the artist exposes his inner being more than he intends. Did Whitman know his own meanings in "Calamus"? The question cannot, probably, be finally answered. But the problem as to what Whitman meant "Calamus" to mean can surely be solved. Abundant evidence as to the intended meaning of "Calamus" exists in Whitman's prose works, and, though not conclusive, as external data never are, such evidence is highly revealing and surely relevant. All the more valuable is this evidence in the case of "Calamus," in which intentional ambiguity—ambiguity used consciously as a poetic device—abounds, resulting in a language always something more or something less than appears on the surface. Wherever such ambiguity exists, a poet may always be quoted against himself.

It is surely significant that in his greatest prose piece, *Democratic Vistas*, Whitman does not silently pass over the "Calamus" emotion but rather dwells at length on it as central to the realization of his ideal democratic state. Of primary importance in understanding the distinctions Whitman would make in a precise definition of this emotion is the word he derived from phrenology, "adhesiveness." In a passage in *Democratic Vistas* Whitman cites adhesiveness as one of the two halves that together constitute the essence—and tension—of democracy: "It [democracy] is the old, yet ever-modern dream of earth, out of her eldest and her youngest, her fond philosophers and poets. Not that half only, individualism, which isolates. There is another half, which is adhesiveness or love, that fuses, ties and aggregates, making the race comrades, and fraternizing all. Both are to be vitalized by religion . . ." (V, 80). . . .⁴

The purity, innocence, and spirituality of the "Calamus" concept as expressed in *Democratic Vistas* cannot be missed. The idea is not original with Whitman. As he states, the "Calamus" idea was expressed by all mankind's saviors and has frequently been expressed by the term "brotherly love." In short, it is a basic Christian concept Whitman has found indispensable to the democratic ideal. The "Calamus" emotion has two facets—personal and social: on the one hand, adhesiveness merges particular individuals in a deeply personal, yet purely spiritual, attachment; on the other hand, a multitude of such attachments interpenetrating and binding a nation creates a democratic state rooted deeply in genuinely moral human character rather than in convention or law.

Although Whitman did not live to see his ideal state, he did experience the kind of personal attachment he celebrated. If further proof of the purity of Whitman's intended meaning is needed, it may be found in the series of letters he wrote to his Civil War companion, Peter Doyle, the unsophisticated Washington horsecar conductor. The letters have been published under the appropriate title *Calamus*, as they constitute a record of precisely the kind of relationship Whitman meant to describe by that title. The terms of endearment Whitman uses in these letters are lavish and suggest metaphorically the character of the emotion motivating his attachment: "Dear Pete, dear son, my darling boy, my young and loving brother . . ." (VIII, 42).⁵ It would be difficult to challenge the purity and spirituality of the feelings Whitman and Doyle had for each other, at least as they emerge in these letters, but, on the other hand, there can be no doubt that these feelings transcend those usual to friends or companions of the same sex. . . .

II. *Revisions* . . .

Contrary to frequent implications by Whitman's critics, his revisions of "Calamus" over a period of some thirty years do not reveal that he was trying to "cover up" or change the original character of the group of poems. Perhaps the most significant and revealing revision made was in the poem now titled "Sometimes with One I Love," which ended originally: "Doubtless I could not have perceived the universe, or written one of my poems, if I had not freely given myself to comrades, to love."[6] Through revision this line became: "(I loved a certain person ardently and my love was not return'd, / Yet out of that I have written these songs"). Two highly significant conclusions may be drawn from this revision: first, changes in "Calamus" were not intended to make the poems less personal—indeed, in this instance, the poem has been made to appear more personal; and, second, and more important, biographical interpretation, the acceptance of Whitman's poetry at "face value," is highly dangerous and likely to be misleading. It would seem safe to assume that revision of "Sometimes with One I Love" from a statement of generalized experience to a suggestion of a highly personal and specific experience was made not for biographical but for poetic or dramatic reasons. How often has the first version of Whitman's poetry contained such seemingly specific references for similar reasons? If, in "Sometimes with One I Love," the "certain person" loved ardently is a figment of Whitman's poetic imagination, it would seem the duty of the impartial critic to distinguish carefully, in the study of Whitman, his poetic from his real world and to refrain from passing so easily and superficially from one to the other on the naïve assumption that there is no difference.

The forty-five poems of the 1860 version of "Calamus" had, by the time of the appearance of Whitman's last edition, been reduced to thirty-nine. Three poems were rejected, four were transferred to other sections of *Leaves of Grass*, and one new poem was added. At first glance it might seem that the three poems were deleted because of their personal nature, because they revealed more than the author intended. But equally "personal" poems were allowed to stay. Close examination of the discarded poems reveals that there were other valid reasons for rejection. In "Long I Thought That Knowledge," the poet says that for a time he found the essence or meaning of life in a series of interests—obtaining knowledge, becoming the orator of America, emulating "old and new heroes," and finally, composing the "songs of the New World"—but he discovered that he could be the "singer of songs no longer": "One who loves me is jealous of me, and withdraws me from all but love." This emotional dilemma becomes the central idea of the poem, which concludes: "I am indifferent to my own songs—I will go with him I love, / It is to be enough for us that we are together—We never separate again.'" There are two good reasons for the deletion of this poem: it introduces the emotion of jealousy into "Calamus" love, an emotion which was avoided in the other poems and which Whitman probably decided was foreign to his concept of comradely attachment; and the poem contradicts certain basic ideas that recur throughout the "Calamus" section. It would be difficult to reconcile the poet's attitude of indifference toward his songs as expressed in this rejected poem with the determination, announced in the opening poems of "Calamus," to sing the songs of "manly attachment," to "celebrate the need of comrades." And it would be equally difficult to reconcile this indifference with the frequently expressed sentiment in "Calamus" that it was the love of comrades that initiated the poetic impulse and granted the poetic power. . . .

Although the revisions here discussed are by no means all that Whitman made in "Calamus," they are the most expensive and significant, and they certainly do not reveal a pattern of suppression or concealment. In almost every instance, sufficient artistic reasons can be found to justify the change undertaken. By and large, the "Calamus" section remained in essence the same through some thirty years of revision. There exists no evidence that Whitman ever genuinely regretted the form "Calamus" had originally taken. Indeed, in 1874, in a review he prepared for John Burroughs' signature, Whitman singled out the "Calamus" emotion as a primary virtue of his *Leaves:* "Yet it [Walt Whitman's verse] is singularly emotional; probably no one has so daringly and freely carried 'manly attachment' into expression as this author."[8]

III. *Major Themes*

The germ of the principal theme in "Calamus" is found in a paper discovered among Whitman's manuscripts with notations indicating that the poet had at one time planned to develop a lecture on the topic: "Why should there be these modesties and prohibitions that keep women from strong actual life—from going about there with men: I desire to say to you, and let you ponder well upon it, the fact that under present arrangement, the love and comradeship of a woman, of his wife however welcome, however complete, does not and cannot satisfy the grandest requirements of a manly soul for love and comrade-ship,—The man he loves, he often loves with more passionate attachment than he ever bestows on any woman, even his wife. —Is it that the growth of love needs the free air—the seasons, perhaps more wildness more rudeness? Why is the love of women so invalid, so transient?"[9] Some of the ideas expressed in this crude early note become embodied in "Calamus" in Whit-man's poetic expression of the distinction between the two kinds of love—amativeness and adhesiveness:

Fast-anchor'd eternal O love! O woman I love!
O bride! O wife! more resistless than I can tell, the thought of you!
Then separate, as disembodied or another born,
Ethereal, the last athletic reality, my consolation,
I ascend, I float in the regions of your love O man,
O sharer of my roving life.

Critics have frequently noted that "Children of Adam" cele-brates love of man for woman, while "Calamus" celebrates love of man for man; in the former, emphasis is on the physical or sexual aspects of love, in the latter on the spiritual. The above poem would bear out this distinction: love of man for man is "disembodied," "ethereal," "the last athletic reality." For Whitman, "athletic" had connotations of a desirable robustness or health: the "last athletic reality" would, surely, be a robust-ness of the soul or spirit that enables it to encompass more than self. Man is the "sharer" of the poet's "roving life," the companion on his spiritual journey.

In "Calamus" variations on the central theme are developed, dropped, reintroduced and treated from a fresh point of view, dropped again, echoed later, and so on, through the thirty-nine poems. This ebb and flow, or symphonic treatment of theme, suggests, as is natural in poetry, not a logical but an emotional development of ideas. In order to see the several aspects of the "Calamus" emotion, in order to understand its varied facets, it should prove useful to isolate and examine the major variations of the basic theme that thread their way through the section.

First, as in almost all sections of *Leaves of Grass*, is the announcement of the poetic program by the chanting poet:

> I proceed for all who are or have been young men,
> To tell the secret of my nights and days,
> To celebrate the need of comrades.

As "In Paths Untrodden" introduces this resolve, "Scented Herbage of My Breast" extends it and, later, it is reintroduced in "These I Singing in Spring" and elsewhere. In these poems the poet seems to consider himself in some way eminently fit, perhaps through experience, for the task he has assumed: "For who but I should understand lovers and all their sorrow and joy? / And who but I should be the poet of comrades?" And the resolution to celebrate "manly attachment" calls forth a renunciation of other interests, a dedication almost religious in its intensity in "Scented Herbage of My Breast":

> I will sound myself and comrades only, I will never again utter a call
> only their call,
> I will raise with it immortal reverberations through the States.

The hyperbole in the first line (Whitman did "utter" other "calls") is a poetic device used throughout "Calamus" for intensifying the felt or evoked emotion; such exaggeration must be taken into account in any honest interpretation of the poems.

Closely allied with these poems announcing the poetic intent are the poems, usually addressed directly to the reader, that are cast in the form of a warning:

> I give you fair warning before you attempt me further,
> I am not what you supposed, but far different.

[*309*

The poet insists upon his "difference" in a number of poems, beginning with "Whoever You Are Holding Me Now in Hand" and including "Recorders Ages Hence," "Are You the New Person Drawn toward Me?" and "To a Western Boy." In "Recorders Ages Hence" the poet confides that he will take his future reader "underneath this impassive exterior" and reveal his genuine personality—"the tenderest lover." In "Are You the New Person Drawn toward Me?" the poet again admonishes, "To begin with take warning, I am surely far different from what you suppose." And in "To a Western Boy," he advises the lad that he cannot become an "eleve" of the poet's unless "blood like mine circle . . . in your veins."

The poet differs from others only in his capacity for "Calamus" love; his exterior, what he appears to be, gives no indication whatsoever of the depths possible to him in spiritual attachment to others. A large number of poems are devoted to portrayal of the impact and achievement of such attachments. In "Of the Terrible Doubt of Appearances," the poet asserts that, in the doubt and uncertainty about reality and "identity beyond the grave," such love grants "untold and untellable wisdom," a knowledge similar to the intuitive knowledge of the mystic: "He ahold of my hand has completely satisfied me."[10] "When I Heard at the Close of the Day" dramatically portrays the importance of such love to the individual: the "plaudits in the capitol" or the accomplishment of plans was as nothing to the knowledge that "my dear friend my lover was on his way coming." In this brief drama, the poet utilizes the language and conventions of romantic love in such details as "all that day my food nourish'd me more," and particularly in the vivid closing picture:

In the stillness in the autumn moonbeams his face was inclined
    toward me,
And his arm lay lightly around my breast—and that night I was
    happy.

Similar portraits, in which the physical comradeship becomes a token of deep spiritual attachment, are vividly drawn in "A Glimpse" and "We Two Boys Together Clinging."

In "Not Heat Flames Up and Consumes" the poet describes

the "Calamus" love as even more intense and consuming than flames (called the "subtle electric fire" in "O You Whom I Often and Silently Come"), and as inevitable and mystical as sea waves. Indeed, the "Calamus" experience seems at some point to merge with the mystical: the "last athletic reality" becomes the reality of the spiritual as opposed to the material universe. The poet's soul is "borne through the open air, / Wafted in all directions O love, for friendship, for you." This image of the floating self, which appears also in "Fast-Anchor'd Eternal O Love!" ("I float in the regions of your love O man"), aptly suggests the spiritual merge of the mystic with the Transcendent. It is surely significant (and illuminating) that in "Song of Myself" God is conceived as the "great Camerado, the lover true for whom I pine."[11] At the center of the "Calamus" emotion is a profound religious feeling, a feeling of spiritual identity and oneness with other beings.

Perhaps the most curious of these intensely personal poems cast in the language of romantic love is "Earth, My Likeness." In this poem one can imagine the poet contemplating a globe representing the earth:

Though you look so impassive, ample and spheric there,
I now suspect that is not all;
I now suspect there is something fierce in you eligible to burst forth.

The association of the earth with a relatively fragile balloon is inevitable upon the introduction of the term "burst forth." But more important than this secondary image is the implication of the object of the poet's contemplation—the earth, the world as we know it through our physical senses. Although the material globe seems "impassive, ample," in reality there is "something fierce" underneath ready to "burst forth." What could this "something" be but the spiritual reality behind the material illusion, "fierce" because it has been ignored or suppressed for so long? This interpretation seems mandatory if the remainder of the poem is to be coherent:

For an athlete is enamour'd of me, and I of him,
But toward him there is something fierce and terrible in me eligible
    to burst forth,
I dare not tell it in words, not even in these songs.

The spiritual reality, in this case a deep and agitated spiritual love, is "fierce and terrible" only in the sense that any spiritual passion could be when pent up for long without object on which to bestow its emotional intensity. If the language seems too intense for the spiritual meaning,[12] one need but note Whitman's use of almost identical language in a prose context which leaves no doubt as to meaning: "To this terrible, irrepressible yearning (surely more or less down underneath in most human souls)—this never-satisfied appetite for sympathy, and this boundless offering of sympathy—this universal democratic comradeship—this old, eternal, yet ever-new interchange of adhesiveness, so fitly emblematic of America—I have given in that book [*Leaves of Grass*], undisguisedly, declaredly, the openest expression" (V, 199). As the mystic cannot describe the source of his certainty, as it would be audacious for him to attempt to define the nature of the Transcendent with which he has merged, so the poet "dare" not attempt to convey the meaning of the feeling that possesses him. There is terror in an alien spirituality, a spirituality so long foreign to man's experience.

As it is dishonest to extract lines without regard to context, so it is misleading to discuss any single poem in "Calamus" without regard for the poems that surround it and modify or qualify its meaning. The poems in which the "Calamus" emotion appears to be a highly personal and intensely passionate spiritual attachment are informed and qualified by the many interspersed poems that celebrate the "Calamus" emotion as a social and democratic force. Indeed, poems of this latter kind make up the bulk of "Calamus." The poet thus finds in the "Calamus" concept the basic impulse necessary to the two conflicting elements in his ideal state, individuality and equality, or "one's-self" and "en-masse." The "Calamus" emotion provides, however, not only these contrary impulses but also their means of reconciliation: the same spiritual love that attaches one closely to an individual will also merge him with the mass. Whitman asserted in prose: ". . . important as they are in any purpose as emotional expressions for humanity, the special meaning of the *Calamus* cluster of *Leaves of Grass*, (and more or less running through the book, and cropping out in *Drum-Taps*,) mainly resides in its political significance. In my opinion, it is by a fervent, accepted development of comradeship, the beautiful and sane affection of man for man, latent in all the young fellows, north and south, east and west—it is by this, I say, and by what goes directly and indirectly along with it, that the United States of the future (I cannot too often repeat) are to be most effectually welded together, intercalated, anneal'd into a living union" (V, 199).

In "I Hear It Was Charged against Me" the poet seems to acknowledge the possibility of misinterpretation of his message:

I hear it was charged against me that I sought to destroy institutions,
But really I am neither for nor against institutions.

The only institution the poet is concerned with is one which, without "edifices or rules or trustees or any argument," he wishes to establish throughout "these States": "The institution of the dear love of comrades." In "The Base of All Metaphysics" the poet indicates, in stating the essence of all philosophies, the hierarchical relationship of the various kinds of love:

The dear love of man for his comrade, the attraction of friend to friend,
Of the well-married husband and wife, of children and parents,
Of city for city and land for land.

The "Calamus" friendship, conceived here as a kind of base on which all of the other relationships of society are constructed, is celebrated in one of the most famous "chants" as the magic ingredient that will transform America into the ideal indestructible state:

Come, I will make the continent indissoluble,
I will make the most splendid race the sun ever shone upon,
I will make divine magnetic lands,
   With the love of comrades,
   With the life-long love of comrades. . . .

In direct emotional contrast to this broad social theme is a theme that delicately, almost shyly, threads its way through the section and that, in the way it is presented, seems almost a confession. The theme is introduced in the sixth poem of the section, "Not Heaving from My Ribb'd Breast Only," which, after a catalogue of the physical manifestations normally associated with romantic love (such as "husky pantings through clinch'd teeth" and "murmurs of my dreams while I sleep"), concludes:

Not in any or all of them O adhesiveness! O pulse of my life!
Need I that you exist and show yourself any more than in these
songs.

In other words, the songs become the only *necessary* outlet for the poet's adhesiveness. The idea that the writing of the poetry offers emotional release is contained also in that strange poem, "Trickle Drops": "From my breast, from within where I was conceal'd, press forth red drops, confession drops." Particularly curious is the poet's calling upon the drops, "ashamed" and "blushing," to "glow upon all I have written."[13]

We have already seen, in "Sometimes with One I Love," that Whitman relates the inspiration or motive for "these songs" to his love that "was not return'd." The poetry becomes the "pay" that is "certain one way or another" in the experience of love, the "pay" which confirms that, in reality there "is no unreturn'd love." But the best known of these "confession" poems is "Here the Frailest Leaves of Me," which originally stood as the next to last poem in the section and whose first line ("Here my last words, and the most baffling") was subsequently deleted. This short poem now appears near the middle of "Calamus":

Here the frailest leaves of me and yet my strongest lasting,
Here I shade and hide my thoughts, I myself do not expose them,
And yet they expose me more than all my other poems.

All these poems suggest that the poet has found sufficient fulfilment in art for certain emotional needs in his personality frustrated in real life. There seems to be frank recognition by the poet that his poetry represents the sublimation of his adhesiveness. It is these poems that those who have sought so diligently for abnormality have seized upon as open admission by the poet. Why does he "shade and hide" his thoughts? The answer to this question must lie in an examination of "Calamus" not as rhetoric or philosophy but as poetry. The poet reveals here not his guilt but his poetic method—ambiguity.

IV. Poetic Technique

We have noted in a number of poems Whitman's use of the diction and tokens of romantic love to describe the "Calamus" comradeship. Such transference from the physical to the spiritual results, whether intentionally or not, in an ambiguity of meaning that gives rise to endless controversy. There is no doubt, however, that a good deal of the ambiguity in "Calamus" is intentional and is consciously used to achieve certain poetic effects. Central to the section's ambiguity is the symbol introduced in the title—"Calamus"—and developed extensively in several key poems. Whitman himself, in one of his rare comments touching on specific meanings in his work, explains the symbol: "Calamus is the very large and aromatic grass, or rush, growing about water ponds in the valleys—spears about three feet high; often called Sweet Flag; grows all over the Northern and Middle States. The recherché or ethereal sense of the term, as used in my book, arises probably from the actual Calamus presenting the biggest and hardiest kind of spears of grass, and their fresh, aquatic, pungent bouquet."[14]

There is a fundamental value, of course, in the use of calamus as an extension of the metaphor, "leaves of grass," which in its common meaning has been elaborated more or less fully in "Song of Myself." Calamus is a very special kind of "grass" with unique connotations, just as "manly attachment" or "athletic love" is an emotion limited rather than universal, with distinct differences in its intense spirituality from other kinds of love. The calamus plant, in addition to having "the biggest and hardiest kind of spears of grass" and a "pungent bouquet," is found growing in clusters of several fascicles each, usually in out-of-the-way, secluded spots in and around ponds. As they are developed in "Calamus" each of these attributes of the plant suggests some aspect of the love of comrades: the size and toughness of the spears symbolize the depth and hardiness of such love; the distinctive odor suggests the spirituality of the attachments; growth in clusters suggests the twofold results of the realization of such emotion: personal attachment and democracy; the seclusion of the plant indicates the rarity of such revolutionary friendships.

Development of the calamus as a symbol is a part of the drama of the section. In the elaboration of the calamus image the poet achieves some of his most successful effects. Not only are all the attributes of the calamus plant utilized as symbolic, but the parts of the plant, the leaf and the root, are fully exploited in all their possible meanings. It is in such exploitation, where meaning on one level frequently expands to include meaning on another level, that ambiguity becomes a conscious poetic device. Although the resulting complexity makes for an enriched poetry, it is the kind of poetry easily open to distortion in interpretation. Such has been the fate of "Calamus."

In the opening poem of the section, "In Paths Untrodden," the untrodden paths by the pond waters quickly become more than the out-of-the-way places where the calamus grows: they become untried or infrequent patterns of human behavior, the action of the dissenter, the thought of the skeptic, the belief of the individualist. (Throughout "Calamus" the recurring image of the secluded, quiet pond is in significant contrast in its emotional connotations to the "pent-up aching river" that served as a basic image throughout "Children of Adam": the pond suggests a serene soul, the river a soul perturbed.) The long, sturdy blades of the fragrant calamus plant becomes "tongues aromatic" to which the poet responds "in this secluded spot." Here he has found something greater than the materialistic "pleasures" and "profits" and "conformities" he had been trying to feed his soul. He has found spiritual love ("manly attachment" or "athletic love"): the calamus blades (as tongues) "inform" by serving, in their fascicle clusters where "many" are brought together as one, as examples of close personal attachment as well as of broadly diffused love, and as examples of seclusion from the "clank of the world." That the "tongues" convey a spiritual message is indicated by their aroma: always in *Leaves of Grass*, odor or fragrance, a reality that has no apparent materialistic existence, symbolizes the spiritual, the ultimate reality that is impalpable and unknowable by any of the ordinary methods of knowing.[15]

While the calamus blades are conceived as tongues in "In

Paths Untrodden," they take on greater complexity in "Scented
Herbage of My Breast." The title evokes a concrete, physical
image of the robust, hirsute chest, an image that suggests the
solidity and strength of the spiritual love symbolized. The herbage is scented; it is the spiritual emanation of the seat of
love—the breast or heart. But the herbage is soon involved in
further meanings:

> Leaves from you I glean, I write, to be perused best afterwards,
> Tomb-leaves, body-leaves growing up above me above death.

The herbage thus becomes first the grain (fruit of his being,
thought) collected (gleaned) by the poet, and next the "leaves"
of a book where the message from his heart can be preserved
and "perused best afterwards"—after the strong emotional grip
has passed. None of these meanings is abandoned even as new
ones are sought out. "Tomb-leaves" are leaves that symbolize
the immortality of man—man embodied in a book of leaves or,
more literally, the "leaves of grass" that grow above one's grave
(note section 6 of "Song of Myself"); "body-leaves" fuse the
image of hair with the image of the grass growing above graves,
out of the dead buried beneath.

But real death is denied: "Perennial roots, tall leaves, O the
winter shall not freeze you delicate leaves." These physical
details, applicable to the calamus plant, suggest the attributes of
spiritual love. The root is the heart, the leaf the manifestation—
the human as well as the poetic gesture (the poet exclaims later,
"O blossoms of my blood! I permit you to tell in your own way
of the heart that is under you"); the winter is the hostility of
society toward the spiritual. Genuine spiritual love cannot be
killed by such hostility. In its seclusion, in the life it finds
withdrawn from society, such love flourishes: "O I do not know
whether many passing by will discover you or inhale your faint
odor, but I believe a few will." But spiritual love is not the
source of mere pleasure: "O I do not know what you mean there
underneath yourselves, you are not happiness." This elusive
meaning takes on a mystical cast as the poet indicates the close
relationship of love and death:

> Yet you are beautiful to me you faint tinged roots, you make me
>   think of death,

Death is beautiful from you, (what indeed is finally beautiful except death and love?)
O I think it is not for life I am chanting here my chant of lovers, I think it must be for death.

The "faint tinged roots" of the calamus plant, symbolizing on one level the heart, the organ from which love takes its origin, on another level suggests the phallus, in turn a token of "manly attachment." "Death is beautiful" from such roots: that is, death from a surfeit of spiritual love, from a yearning for the final merge with the great Camerado (as in "Song of Myself") is a beautiful experience. As death releases the confined soul for final and lasting union with other souls, death really becomes the genuine consummation of spiritual love: "I am not sure but the high soul of lovers welcomes death most."

At no time in this first part of "Scented Herbage of My Breast" is the central symbol dropped or are any of its meanings forgotten:

Indeed O death, I think now these leaves mean precisely the same as you mean,
Grow up taller sweet leaves that I may see! grow up out of my breast!
Spring away from the conceal'd heart there!
Do not fold yourself so in your pink-tinged roots timid leaves!
Do not remain down there so ashamed, herbage of my breast!

Throughout these lines, all the complex meaning of the symbol is operative. Never is the vividness of the actual calamus plant sacrificed or any of its natural attributes distorted for symbolic purposes. The leaves in this passage are, simultaneously, the leaves of the calamus plant, the hair on the chest (a suggestion utilized later when the poet asserts, "Come I am determin'd to unbare this broad breast of mine"), the grass growing atop the grave, pages of a book (*Leaves of Grass* itself), the outward manifestation of the hidden heart, and the capacity for spiritual love and the yearning for its return. The root is, of course, the calamus root with its distinctive color and odor; but at the same time it suggests the flesh where the hair is imbedded, the phallus in all its mystic associations (these meanings suggesting the vitality and virility of the "robust" spiritual love the poet describes), the buried corpse that feeds the grass above its grave, and the unseen heart as the source of the blood (passion) that has nourished the spiritual love.

The poet himself appears to admit that his symbol has become so burdened with meaning that it ceases to function effectively:

Emblematic and capricious blades I leave you, now you serve me
    not,
I will say what I have to say by itself.

After all the serious punning on "leaves," one might well read "I leave you" as a sly bit of humor into which the poet has been tempted as a farewell to the calamus, which has proved not only "emblematic" but "capricious." Perhaps the calamus is a capricious symbol because, although it was intended primarily to suggest the spiritual, it inevitably by the very nature of its form gave rise to physical associations: although these associations might in turn prove useful in suggesting attributes of the spiritual, they are also rather easily open to misinterpretation. After dropping the symbol, what the poet says "by itself" is a reiteration of what has been said through the symbol. He addresses death:

That you hide in these shifting forms of life, for reasons, and that
    they are mainly for you,
That you beyond them come forth to remain, the real reality,
That behind the mask of materials you patiently wait, no matter
    how long. . . .

Here the poet glimpses the truth asserted by all mystics, that the physical world that we know through our senses is a "mask of materials," a "show of appearance," that the world beyond to which death brings us is the "real reality." Death, then, represents the only means to the consummation of genuine and deeply felt spiritual love. It is surely needless to point out that such love is not confined to males; it may exist wherever the physical is not the primary motive in close personal, passionate attachment. . . .

Throughout "Calamus" ambiguity is used to create drama. Doubtless, Whitman has introduced the physical image into his poems in such a way as to multiply his meaning or to blur it. One vividly sees, hears, smells, tastes, or touches, and if he does no more he is prepared to question the poet's motives and psychology. If, however, the reader understands that the suggestive or symbolic image is, in Whitman's belief, the essence of poetry and that only the physical (what is knowable through the senses) can be imaged, he may then realize that the tokens of amative love in "Calamus" are but metaphors, a poetic attempt to associate with spiritual love the intensity and personal passion of traditional romantic attachment. Mark Van Doren widely misses the mark when he questions Whitman's "democratic dogmas" because of their basis in "abnormal" love. In the first place, Whitman did not proclaim "dogmas" but rather suggested an ideal. In the second place, there exists no evidence that Whitman's ideal is grounded in abnormality. Outside of "Calamus," in his prose, Whitman indicated rather clearly that his belief in adhesiveness was an intense belief in the Christian concept of brotherly love. There are only two ways of reading "Calamus" as a proclamation of the unwholesome: superficially, without going beneath the surface meanings, without attention to the intentional ambiguity; or psychoanalytically, with no attention whatever to either surface or symbolic meaning, but with intensive (and wild) speculation as to personal motives and unintended revelations. Surely neither of these methods is valid in the reading and interpretation of poetry. But even if one grants the as yet unproved charge against the poet, there is still the necessity of showing that such a biographical fact is relevant to an evaluation of Whitman's ideas or his poetry. Should knowledge of Keats's tuberculosis modify or condition in any way our response to "Ode to a Nightingale"?

GAY WILSON ALLEN

[1 9 0 3 –   ]

and

CHARLES T. DAVIS

[1 9 1 8 –   ]

Introduction to WALT WHITMAN'S POEMS (*1955*)

. . . Whitman himself was at least partly to blame for this aesthetic neglect of his poems, for in 1855 he defined the function of his ideal poet entirely in terms of moral and spiritual leadership, and he reacted to the ensuing hostility of the conventional literary world by rationalizing his artistry as an art without art. The romantic theory on which he had grown up made it easy for him to accept this obscurantism. To the romanticist, only Nature was real; art meant artifice and artificiality. Or as Whitman expressed it in *Specimen Days:* "Nature seems to look on all fixed-up poetry and art as something almost impertinent." His ambition was to write with such natural power that his reader would forget he was reading a poem and believe: ". . . this is no book, / Who touches this touches a man. . . ."

    In order to produce this illusion Whitman exploited his own personality. No doubt he satisfied his inner needs in doing so, but this is a problem for the biographer, whose solution may

Reprinted by permission of New York University Press from *Walt Whitman's Poems* (New York, 1955), pp. 1–21, abridged.

[*3 2 1*

increase our sympathy for the poet while distracting our attention from his achievement, or lack of it. No doubt, too, Whitman inherited from romanticism the convictions that all art is subjective and that the best poetry is that which is most personal. But whatever the source, few poets ever exploited themselves more relentlessly than Whitman did, or more misled themselves and their readers by so doing.

The title page of the first *Leaves of Grass* did not bear the poet's name. Whitman revealed his authorship, during that age of rigid formality in dress and manners, by printing as Frontispiece a photograph of himself in shirt sleeves and by inserting in the middle of his leading poems these lines:

Walt Whitman, an American, one of the roughs, a kosmos,
Disorderly fleshy and sensual . . . . eating drinking and breeding,
No sentimentalist . . . . no stander above men and women or apart
    from them . . . . no more modest than immodest.

From this time until the end of his life Whitman made his unconventional dress and bearded face a trade-mark. "Washes and razors for foofoos . . . . for me freckles and a bristling beard." He advertised his literary wares by newspaper interviews and anonymously written articles in which he paraded his eccentricities. In his poems he emphasized his huge physique, his shaggy appearance, and his undiscriminating sympathy. In 1874 he declared, ". . . poems of the first class (poems of the depth, as distinguished from those of the surface) are to be sternly tallied with the poets themselves, and tried by them and their lives."

Whitman's first biographers, who reverently followed his own wishes, insisted that one must know the man to understand and appreciate his poems, and to a surprising extent later critics —friendly and unfriendly, even to the present day—have usually agreed with this theory. Whitman and his co-operative biographers really meant *sympathy*, not understanding. One can understand almost any good poem, as a poem, with little or no knowledge of the poet's life, though such knowledge may stimulate interest and arouse sympathy—or antipathy. Yet, while sympathy often leads to understanding, it is no substitute for critical judgment.

Actually, Whitman's obtruding his personality in his poems conflicted with his more fundamental themes and achievements, which he often seemed to be the last to comprehend. He began his first poem in the 1855 edition, later called "Song of Myself," by announcing, "I celebrate myself," but he quickly added that he spoke vicariously for all men and women. The "I" of his lyrics was thus from the beginning symbolical. Of course he had to draw upon his own experience, and his imagination was most stimulated (as with any artist) when he could tap the energy of his inner desires and drives, but so far as the finished poem was concerned, "expressing" himself was secondary in importance to his creating a form for the expression of a more universal experience in which his finite life was only an interlude.

For a generation after the War of 1812 American patriotism developed in the direction of a cosmic philosophy of social evolution. Or it might more accurately be called a religion based on the faith that the Creator had selected the North American continent for the scene of the culminating civilization in world history. In 1839 an editorial in the *Democratic Review* (a magazine to which Whitman contributed a few years later) declared: "It would, perhaps, not be too extravagant to say that the poetical resources of our country are boundless. Nature has here granted everything to genius which can excite, exalt, enlarge, and ennoble its powers. Nothing is narrow, nothing is confined. All is height, all is expansion. . . . Our history, too, is poetical."

Whitman's exploitation of size, therefore, was not the result merely of the fact that his own body was large and strong, for spatial dimensions symbolized Americans' conceit of themselves and their cultural and moral aspirations, and Whitman's consciousness was saturated by the national consciousness. "Here at last is something in the doings of man that corresponds with the broadcast doings of the day and night. . . . Here are the roughs and beards and space and ruggedness and nonchalance that the soul loves." This wide, fertile, seemingly inexhaustible continent invited "a corresponding largeness and generosity of the spirit of the citizen." It called for amplitude in the poet, too. "The greatest poet hardly knows pettiness or triviality. If he breathes into anything that was before thought small it dilates with the grandeur and life of the universe.["]1

There can be no doubt that Whitman's personal life was profoundly influenced by this national dream of expansion and development, but the point is that he expressed in his poems not the character and personality actually his in everyday life so much as the vision of physical and spiritual power he shared with the nation. The folk mind created its mythical heroes of supernatural strength: Paul Bunyan, Davy Crockett, John Henry, Mike Fink—demigods of untamed forests and rivers and a raw civilization. On the same scale Walt Whitman created his mythical poet, whom he personified in himself. In writing his 1855 Preface he knew that this poet was a myth, though a very intoxicating one, and in writing his best early poems he drew strength from the potency of the myth. But in a short time he began to confuse the myth with his deliberately cultivated personality, and in subsequent attempts to elucidate his *Leaves of Grass* he was as likely to obscure as to clarify his purpose in writing his poems—and still more to obscure what he had actually accomplished in a given poem.

Despite many discouragements, Whitman lived a long and productive life, and his artistic motives varied from time to time. Sometimes he wrote, as he confessed in 1876, to express his "irrepressible yearning" for love, to appease his "never-satisfied appetite for sympathy."2 Indeed, such psychological motives may have nurtured his poetic faculties, but in his greatest lyrics, such as "Out of the Cradle" and "When Lilacs Last," he created an artistic form as a vehicle for the mythopoeic experience of the race. Here his themes were birth, death, and resurrection—the basic themes of nearly all the world's greatest religious and cultural myths—for which he found appropriate symbolic imagery and rhythms. In these masterpieces the poet transcended his personality, and even the national consciousness.

Three motives, then, competed in Whitman's mind when he attempted to exercise his poetic faculties: the desire to celebrate himself and exploit his own real or imagined personality, the ambition to celebrate his nation and give artistic embodiment to its highest aspirations, and an intuition of the meaning of the great life mysteries: birth, death, and the hope of resurrection.

Since this third motive will lead us into Whitman's doctrine of poetry as knowledge, let us postpone discussion of it until we have approached his emerging art from another side—so that we may see his poetic art in its true depth and perspective.

IMAGERY AND "SPATIAL FORM"

In his youth Whitman wrote a number of poems in conventional rhyme and meter, but they were so mediocre that we do not ordinarily consider them when speaking of his poetry. About 1850, or slightly earlier, he began the experimental development of a new poetic technique, and one of these early compositions, called simply "Pictures" and never published in its entirety by Whitman himself, reveals quite plainly that he devoted his attention first of all to imagery.

Although no entirely satisfactory definition of "imagery" has ever been given (as Caroline Spurgeon[3] has pointed out), most users of the term would agree that it is a figurative use of words by which the poet suggests to the reader's senses a physical object—or the momentary interaction of objects—that has an analogical and subjective meaning. Ezra Pound has defined the image as "that which presents an intellectual and emotional complex in an instant of time." The image may appeal to any of the senses, but one of the simplest varieties is the brief reflection of a physical object or action on the retina of the human eye or in the lens of a camera, hence the appropriateness of Whitman's rudimentary term "picture." It is a snapshot of experience—real or fictitious. To judge by the sound of the lines, Whitman gave little if any thought to rhythm while writing "Pictures." But as he explored his image-making faculty, he discovered an order based solely on association in his memory, and thereby he began to find a natural structure congenial to his own mind and disposition and suitable for his emerging poetic art.

In a little house pictures I keep,
Many pictures hanging suspended—
It is not a fixed house,
It is round—it is but a few inches from one side of it to the other side,
But behold! it has room enough—in it, hundreds and thousands,—
all the varieties;

[325

Here! do you know this? this is cicerone himself;
And here, see you, my own States—and here the world itself
    bowling through the air;
And there, on the walls hanging, portraits of women and men,
    carefully kept,
This is the portrait of my dear mother—and this of my father—and
    these of my brothers and sisters;
This, (I name every thing as it comes,) This is a beautiful statue,
    long lost, dark buried, but never destroyed—now found by me,
    and restored to the light;[4]

Most of this is abstract: Whitman merely alluded to the picture
in his mind without attempting to project it for the reader. The
composition is, therefore, not so much a poem as a rough plan
for a poem, or rather for the process of poetic creation, and the
"round house" on the walls of which hang the poet's images is a
naïve though accurate analogy of this process. These images
come from reading as well as seeing at firsthand, but reading is
experience too. Everything that the poet has seen, heard, felt, or
thought is stored up somewhere in his private gallery. Impressions of the events of the day and intimate portraits of his
immediate family stand side by side with mental images of men
and customs of antiquity: Cicero, Socrates, Athens on a clear
afternoon, Adam and Eve in the Garden of Eden, the world
itself revolving around the sun (Whitman first wrote "rolling"
and then changed that to "bowling," which more accurately describes the motion of the earth traveling around the sun). And
the marvel is that each picture leads the poet's attention to
another, so that no matter in what direction his inward eye turns
it always sees another picture. He begins on the conscious level,
but the associations (which psychologists to the present day
cannot adequately explain) carry his attention to the fringe of
the subconscious. "I name every thing as it comes," the poet
says. And the images come as if propelled by some hidden force,
out of the secret depths of memory into the light of consciousness.

    These images have no logical order in their coming. The
"naming" process itself is ambiguous. It may be that the act of
recognition, or thinking of the "name," may enable the poet to
bring the picture to the surface by an act of his will, though in
the latter sense it will have attached to it other images that the

conscious mind did not expect or perhaps even want. What this amounts to is that Whitman had discovered the "stream-of-consciousness" many years before William James suggested a term for it, and thereby he also discovered literary techniques for which he was searching.

In the mid-nineteenth century all literary compositions that had any standing as literature were constructed on the order of Aristotelian logic: beginning, middle, and end, or, in narration, time sequence. Language itself, in fact, is regulated by the laws of syntax, which are but conventions of time and logic. All actions are fitted into the clearly defined categories of "tense." As a consequence, for centuries time-logic governed the literary forms. For example, the sonnet is a metaphorical syllogism. Most narrative poems begin at a certain point in history (real or fictitious) and proceed episode by episode to a later point in historical time or in imagined history. By analogy, the conventional poet projects his images onto a flat rectangular surface. The "pictures" in his literary gallery hang in rows, or at least in neat geometrical patterns.

But Whitman's "round house" had no beginning and no end; roundness described not only the shape of his skull but also the poetic structure with which he was experimenting. The images that floated into the conscious mind of the poet, the "namer," were arranged only by their mysterious associations. Their order, therefore, may be called "spatial" rather than temporal; they spread out and form a panorama. Near the end of the unfinished manuscript Whitman repeated, "still I name them [the pictures] as they come." This is the order of scenes recalled in a dream. A poem based on such an order could never be completed; as in Eliot's phrase in *The Waste Land* (a very different context), the poet could only give "fragments shored against time."

With the exception of "Pictures," which could scarcely be called a real poem—certainly not a work of art—Whitman never constructed any finished poem on such an order (he probably came nearest to doing so in "The Sleepers"). But in writing "Pictures" he made several discoveries that he later used in more successful attempts to write poems. First of all he learned that images were the bricks for his poetic building. Bricks, of course, are manufactured from other substances, just as sentences and phrases are made up of smaller linguistic units. But as the speaker or writer articulates his thought, he thinks not in terms of phonemes or syllables but phrases, clauses, and sentences. In the same way, as Whitman articulated his poetic thought, he manipulated images or mental pictures conveyed by words, which he arranged on the page as separate lines or verses, each image or closely related cluster forming the core of the individual verse.

In his experiment with the "round house" Whitman also discovered the exhilarating sense of freedom that he could gain by casting off the ballast of time and letting his image-recalling faculty roam at will through space. This gave him the sensation of possessing all geography for his intellectual demesne. As a poet he was to make a conscious practice of imagining (or image-ing) himself high up over the revolving globe, peering down with telescopic sight at the topography, animate nature, and occupations of men and women. Thus the so-called "catalogue" device became a basic feature of his structural technique. He wanted to see and share all creation. This desire he satisfied and conveyed to the reader by selecting or arranging, to use Muriel Rukeyser's[5] term, a montage of images to fit a symbolical pattern, a geography of his mind. "Song of Myself," for instance, is constructed on a basic spatial order of images, but the poet did not literally "give them as they come," unless in one or two of the catalogue passages. Only fragments of the manuscript have survived, but both the length of the poem and the arrangement of the parts indicate very plainly that it was composed in segments, probably over a period of several years, and these segments were then fitted together, as Roger Asselineau[6] says, like mosaics. We thus have smaller patterns composing larger patterns . . . arranged on a scale of an allegorical hierarchy of values.

Many critics of "Song of Myself," even some who have most admired it, have failed to find in it any conscious structure whatever. Others have professed to find in it a "symphonic" structure. But since the poem is not a musical composition, this is only a metaphor—of some value, however, because it does suggest that there is an order in the reader's aesthetic experience, expectations raised and satisfied, and a sense of completion at the end. Indeed, many of Whitman's longer poems that seem chaotic on first reading turn out on rereading to have a kind of musical logic, a pattern of symbolic structure and a progression of emotional intensification that culminates in a genuine climax and denouement. And just as learning to hear and identify the motifs in a symphony enriches one's enjoyment of the music, so will the recognition of Whitman's structural devices and arrangements lead to a greater appreciation of his poems and surer judgment of his poetic successes or failures.

POETRY AS KNOWLEDGE: THE POET AS "TIME-BINDER"

Although in "Pictures" Whitman experimented with arranging his imagery spatially instead of logically or temporally, he was profoundly interested in *time*—another of his anticipations of twentieth-century literary theories and techniques. In fact, his theory of the function of the poet (as expressed in his 1855 Preface and used in several major poems) might be called that of "time-binding," to borrow a term from a contemporary semanticist. Standing firmly on present reality, the poet receives into his mind and character the accumulated wisdom, heroism, and grandeur of past generations. By mystic sympathy and intuition he makes these his own, and then through his art he brings them to bear upon the present and future, so that he himself becomes a link between past and future.

Without effort and without exposing in the least how it is done the greatest poet brings the spirit of any or all events and passions and scenes and persons some more and some less to bear on your individual character as you hear or read. To do this well is to compete with the laws that pursue and follow time. What is the purpose must surely be there and the clue of it must be there . . . . and the faintest indication is the indication of the best and then becomes the clearest indication. Past and present and future are not disjoined but joined. The greatest poet forms the consistence of what is to be from what has been and is. He drags the dead out of their coffins and stands them again on their feet . . . . he says to the past, Rise and walk before me that I may realize you. He learns the lesson . . . . he places himself where the future becomes present.[7]

This concept of "past and present and future [as] not disjoined but joined" anticipates Bergson's philosophy in *Time and Free Will* and *Creative Evolution*. It is the metaphysical foundation of Whitman's philosophy of art; poetry is to him the supreme art because it is the supreme wisdom of the race. The main reason for his consistent neglect of aesthetics in talking or writing about his poetry was his deep conviction that poetry is the highest form of spiritual teaching. The poet, therefore, is a seer, a prophet. He understands the purposes of life, death, and eternity; "he knows the soul." What he gives his hearers or readers, however, is no formula or creed but a hint, a clue, an "indirection" (one of his favorite words) to the meaning of existence and the path to eternal happiness.

A great poem is for ages and ages in common and for all degrees and complexions and all departments and sects and for a woman as much as a man and a man as much as a woman. A great poem is no finish to a man or woman but rather a beginning. Has any one fancied he could sit at last under some due authority and rest satisfied with explanations and realize and be content and full? To no such terminus does the greatest poet bring . . . he brings neither cessation or sheltered fatness and ease. The touch of him tells in action . . . . The companion of him beholds the birth and progress of stars and learns one of the meanings. Now there shall be a man cohered out of tumult and chaos . . . .[8]

This poet sounds more like a god than a man, but through his art Whitman could perform some of these marvels, as in "Crossing Brooklyn Ferry." Here, beginning on the factual, realistic level, the poet considers his ties with the past, present, and future. As he thinks sympathetically of all the men and women who have crossed the river on this same ferry, he feels an identity, a oneness in spirit with them, and when he projects his thoughts into the future he feels the same identity with the generations to come who will share with him the same experience. This "identity" exists, of course, only in the fantasy of the poet (and his intuition fails to warn him that the ferry will give way to a bridge!), but in another sense he turns the dream into reality. The poem itself is a ferry, shuttling across the river of time. Since the poet's death thousands of people have read his poem and shared vicariously his experience and identification. Thus he truthfully prophesied:

It avails not, time nor place—distance avails not,
I am with you, you men and women of a generation, or ever so many
    generations hence
. . . .
What is it then between us? . . . .
Whatever it is, it avails not—distance avails not, and place avails
    not,
I too lived . . . . .
I too had been struck from the float forever held in solution.[9]

The "float forever held in solution" is, of course, life in the transcendental sense (cf. Emerson's "Over-Soul"). Whatever the life force may be (and here again Whitman seems to anticipate Bergson's *élan vital*),[10] it does seem like an ocean, out of which individual drops emerge from time to time (clock time as opposed to Whitman's intuition of tenseless time), only to return and be lost again in the great womb of time. This mystical doctrine gave Whitman his key symbol, the ocean as mother—death—resurrection (cf. "Out of the Cradle Endlessly Rocking"). And it is significant that in the myths of all lands the ocean (sometimes lake or river) has been used with the same symbolism. Whether by studying these myths (and he was a great reader) or by actual mystical intuition, the poet somehow attained a universal view of the meaning of life, and a sympathetic identification that transcended time and space, thus realizing the fantasy in "Song of Myself":

Space and Time! now I see it is true, what I guess'd at,
. . . .
My ties and ballasts leave me, my elbows rest in sea-gaps,
I skirt sierras, my palms cover continents,
I am afoot with my vision.[11]

THE ROLE OF THE "FANCY"

The poetic faculty that enabled Whitman to cast off his "ties and ballasts" and cover continents with his palms he later called "Fancy." In 1855 he did not use this term, though in some ways he anticipated it. In "Song of Myself" he speaks of himself (his physical self) and his "soul," which he seems to regard as the real Me. But his soul is not what he later calls his Fancy. The soul must be invited to "loafe" with him on the grass, to "loose the stop" from her throat. After a soothing "lull," the poet hears the "hum of your valved voice," and he remembers a summer morning in June when he felt himself to be in rapport with his soul and experienced "the peace and joy and knowledge that pass all the art and argument of the earth."[12] Doubtless out of such mystical experiences Whitman derived many of the moods and convictions that permeated his earlier poems. But the soul did not in any sense write or dictate the poems.

The creative process of the poet, as Whitman describes it in the 1855 Preface, proceeds in two stages. First, the poet floods himself with his immediate age, with every variety of sensory stimuli. Second, he experiences an "opening to eternity," such as the revelation the soul made to him on that memorable June morning. Such experiences give "similitude to all periods and locations and processes and animate and inanimate forms" and are "the bond of time."[13] In simpler language, while in rapport with his soul Whitman learned this spiritual fact: "a kelson of the creation is love."[14] Yet it is not the soul but the Fancy that finds means for expressing this truth. Fancy is that wholly practical energy which describes the sensory stimuli and prepares for the spiritual perception by imposing upon varied physical experiences at least a rough and informal order.

In Whitman's early poetry the concept of the Fancy remains rudimentary. In "Song of Myself" it functions within the familiar dualism of body and spirit, which appear as "My tongue" (the beginning of the description of the organic self, line 6 in the final version) and "my soul." The poet immerses himself completely in his physical existence, discovers the luxuriant richness of all his senses, and bids "Welcome" to "every organ and attribute." The activity of Fancy in the Preface is a "tally" of particular facts of the physical universe; that is, it creates artistic symbols that enable the human mind to comprehend the meaning and significance of the phenomenal world (cf. Emerson's theory of "symbols" in his essay "Nature"). "Tally" becomes "loafe" in "Song of Myself," and it makes possible a listing of the details of the poet's origin and a catalogue of his body's sense impressions, ranging from primitive *smell* to the more complicated *sight*. The form of the creative process described in the Preface appears here. At a point in the total intoxication with the vivid pleasures of the body, the experience of eternity comes, the "lull" followed by the "hum" that heralds the identification (through the soul) with God, and the perception of the body's fitness for the harmony of the divine whole. What is communicated in the poem is the sense of being uplifted, or absorbed, into something that Whitman indicates by "float." The opening to eternity occurs in its own time, uncontrolled, though sought by the poet.

Although the spiritual intimation the poet received while loafing in the grass affirmed the divine nature of the body and suggested a harmony extending beyond it, the spiritual meaning of "all else"—the world of things and persons that meets the eye, the ear, the hand, and the intelligence of the poet—requires a "tally." The world-in-time proves itself equally as divine as the body, which touches it. Indeed, Whitman says:

> All truths wait in all things,
> They neither hasten their own delivery nor resist it,
> They do not need the obstetric forceps of the surgeon.[15]

Awareness of the facts of vegetable, animal, and human life can lead the poet to the opening to eternity.

"Loafe" is the principal descriptive term in "Song of Myself" for the activity of Fancy when the poet invites the mystic union of body and soul. Several terms appear in "Song of the Open Road" . . . , but the one that is employed with most frequency is "travelling," suggesting a more aggressive role for Fancy than "tallying" or "loafing." The inducements for the poet, "afoot and light-hearted" on the open road, are more confidently anticipated, more positively presented, than they are in "Song of Myself": happiness for the soul, the "freshness and sweetness of man and woman," "divine things well envelop'd," and "divine things more beautiful than words can tell." Though "travelling" suggests the major activity of Fancy, "sailing" and even "walking" also prove to be useful terms.

The relationship between Fancy and soul in "Song of Myself" differs somewhat from their relationship in "Song of the

Open Road." In the former the soul is invited to join the body, to inspire physical reality, and it does so under compulsions that seem inherent in its own nature. In "Song of the Open Road" the soul is a traveling companion in need of testing, or of being "provoked."

Here is the test of wisdom,
Wisdom is not finally tested in schools,
Wisdom cannot be pass'd from one having it to another not having
    it,
Wisdom is of the soul, is not susceptible of proof, is its own proof,
Applies to all stages and objects and qualities and is content,
Is the certainty of the reality and immortality of things, and the
    excellence of things;
Something there is in the float of the sight of things that provokes it
    out of the soul.[16]

The special faculty of the poet, Fancy, acquires additional strength in "Crossing Brooklyn Ferry," where it gives meaning to the ferry ride from Brooklyn to New York, prosaic enough in itself, and to the physical context of the boat trip. Of the physical details—the river, the clouds at sunset, the tall masts of Manhattan, the hills of Brooklyn—Whitman says:

You have waited, you always wait, you dumb, beautiful ministers,
We receive you with free sense at last, and are insatiate hencefor-
    ward,
Not you any more shall be able to foil us, or withhold yourselves
    from us,
We use you, and do not cast you aside . . . .

What "use" means here is the ability of Fancy to dissolve reality, the particular facts of the crossing, and to reveal the "simple, compact, well-joined scheme" of which the poet and the ferry ride constitute a part. Fancy prepares for a perspective that can only come to the poet from the wisdom of eternity:

It avails not, time nor place—distance avails not,
I am with you, you men and women of a generation, or ever so many
    generations hence.[17]

Whitman's Fancy, like Coleridge's, has the ability to leap beyond "fixities and definites." In its power to disintegrate the real world and to create a new and ideal unity it resembles Coleridge's "Secondary Imagination." The mediating services of Fancy are amply illustrated in this poem: they join Nature and man's physical existence to eternity and the soul.

"Passage to India" uses one of the enegetic verbs of "Song of the Open Road," "sailing," to describe the mediating power of Fancy. The poet accompanies the soul to India. As in "Crossing Brooklyn Ferry," the peculiar function of the poet is wholly identified with the extraordinary ability of Fancy. Here it absorbs the details of the westward movement of discovery, as well as the most recent developments in communication and transportation, and fits them into a clear and inevitable spiritual design:

> Passage indeed O soul to primal thought,
> Not lands and seas alone, thy own clear freshness,
> The young maturity of brood and bloom,
> To realms of budding bibles.

The purpose of the "return" is a grand union of nature and man, which "shall be disjoined and diffused no more." And there is a union in time as well, with the "retrospect brought forward" to the "year at whose wide-flung door I sing!" The reconciling agent is the "true son of God, the poet," who shall complete the "Trinitas divine" against the backdrop of all time. The "sailing" of both the poet and the soul is toward eternity, and the journey is the justification of more material forms of circumnavigation. The voyage, too, suggests the condition of being suspended in the divine float:

O soul thou pleasest me, I thee,
Sailing these seas or on the hills, or waking in the night,
Thoughts, silent thoughts, of Time and Space and Death, like
    waters flowing,
Bear me indeed as through the regions infinite.[18]

Whitman's terms for Fancy, the mediating faculty of the poet, are not always highly descriptive words like "sail," or even "loafe," but often comparatively dull words like "think" and "remind." "Filter'd" is also associated with Fancy. In "Song of Myself" "filter'd" suggests, though somewhat ambiguously, the evaluation of sense experience. In "Good-Bye My Fancy!" it seems to have the power not only to screen sense experience but even to remake physical reality. As the poet

nears the end of his corporeal life, his faith in Fancy is boundless and he wonders if death means only that Fancy will usher
him "to the true songs."

⟨ Whitman's Fancy has the general function of reconciling and
unifying two opposing forces. One is the body, perhaps "Myself" of "Song of Myself," but it extends to the whole organic
world and is ultimately incorporated by the more comprehensive
category, Nature. The other is the soul, the real "Me" in "Song
of Myself," always removed, unitary, and complete. It becomes
an "eidólon" in the late poems, a "round, full-orb'd"[19] image,
which is directed and cajoled by the Fancy to undertake new
ventures. Then there is Fancy, which assumes increasing importance as Whitman matures as a poet and makes it possible for
him to achieve a rich integration of the most varied organic,
intellectual, and spiritual impulses and interests. In a late poem,
"When the Full-grown Poet Came," Whitman personified this
integration of Nature and soul:

Then the full-grown poet stood between the two, and took each by
the hand;
And to-day and ever so stands, as blender, uniter, tightly holding
hands,
Which he will never release until he reconciles the two,
And wholly and joyously blends them.

The diplomatic power here is Fancy, and the trinity of Nature,
soul, Fancy, with its two passive elements and one aggressive
agent, represents Whitman's mature conception of the poet's
creative process. . . .

What misled Whitman himself regarding the "aestheticism"
(his own word) of his poems was the absence in them of the
conventional techniques as guiding principles. They actually
contained more conventional techniques, such as alliteration,
assonance, personification, rhetorical patterns, and "poetic diction," than he realized, but except in a few poems (e.g., "O
Captain! My Captain!" and "Pioneers! O Pioneers!") he did not
consciously use rhyme, meter, stanzas, refrains, and similar
devices. The "readjustment of the whole theory and nature of
poetry" for which he called in this same essay was already
taking place, though faster in Europe than in America, and
because of this readjustment it is possible today to see that his

greatest achievement was actually in the realm of aesthetics. As T. S. Eliot has remarked, "When Whitman speaks of the lilacs or the mocking-bird his theories and beliefs drop away like a needless pretext."[20] This is another way of saying that Whitman's importance as a poet is in his artistry, not in his didactic message.

N O T E S

The following abbreviations appear in the Notes:

CRE   *Leaves of Grass—Comprehensive Reader's Edition*, ed. Harold W. Blodgett and Sculley Bradley (New York, 1965).

Complete Writings   *The Complete Writings of Walt Whitman*, ed. Richard Maurice Bucke, Thomas B. Harned, and Horace L. Traubel (New York, 1902), 10 vols.

Correspondence   *The Correspondence of Walt Whitman*, ed. Edwin Haviland Miller (New York, 1961–1968), 4 vols.

Traubel   *With Walt Whitman in Camden*, ed. Horace Traubel (Vols. 1–3, New York; Vol. 4, Philadelphia; Vol. 5, Carbondale, Ill.; 1906–1964), 5 vols.

Introduction

1. Quoted by Emory Holloway, *Whitman—An Interpretation in Narrative* (New York, 1926), 250.
2. Traubel, I, 58; I, 104–105; II, 4; *Specimen Days*, ed. Floyd Stovall, 412, 421; Traubel, I, 350.
3. Traubel, V, 310–311.
4. Letter from Whitman to Richard Maurice Bucke, October 31, 1889; see *Correspondence*, IV, letter 2142.
5. Quoted by Gay Wilson Allen, *The Solitary Singer* (New York, 1955), 169.
6. Traubel, IV, 440.
7. Traubel, IV, 211.
8. *A Small Boy and Others* (1913), 77, 310–311.
9. Traubel, IV, 17, 23.
10. Traubel, I, 78; II, 233.
11. Clara Barrus, *Whitman and Burroughs, Comrades* (Boston, 1931), 13, 280.
12. Herbert H. Gilchrist, *Anne Gilchrist: Her Life and Writings* (New York, 1887), 287; and Traubel, I, 308.
13. See *Correspondence*, II, 134–138.
14. See *Correspondence*, II, 133n.; and Traubel, I, 133–135. Dowden's letter is in the Charles E. Feinberg Collection.
15. Traubel, I, 299.
16. Traubel, I, 333 and 145–146.
17. Traubel, I, 208. Lanier's letter is in the Charles E. Feinberg Collection.
18. Traubel, I, 209.
19. *Correspondence*, II, 49n.
20. Traubel, V, 320; and *Correspondence*, IV, letter 1923.
21. Traubel, IV, 127; II, 276–277.
22. Quoted by Gay Wilson Allen, *William James—A Biography* (New York, 1967), 200.
23. "By Blue Ontario's Shore," ll. 248–249.
24. Allen, *William James—A Biography*, 414.
25. *Correspondence*, IV, letter 2133.
26. Traubel, III, 418.
27. Traubel, II, 252.
28. Traubel, V, 310–311.

Charles Eliot Norton

1. I have corrected Norton's few misquotations. *CRE*, 717.
2. There follow three pages of extracts from "Song of Myself," "I Sing the Body Electric," "Faces," and "Great Are the Myths."

Henry David Thoreau

1. Henry Ward Beecher (1813–1887), pastor of the Plymouth Congregational Church in Brooklyn and one of the celebrated (and somewhat notorious) orators of the century.
2. "Crossing Brooklyn Ferry" was called "Sun-Down Poem" in the 1856 edition of *Leaves of Grass*.

William Dean Howells

1. Howells' adaptation of a line from Section 26 of "Song of Myself": *"Walt, you understand enough—why don't you let it out then?"* (1860 edition).
2. Both quotations in this paragraph are from "A Backward Glance O'er Travel'd Roads," *November Boughs* (Philadelphia, 1888), 16.

Henry James

1. Martin Farquhar Tupper (1810–1889) developed an international reputation for his meterless commonplaces in *Proverbial Philosophy* (1838–1842), but was enshrined by artists and critics in the nineteenth-century "Dunciad."
2. *Drum-Taps* (1865), 8.
3. *Drum-Taps* (1865), 18. James selected for quotation two of the weakest poems in a collection which is admittedly uneven but which includes that beautifully understated lyric "Vigil Strange I Kept on the Field One Night."
4. Pierre Jean de Béranger (1780–1857).

William D. O'Connor

1. This is an exaggeration, one to which the poet himself was prone. Except for his trip to New Orleans in 1848, Whitman knew the United States west of the Mississippi River only from books and newspapers. It was not until 1879 that he traveled in the Western part of the country.

2. O'Connor goes on to cite the praise of Emerson and others and to argue ingeniously that "even the copious torrents of abuse" are a kind of tribute.

3. Gaius Petronius, Roman author of *Satyricon;* James Shirley (1596–1666), English dramatist; Jean Baptiste Louvet de Couvrai (1760–1797), French politician and author of *Aventures du Chevalier de Faublas* (1787–1789). Immediately after this passage O'Connor surveys world literature, from the Bible to Byron, to point out that "indecent passages" abound—quite a catalogue.

4. Lysander Spooner (1808–1887), author of books on law, banking, and the Constitution.

5. Richard Hildreth (1807–1865), author of a six-volume *History of the United States* (1849–1852).

6. Sylvester Judd (1813–1853), a Unitarian minister, wrote *Margaret* (an account of a Fourier community) in 1845 and revised it in 1851.

7. American poet (1816–1850).

8. Delia Bacon (1811–1859) was one of the early Baconians, that strange and strained cult which later claimed O'Connor's polemical sound and fury. Hawthorne wrote the preface to her *Philosophy of the Plays of Shakspere Unfolded* (1857).

9. Henry Charles Carey (1793–1879) was the author of *The Principles of Political Economy* (1837–1840) and *The Principles of Social Science* (1858–1859).

10. The famous abolitionist (1811–1884), whose *Speeches, Lectures, and Letters* appeared in 1863.

11. O'Connor proceeds to catalogue the virtues of America and Americans with extravagant gusto.

12. The rest of O'Connor tract is a tribute to Whitman the man.

John Burroughs

1. "Laws for Creations," 1. 4. Burroughs wrote "whole" instead of "world."

Ferdinand Freiligrath

1. Johann Georg Hamann (1730–1788), the "Magus of the North."
2. Félicité Robert de Lamennais (1782–1854), French priest and philosopher, published *Paroles d'un Croyant* in 1834. Saintsbury (see below) makes the same comparison.

Anne Gilchrist

1. "Out of the Cradle Endlessly Rocking"; the title in the editions of 1860 and 1867 was "A Word Out of the Sea."
2. "Tears" was one of the new poems included in the 1867 edition of *Leaves of Grass*.
3. "Song at Sunset," 1. 20.
4. At this point Mrs. Gilchrist quotes in entirety "Roots and Leaves Themselves Alone," one of the "Calamus" poems.
5. The last line of "A Song of Joys" in the 1860 and 1867 editions.
6. "A Song of the Rolling Earth," 1. 41.
7. Mrs. Gilchrist again quotes from "A Song of Joys" at the conclusion of this paragraph; some of the lines she admired, incidentally, were deleted by the poet in 1881.
8. "Starting from Paumanok," 1. 92; for syntactical reasons she has made "poem" plural.
9. The closing lines of "The Wound-Dresser."
10. "Vocalism," 1. 1 (1860).
11. "I Sing the Body Electric," 1. 80.
12. "A Song of Joys," 1. 100.
13. Probably an adaptation, from memory, of the following line in "To the East and to the West," ". . . the main purport of these States is to found a superb friendship, exaltè, previously unknown."

14. "Song of the Open Road," l. 81.
15. Misquoted from "Starting from Paumanok," l. 208: "Far breath'd land! Arctic braced! Mexican breez'd!"

Edward Dowden

1. At this point Dowden quotes "Starting from Paumanok," ll. 49–62, which concludes: "I stand in my place with my own day here."
2. "Passage to India," a fusion of ll. 103–104, 115.
3. "As I Ebb'd with the Ocean of Life," ll. 28–30, 32–34.
4. "Outlines for a Tomb," ll. 41–42. Peabody (1795–1869), a philanthropist, endowed the museums bearing his name at Yale and Harvard; see *Correspondence*, II, 91.
5. Here Dowden quotes de Tocqueville's celebrated discussion of poetry in a democracy, *Democracy in America*, II (New York, 1945), 76–78.
6. From 1860 to 1881, "Song of Myself" was titled "Walt Whitman."
7. Based on l. 148, "A Song for Occupations."
8. "Song of Myself," ll. 653–654.
9. "The Prairie-Grass Dividing," l. 5.
10. Wordsworth, "Tintern Abbey," ll. 100–102.
11. "Starting from Paumanok," l. 163.
12. Marquis de Vauvenargues (1715–1745), French soldier and author of *Introduction à la Connaissance de l'Esprit Humain*.

George Saintsbury

1. "A Promise to California," l. 3.
2. John Addington Symonds, *Studies of the Greek Poets* (London, 1873), 422.
3. "Song of Myself," ll. 35–37.
4. Saintsbury quotes the "Death Carol," ll. 135–162, in entirety.
5. "I Sing the Body Electric," Section 4.
6. Eby in his *Concordance* cites eighteen appearances of this word in the poetry.
7. "To a Historian."
8. "To a Western Boy."

9. "Starting from Paumanok," l. 173.
10. Sir Richard Owen (1804–1892) was a professor of comparative anatomy and physiology; Eduard Sievers (1850–1932), a famous German philologist.
11. "Song of Myself," ll. 102–104.
12. "Song of Prudence," ll. 8–9. Saintsbury quotes from an early edition of *Leaves of Grass;* the passage appears in two lines, the second beginning with "but the same affects . . . ," in the 1881 and later editions.

Standish James O'Grady

1. "Song at Sunset," l. 52: "Wherever I have been I have charged myself with contentment and triumph."
2. Perhaps an adaptation of a line in "To a Historian" later excised: "Me, a Manhattanese, the most loving and arrogant of men."
3. "Starting from Paumanok," ll. 184–186.
4. "Song of Myself," l. 150.
5. "Starting from Paumanok," ll. 234–235; the "I" was altered to "he."
6. This and the next paragraph are quoted by Bucke in *Walt Whitman* (Philadelphia, 1883), 166–167.
7. "Starting from Paumanok," ll. 86–94.
8. "Thought" ("As I sit with others at a great feast . . ."), l. 5.
9. "Tears."
10. "Dirge for Two Veterans"; see ll. 25–28.
11. "The Wound-Dresser."

Robert Louis Stevenson

1. Preface 1855; see *Prose Works 1892*, ed. Floyd Stovall (New York, 1963–1964), 438.
2. "When Lilacs Last in the Dooryard Bloom'd," l. 154.
3. "Song of Myself," l. 1039.
4. "Song of Myself," l. 1059.
5. A reference to Swinburne's laudatory comments about Whitman in *William Blake: A Critical Essay* (London, 1868), 300–303.
6. "By Blue Ontario's Shore," l. 240: "Dismiss'd whatever insulted my own soul or defiled my body."

Sidney Lanier

1. The quotations are from "Poetry To-day in America—Shakspere —The Future," which appeared in *The North American Review* in February 1881; see *Prose Works 1892*, ed. Stovall, 477, 478, and 490.
2. Lanier's discussion of Whitman was divided between two lectures; the material up to this point appears in his second lecture.
3. Here Lanier repeats the quotations from "Poetry To-day in America."
4. "By Blue Ontario's Shore," ll. 44–45.
5. "By Blue Ontario's Shore," l. 326.
6. Lanier is misleading here, although he had no way of knowing Whitman's eminently just appreciation of Tennyson's genius; see "A Word about Tennyson," ed. Stovall, 568–572. Their letters also testify to mutual respect.
7. WW deleted this line in the 1881 revisions. The preceding lines are from "Song of Myself," ll. 4–5, 413–415. The reading "Walt Whitman etc." appears in the 1871 and 1876 editions.

Gerard Manley Hopkins

1. "Come Up from the Fields Father": "Come up from the fields father, here's a letter from our Pete."
2. "To the Man-of-War Bird" and "Spirit That Form'd This Scene." "The last was printed in *The Academy* of 24 Sept. 1881, from the New York *Critic* of 10 Sept., and headed 'Original Verse'" [CCA].
3. See Saintsbury's review above.
4. "Three pictures by John Constable were exhibited at the Paris Salon of 1824" [CCA].
5. "*The Leaden Echo and the Golden Echo*, Poems, 36. Dated: Stonyhurst, 13 Oct. 1882" [CCA].
6. Robert Greene (1560?–1592), poet and dramatist.

Algernon Swinburne

1. At the conclusion of *William Blake: A Critical Essay* (London, 1868), 300–303, Swinburne points out similarities between

Blake and Whitman, and terms "When Lilacs Last in the Dooryard Bloom'd" "the most sweet and sonorous nocturn ever chanted
in the church of the world." "To Walt Whitman in America"
appeared in *Songs before Sunrise* (1871).
2. "To a Certain Civilian," first and last lines.
3. "O Captain! My Captain!," ll. 4–5, 11–12.
4. James Hogg (1770–1835), writer of ballads; Charles Dibdin
   (1745–1814), dramatist and song-writer; James Catnach
   (1792–1841), London publisher of chap-books and broadsides.
5. A Thracian goddess associated with licentious rites.
6. Italian poet and dramatist (1698–1782).
7. English poet (1781–1849), remembered as the "Corn-Law Rhy-
   mer."

Gabriel Sarrazin

1. Proclus or Proculus (410?–485), Greek neoplatonic philosopher; Abū Saīd (967–1049), Persian mystic.
2. The last two lines of "All Is Truth."
3. Sarrazin quotes here so-called mystical or pantheistic passages
   from *Leaves of Grass*, beginning with Section 5 of "Song of
   Myself."
4. In a note Sarrazin cites "I Sit and Look Out," "Of the Terrible
   Doubt of Appearances," and "Yet, Yet, Ye Downcast Hours."
5. At this point Sarrazin refers to the Harlan incident.
6. He mentions in a note the following "magnificent pieces": "The
   Mystic Trumpeter," "As I Walk These Broad Majestic Days,"
   "So Long!" and "Roaming in Thought."
7. Gautama Buddha, called Sakyamuni (Sage of the Sakyas).
8. French Catholic priest (1581?–1660), renowned for his charitable organizations.
9. Juan de Dios, or Juan Ciudad (1485–1550), and Juan de Avila
   (1494?–1569).

John Addington Symonds

1. In the previous section "Fast-Anchor'd Eternal O Love!" is
   quoted in entirety.
2. Words and phrases from the above poem.
3. Symonds quotes from "Scented Herbage of My Breast," ll.
   12–20; "These I Singing in Spring," ll. 19–21; and "O You
   Whom I Often and Silently Come," in entirety.

4. *Notes on Walt Whitman As Poet and Person* (New York, 1871), 31.
5. At this point Symonds quotes from the Preface to the 1876 edition of *Leaves of Grass* and *Two Rivulets*, *CRE*, 751.
6. Whitman read *Phædrus* in the 1860s; see E. H. Miller, *Walt Whitman's Poetry: A Psychological Journey* (Boston, 1968), 146.
7. "To the East and to the West," ll. 5–6.
8. "Earth, My Likeness," l. 4. Curiously (unless we are to be Freudian) Symonds substitutes "me" for "you," although earlier he quotes the line correctly.
9. "Fast-Anchor'd Eternal O Love!," l. 4.
10. Whitman's letter on August 19, 1890, an excerpt from which Symonds sent to Edward Carpenter: "That the *Calamus* part has ever allowed the possibility of such construction as mentioned is terrible. I am fain to hope that the pages themselves are not to be even mentioned for such gratuitous and quite at the time un-dreamed and unwished possibility of morbid inference—which are disavowed by me and seem damnable."
11. *Democratic Vistas*, ed. Stovall, 415.

John Jay Chapman

1. Earlier in his essay Chapman attacks those English critics (un-named) who utilize "a few old canons and shibboleths out of Horace and Aristotle" (141). Obviously Chapman was little acquainted with English criticism of Whitman and was intent more upon making a point than in dealing with reality.

Barrett Wendell

1. Wendell quotes the last section of the poem in entirety.
2. In the preceding paragraph he quotes completely "Ethiopia Salut-ing the Colors" and "O Captain! My Captain!"

Richard Maurice Bucke

1. The tale was later entitled "One Wicked Impulse"; see Thomas L. Brasher, *The Early Poems and the Fiction* (New York, 1963), 309*n*.

2. "Song of Myself," l. 176.
3. I have corrected the errors in Bucke's transcription.
4. For the history of this poem (1876), see *CRE*, 619.
5. "Hast Never Come to Thee an Hour" (1881).
6. The quotations are from *Democratic Vistas*, ed. Stovall, 376, 391, 394, 398–399, 420.
7. "Prayer of Columbus," ll. 16, 26–30, 40–46, 51–55. I have inserted the omitted ellipses.
8. The last two lines of the poem. In the preceding lines Whitman matter of factly looks back at his early poems, but it is doubtful that Bucke's explication bears much relationship to the facts.
9. "To the Sun-Set Breeze," ll. 6, 13–15, slightly misquoted. "To the Sun-Set Breeze" was one in a "cluster" which Whitman sent to *Harper's Monthly* on October 18, 1889. The editor, Henry M. Alden, in rejecting the work called it "too much of an improvisation for our use." *Nineteenth Century* also rejected the sequence. Finally, "To the Sun-Set Breeze" appeared in *Lippincott's Monthly Magazine* in December 1890. Thus the poem was written almost three years before the poet's death.
10. The quotations are from "Starting from Paumanok," l. 100; "Song of Myself," l. 52 and ll. 131–132.

William James

1. "Song of Myself," ll. 684–691. James omits, without notation, line 688: "They do not make me sick discussing their duty to God."
2. *The Iliad*, Book XXI, E. Meyer's translation [WJ].
3. "To Think of Time," l. 114.
4. James quotes "Crossing Brooklyn Ferry," ll. 1–49, with (unindicated) omissions.
5. *Calamus: A Series of Letters . . . by Walt Whitman to a Young Friend (Peter Doyle)*, ed. Richard Maurice Bucke (Boston, 1897), 41–42; *Correspondence*, II, 56–57. James omits the latter part of the letter.

Ezra Pound

1. Bliss Carman (1861–1929) and Richard Hovey (1864–1900) collaborated in *Songs from Vagabondia* (1894) and two sequels.
2. Marcel Schwob (1867–1905), French translator and poet.

Basil De Selincourt

1. "Song of the Open Road," Section 7.
2. "Song of the Open Road," Section 9.
3. "Full of Life Now."
4. "Crossing Brooklyn Ferry," ll. 126–127.
5. "This Compost," l. 17.
6. "Crossing Brooklyn Ferry," ll. 1–2, 92–93, 101–105, 126–132.

John Cowper Powys

1. French symbolist poet (1872–1960), editor of *Vers et Prose* and author of *Ballades françaises*.
2. Il Pisanello, or Antonio Pisano (1397?–1455?), Veronese painter and medalist; El Greco (1548?–1614?), Spanish mystical painter; Sandro Botticelli (1444?–1510), Italian painter; Scopas, Greek sculptor of 4th century B.C.
3. "For You O Democracy," ll. 1–2. The "vulgar" conclusion reads: "For you these from me, O Democracy, to serve you ma femme! / For you, for you I am trilling these songs."
4. "In Paths Untrodden," l. 2.
5. "Song of Myself," l. 246: "*Ya-honk* he [the wild gander] says, and sounds it down to me like an invitation."
6. "Out of the Cradle Endlessly Rocking."
7. "To Him That Was Crucified."

D. H. Lawrence

1. "Starting from Paumanok," l. 189; "Song of Myself," l. 329; and "City of Orgies," l. 9: "Lovers, continual lovers."
2. "I Am He That Aches with Love."
3. "Song of Myself," l. 1272.
4. Apparently Lawrence quoted from memory. The closest line I can find appears in "Our Old Feuillage," l. 63: "The athletic American matron."
5. "I Sing the Body Electric," ll. 72–74. I have corrected Lawrence's faulty transcription.
6. "I Sing the Body Electric," ll. 64–65.

7. A similar passage in *Studies in Classic American Literature* is interlaced with questions: "Will it though? Will it? . . . Is it? Are you sure?," (181).
8. "Scented Herbage of My Breast," ll. 9–16, corrected.
9. "Out of the Cradle Endlessly Rocking," ll. 165–173, corrected.

Vernon Parrington

1. Parrington reviews Whitman's early life with particular attention to his political views.
2. The quotations are from Traubel, I, 215, 65, 79–80 [VP].
3. *Democratic Vistas*, ed. Stovall, 381.
4. "Passage to India," ll. 192–193.
5. The quotations appear in Traubel, I, 232, 174, 285 [VP].
6. Traubel, I, 101, 193, 215, 223, 363 [VP].
7. "To the Sun-Set Breeze," l. 4.
8. "Thanks in Old Age."

F. O. Matthiessen

1. "Slang in America," in *Prose Works 1892*, ed. Stovall, 572.
2. "Shut Not Your Doors," l. 4.
3. "From Pent-up Aching Rivers," l. 9.
4. *CRE*, 737.
5. *Complete Writings* (1902), X, 15.
6. "I Sing the Body Electric," l. 8.
7. *Complete Writings* (1902), IX, 170–171.
8. Preface 1872, *CRE*, 742.
9. "The Sleepers," ll. 46–47. I fail to follow Matthiessen's point in this comment upon the beginning of an extraordinary dream sequence.
10. "Faces," ll. 17–19.
11. "The Sleepers," ll. 38, 119; "Song of Myself," ll. 1215, 989–990.
12. "Song of Myself," ll. 217–218, 222, 225, 232, 154.
13. "The reported figures, 13,447 and 6,978, are those of W. H. Trimble's unpublished concordance" [FOM].
14. "Song of the Open Road," ll. 129, 214.
15. "Starting from Paumanok," l. 233. I suspect that Whitman here is deliberately humorous.

16. "A Carol Closing Sixty-nine," l. 3.
17. "Song of Myself," l. 1327.

Muriel Rukeyser

1. "The Sleepers," l. 4.
2. "There Was a Child Went Forth," l. 27.
3. "That Shadow My Likeness," l. 5.
4. "As Adam Early in the Morning," l. 5.
5. "The Sleepers," l. 32.
6. "By Blue Ontario's Shore," l. 213.
7. "Song of the Open Road," ll. 19–22.
8. "Passage to India," ll. 233–239.
9. "When Lilacs Last in the Dooryard Bloom'd," ll. 84–88.
10. Steven Foster has stimulating suggestions to make in this connection in "Bergson's 'Intuition' and Whitman's 'Song of Myself,' " *Texas Studies in Literature and Language*, VI (1964), 385–387.

Henry Miller

1. See Bucke above, p. 120. Miller draws heavily for biographical material upon *Cosmic Consciousness*.

Gustav Bychowski

1. "There Was a Child Went Forth," ll. 2–4, 19–21, 26–30.
2. "Out of the Cradle Endlessly Rocking," ll. 150–157, 144–145.
3. "Night on the Prairies," ll. 16–17. This poem was written in 1860, not in "the period of decline." "Assurances" appeared in 1856. Evidently Bychowski did not realize that most of the poems in this group were written earlier.
4. "I Sing the Body Electric," ll. 5–8, 127–128.
5. Bychowski proceeds to discuss briefly the eye and the mouth or voice as "channels of perception."
6. "As If a Phantom Caress'd Me."
7. "Song of Myself," ll. 17–20.
8. "Song of Myself," ll. 614–622, 640–643.

9. Quoted by Emory Holloway, *Whitman: An Interpretation in Narrative* (New York, 1926), 69–70 [GB].

10. *Correspondence*, II, 258, 101, 85.

11. The wife of William D. O'Connor, then Mrs. Calder, published "Personal Recollections of Walt Whitman" in *The Atlantic Monthly* in June 1907.

12. Bychowski quotes from "Song of the Broad-Axe" and "Rise O Days from Your Fathomless Deeps."

13. Passages are quoted from "Native Moments," "A Woman Waits for Me," and "Song of Myself" (ll. 817–819, 1006). In the last instance Bychowski is so intent on demonstrating his (valid) point that he runs the lines together without indicating the ellipsis.

14. A misquotation. Perhaps the reference is to "For You O Democracy": "I will make the most splendid race the sun ever shone upon."

15. "A Song of Joys," ll. 40–42.

16. "Starting from Paumanok," l. 164: "I will effuse egotism."

17. *The Uncollected Poetry and Prose of Walt Whitman*, ed. Emory Holloway (New York, 1921), II, 64 [GB].

18. "A Backward Glance O'er Travel'd Roads," ed. Stovall, 726.

19. Bychowski cites the reference to the father in "The Sleepers" (l. 166) and in "There Was a Child Went Forth." He also discusses the tyrant father who abuses his son in the early short story "Bervance: or, Father and Son." He neglects to mention that these early tales are filled with vicious father figures.

20. "Chanting the Square Deific," ll. 5–7, 13–19, 21, 36–45.

21. Bychowski quotes from "By Blue Ontario's Shore," ll. 132–133, 137–138, 140, 147, 149–154, 161. He is not convincing in this argument: he writes as though there is a steady, unchecked growth to "full compensation for all the gloomy years of weakness," when in actuality "As I Ebb'd with the Ocean of Life" and many of the "Calamus" poems, written in 1859 and 1860, reveal uncertainty about artistic sublimation.

22. "Passage to India," ll. 169–174, 175–181.

23. Quoted in Holloway, 245 [GB]. At this point Bychowski quotes in entirety "A Noiseless Patient Spider," as does Holloway.

24. *Democratic Vistas*, ed. Stovall, 381.

25. *Democratic Vistas*, 380–381.

26. *Democratic Vistas*, 394.

Randall Jarrell

1. See Hopkins, p. 78.
2. Edith Wharton, *A Backward Glance* (New York, 1936), 186.
3. "Song of the Open Road," ll. 138–139.
4. Except for the second one ("Song of the Open Road," l. 202), all quotations in this sentence are from "Song of Myself," ll. 642, 844, 101, 727, 265, 278.
5. "Song of Myself," ll. 457, 449, 806, 840, 1029–30, 1078–79.
6. "Song of Myself," ll. 670–671 and 691.
7. "Song of Myself," ll. 501–502.
8. "Song of Myself," ll. 399–400.
9. "Song of the Exposition," ll. 16–17, 57–59.
10. "Song of Myself," ll. 1043–45.
11. "Song of Myself," ll. 958–962.
12. "Song of Myself," ll. 1114–16.
13. "Song of Myself," ll. 60–61.
14. "Song of Myself," l. 987.
15. "Song of Myself," ll. 1322, 1338.
16. "Crossing Brooklyn Ferry," l. 126; "A Song for Occupations," ll. 53–54; "Song of Myself," ll. 1300–01.
17. "I Sing the Body Electric," l. 159; "Out of the Cradle Endlessly Rocking," ll. 141–142; "We Two, How Long We Were Fool'd."
18. "You Felons on Trial in Courts," l. 7.
19. "Salut Au Monde!," l. 132.
20. "Song of Myself," l. 544.
21. "Song of Myself," ll. 553–556.
22. "Song of Myself," ll. 604–610.
23. "The Sleepers," ll. 32–41.
24. "Song of Myself," ll. 148–153.
25. The three lists are from "Song of Myself," ll. 264–278, 303–305, 1063–69.
26. "Song of Myself," Section 36.
27. "To a Foil'd European Revolutionaire," ll. 22–23.
28. "To the States," ll. 5–8.
29. "Crossing Brooklyn Ferry," ll. 67–84.
30. "Song of Myself," l. 244.
31. "Song of Myself," ll. 1083–84.
32. "Song of Myself," ll. 822–832.

33. " 'The Rounded Catalogue Divine Complete.' "
34. "I Sit and Look Out," ll. 9–10.
35. "Song of Myself," ll. 49–51.
36. "Song of Myself," ll. 75–79.
37. "Are You the New Person Drawn toward Me?," ll. 6–9.

Malcolm Cowley

1. Interestingly, Whitman held no such lofty opinion of Bucke's acumen, and it is of significance that the poet consistently (and almost ruthlessly) excised from Bucke's biography the "cosmic consciousness" encrustrations, a point made abundantly clear in Harold Jaffe's study of the manuscripts of *Walt Whitman* (1883) in his as yet unpublished dissertation (New York University, 1968).
2. Note James E. Miller's discussion below of the Christian brotherhood unfolded in the "Calamus" sequence.
3. See the following essay by Richard Chase.
4. Carl F. Strauch, "The Structure of Walt Whitman's 'Song of Myself,' " *The English Journal*, XXVII (1938), 597–607; and James E. Miller, Jr., " 'Song of Myself' as Inverted Mystical Experience," in *A Critical Guide to Leaves of Grass* (Chicago, 1957), 6–35. It is hardly accurate at this date to state that "scholars" find "Song of Myself" deficient in structure. Note the comments of Chase and Adams, reprinted in this volume, and also see Roy Harvey Pearce, *The Continuity of American Poetry* (Princeton, 1961), 69–83.
5. See Miller, 7; he expands to seven the five "phases of the mystical life" outlined by Evelyn Underhill in *Mysticism: A Study in the Nature and Development of Man's Spiritual Consciousness* (London, 1926).
6. An excellent discussion of the grass imagery appears in Richard P. Adams, "Whitman: A Brief Revaluation," *Tulane Studies in English*, V (1955), 131–132.
7. It can as plausibly be argued that the "sexual union" here is no less autoerotic fantasy—and therefore "figurative"—than the union described in Section 5.
8. It hardly seems necessary to attribute Whitman's monism to Eastern sources when it appears in Milton and Goethe.
9. "Song of the Open Road," l. 180.

Richard Chase

1. Line 389. This line has been set to music by that great eccentric Charles Ives.
2. Conway visited Whitman in 1855, not 1857, and recounted the meeting in *The Fortnightly Review*, VI (1866), 538–548; see Allen, *The Solitary Singer*, 170–171, 372–373.

Edwin Haviland Miller

1. Erik H. Erikson, *Childhood and Society* (New York, 1963), 252. Quoted by permission of the publisher, W. W. Norton & Company.
2. Marie Bonaparte's discussion of the "bridge" in *The Life and Works of Edgar Allan Poe: A Psycho-Analytic Interpretation* (London, 1949), 525–536, is summarized in Paul Friedman's "The Bridge: A Study in Symbolism," *Psychoanalytic Quarterly*, XXI (1952), 51.
3. Bruno Bettelheim, *Symbolic Wounds: Puberty Rites and the Envious Male* (New York, 1962), 115. Quoted by permission of The Macmillan Company; copyright 1954, 1962 by The Free Press.

Leo Spitzer

1. These references are elaborated in the omitted "survey": Shelley's skylark teaches "the knowledge of ultimate things inaccessible to the poet" (18); "This minstrel of God [St. Francis], feeling that one human being alone would not be worthy of praising the Lord, brings into his poem all creatures which may testify with him to the greatness of the Creator" (16); Arnold's Philomela sings of "eternal passion, eternal pain" (21); Hugo's *Le satyre* in which the poet sees "himself as that animal-God" (20).
2. "Song of Myself," ll. 330, 333, 334, 346. In a lengthy footnote, Spitzer notes that "Whitman could not realize that he was repeating Dante's procedure, that the poet of democracy must impersonate this sublime abstraction with the same consistency that made

Dante impersonate the universal Christian quest for the Beyond. The sea must whisper its oracle 'privately' to Whitman just as Beatrice in the Beyond calls Dante by his personal name" (23*n*.).
3. Earlier Spitzer notes: "In surging prose Ambrose offered a powerful acoustic description of the harmony . . . in which are fused the song of the waves and the choirs of the devout congregation in an island sanctuary" (15).
4. "Song of Myself," l. 665.
5. "Les plus désespérés sont les chants les plus beaux, / Et j'en sais d'immortels qui sont de purs sanglots" (quoted 20).
6. "Scented Herbage of My Breast," ll. 10–15.

Stephen E. Whicher

1. I have omitted Whicher's biographical reconstruction of the years 1856–1860, where, as he acknowledges, he follows Jean Catel, Frederik Schyberg, and Roger Asselineau in accepting an "emotional crisis" stemming from "some sort of homosexual 'love affair.' " Although Whitman may have had an unsuccessful affair during this period, all commentators ignore two important matters: the death of the poet's father in 1855 and preoccupation with ardent male relationships in the tales composed in the early 1840's.
2. See Bychowski above, p. 205. If his interpretation is accepted, it is not necessary to postulate an abortive love relationship in the period immediately prior to the composition of the poems.
3. Earlier Whicher quotes ll. 1302–08 of "Song of Myself."
4. This autobiographical "Calamus" poem appeared only in the 1860 edition.

Kenneth Burke

1. Earlier Burke refers to "Respondez!" as "a kind of Saturnalia-in-reverse" since it plays upon "a ritualistic reversal of roles" (96).
2. "Long, Too Long America," ll. 1–2.
3. "Not Youth Pertains to Me," l. 6; "By Blue Ontario's Shore," l. 243; "The Wound-Dresser," ll. 64–65.
4. "To Old Age" (1860).
5. Burke observes earlier that the " 'ecstatic' champion of the 'athletic' and 'electric' body [turns] from identification with the feller

of trees (as in *Song of the Broad-Axe*) to identification with the fallen tree itself (as in *Song of the Redwood-Tree*)" (76).
6. *Democratic Vistas*, ed. Stovall, 401.
7. "Starting from Paumanok," ll. 13–14.
8. "A Broadway Pageant," ll. 26–29, and ll. 72–73, 75.
9. "Over the Carnage Rose Prophetic a Voice."
10. "Song of Myself," ll. 1319–22.
11. "Unfolded Out of the Folds," l. 1.
12. "Song of Myself," ll. 477, 483–484.
13. "Roots and Leaves Themselves Alone," l. 8.
14. "Give Me the Splendid Silent Sun," l. 8: "Give me for marriage a sweet-breath'd woman of whom I should never tire"; "When I Heard at the Close of the Day," l. 3; "Song of Myself," ll. 14–15.
15. "Song of Myself," ll. 114–120.

James E. Miller, Jr.

1. Bliss Perry, *Walt Whitman: His Life and Work* (Boston, 1906), 286 [JEM].
2. *Reminiscences of Walt Whitman* (London, 1896), 133–134 [JEM].
3. "Walt Whitman, Stranger," in his *The Private Reader* (New York, 1942), 82 [JEM]; the article appeared earlier in *American Mercury*, XXXV (1936), 277–285.
4. "Quotations from Whitman are where possible identified in the text by volume and page number of *The Complete Writings of Walt Whitman*, ed. Richard M. Bucke *et al.* (New York, 1902)" [JEM]. In the following paragraph, omitted here, Miller refers to another lengthy passage on comradeship (V, 131).
5. Letter to Doyle on August 21, 1869; see *Correspondence*, II, 85.
6. *Leaves of Grass* (1860), 376 [JEM].
7. *Leaves of Grass* (1860), 354–355 [JEM].
8. Clara Barrus, *Whitman and Burroughs, Comrades* (Boston, 1931), 108 [JEM].
9. Clifton Joseph Furness, ed., *Walt Whitman's Workshop* (Cambridge, Mass., 1928), 63–64 [JEM].
10. This appears to be a strained and depersonalized reading of a personal passage.
11. "Song of Myself," l. 1200.
12. De Selincourt, in *Walt Whitman, a Critical Study* (London,

1914), 206, characterizes this passage as descriptive of sodomy.
13. Note Burke's comment on this poem, p. 299.
14. William Sloane Kennedy, *The Fight of a Book for the World* (West Yarmouth, Mass., 1926), 177 [JEM]; but see *Correspondence*, I, 347, and *Poems by Walt Whitman* (London, 1868), ed., W. M. Rossetti, 390*n*.
15. Burke's observations on scent should also be noted, p. 294.

Gay Wilson Allen and Charles T. Davis

1. Preface 1855, *CRE*, 709, 710, 713.
2. Preface 1876, *CRE*, 751.
3. *Shakespeare's Imagery, and What It Tells Us* (New York, 1935) [GWA].
4. The opening lines of "Pictures," which is printed in entirety in *CRE*, 642-649.
5. See p. 193.
6. Roger Asselineau, *L'Évolution de Walt Whitman: après la première edition des Feuilles d'Herbe* (Paris, 1954); later translated by the author (Cambridge, Mass., 1960, 1962).
7. Preface 1855, *CRE*, 716.
8. Preface 1855, *CRE*, 727.
9. "Crossing Brooklyn Ferry," ll. 20–21, 54, 56–57, 62.
10. For a later discussion, see Steven Foster, "Bergson's 'Intuition' and Whitman's 'Song of Myself,'" *Texas Studies in Literature and Language*, VI (1964), 376–387.
11. "Song of Myself," ll. 710, 714–716.
12. "Song of Myself," Section 5.
13. Preface 1855, *CRE*, 726.
14. "Song of Myself," l. 95.
15. "Song of Myself," ll. 648–650.
16. "Song of the Open Road," ll. 76–82.
17. "Crossing Brooklyn Ferry," ll. 126–129, 20–21.
18. "Passage to India," ll. 165–168, 187–190.
19. "Eidólons" (1876), last line.
20. See p. 163.

I N D E X

A NOTE ON THE TYPE

The text of this book was set on the Linotype in a face called MONTICELLO. This type, issued by The Mergenthaler Linotype Company in 1950 is based on a cutting called "Ronaldson Roman No. 1", a late eighteenth-century production of the Binny & Ronaldson foundry of Philadelphia. Monticello belongs to the family of transitional faces which includes Bell Roman, Baskerville, Bulmer and Fournier. The Transitionals fall between the hearty "Old Style" taste represented by Caslon's letters, and the graver-styled nineteenth-century "Moderns".

The book was printed and bound by The Kingsport Press, Inc., Kingsport, Tenn. Paper was manufactured by P. H. Glatfelter, Spring Grove, Pa. Designed by Guy Fleming.